Renew by phone or online
0845 0020 777
www.bristol.gov.uk/libraries
Bristol Libraries

PLEASE RETURN BOOK BY LAST DATE STAMPED

04 JAN 11.

8 - 11 - 11

BRISTOL LIBRARIES
WITHDRAWN

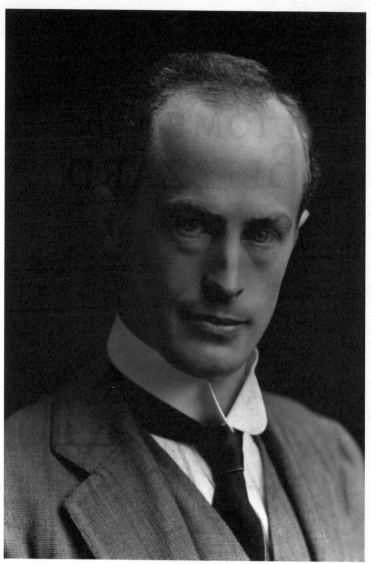

Sir Douglas Mawson

THE
HOME *of the*
BLIZZARD

A TRUE STORY OF ANTARCTIC SURVIVAL

SIR DOUGLAS MAWSON
Foreword by SIR RANULPH FIENNES

This edition first published in 2000 by
Birlinn Limited
West Newington House
10 Newington Road
Edinburgh EH9 1QS

www.birlinn.co.uk

2

First published in 1915 by William Heinemann, London (two volumes)
Abridged popular edition first published in 1930 by
Hodder & Stoughton Ltd, London

ISBN 978 1 84158 077 7

The photographs in this book were provided by the Mawson Collection,
University of Adelaide, from their collection of original prints and glass plates.

Printed and bound in China for Imago

CONTENTS

FOREWORD

ANYONE INTERESTED in the history of polar exploration has heard of Robert Peary, Frederick Cook, Robert Falcon Scott, Ernest Shackleton and Roald Amundsen, but who is Douglas Mawson? His polar exploits and accomplishments easily rank with his better-known colleagues but, because he neither reached nor claimed to reach either of the Geographical Poles, the international media of his day never quite latched onto Mawson as they did to the others. Yet his story is every bit as dramatic, as heroic and tragic, perhaps more so. I am sure you will agree when you have read this remarkable book.

On the day Mawson's expedition ship returned home to Australia, she received the news that Amundsen and his Norwegian team had conquered the great human challenge of reaching the South Pole and not long afterwards banner headlines all over the world screamed out the tragic news of Scott's death. The age of "heroic exploration" (coined by romantically inclined editors) had ended, soon to be replaced by the endless heroes and tragedies of the two World Wars. Mawson's amazing tale hardly ruffled the surface of international awareness when his original two-volume account was published in 1915. Between the wars, however, his 1930 abridged edition, less expensive and shorn of much scientific data, was a best-seller in America and throughout the Commonwealth countries. This book is a facsimile edition of the popular 1930 issue with the benefit of photographs largely taken by the famous polar photographer Frank Hurley (also responsible for the remarkable photographic record of Shackleton's *Endurance* expedition).

Mawson was born in Yorkshire in 1882 and had moved to Australia two years later with his family at a time when many British emigrants were heading for the colonies to set up new lives in sunnier climes. The young Mawson became a geologist and had enjoyed many tough journeys into the outback by the time he was approached by both Scott and Shackleton as a prospective member of their respective teams that were trying to reach the South Pole.

Mawson ended up on Shackleton's team, not for the main polar attempt, but in 1908, as part of the first successful ascent of Mount Erebus, the only active volcano in Antarctica and, in 1909, with two other Australians, in the first journey to the South Magnetic Pole. This incredible unsupported journey of 1,260 miles later prompted its notable leader, Professor Edgar David, to say of Mawson, "In him we had an Australian [Fridtjov] Nansen, a man of infinite resources, splendid spirit, marvelous physique and an indifference to frost and cold that was astonishing—all the attributes of a great explorer."

Mawson himself was bitten by the polar bug and wrote of the terrain they had crossed: "we came to probe its mystery, to reduce this land to terms of science but there is always the indefinable which holds aloof yet which rivets our souls." He was hooked and immediately made plans to lead his own ventures as soon as he feasibly could.

Mawson went to London where he asked if Scott would take an Australian team on his ship in 1910 to complete exploration work during the main South Pole attempt. Scott demurred but offered Mawson a place on his South Pole team. Mawson, taking Shackleton's advice, turned down the offer and pressed forward with his own plans to investigate the great quadrant of Antarctica lying adjacent to his motherland Australia. He set about raising funds from wealthy Australians living in London. The expedition was ready to go by the polar spring of 1911. Because Scott's preparations for his final fated journey were based on Ross Island, Mawson's intended base site, Mawson was forced to set up a base further west in an unknown region. This region turned out to be riven with year-long windstorms of unprecedented ferocity. That he persevered with all his plans in this uniquely hellish territory was, in itself, a testament to the quality of the team and to his personal leadership. This book, which tells the story of Mawson's expedition, has become one of the greatest accounts of polar survival in history.

By the time Mawson left Antarctica, he and his men had added more to the maps of the world's sixth continent than any one else of their time. Though he loved adventure and was proud of his Australian identity, scientific curiosity was Mawson's driving force. He was openly derisive of Pole-hunting for its own sake. When Mawson returned to Australia in 1913 his expedition had explored and mapped some 2,000 miles of the unknown coastline of Earth's last unmapped continent and added a huge amount of data to our scientific knowledge of this forbidding place.

In the 1980s and 1990s I led a series of expeditions to the North and South Poles. A Canadian magazine recently stated that these endeavors had no scientific value, so I sued them for libel and won. Though I am not a scientist, many of my colleagues are. Like Mawson, our journeys combined the two elements of adventure and scientific research, and this dedication to science may be one explanation of why Mawson is not as well known as many of his contemporaries.

In 1979 I led a team of three across another vast chunk of unexplored Antarctica on the opposite side of the continent and mapped it for the first time using aneroid barometers. That was a mere sixty-six years after Mawson's epic journey yet, at the time, I knew little or nothing of Mawson's feats. He had been a true hero in his own country, but by the 1970s Mawson was little known outside the world of polar historians. By the 1970s explorers were thought of as eccentrics. True heroes were the stars of film, pop and sports and it was not until the mid 1980s that, by sheer chance, I came across a copy of *The Home of the Blizzard*. I was entranced by the book which, to me, outshone that other survival epic, *The Worst Journey in the World* by Apsley Cherry-Garrard, one of Scott's team.

For the past fifteen years I have made a practice of re-reading *The Home of the Blizzard* during the planning stage of each new expedition. In many ways, the polar expeditions of today are no different than they were in Mawson's day. Much of the equipment Mawson had used remained virtually unchanged in the 1970s and early 1980s. Some of it is still used, but the 1990s have produced a surge in research and development and many improvements have been made. For example, Mawson's men used theodolites to locate their position on their sledge journeys. In the 1970s I, too, carried this unwieldy instrument, but in the 1980s research into plastics produced a light (two-pound) plastic sextant which was a great improvement. In the 1990s the ubiquitous Global Positioning Satellite tells you your location in seconds and the equipment weighs only four ounces. In the 1970s, we used the same heavy pyramid tents as did Mawson but in 1981 the light geodesic tent took over. Then, as now, the equipment was expensive to buy and Mawson, like today's expedition leaders, knew all about sponsorship. He even dedicated his book to his sponsors, his team and his family—in that order! His main cost was his ship, the *Aurora*. Incidentally, sixty years later my polar ship the *Kista Dan* was sponsored by the Bowring family business who also had owned the *Aurora*. Many of his food sponsors, including Cadbury's chocolate, are our sponsors to this day, with some of their products being little altered from the early part of the century.

When Mawson sought volunteers for his team, they, like mine six decades later, almost exclusively came from Commonwealth countries. The very day the *Aurora* returned to Australia she passed Amundsen' ship, the *Fram*, and learned, as did the entire world, that the Norwegian, not Scott, had conquered the South Pole. This, too, has not changed much. In the 1980s and 1990s my expeditions to achieve the remaining polar "firsts" consistently have contended for the titles with chiefly Norwegian rivals.

Mawson vividly describes the troubles of erecting and maintaining his base camp hut in Antarctica. Winds in excess of 200 miles per hour battered his base on its rock formations close by the sea. Our own 1980–1981 crossing of Antarctica was preceded by an eight-month sojourn at a base with a radio operator (my wife) and two others at 6,000 feet above sea level and living in snow. We experienced winds up to 125 miles per hour and the wind-chill factor dropped to minus 84 degrees centigrade. Because our huts were made of light cardboard, we relied entirely on snowdrifts to cover them for wind protection and insulation. Like Mawson's men we dug deep trenches, 200 yards in all, for stores, lavatories, 80-foot-deep slop pits and sledge workshops. We experienced the same camaraderie as did the Australians, the same busy lives of survival chores, drift removal and science programmes. The lack of contact with other humans, news or entertainment was missed by no one. We suffered the same dangers from blizzards and from near-deaths by carbon monoxide poisoning. It is surprising that Mawson's men omitted placing guide ropes between their huts and the out-houses, which was more than once the cause of death by exposure. We placed 700 yards of rope or string on posts in order to avoid becoming fatally disoriented on the way to the out-houses.

In 1993 I led a two-man team across the Antarctic continent. The Guinness Book of Records describes that trip as "the longest totally self-supporting polar sledge journey ever made and the first totally unsupported crossing of the Antarctic landmass, a distance of 1,350 miles." The previous unsupported record of 1,245 miles had stood for 84 years and was set by Mawson. His sledge loads weighed 574 pounds each. Ours weighed 485 pound each. The difference in progress was that Mawson used dogs to pull the loads and we man-hauled. Like Mawson's team, we slowly starved. I reduced in weight from over 210 pounds to 140 pounds. Mawson, however, was reduced down to just 125 pounds, so he was clearly the closer to death.

Man-hauling sledges of some 500 pounds makes you sweat even at minus 40 degrees centigrade. No modern fabrics are truly 100 per cent breathable, so they block the sweat. We had no space to carry spare clothes or fuel to heat the tent, so sweat-damp clothes would be lethal. As a result, we, like Mawson, relied on cotton clothing that was 100 per cent breathable and was available in 1909. On our skis we, like some of Mawson's men, used seal-skins to provide traction. On our Antarctic crossing 1993 we fashioned crampons from spare rope, as did Mawson, in order to man-haul over steep areas of blue-ice glaciers.

As Scott, Shackleton and Amundsen had done before him, Mawson used a mast and sail to add wind-power to the efforts of his dogs. In 1993 we did likewise with updated versions. The principle was the same: If he wind was behind you, it could help you progress. However, in 1996 I attempted to cross Antarctica solo using a sophisticated kite. Despite having no sailing know-how, I found that unlike the 1993 equipment, this new-fangled device could add enormous advantages. Indeed, in one day I traveled 117 miles instead of my normal hard-won daily 10 miles. At the end of the sailing day I was fresh and had used little effort, whereas a man-haul day used far more effort, calories and food than a marathon run.

Nowadays new sails called parawings have further revolution-ized "man-haul" travel in Antarctica. They can take you south even though the wind comes from the west or east. This means that a huge amount of sheer effort is removed and any fit person with good sailing knowledge could—theoretically—cross Antarctica in less than two months.

Of course, they still could fall into crevasses as easily as Mawson's men unfortunately did, and this will remain a menace until some clever scientist produces a pocket-sized crevasse detection radar.

I will not spoil the book by dwelling on details of the human tragedy which overtook his journey, but the resulting struggle by Mawson to get back to his coastal base, the unspeakable horrors that he suffered en route and the remark-able tale of endurance that he tells so well will make this a story you cannot put down.

The subsidiary journeys of Mawson's colleagues are equally well-told and are classics of exploration in their own right, especially that of Frank Wild. Wild had distinguished himself on the expeditions of both Scott and Shackleton even before his involvement with Mawson's team, yet his autobi-ography will be published for the first time in 1999.

Mawson was knighted for his polar work and, in 1958 when he died, he was given a full Australian state funeral.

I hope that this new edition of *The Home of the Blizzard* will serve to widen the circle of his admirers worldwide as his posthumous reputation so richly deserves.

Sir Ranulph Fiennes
February 27, 1998

TO THOSE WHO MADE IT POSSIBLE

THE SUBSCRIBERS AND CO-OPERATORS

TO THOSE WHO MADE IT A SUCCESS

MY COMRADES

AND TO

THOSE WHO WAITED

AUTHOR'S PREFACE

In this edition of "The Home of the Blizzard" it has been my endeavour to present a connected narrative of the Expedition in a less expensive and more concentrated form than in the large two-volume work. The account has been made even more popular by the retention of only such matter as is of general interest. This has necessitated the re-writing of certain sections and the revision of the whole.

The illustrations in this volume, though few in number compared with those of the larger work, are many of them new and never before published, giving to this edition a special interest.

Those who wish for fuller information and more copious illustrations should refer to the two-volume work or to the Scientific Publications published separately as ready.

The reports handed to me by the leaders concerning the work of the sledging journeys and of the respective bases were written in a clear and popular style. It is to be regretted that space does not allow of their publication *in extenso*, it being found necessary to make excisions and extracts to keep the narrative within limits. I wish to assure the various authors of my appreciation of their contributions and hope that some day they will themselves publish a fuller account of their adventures.

For the photographic illustrations, the book is indebted to the members of the staff whose names appear under the respective reproductions; but our thanks are chiefly due to Frank Hurley, whose artistic taste and perseverance under conditions of exceptional difficulty receive our utmost commendation. Alfred J. Hodgeman has done good service in connection with the preparation of diagrams and maps.

With regard to the writing of the original two-volume edition, I found leisure during the second winter in Adelie Land to prepare the first seven chapters; but the greater part had to be completed on return to civilization in a period which, owing to arrangements for publication, was limited to several months. Even that short time was not entirely free for the task, for many details had to be settled in connection with the winding up of the Expedition, its finances, and preparations for dealing with the scientific collections and data. In such circumstances it was well for the book that I was able to enlist the services of Dr. A. L. McLean. His journalistic talent had been revealed when he occupied the post of editor of the *Adelie Blizzard*, a monthly volume which helped to relieve the monotony of our second year in Adelie Land. I was very greatly assisted by Dr. McLean, who was occupied for months revising, cutting down and amplifying the material of the story. Later, when I was in Australia on a lecturing tour on behalf of the finances of the Expedition, he remained in London to revise the proofs and see the book through the press.

Finally, I wish to express my thanks to Dr. Hugh Robert Mill for hints and criticisms by which we have greatly profited.

DOUGLAS MAWSON.

PREFACE

ONE of the oft-repeated questions, for which I usually had a ready answer, at the conclusion of Sir Ernest Shackleton's Expedition (1907–9) was, "Would you like to go to the Antarctic again?" In the first flush of the welcome home and for many months, during which the keen edge of pleasure under civilized conditions had not entirely worn away, I was inclined to reply with a somewhat emphatic negative. But, once more a man in the world of men, lulled in the easy repose of routine, and performing the ordinary duties of a workaday world, old emotions awakened, the grand sweet days returned in irresistible glamour, far away "voices" called:

> ". . . from the wilderness, the vast and Godlike spaces,
> The stark and sullen solitudes that sentinel the Pole."

There always seemed to be something at the back of my mind, stored away for future contemplation, and it was an idea which largely matured during my first sojourn in the far South. At times, during the long hours of steady tramping across the trackless snow-fields, one's thoughts flow in a clear and limpid stream, the mind is unruffled and composed and the passion of a great venture springing suddenly before the imagination is sobered by the calmness of pure reason. It may have been in one such phase that I suddenly found myself eager for more than a glimpse of the great span of Antarctic coast lying nearest to Australia.

Professor T. W. E. David, Dr. F. A. Mackay and I, when seeking the South Magnetic Pole during the summer of 1908–9, had penetrated farthest into that region on land. The limiting outposts had been defined by other expeditions; at Cape Adare on the east and at Gaussberg on the west. Between them lay my "Land of Hope and Glory," of whose outline and glacial features only the barest evidence had been furnished.

The idea of exploring this unknown coast took firm root in my mind while I was on a visit to Europe in February 1910. The prospects of an expedition operating to the west of Cape Adare were discussed with the late Captain R. F. Scott, and I suggested that the activities of his expedition might be arranged to extend over part of the area in question. However, after mature thought, Captain Scott decided that his hands were already too full to make any definite proposition for a region so remote from his own principal objective.

Sir Ernest Shackleton was warmly enthusiastic when the scheme was laid before him, and planned to lead the undertaking himself. Later in the year pressure of private affairs required his continuous presence in London, and so, in agreement with an arrangement between us, the leadership of the projected expedition relapsed to myself.

For many reasons, besides the fact that it was the country of my home and Alma Mater, I was desirous that the Expedition should be maintained by Australia. It seemed to me that here was an opportunity to prove that the young men of a young country could rise to those traditions which have made the history of British Polar exploration one of triumphant endeavour as well as of tragic sacrifice. And so I was privileged to rally the "sons of the younger son."

A provisional plan was drafted and put before the Australasian Association for the Advancement of Science at their meeting held at Sydney in January 1911, with a request for approval and financial assistance. Both were unanimously granted, a sum of £1000 was voted and committees were formed to co-operate in the arrangement of a scientific programme and to approach the Government with a view to obtaining substantial help.

The three leading members of the Committees were Professor Orme Masson (President), Professor T. W. Edgeworth David (President Elect) and Professor G. C. Henderson (President of the Geographical Section). All were zealous and active in furthering the projects of the Expedition.

Meanwhile I had laid my scheme of work before certain prominent Australians and some large donations* had been promised. The sympathy and warm-hearted generosity of these gentlemen was an incentive for me to push through my plans at once to a successful issue.

I therefore left immediately for London with a view to making arrangements there for a vessel suitable for polar exploration, to secure sledging dogs from Greenland and furs from Norway, and to order the construction of certain instruments and equipment. It was also my intention to gain if possible the support of Australians residing in London. The Council of the University of Adelaide, in a broad-minded scientific spirit, granted me the necessary leave of absence from my post as lecturer, to carry through what had now resolved itself into an extensive and prolonged enterprise.

During my absence, a Committee of the Australasian Association for the Advancement of Science approached the Commonwealth Government with an appeal for funds. Unfortunately it was the year of the Coronation of His Majesty King George V, and the leading members of the Cabinet were in England, so the final answer to the deputation was postponed. I was thus in a position of some difficulty, for many requirements had to be ordered without delay if the Expedition were to get away from Australia before the end of the year.

At length, through the kindness of Lord Northcliffe, the columns of the *Daily Mail* were opened to us, and Sir Ernest Shackleton made a strong appeal on our behalf. I am very much indebted to Sir Ernest Shackleton's energy and efforts which secured some large donations towards the

* The following is a list of donations of £1000 and over received from private individuals.

Samuel Hordern (Sydney), £2500; Robert Barr Smith (Adelaide), £1000; Hugh Dixson (Sydney), £1000; Roderick Murchison (Melbourne), £1000; William A. Horn (Adelaide), £1000; Hugh Denison (Sydney), £1000; Sir Lucas Tooth (Sydney), £1000; Lord Strathcona (Canada), £1000; Eugene Sandow (London), £1050; and towards outstanding accounts on return of the Expedition a sum of £1100 from Lady Scott (Robert F.). A complete list of all donations to the funds and an audited statement of accounts will appear in connection with the series of scientific volumes already published or in hand.

funds. The Royal Geographical Society set the seal of its approval on the aims of the Expedition, and many donations were soon afterwards received.

At this rather critical period I was fortunate in securing the co-operation of Captain John King Davis, my old friend and colleague of the Shackleton Expeditions. He was in future to act as Master of the vessel and Second in Command of the Expedition. Davis joined me in April 1911, and rendered valuable help in the preliminary arrangements. Under his direction the S.Y. *Aurora* was purchased and refitted; eventually sailing from London flying the burgee of the Royal Thames Yacht Club.

The few months spent in London were anxious and trying, but the memory of them is pleasantly relieved by the generosity and assistance which were meted out on every hand. Sir George Reid, High Commissioner for the Australian Commonwealth, I shall always remember as an ever-present friend. The preparations for the scientific programme received a strong impetus from well-known Antarctic explorers, notably Dr. W. S. Bruce, Dr. Jean Charcot, Captain Adrian de Gerlache, and the late Sir John Murray and Mr. J. Y. Buchanan of the *Challenger* Expedition. In the dispositions made for oceanographical work I was indebted for liberal support to H.S.H. the Prince of Monaco.

In July 1911 I was once more in Australia, a large proportion of my time being occupied with finance, the purchase and concentration of stores and equipment, and the appointment of the staff. In this work I was aided by Professors Masson and David and by Miss Ethel Bage, who throughout this busy period acted in an honorary capacity as secretary in Melbourne.

Time was drawing on and the funds of the Expedition were wholly inadequate to the needs of the moment, until Mr. T. H. Smeaton, M.P., introduced a deputation to the Hon. John Verran, Premier of South Australia. The deputation, organized to approach the State Government for a grant of £5000, was led by the Right Hon. Sir Samuel Way, Bart., Chief Justice of South Australia and Chancellor of the Adelaide University, and supported by Mr. Lavington

Bonython, Mayor of Adelaide, T. Ryan, M.P., the President of several scientific societies and members of the University staff. This sum was eventually forthcoming and it paved the way to greater things.

In Sydney, Professor David approached the State Government on behalf of the Expedition for financial support, and, through the Acting Premier, the Hon. W. A. Holman, £7000 was generously promised. The State of Victoria through the Hon. W. Watt, Premier of Victoria, supplemented our funds to the extent of £6000.

Upheld by the prestige of a large meeting convened in the Melbourne Town Hall during the spring, the objects of the Australasian Antarctic Expedition were more widely published. On that memorable occasion the Governor-General, Lord Denman, acted as chairman, and among others who participated were the Hon. Andrew Fisher (Prime Minister of the Commonwealth), the Hon. Alfred Deakin (Leader of the Opposition), Professor Orme Masson (President A.A.A.S. and representative of Victoria), Senator Walker (representing New South Wales) and Professor G. C. Henderson (representing South Australia).

Soon after this meeting the Commonwealth Government voted £5000, following a grant of £2000 made by the British Government at the instance of Lord Denman, who from the outset had been a staunch friend of the Expedition.

At the end of October 1911 all immediate financial anxiety had passed, and I was able to devote myself with confidence to the final preparations.

Captain Davis brought the *Aurora* from England to Australia, and on December 2, 1911, we left Hobart for the South. A base was established on Macquarie Island, after which the ship pushed through the ice and landed a party on an undiscovered portion of the Antarctic Continent adjacent to d'Urville's Adelie Land. After a journey of fifteen hundred miles to the west of this base another party was landed and then the *Aurora* returned to Hobart to refit and to carry out oceanographical investigations, during the year 1912, in the waters south of Australia and New Zealand.

In December 1912 Captain Davis revisited the Antarctic to relieve the two parties who had wintered there. A calamity befell my own sledging party, Lieut. B. E. S. Ninnis and Dr. X. Mertz both lost their lives, and my arrival back at winter quarters was delayed for so long that the *Aurora* was forced to leave six men for another year to prosecute a search for the missing party. The remainder of the men and the party fifteen hundred miles to the west were landed safely at Hobart in March 1912.

Thus the prearranged plans were upset by my non-return, and the administration of the Expedition in Australia was carried out by Professor David, whose special knowledge was invaluable at such a juncture.

Funds were once more required, and, during the summer of 1912, Captain Davis visited London and secured additional support, while the Australasian Association for the Advancement of Science again successfully approached the Commonwealth Government (The Right Hon. J. H. Cook, Prime Minister). In all, the sum of £8000 was raised to meet the demands of a second voyage of relief.

The party left on Macquarie Island, who had agreed to remain at the station for another year, ran short of food during their second winter. The New Zealand Government rendered the Expedition a great service in dispatching stores to them by the *Tutanekai* without delay.

Finally, in the summer of 1913, the *Aurora* set out on her third cruise to the far South, picking up the parties at Macquarie Island and in the Antarctic, carried out observations for two months amid the ice, and reached Adelaide late in February 1914.

Throughout a period of more than three years Professors David and Masson—the fathers of the Expedition—worked indefatigably and unselfishly in its interests. To these gentlemen the success of the Expedition is ever so deeply indebted.

In shipping arrangements Captain Davis was assisted throughout by Mr. J. J. Kinsey, Christchurch, Capt. Barter, Sydney, and Mr. F. Hammond, Hobart. Many favours were also received from Admiral King Hall (in charge of the Imperial Squadron in Australasian waters), Admiral Creswell (in charge of the Commonwealth forces), and Captain J. P. Rolleston (Naval stores at Garden Island).

Such an undertaking is the work of a multitude, and it is only by sympathetic support from many sources that a measure of success can be expected. In this connection there are many names which I recall with warm gratitude. It is impossible to mention all to whom the Expedition is indebted, but I trust that none of those who have taken a prominent part will fail to find an acknowledgment somewhere in this volume.

I should specially mention the friendly help afforded by the Australasian Press, which has at all times given the Expedition favourable and lengthy notices, insisting on its national and scientific character.

With regard to the conduct of the work itself, I was seconded by the whole-hearted co-operation of the members, my comrades, and what they have done can only be indicated in this narrative. The reader will not fail to be struck with the great part played by our lion-hearted Davis; with the highly satisfactory operations conducted by the intrepid Frank Wild; and with the sound and able leadership of George Ainsworth.

INTRODUCTION

AT the southern extremity of the globe there is a vast unknown region touched upon, even to the present day, only at widely separated intervals.

The Antarctic problem* assumed its modern aspect after Captain Cook's circumnavigation of the globe in high southern latitudes, accomplished between 1772 and 1775. Fact replaced the fiction and surmise of former times, and maps appeared showing a large blank area at the southern extremity of the earth, where speculative cartographers had affirmed the existence of habitable land extending far towards the Equator. Cook's voyage made it clear that if there were any considerable mass of Antarctic land, it must indubitably lie within the Antarctic Circle, and be subjected to such stringent climatic conditions as to render it an unlikely habitation for man.

Cook's reports of seals on the island of South Georgia initiated in the Antarctic seas south of America a commercial enterprise, which is still carried on, and has incidentally thrown much light upon the geography of the South Polar regions. Indeed, almost the whole of such information, prior to the year 1839, was the outcome of sealing and whaling projects.

About the year 1840 a wave of scientific enthusiasm resulted in the dispatch of three national expeditions by France, the United States, and Great Britain; part at least of whose programmes was Antarctic exploration. Russia had previously sent out an expedition which had made notable discoveries.

The contributions to knowledge gained at this period were considerable. Those carried back to civilization by the British expedition under Ross are so well known that

* Dr. H. R. Mill has compiled a summary of Antarctic exploration in his "Siege of the South Pole."

they need not be described. The French under Dumont d'Urville and the Americans under Wilkes visited the region to the southward of Australia—the arena of our own efforts—and frequent references will be made to their work throughout the story.

What has been termed the period of inverted interest now intervened, before the modern movement set in with overpowering insistence. It was not till 1897 that it had commenced in earnest. Since then many adventurers have gone forth; most of the prominent civilized nations taking their share in exploration. By their joint efforts some, at least, of the mystery of Antarctica has been dispelled.

The Continent itself appears to have been sighted for the first time in the year 1820, but no human being actually set foot on it until 1895. The Belgian expedition under de Gerlache was the first to experience the Antarctic winter, spending the year 1898 drifting helplessly, frozen in the pack-ice to the southward of America. In the following year a British expedition under Borchgrevinck, wintering at Cape Adare, on the Australasian side, passed a year upon the Antarctic mainland.

The main efforts of recent years have been centred upon the two accessible areas, namely, that in the American Quadrant* which is prolonged as a tongue of land outside the Antarctic Circle, being consequently less beset by ice; secondly, the vicinity of the Ross Sea in the Australian Quadrant. It is because these two favoured domains have for special reasons attracted the stream of exploration that the major portion of Antarctica is unknown. Nevertheless, one is in a position to sketch broad features which will probably not be radically altered by any future expeditions.

---

* For convenience, the Antarctic regions may be referred to in four main divisions, corresponding with the quadrants of the hemispheres. Of the several suggestions thrown out by previous writers, the one that appears to have most to recommend it and is adopted here is that based on the meridian of Greenwich, referring the quadrants to an adjacent continent or ocean. Thus the American quadrant lies between 0° and 90° W., the African Quadrant between 0° and 90° E., and the Australian Quadrant between 90° and 180° E. The fourth division is called the Pacific Quadrant, since ocean alone lies to the north of it.

Certain it is that a continent approaching the area of North America lies more or less buried beneath the South Polar snows; though any statement of the precise area is insufficient for a proper appreciation of the magnitude, unless its elevated plateau-like character be also taken into consideration. It appears to be highest over a wide central crown rising to more than ten thousand feet. Of the remainder, there is little doubt that the major portion stands as high as six thousand feet. The average elevation must far exceed that of any other continent, for, with peaks nineteen thousand feet above the sea-level, its mountainous topography is remarkable. Along the coast of Victoria Land, in the Australian Quadrant, are some of the most majestic vistas of alpine scenery that the world affords. Rock exposures are rare, ice appearing everywhere except in the most favoured places.

Regarding plant and animal life upon the land there is little to say. The vegetable kingdom is represented by plants of low organization such as mosses, lichens, diatoms and alga. The animal world, so far as true land-forms are concerned, is limited to types like the protozoa (lowest in the organic scale), rotifera and minute insect-like mites which lurk hidden away amongst the tufts of moss or on the under-side of loose stones. Bacteria, most fundamental of all, at the basis, so to speak, of animal and vegetable life, have a manifold distribution.

It is a very different matter when we turn to the life of the neighbouring seas, for that vies in abundance with the warmer waters of lower latitudes. There are innumerable seals, many sea birds and millions of penguins. As all these breed on Antarctic shores, the coastal margin of the continent is not so desolate.

In view of the fact that life, including land-mammals, is abundant in the North Polar regions, it may be asked why analogous forms are not better represented in corresponding southern latitudes. Without going too deeply into the question, it may be briefly stated, first, that a more wide-spread glaciation than at present prevails invested the great southern continent and its environing seas, within recent geological times, effectually exterminating any pre-existing land life. Secondly, since that period the continent has been isolated by a wide belt of ocean from other lands, from which restocking might have taken place after the manner of the North Polar regions. Finally, climatic conditions in the Antarctic are, latitude for latitude, much more severe than in the Arctic.

With regard to climate in general, Antarctica has the lowest mean temperature and the highest wind-velocity of any land existing. This naturally follows from the fact that it is a lofty expanse of ice-clad land circumscribing the Pole, and that the Antarctic summer occurs when the earth is farther from the sun than is the case during the Arctic summer.

There are those who would impatiently ask, "What is the use of it all?" The answer is brief.

Bound up with the mystery of this seventh continent are volumes of data of vital importance to science, and economic problems which may become of moment in the near future.

The polar regions, like any other part of the globe, may be said to be paved with facts, the essence of which it is necessary to acquire before knowledge of this special zone can be brought to even a provisional exactitude. On the face of it, polar research may seem to be specific and discriminating, but it must be remembered that an advance in any one of the departments into which, for convenience, science is artificially divided, conduces to the advantage of all. Science is a homogeneous whole. If we ignore the facts contained in one part of the world, surely we are hampering scientific advance. It is obvious to everyone that, given only a fraction of the pieces, it is a much more difficult task to put together a jig-saw puzzle and obtain an idea of the finished pattern than were all the pieces at hand. The pieces of the jig-saw puzzle are the data of science.

Though it is not sufficiently recognized, the advance of science is attended by a corresponding increase in the creature comforts of man. Again from an economic aspect, the frozen South may not attract immediate attention. But who can say what a train of enterprise the future may bring?

Captain James Cook, on his return to London after the circumnavigation of Antarctica, held that the far-southern lands had no future. Yet, a few years later, great profits were being returned to Great Britain and the United States from sealing-stations established as a result of Cook's own observations. At the present day, about twenty whaling companies have flourishing industries in the Antarctic waters within the American Quadrant.

Even now much can be said in regard to the possibilities offered by the Antarctic regions for economic development, but, year by year, the outlook will widen, since man is constantly resorting to subtler and more ingenious artifice in applying Nature's resources. It will be remembered that Charles Darwin, when in Australia, predicted a very limited commercial future for New South Wales. But the mastery of man overcame the difficulties which Darwin's too penetrating mind foresaw.

What will be the rôle of the South in the progress of civilization and in the development of the arts and sciences is not now obvious. As sure as there is here a vast mass of land with potentialities, strictly limited at present, so surely will it be cemented some day within the universal plinth of things.

An unknown coast-line lay before the door of Australia. Following on the general advance of exploration, and as a sequel to several important discoveries, the time arrived when a complete elucidation of the Antarctic problem was more than ever desirable. In the Australian Quadrant, the broad geographical features of the Ross Sea area were well known, but of the remainder and greater portion of the tract only vague and imperfect reports could be supplied. It was with a view to clearing up some of the mystery connected with the tract that the Australasian Antarctic Expedition was formed.

Before proceeding with our story it will be as well to review the stage at which discovery had arrived when our expedition came upon the scene.

The coast-line of the eastern extremity of the Australian Quadrant, including the outline of the Ross Sea and the coast west-north-west of Cape Adare as far as Cape North, was charted by Ross and has been amplified by seven later expeditions. In the region west of Cape North, recent explorers had done very little. Scott in the *Discovery* had disproved the existence of some of Wilkes's land in that direction; Shackleton in the *Nimrod* had viewed some forty miles of high land beyond Cape North; lastly, on the eve of our departure, Scott's *Terra Nova* had met two patches of new land—Oates Land—still farther west, making it evident that the continent ranged at least two hundred and eighty miles in a west-north-west direction from Cape Adare.

Just outside the western limit of the Australian Quadrant lies Gaussberg in Kaiser Wilhelm Land, discovered by a German Expedition under Professor von Drygalski in 1902. In that vicinity also, the *Challenger* (1872) secured several valuable soundings. Between the most westerly point sighted by the *Terra Nova* and Gaussberg, there is a circuit of two thousand miles, bordering the Antarctic Circle, in which no vessels had navigated other than those of Balleny, Wilkes and d'Urville in the years 1839 and 1840.

This was the area of our activities and, therefore, a synopsis of the voyages of those early mariners will be enlightening.

Balleny, a British whaling-master, with the schooner *Eliza Scott* of one hundred and fifty-four tons, and a cutter, the *Sabrina* of fifty-four tons, was the first to meet with success in these waters. Proceeding southward from New Zealand in 1839, he located the Balleny Islands, a group containing active volcanoes, lying about two hundred miles off the nearest part of the mainland and to the north-west of Cape Adare. Leaving these islands, Balleny sailed westward keeping a look-out for new land. During a gale the vessels became separated and the *Sabrina* was lost with all hands. Balleny in the *Eliza Scott* arrived safely in England and reported doubtful land in 122° E. longitude, approximately.

Admiral Dumont d'Urville, leader of a very notable French Expedition, in command of two corvettes, the *Astrolabe* and the *Zelée*, steered southward from Hobart on

January 1, 1840. Without much obstruction from floating ice, he came within sight of the Antarctic coast, thenceforth known as Adelie Land. The expedition did not set foot on the mainland, but a landing was effected on an adjacent islet. They remained in the vicinity of the coast for a few days, when a gale sprang up which was hazardously weathered amongst large bergs and scattered pack-ice. The ships then cruised along the face of flat-topped ice-cliffs, of the type known as barrier-ice or shelf-ice, which were taken to be connected with land and named Côte Clarie. At the present day at least, as will be seen later, Côte Clarie does not exist.

Lieutenant Charles Wilkes, the leader of a world-renowned exploring expedition to circumnavigate the world, having already executed an excellent programme amongst the islands of the Pacific Ocean, proceeded south from Sydney at the close of the year 1839. His vessels were the *Vincennes*, a sloop of war of seven hundred and eighty tons, the *Peacock*, another sloop of six hundred and fifty tons, the *Porpoise*, a gun-brig of two hundred and thirty tons, and a tender, the *Flying Fish*, of ninety-six tons. The scientists of the expedition were precluded from joining in this part of the programme, and were left behind in Sydney. The ships, which were in no way suited for the requirements of exploration in ice-infested seas, spent a period of forty-two days in Antarctic waters, most of the time separated by gales, during which the crews showed great skill in navigating their ill-fitted crafts and suffered great hardships.

Land was reported almost daily, but, unfortunately, subsequent exploration has shown that many of the landfalls do not exist. Several soundings made by Wilkes were indicative of the approach to land, but he must have frequently mistaken for it distant ice-masses frozen in the pack. Experience has proved what deceptive light-effects may be observed amid the ice and how easily a mirage may simulate reality.

The only spot where Wilkes reported rocks *in situ* was in Adelie Land, where Admiral Dumont d'Urville had anticipated him by seven days. Farther west, earth and stones had been collected by Wilkes from material embedded in floating masses of ice off the coast of his Knox Land. These facts lend credence to Wilkes's claims of land in this latter vicinity. His expedition did not once set foot on Antarctic shores, and, possibly on account of the absence of the scientific staff, his descriptions tend to be obscure. Certain soundings made by Wilkes were sufficient to show that he was probably in some places at no great distance from land. Considering that his work was carried out in the days of sailing-ships, in unsuitable craft, under the most adverse weather conditions, with crews scurvy-stricken and discontented, it is wonderful how much was achieved. We may amply testify that he did more than open the field for future expeditions.

With these few references is comprised, in brief outline, our knowledge concerning the region to which our own effort was to be directed, at the time when the plans of the Australasian Antarctic Expedition were being formulated.

CHAPTER I

PLAN AND PREPARATION

THE chief object of this Australasian Antarctic Expedition was to investigate, as far as possible, the stretch of prospective but practically unknown Antarctic coast extending almost two thousand miles in an east and west direction, between the farthest west of the *Terra Nova** and the farthest east of the *Gauss*†—a new sphere west of the region visited by Scott and Shackleton. The programme also included the scientific examination of Macquarie Island, a sub-Antarctic possession of the Commonwealth, lying some eight hundred and fifty miles south-south-east of Hobart. In addition to work to be conducted from land bases, provision was to be made for the ship's party to carry out extensive investigations of the ocean and its floor over the broad belt between Australia and the Antarctic Continent. This latter was an important item of the programme, for science is just as much interested in problems connected with the depths of the ocean as with those arising from a study of the dry land.

These plans were formulated with no idea of the attainment of the South Geographic Pole; but this reflected in no way adversely upon the prospects. As it happened the experiences and discoveries proved unusually absorbing.

The procedure adopted to achieve these objects was briefly as follows. A suitable vessel was to be acquired, fitted and equipped. Hobart was selected as the final port of departure, and from thence a course was to be set for Macquarie Island. There it was intended to land a small party with stores and a hut, to chart the Island and prosecute general scientific investigations during the ensuing year. Leaving

* Scott's British Antarctic Expedition of 1910.
† German Antarctic Expedition of 1902.

1

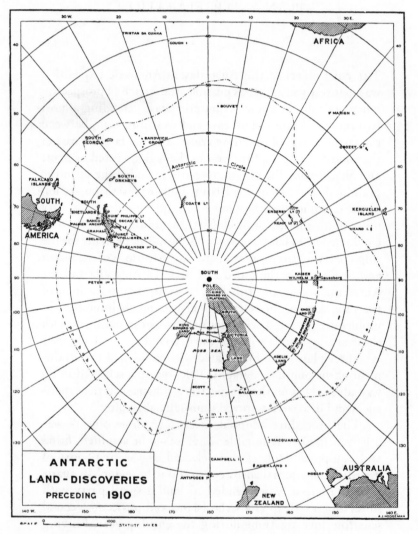

Map showing Antarctic Lands as known when the plans
of the Australasian Antarctic Expedition were first
formulated.

Macquarie Island the vessel was to proceed south to the ice on the meridian of 158° E. longitude, to the westward of which the Antarctic programme was to be conducted. After reaching the pack-ice, every endeavour was to be made to penetrate to the South to reach the supposed continent. A main party, provisioned and equipped for a year's campaign, was to be landed in Antarctica on the first opportunity; there a hut would be built to constitute a Main Base station, from which to prosecute explorations on land. Thereafter, the ship was to proceed westward with the set of the drift in those seas, and it was confidently hoped that further landings would be made and at least one more shore station, a Western Base party, be established before the end of the summer season. Having landed several parties the vessel was to return to Hobart. The following summer, the ship was to go South once more and conclude the Expedition by relieving the several land parties.

The scope of our intentions was regarded by some as over ambitious, but seeing nothing impossible in these arrangements, we continued to adhere to them as closely as possible with what fortune remains to be told.

To secure a suitable vessel was a matter of fundamental importance. The primary consideration in the design of a vessel built to navigate amid the ice is that the hull be very staunch, capable of driving into the pack and of resisting lateral pressure, if the ice should close in around it.

So a thick-walled timber vessel, with adequate stiffening in the framework, would meet the case. The construction being of wood imparts a certain elasticity, which is of great advantage in easing the shock of impacts with floating ice. The ordinary steel ship would be ripped on its first contact with the ice. Another device, to obviate the shock and to assist in forging a way through the pack-ice, is to have a cut-away bow. Thus, instead of presenting to the ice a vertical face, which would immediately arrest the ship and possibly cause considerable damage on account of the sudden stress of the blow, a sloping, over-hanging bow is adopted. This arrangement enables the bow to rise over the impediment, with a gradual slackening of speed. The immense

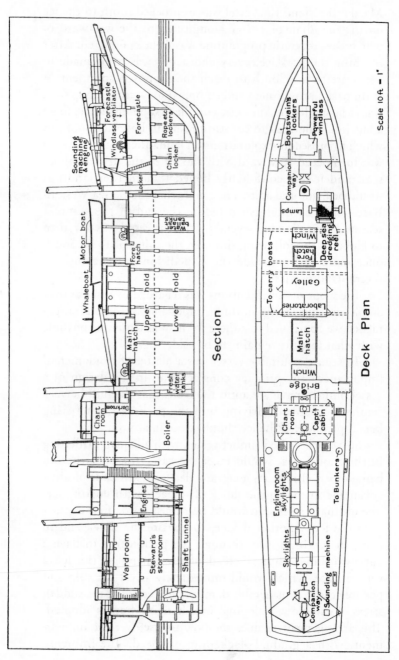

Plan and Section of the S.Y. *Aurora.*

weight put upon the ice crushes it and the ship settles down, moving ahead and gathering speed to meet the next obstacle.

Of importance second only to a strong hull is the possession of sails in addition to engines. The latter are a *sine qua non* in polar navigation, for sails allow of economy in the consumption of coal, and always remain as a last resort should the coal-supply be exhausted or the propeller damaged. Such craft are not to be had in southern waters, being exclusively engaged upon arctic sealing and whaling.

The *Aurora*, of the Newfoundland sealing fleet, was ultimately purchased and underwent necessary alterations. She was built in Dundee, and though by no means young was still in good condition and capable of buffeting with the pack for many a year.

The hull was made of stout oak planks, sheathed with greenheart and lined with fir. The bow, fashioned on cut-away lines, was a mass of solid wood, armoured with steel plates. The heavy side frames were braced and stiffened by two tiers of horizontal oak beams, upon which were built the 'tween decks and the main deck. Three bulkheads isolated the forepeak, the main hold, the engine-room and the after living-quarters respectively.

The principal dimensions were, length one hundred and sixty-five feet, breadth thirty feet, and depth eighteen feet. The actual carrying capacity we found to be about six hundred tons.

The engines, situated aft, were compound, supplied with steam from a single boiler. The normal power registered was ninety-eight horse-power, working a four-bladed propeller, driving it at the rate of sixty or seventy revolutions per minute (six to ten knots per hour).

Steam was also laid on to a winch, aft, for handling cargo in the main hold, and to a forward steam-windlass. The latter was mainly used for raising the anchor and manipulating the deep-sea dredging-cable.

The ship was square on the foremast and schooner rigged on the main and mizen masts.

Between the engine-room bulkhead and the chain and sail locker was a spacious hold. Six large steel tanks built into the bottom of the hold served for the storage of fresh water, and at any time when empty could be filled with sea-water, offering a ready means of securing emergency ballast.

On the deck, just forward of the main hatch, was a deck-house, comprising cook's galley, steward's pantry and two laboratories. Still farther forward was a small lamp-room for the storage of kerosene, lamps and other necessaries. A lofty fo'c'sle-head gave much accommodation for carpenters', ship-wrights' and other stores. Below it, a capacious fo'c'sle served as quarters for a crew of sixteen men.

Aft, the chart-room, captain's cabin and photographic dark-room formed a block leading up to the bridge, situated immediately in front of the funnel. Farther aft, behind the engine-room and below the poop deck, was the ward-room, a central space sixteen feet by eight feet, filled by the dining-table and surrounded by cabins and bunks for twenty persons.

The expedition was most fortunate in securing Captain John King Davis of *Nimrod* fame as second in command. His special charge was the command of the S.Y. *Aurora*, and it was under his direction that she was purchased and refitted. The burden of the few anxious months spent in London at that time was greatly relieved by Davis's cheerful co-operation and inex-haustible energy.

From the time that the *Aurora* arrived in London to her departure for Australia, she was a scene of busy activity, as alterations and replacements were necessary to fit her for her future work.

In the meantime stores and gear were being assembled. Purchases were made and valuable donations received both in Europe and Australia.

On June 22, 1911, I departed from London for Australia, where much required my attention, leaving Davis to complete necessary arrangements and to bring the *Aurora* out to Hobart. In Australia there was much to be done, and the ensuing months were kept busy in completing the finances of the expedition and dealing with a multitude of other matters connected with the stores, gear and staff.

In no department can a leader spend time more profitably than in the selection of the men who are to accomplish the work. For a polar campaign the great desideratum is tempered youth. It is the vigour, the dash and the recuperative power of youth that is so necessary to cope with the extreme discomforts and trials of such exploration, which approximate to the limit of human endurance and often enough exceed it.

Ours proved to be a very happy selection. The majority of the men chosen as members of the land parties were young graduates of the Commonwealth and the New Zealand Universities, and with few exceptions all were representative of Australasia.

Among the exceptions was Mr. Frank Wild, who was appointed in charge of one of our Antarctic wintering stations. Wild had already distinguished himself in the South on both the Scott and the Shackleton expeditions. He is now in the unique position of being, as it were, the oldest resident of Antarctica. Our sojourn together at Cape Royds, as fellow members of the Shackleton Expedition, had acquainted me with Wild's high merits as an explorer and leader.

Lieutenant B. E. S. Ninnis of the Royal Fusiliers, Dr. X. Mertz, an expert Swiss ski-runner and mountaineer, and Mr. F. H. Bickerton, in charge of the air-tractor sledge, were also appointed in London.

All arrangements regarding the ship's complement were left to Captain Davis.

The staff,* as eventually disposed, was as follows:

STAFF OF THE ADELIE LAND STATION.
(*Main Base.*)†

Dr. D. Mawson.	Commander of the Expedition.
Lieut. R. Bage.	Astronomer, Assistant Magnetician and Recorder of Tides.
C. T. Madigan.	Meteorologist.
Lieut. B. E. S. Ninnis.	In charge of Greenland dogs.
Dr. X. Mertz.	In charge of Greenland dogs.

---

* For further details refer to Appendix I.

† During the second year of occupation the Party at the Main Base was reduced to seven: Bage, Madigan, Bickerton, McLean, Hodgeman and myself together with S. N. Jeffryes, a new-comer, who relieved Hannam with the wireless.

A. L. McLean.	Chief Medical Officer, Bacteriologist.
F. H. Bickerton.	In charge of air-tractor sledge.
A. J. Hodgeman.	Cartographer and Sketch Artist.
J. F. Hurley.	Official Photographer.
E. N. Webb.	Chief Magnetician.
P. E. Correll.	Mechanic and Assistant Physicist.
J. G. Hunter.	Biologist.
C. F. Laseron.	Taxidermist and Biological Collector.
F. L. Stillwell.	Geologist.
H. D. Murphy.	In charge of Expedition stores.
W. H. Hannam.	Wireless Operator and Mechanic.
J. H. Close.	Assistant Collector.
L. A. Whetter.	Surgeon.

STAFF OF THE QUEEN MARY LAND STATION.
(*Western Base.*)

F. Wild.	Leader, Sledge-master.
A. D. Watson.	Geologist.
S. E. Jones.	Medical Officer.
C. T. Harrisson.	Biologist.
M. H. Moyes.	Meteorologist.
A. L. Kennedy.	Magnetician.
C. A. Hoadley.	Geologist.
C. Dovers.	Cartographer.

STAFF OF THE MACQUARIE ISLAND STATION.

G. F. Ainsworth.	Leader: Meteorologist.
L. R. Blake.	Cartographer and Geologist.
H. Hamilton.	Biologist.
C. A. Sandell.	Wireless Operator and Mechanic.
A. J. Sawyer.	Wireless Operator.

THE SHIP'S PARTY.

J. K. Davis.	Master of S.Y. *Aurora* and Second-in-Command of the Expedition.
J. H. Blair.	First Officer during the final Antarctic Cruise.
P. Gray.	Second Officer.
C. P. de la Motte.	Third Officer.
F. J. Gillies.	Chief Engineer.

Added to these officers was a crew of nineteen, making a total of twenty-four in the ship's company. N. C. Toucher, and later F. D. Fletcher, served in the capacity of Chief Officer during the earlier voyages.

In the matter of clothes for the Antarctic land parties, we were provided with abundance of thick woollen under-clothing, and with outer garments of Jaeger fleece. These latter were union-suits, combining trousers and waistcoast, so arranged as to meet the requirements of the most severe climatic conditions. An over-suit of wind-proof material, Burberry gabardine, made to our own designs, was also supplied to be worn when necessary. For the extremities there were fur mitts made of wolf's skin, as well as woollen ones; and, in addition to the usual heavy leather ski-boots, we had fur boots from Lapland (finnesko) of reindeer skin.

The food-stuffs were selected with at least as much consid-eration as was given to any other of the requisites. The successful work of an expedition depends on the health of the men, and good and suitable food reduces to a minimum the danger of scurvy. With this end in view, canned fruit and vegetables figured largely in our commissariat. Preserved meats were taken only in comparatively small quantities, for in the matter of meat we intended to rely chiefly upon seal and penguin flesh.

Scientific appliances were accumulated from divers sources. Finally there were fur sleeping-bags of reindeer skin, sledges from Norway, mountaineering equipment from Switzerland and Esquimaux dogs from Greenland.

Many of these requirements had been assembled in London and there taken on board the *Aurora*. The rest streamed into the base at Hobart during the latter months of the year.

At length on November 4, 1911, Captain Davis arrived at Hobart with the *Aurora*, after a voyage from London of one hundred days including stoppages for coal at Cardiff and Capetown.

Before the ship had reached Queen's Wharf, the berth generously provided by the Harbour Board, the Greenland dogs were transferred to the quarantine ground, and with them went Dr. Mertz and Lieutenant Ninnis, who had accompanied the vessel on her long voyage and now gave up all their time during the stay in Hobart to the care of those important animals. A feeling of relief spread over the whole ship's company as the last dog passed over the side, for travelling with a deck cargo of dogs is not the most enviable thing from a sailor's point of view. Especially is this the case in a sailing vessel where room is limited and, consequently, dogs and ropes are mixed indiscriminately.

The date of departure south was fixed for 4 p.m. of Saturday, December 2, and a truly appalling amount of work had to be done before then.

Throughout the month of November, the staff continued to arrive in contingents at Hobart, immediately busying themselves in their own departments, and in sorting over the many thousands of packages in the great Queen's Wharf shed. Wild was placed in charge, and all entered heartily into the work. The execution of it was just what was wanted to make us fit, and prepared for the sudden and arduous work of discharging cargo at the various bases. It also gave me the opportunity of personally gauging certain qualities of the men, which are not usually evoked by a university curriculum.

Some five thousand two hundred packages were in the shed, to be sorted over and checked. The requirements of several land parties, as well as those of the ship, were being provided for, and consequently the most careful supervision was necessary to prevent mistakes, especially as the omission of a single article might fundamentally affect the work of a whole party. To assist in discriminating the impedimenta, coloured bands were painted round the packages, distinctive of the various bases.

It had been arranged that, wherever possible, everything should be packed in cases of a handy size, to facilitate unloading and transportation; each about fifty to seventy pounds in weight.

In addition to other distinguishing marks, every package bore a different number, and the detailed contents were listed in a schedule of reference.

Concurrently with the progress of this work, the ship was again overhauled, repairs effected, and many deficiencies made good. The labours of the shipwrights did not interfere with the loading, which went ahead steadily during the last fortnight in November.

The tanks in the hold not used for our supply of fresh water were packed with reserve stores for the ship. The remainder of the lower hold and the bunkers were filled with coal. Slowly the contents of the shed diminished as they were transferred to the 'tween decks. Then came the overflow. Eventually, every available space in the ship was flooded with a complicated assemblage of gear, ranging from the oregon timber masts of the wireless equipment occupying a portion of the deck amidships, to a selection of prime Australian cheeses which filled one of the cabins, and pervaded the ward-room with an odour which remained one of its permanent associations.

Yet, heterogeneous and ill-assorted as our cargo may have appeared to the crowds of curious onlookers, Captain Davis had arranged for the stowage of everything with a nicety which did him credit. The complete effects of the four bases were thus kept separate, and available in whatever order was required. Furthermore, the removal of one unit would not break the stowage of the remainder, nor disturb the trim of the ship.

At a late date the air-tractor sledge arrived. This was a monoplane body on a sledge-runner undercarriage, constructed by Messrs. Vickers, Ltd. The body was contained in one huge case which, though awkward, was comparatively light, the case weighing much more than the contents. This was securely lashed above the main deck, resting on the fo'c'sle and two boat skids.

Air tractors are great consumers of petrol of the highest quality. This demand, in addition to the requirements of two wireless plants and a motor-launch, made it necessary to take larger quantities than we liked of this dangerously inflammable stuff. So a large quantity of Shell benzine and kerosene, packed in the usual four-gallon export tins, was carried as a deck cargo.

For the transport of the requirements of the Macquarie Island Base, the S.S. *Toroa*, a small steam-packet of one hundred and twenty tons, trading between Melbourne and Tasmanian ports, was chartered. It was arranged that this auxiliary should leave Hobart several days after the *Aurora*, so as to allow us time, before her arrival, to inspect the island, and to select a suitable spot for the location of the base. As she was well provided with passenger accommodation, it was arranged that the majority of the land party should journey by her as far as Macquarie Island.

The Governor of Tasmania, Sir Henry Barron, the Premier, Sir Elliot Lewis, and the citizens of Hobart extended to us the greatest hospitality during our stay, and, when the time came, gave us a hearty send off.

CHAPTER II

THE VOYAGE TO MACQUARIE ISLAND

"Let us probe the silent places, let us seek what luck betide us;
Let us journey to a lonely land I know.
There's a whisper on the night-wind, there's a star agleam to guide us.
And the wind is calling, calling—Let us go."—SERVICE.

SATURDAY, December 2, arrived and then began final leave-taking. "God speed" messages were received from far and wide, and intercessory services were held in the cathedrals of Sydney and Hobart.

We were greatly honoured at this time in receiving a message of kind wishes for success from Queen Alexandra and, at an earlier date, from His Majesty the King.

Proud of such universal sympathy and interest, we felt stimulated to even greater exertions.

All the staff were united for the space of an hour at luncheon. Then, proceeding to the vessel, I had to push my way through a vast crowd assembled at the wharf to give us a parting cheer.

At 4 p.m. sharp, the telegraph was rung for the engines, and, with a final expression of good wishes from the Governor and Lady Barron, we glided out into the channel, where our supply of dynamite and sporting cartridges was taken on board. Captain G. S. Nares, whose kindness we had previously known, had the H.M.S. *Fantome* dressed in our honour, and lusty cheering reached us from across the water.

As we proceeded down the river Hobart looked its best, with the glancing sails of pleasure craft skimming near the foreshores, and backed by the stately, sombre mass of Mount Wellington.

A halt was made in mid-stream opposite the Quarantine Station, and there the thirty-eight surviving dogs were delivered from a ketch, passed over the side and secured at intervals on top of the deck cargo.

The engines began to throb again, not to cease until the arrival at Macquarie Island. A few miles lower down the channel, the Premier, and a number of other friends and well-wishers who had followed in a small steamer, bade us a final adieu.

Behind lay a sparkling sea-scape and the Tasmanian littoral; before, the blue southern ocean heaving with an ominous swell. A glance at the barograph showed a continuous fall, and a telegram from Mr. Hunt, Director of the Commonwealth Weather Bureau, received a few hours previously, informed us of a storm-centre to the south and the expectation of fresh south-westerly winds.

The piles of loose gear presented an indescribable scene of chaos, and, even as we rolled lazily in the increasing swell, the water commenced to run about the decks. There was no time to be lost in securing movable articles and preparing the ship for heavy weather. All hands set to work.

On the main deck the cargo was brought up flush with the top of the bulwarks, and consisted of the wireless masts, two huts, a large motor-launch, cases of dog biscuits and many other sundries. Butter to the extent of a couple of tons was accommodated chiefly on the roof of the main deck-house, where it was out of the way of the dogs. The roof of the chart-house, which formed an extension of the bridge proper, did not escape, for the railing offered facilities for lashing sledges; besides, there was room for tide-gauges, meteorological screens, and cases of fresh eggs and apples. Somebody happened to think of space unoccupied in the meteorological screens, and a few fowls were housed therein.

On the poop-deck there were the cases of benzine, sledges, and the timbers for constructing the chief magnetic observatory. An agglomeration of instruments and private gear rendered the ward-room well nigh impossible of access.

The deck was so encumbered that only at rare intervals was it visible. However, by our united efforts everything was well secured by 8 p.m.

It was dusk, and the distant highlands were silhouetted against the twilight sky. A tiny, sparkling lamp glimmered from Signal Hill its warm farewell. From the swaying poop we flashed back, "Good-bye, all snug on board."

Onward with a dogged plunge pressed our laden ship. Home and the past were effaced in the shroud of darkness, and thought leapt to the beckoning South—to the "dawn" of undiscovered lands.

During the night the wind and sea rose steadily, developing into a full gale. In order to make Macquarie Island, it was important not to allow the ship to drive too far to the east, as at all times the prevailing winds in this region are from the west. Partly on this account, and partly because of the extreme severity of the gale, the ship was hove to with head to wind, wallowing in mountainous seas. Such a storm, witnessed from a large vessel, would be an inspiring sight, but was awe-inspiring in so small a craft, especially where the natural buoyancy had been largely impaired by over-loading. With an immense quantity of deck cargo, amongst which were six thousand gallons of benzine, kerosene and spirit, in tins which were none too strong, we might well have been excused a lively anxiety during those days. It seemed as if no power on earth could save the loss of at least part of the deck cargo. Would it be the indispensable hut timbers amidships, or would a sea break on the benzine aft and flood us with inflammable liquid and vapour?

By dint of strenuous efforts and good seamanship, Captain Davis with his officers and crew held their own. The land parties assisted in the general work, constantly tightening up the lashings and lending "beef," a sailor's term for manpower, wherever required. For this purpose the members of the land parties were divided into watches, so that there were always a number patrolling the decks.

Most of us passed through a stage of sea-sickness, but except in the case of two or three, it soon passed off. Seas deluged all parts of the ship. A quantity of ashes was carried down into the bilge-water pump and obstructed the steam-pump. Whilst this was being cleared, the emergency deck pumps had to be requisitioned. The latter were available for working either by hand-power or by chain-gearing from the after-winch.

The deck-plug of one of the fresh-water tanks was carried away and, before it was noticed, sea-water had entered to such an extent as to render our supply unfit for drinking. Thus we were, henceforth, on a strictly limited water ration.

The wind increased from bad to worse, and great seas continued to rise until their culmination about 4 a.m. on the morning of December 5, when one struck the bridge, carrying the starboard side clean away. Toucher, the officer on watch, had a narrow escape; fortunately he happened to be on the other side of the bridge at the time.

The deck-rings holding the motor-launch drew, the launch itself was sprung and its decking partly stove in.

On the morning of December 8 we found ourselves in latitude 49° 56' S., and longitude 152° 28' E., with the weather so far abated that we were able to steer a course for Macquarie Island.

During the heavy weather food had been prepared only with the greatest difficulty. The galley was deluged time and again. It was enough to dishearten any cook, repeatedly finding himself amongst kitchen debris of all kinds, including pots and pans full and empty. Nor did the difficulties end in the galley, for food which survived until its arrival on the table, though not allowed much time for further mishap, often ended in a disagreeable mess on the floor or, tossed by a lurch of more than usual suddenness, entered an adjoining cabin. From such localities the elusive *pièce de résistance* was often rescued.

As we approached our rendezvous, whale-birds * appeared. During the heavy weather, Mother Cary's chickens only were seen, but, as the wind abated, the majestic wandering albatross, the sooty albatross and the mollymawk followed in our wake. Whales were observed spouting at intervals in the distance.

At daybreak on December 11 land began to show up, and by 6 a.m. we were some sixteen miles off the west coast of Macquarie Island, bearing on about the centre of its length.

---

* For the specific names refer to Appendix II.

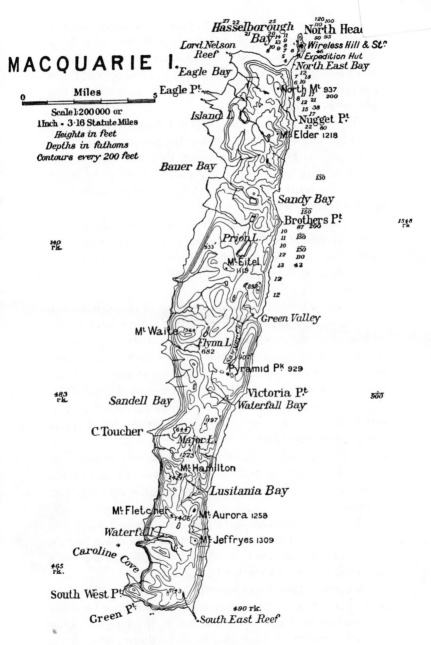

Map of Macquarie Island.

In general shape it is long and narrow, the length over all being twenty-one miles. A reef runs out for several miles at both extremities of the main island, reappearing again some miles beyond in isolated rocky islets; the Bishop and Clerk nineteen miles to the southward and the Judge and Clerk eight miles to the north.

The land everywhere rises abruptly from the sea or from an exaggerated beach to an undulating plateau-like interior, reaching a maximum elevation of one thousand four hundred and twenty-five feet. Nowhere is there a harbour in the proper sense of the word, though several anchorages in open road-steads are recognized.

The island is situated in about 55° S. latitude and the climate is comparatively cold, but it is the prevalence of strong winds that is the least desirable feature of its weather.

Sealing, so prosperous in the early days, is still carried on, but only in a desultory fashion.

Captain Davis had visited the island in the *Nimrod*, and was acquainted with the three better-known anchorages, which are on the east side and sheltered from the prevailing westerlies. One of the old-time sealers had reported a cove suitable for small craft at the south-western corner, but the information was scanty, and recent mariners had avoided that side of the island. On the morning of our approach the breeze was from the south-east, and, being favourable, Captain Davis proposed a visit.

By noon, Caroline Cove, as it is called, was abreast of us. Its small dimensions, and the fact that a rocky islet for the most part blocks the entrance, at first caused some misgivings as to its identity.

A boat was lowered, and a party of us rowed in towards the entrance, sounding at intervals to ascertain whether the *Aurora* could make use of it, should our inspection prove it a suitable locality for the land station.

We passed through a channel not more than eighty yards wide, but with deep water almost to the rocks on either side. A beautiful inlet now opened to view. Thick tussock-grass matted the steep hillsides, and the rocky shores, between the tide marks as well as in the depths below, were clothed with a profuse growth of brown kelp. Leaping out of the water in scores around us were penguins of several varieties, in their action reminding us of nothing so much as shoals of fish chased by sharks. Penguins were in thousands on the uprising cliffs, and from rookeries near and far came an incessant din. At intervals along the shore sea-elephants disported their ungainly masses in the sunlight. Circling above us in anxious haste, sea-birds of many varieties gave warning of our near approach to their nests. It was the invasion by man of an exquisite scene of primitive nature.

After the severe weather experienced, the relaxation made us all feel like a band of schoolboys on holiday.

A small sandy beach barred the islet, and the whale-boat was directed towards it. We were soon grating on the sand amidst an army of Royal penguins; picturesque little fellows, with a crest and eyebrows of long golden-yellow feathers. A few yards from the massed ranks of the penguins was a mottled sea-leopard, which woke up and slid into the sea as we approached.

Several hours were spent examining the neighbourhood. Webb and Kennedy took a set of magnetic observations, while others hoisted some cases of stores on to a rocky knob to form a provision depot, as it was quickly decided that the northern end of the island was likely to be more suitable for a permanent station.

The Royal penguins were almost as petulant as the Adelie penguins which we were to meet further south. They surrounded us, pecked at our legs and chattered with an audacity which defies description. It was discovered that they resented any attempt to drive them into the sea, and it was only after long persuasion that a bevy took to the water. This was a sign of a general capitulation, and some hundreds immediately followed, jostling each other in their haste, squawking, whirring their flippers, splashing and churning the water, reminding one of a crowd of miniature surf-bathers. We followed the files of birds marching inland, along the course of a tumbling stream, until at an elevation of some five hundred feet, on a flattish piece of ground, a huge rookery opened out—acres and acres of birds and eggs.

In one corner of the bay were nests of giant petrels in which sat huge downy young, about the size of a football, resembling grotesque, fluffy toys which might be expected to hang on a Christmas-tree.

Here and there on the beach and on the grass wandered bright coloured Maori-hens. On the south side of the bay, in a low, peaty area overgrown with tussock grass, were scores of sea-elephants, wallowing in bog-holes or sleeping at their ease.

Sea-elephants, at one time found in immense numbers on all sub-Antarctic islands, are now comparatively rare, even to the degree of extinction, in many of their old haunts. This is the result of ruthless slaughter prosecuted especially by sealers in the early days. At the present time Macquarie Island is more favoured by them than probably any other known locality. The name by which they are popularly known refers to their elephantine proportions and to the fact that, in the case of the old males, the nasal regions are enormously developed, expanding when in a state of excitement to form a short, trunk-like appendage. These monsters are several tons in weight, and we recorded them close on twenty feet in length; but no doubt they occasionally reach even greater size, for sealers have reported meeting examples up to twenty-five feet long.

Arriving on board the *Aurora* in the evening, we learnt that the ship had had an adventure which might have been most serious. It appeared that after dropping us at the entrance to Caroline Cove, the vessel was allowed to drift out to sea under the influence of the off-shore breeze. When about one-third of a mile north-west of the entrance, a violent shock was felt, and she slid over a rock which rose up out of deep water to within about fourteen feet of high-water level; no sign appearing of it on the surface on account of the tranquil state of the sea. Much apprehension was felt for the hull, but as no serious leak started, the escape was considered a fortunate one. A few soundings had been made proving a depth of four hundred fathoms within one and a half miles of the land.

A course was now set for the northern end of the island. Dangerous looking reefs ran out from many headlands, and cascades of water could be seen falling hundreds of feet from the highlands to the narrow coastal flats.

The anchorage most used was that known as North-East Bay, lying on the eastern side of a low spit joining the main mass of the island to an almost isolated outpost in the form of a flat-topped hill—Wireless Hill—some three-quarters of a mile farther north. It is practically an open roadstead, but, as the prevailing winds blow on to the other side of the island, quiet water can be nearly always expected.

However, when we arrived at North-East Bay on the morning following our adventure, a stiff south-east breeze was blowing, and the wash on the beach put landing out of the question. Captain Davis ran in as near the coast as he could safely venture and dropped anchor, pending the moderation of the wind.

On the leeward slopes of a low ridge, pushing itself out on to the southern extremity of the spit, could be seen two small huts, but no sign of human life. This was not surprising as it was only seven o'clock. Below the huts, upon low surf-covered rocks running out from the beach, lay a small schooner partly broken up and evidently a recent victim. A mile to the southward, fragments of another wreck protruded from the sand.

We were discussing wrecks and the grisly toll which has been levied by these dangerous and uncharted shores, when a human figure appeared in front of one of the huts. After surveying us for a moment, he disappeared within to reappear shortly afterwards, followed by a stream of others rushing hither and thither; just as if he had disturbed a hornet's nest. After such an exciting demonstration we awaited the next move with some expectancy.

Planks and barrels were brought on to the beach and a flagstaff was hoisted. Then one of the party mounted on the barrel, and told us by flag signals that the ship on the beach was the *Clyde*, which had recently been wrecked, and that all hands were safely on shore, but requiring assistance. Besides the shipwrecked crew, there were half a dozen men who resided on the island during the summer months for the purpose of collecting blubber.

The sealers tried repeatedly to come out to us, but as often as it was launched their boat was washed up again on the beach, capsizing them into the water. At length they signalled that a landing could be made on the opposite side of the spit, so the anchor was raised and the ship steamed round the north end of the island, to what Captain Davis proposed should be named Hasselborough Bay, in recognition of the discoverer of the island. This proved an admirable anchorage, for the wind remained from the east and south-east during the greater part of our stay.

The sealers pushed their boat across the spit, and, launching it in calmer water, came out to us, meeting the *Aurora* some three miles off the land. The anchor was let go about one mile and a half from the head of the bay.

News was exchanged with the sealers. It appeared that there had been much speculation as to what sort of a craft we were; visits of ships, other than those sent down specially to convey their oil to New Zealand, being practically unknown.

They were greatly relieved to hear that our auxiliary vessel, the *Toroa*, was expected immediately, and would be available for taking the shipwrecked crew back to civilization.

In company with Ainsworth, Hannam and others, I went ashore to select a site for the station. As strong westerly winds were to be expected during the greater part of the year, it was necessary to erect buildings in the lee of substantial break-winds. Several sites for a hut convenient to a serviceable landing-place were inspected at the north end of the beach. The hut was eventually erected in the lee of a large mass of rock, rising out of the grass-covered sandy flat at the north end of the spit.

As the result of a consultation it was decided that the best site for the wireless station was the summit of the isolated precipitous hill—Wireless Hill. We had then to face the serious difficulty of transportation of the heavy masts and engine parts from the beach to the summit—a vertical height of over three hundred and fifty feet.

To facilitate this latter work the sealers placed at our disposal a "flying-fox"—a wire hoist—which ran from sea-level to the top of Wireless Hill, and which they had erected for the carriage of blubber. On inspecting it, Wild reported that it was serviceable, but would first require to be strengthened. He immediately set about this with the help of a party.

Hurley now discovered that he had accidentally left one of his cinematograph lenses on a rock where he had been working in Caroline Cove. As it was indispensable, and there was little prospect of the weather allowing of another visit by the ship, it was decided that he should go on a journey overland to recover it. One of the sealers, Hutchinson by name, who had been to Caroline Cove and knew the best route to take, kindly volunteered to accompany Hurley. The party was eventually increased by the addition of Harrisson, who was to keep a look-out for matters of biological interest. They started off at noon on December 13.

The dogs were disembarked and remained ashore until we were ready to proceed on the voyage. Although the greater part of the stores for the Macquarie Island party were to arrive by the *Toroa*, there were a few tons on board the *Aurora*. These latter were all transferred to the shore by noon on December 13, thanks to the motor-launch which, after injuries sustained in the recent gale, had been put into good working order again by Bickerton and Gillies.

Everything but the items of the wireless installation was landed on the spit, as near the north-east corner as the surf would allow. Fortunately, the reefs ran out from the shore at intervals, and calmer water could be found in their lee. All gear for the wireless station was taken to a spot about half a mile to the north-west at the foot of Wireless Hill, where the "flying-fox" was situated. Just at that spot there was a landing place at the head of a charming little boat harbour, formed by numerous kelp-covered, rocky reefs rising at intervals above the level of high water. These broke the swell, so that in most weathers calm water was assured at the landing-place.

This boat harbour was a fascinating spot. On the western side was a rookery of blue-eyed cormorants; scattered nests of white gulls relieved the sombre appearance of the reefs on the opposite side: whilst gentoo penguins in numbers were busy hatching their eggs on the sloping ground beyond. Skua-gulls and giant petrels were perched here and there amongst the rocks, watching for an opportunity of marauding the nests of other birds. Sea-elephants raised their massive, dripping heads in shoal and channel. The dark reefs, running out into the pellucid water, supported a vast growth of a snake-like form of kelp, whose octopus-like tentacles, many yards in length, writhed yellow and brown to the swing of the surge, and gave the foreground an indescribable weird-ness. I stood looking out to the sea from here one evening, soon after sunset, the launch lazily rolling in the swell, and the *Aurora* in the offing, while the rich tints of the afterglow paled in the south-west. It was a soul-stirring evening. I felt envious of Wild and his party, whose occupation in connection with the "flying-fox" kept them, during those busy days, permanently camped at the spot.

The *Toroa* made her appearance on the afternoon of December 13, and came to anchor about half a mile inshore from the *Aurora*. Within a few minutes of her arrival, a five-ton motor-boat was launched and unloading commenced.

Fifty sheep were taken on shore to feed on the rank grass until our departure. A continuous stream of coal and stores passed, by motor-launch and whale-boat, from ship to ship and from the ships to the several landing-places on shore. We kept at the work as long as possible—about sixteen hours a day including a short interval for lunch.

Operations progressed so rapidly that on the morning of the 15th the *Toroa* was ready to leave for Hobart. She weighed anchor and we parted with a cheer.

The transportation of the wireless equipment to the top of the hill had been going on simultaneously with the unloading of the ships. Now, however, all were able to concentrate upon it, and the work went forward merrily.

Digging the pits for bedding the heavy, wooden "dead men"—the anchorages—and erecting the wireless masts, the engine-hut and the operating-hut provided plenty of work for all. Here was as busy a scene as one could witness anywhere—some with the picks and shovels, others with hammers and nails, sailors splicing ropes and fitting masts, and a stream of men hauling the loads up from the sea-shore to their destination on the summit.

The distance between the lower and upper terminals of the "flying-fox" was some eight hundred feet. This was spanned by two steel-wire carrying cables. Freight was dispatched to the top of the hill by the simple process of filling a bag at the summit, acting as a counterpoise, with earth, until slightly in excess of the weight to be lifted; then off it would start, gathering speed as it went. Owing to an unexpected evolution of a brake-device, designed to check the speed of the counterpoise as it approached the end of its journey, Wild was temporarily injured. Though incapacitated for a few days he continued to supervise operations at the lower terminal.

Where heavier loads were concerned, the cables of the "flying-fox" would not stand the additional weight of the counterpoise, and so the hauling had to be done by a straight pull on the top of the hill. The hauling was executed to the accompaniment of chanties, and these helped to relieve the strain of the work. It was a familiar sight to see a string of twenty men on the hauling-line at the top of the hill scaring the skua-gulls with popular choruses like "A' roving" and "Ho, boys, pull her along." On calm days the parties at either end of the terminal could communicate by shouting, but were much assisted by megaphones improvised from a pair of leggings.

In the meantime, Hurley, Harrisson, and the sealer, Hutchinson, had returned from their trip to Caroline Cove, after a most interesting though arduous journey. They had camped the first evening at the Nuggets, a rocky point on the east coast some four miles to the south of North-East Bay. From the Nuggets, the trail struck inland up the steep hillsides until the summit of the island was reached; then over pebble-strewn, undulating ground with occasional small lakes, arriving at the west coast near its southern extremity. Owing to rain and fog they overshot the mark and had to spend the night close to a bay at the south end. There Hurley obtained some good photographs of sea-elephants and of the penguin rookeries.

The next morning, December 15, they set off again, this time finding Caroline Cove without further difficulty. Harrisson remained on the brow of the hill overlooking the cove, and there captured some prions and their eggs. Hurley and his companion recovered the lost lens and returned to Harrisson, securing a fine albatross on the way. This solitary bird was descried sitting on the hillside, several hundreds of feet above sea-level. Its plumage was in such good condition that they could not resist the impulse to secure it for our collection, for the moment not considering the enormous weight to be carried. They had neither firearms nor an Ancient Mariner's cross-bow, and no stones were to be had in the vicinity— when the resourceful Hurley suddenly bethought himself of a small tin of meat in his haversack, and with a fortunate throw, hit the bird on the head, killing the majestic creature on the spot.

Shouldering their prize, they trudged on to Lusitania Bay, camping there that night in an old dilapidated hut; a remnant of the sealing days. Close by there was a large rookery of King penguins, a variety of penguin with richly tinted plumage on the head and shoulders, and next in size to the Emperor—the sovereign bird of the Antarctic regions. The breeding season was at its height, so Harrisson secured and preserved a great number of their eggs. Hutchinson kindly volunteered to carry the albatross in addition to his original load. If they had skinned the bird, the weight would have been materially reduced, but with the meagre appliances at hand, it would undoubtedly have been spoiled as a specimen. Hurley, very ambitiously, had taken a heavy camera, in addition to a blanket and other sundries. During the rough and wet walking of the previous day, his boots had worn out and caused him to twist a tendon in the right foot, so that he was not up to his usual form, while Harrisson was hampered with a bulky cargo of eggs and specimens.

Saddled with these heavy burdens, the party found the return journey very laborious. Hurley's leg set the pace, and so, later in the day, Harrisson decided to push on ahead in order to give us news, as they had orders to be back as soon as possible and were then overdue. When darkness came on

Harrisson was near the Nuggets, where he passed the night amongst the tussock-grass. Hurley and Hutchinson, who were five miles behind, also slept by the wayside. When dawn appeared, Harrisson moved on, reaching the north-end huts at about 9 a.m. Mertz and Whetter immediately set out and came to the relief of the other two men a few hours later.

Fatigue and a lame leg reduced Hurley for the rest of the day, but the next morning he was off to get pictures of the work proceeding on Wireless Hill. It was practically impossible for him to walk to the top of the hill, but not to be baffled, he accepted the risk of the "flying-fox." Long before reaching the top he realized how much his safety depended on the strength of the hauling-line and the care of those at the summit.

During the latter part of our stay at the Island the wind blew from the north and north-north-east, at times quite strongly, so that for several days we were unable to reach the shore from the ship.

Our best anchor carried away, and we were reduced to steaming up and down in the partial shelter of Hasselborough Bay. Ashore the boatswain, some of the sailors, and the majority of the members of the land parties were busy completing the erection of the "wireless" masts.

On the morning of December 23 it was found possible to lower the whale-boat, and Wild went off with a complement of sturdy oarsmen, including Madigan, Moyes, Watson and Kennedy, and succeeded in bringing off the dogs. Several trips were made with difficulty during the day, but at last all the men, dogs and sheep were embarked.

Both Wild and I went with the whale-boat on its last trip at dusk on the evening of December 23. The only possible landing-place, with the sea then running, was at the extreme north-eastern corner of the beach. No time was lost in getting the men and the remainder of the cargo into the boat, though in the darkness this was not easily managed. The final parting with our Macquarie Island party took place on the beach, their cheers echoing to ours as we breasted the surf and "gave way" for the ship.

CHAPTER III

FROM MACQUARIE ISLAND TO ADELIE LAND

THE morning following our farewell to Ainsworth and party at the north end of the island found us steaming down the west coast, southward bound.

Our supply of fresh water was scanty, and the only resource was to touch at Caroline Cove. As a matter of fact, there were several localities on the east coast where water might be had, but the strong easterly weather then prevailing made a landing on that side of the island impossible.

On the ship nearing the south end, the wind subsided. She then crept into the lee of the cliffs, a boat was dropped and soundings disclosed a deep passage at the mouth of Caroline Cove and ample water within. There was, however, limited space for manœuvring the vessel if a change should occur in the direction of the wind. The risk was taken; the *Aurora* felt her way in, and, to provide against accident, was anchored by Captain Davis with her bow towards the entrance. A kedge-anchor was then run out to secure the stern.

During the cruise down the coast the missing stock of our only remaining bower-anchor had been replaced by Gillies and Hannam. Two oregon "dead men," bolted together on the shank, made a clumsy but efficient makeshift.

Two large barrels were taken ashore, repeatedly filled and towed off to the ship. It was difficult at first to find good water, for the main stream flowing from the head of the bay was contaminated by the penguins which made it their highway to a rookery. After a search, an almost dry gully was found to yield soakage water when a pit was dug in its bed. This spot was some eighty yards from the beach, and to reach it one traversed an area of tussock-grass where sea-elephants wallowed in soft mire.

A cordon of men was made and buckets were interchanged, the full ones descending and the empty ones ascending. The barrels on the beach were thus speedily filled and taken off by a boat's crew. At 11 p.m. darkness came, and it was decided to complete the work on the following day.

As we rowed to the ship, the water was serenely placid. From the dark environing hills came the weird cries of strange birds. There was a hint of wildness, soon to be forgotten in the chorus of a song and the hearty shouts of the rowers.

About 2 a.m. the officer on watch came down to report to Captain Davis a slight change in the direction of the breeze. At 3 a.m. I was again awakened by hearing Captain Davis hasten on deck, and by a gentle bumping of the ship, undoubtedly against rock. It appeared that the officer on watch had left the bridge for a few minutes, while the wind freshened and was blowing at the time nearly broadside-on from the north. This caused the ship to sag to leeward, stretching the bow and stern cables, until she came in con tact with the kelp-covered, steep, rocky bank on the south side. The narrow limits of the anchorage were responsible for this dangerous situation.

All hands were immediately called on deck and set to work hauling on the stern cable. In a few minutes the propeller and rudder were out of danger. The engines were then started slowly ahead, and, as we came up to the bower anchor, the cable was taken in. The wind was blowing across the narrow entrance to the cove, so that it was advisable to get quickly under way. The kedge-anchor was abandoned, and we steamed straight out to sea. The wind increased, and there was no other course open but to continue the southward voyage.

The day so inauspiciously begun turned out beautifully sunny. There was additional verve in our Christmas celebration, as Macquarie Island and the Bishop and Clerk, in turn, sank below the northern horizon.

For some days we were favoured by exceptional weather;

a moderate breeze from the north-east and a long, lazy swell combining to make our progress rapid.

Regarding the ice conditions over the whole segment of the unknown tract upon which our attack was directed, very little was known. Interpreting Wilkes's report in the light of our own knowledge of Antarctic navigation, we were not encouraged to expect an easy passage through the ice. D'Urville appeared to have reached his landfall without much hindrance by ice, but that was a fortunate circumstance in view of the difficulties Wilkes had met elsewhere in that region. At the western limit of the area we were to explore, the Germans in the *Gauss* had been irrevocably trapped in the ice as early as the month of February. At the eastern limit, only the year before, the *Terra Nova* of Scott's expedition had sighted new land almost south of where we now were, but even though it was then the end of summer, and the sea was almost free from the previous season's ice, they were not able to reach the land on account of the dense pack.

In the early southern summer, at the time of our arrival, the ice conditions were expected to be at their worst. This followed from the fact that not only would local floes be encountered, but also a vast expanse of pack fed by the disintegrating floes of the Ross Sea, since, between Cape Adare and the Balleny Islands, the ice drifting to the northwest under the influence of the south-east winds is arrested in an extensive sheet. On the other hand, were we to wait for the later season, no time would remain for the accomplishment of the programme which had been arranged. So we were forced to accept things as we found them, being also prepared to make the most of any chance opportunity.

At noon on December 27 whales were spouting all round us, and appeared to be travelling from west to east. Albatrosses of several species constantly hovered about, and swallow-like Wilson petrels would sail along the troughs and flit over the crests of the waves, to vanish into sombre distance.

Already we were steaming through untravelled waters, and new discoveries might be expected at any moment. A keen interest spread throughout the ship. On several occasions, fantastic clouds on the horizon gave hope of land, only to be abandoned on further advance. On December 28 and 29 large masses of floating kelp were seen, and, like the flotsam met with by Columbus, still further raised our hopes. So the possibility of undiscovered islands existing in the Southern Ocean, south of Australia and outside the ice-bound region, kept us vigilant.

With regard to the nature of the Antarctic land to be expected ahead, some authorities had held that any such existing in this region would be found to be of the nature of isolated islands. Those personally familiar with the adjacent land, however, were all in favour of it being continental—a continuation of the Victoria Land plateau. The land lay to the south beyond doubt; the problem was to reach it through the belt of ice-bound sea. Still, navigable pack-ice might be ahead, obviating the need of driving too far to the west in efforts to break through to the south.

"Ice on the starboard bow!" At 4 p.m. on December 29 the cry was raised, and shortly after we passed alongside a small caverned berg whose bluish-green tints called forth general admiration. In the distance others could be seen. One larger than the average stood almost in our path. It was of the flat-topped, sheer-walled type, so characteristic of the Antarctic regions; three-quarters of a mile long and half a mile wide, rising eighty feet above the water.

A light fog obscured the surrounding sea and distant bergs glided by like spectres. A monstrous block on the starboard side had not been long adrift, for it showed but slight signs of weathering.

The fog thickened over a grey swell that shimmered with an oily lustre. At 7 p.m. pack-ice came suddenly to view, and towards it we steered, vainly peering through the mists ahead in search of a passage. The ice was closely packed, the pieces being small and well worn. On the outskirts was a light brash which steadily gave place to a heavier variety, composed of larger and more angular fragments. A swishing murmur like the wind in the tree-tops came from the great expanse. It was alabaster-white and through the small, separate chips was diffused a pale lilac coloration. The larger chunks, by their motion and exposure to wind and current, had a circle of clear water; the deep sea-blue hovering round their water-worn niches. Here and there appeared the ochreous-yellow colour of adhering films of diatoms.

As we could not see what lay beyond, and the pack was becoming heavier, the ship was swung round and headed out.

Steering to the west through open water and patches of trailing brash, we were encouraged to find the pack trending towards the south. By pushing through bars of jammed floes and dodging numerous bergs, twenty miles were gained due southwards before the conditions had changed. The fog cleared, and right ahead massive bergs rose out of an ice-strewn sea. We neared one which was a mile in length and one hundred feet in height. The heaving ocean, dashing against its mighty, glistening walls, rushed with a hollow boom into caverns of ethereal blue; Gothic portals to a cathedral of resplendent purity.

The smaller bergs and fragments of the floe crowded closer together, and the two men at the wheel had little time for reverie. Orders came in quick succession—"Starboard! Steady!" and in a flash—"Hard-a-port!" Then repeated all over again, while the rudder chains scraped and rattled in their channels.

Gradually the swell subsided, smoothed by the weight of ice. The tranquillity of the water heightened the superb effects of this glacial world. Majestic tabular bergs whose crevices exhaled a vaporous azure; lofty spires, radiant turrets and splendid castles; honeycombed masses illumined by pale green light within whose fairy labyrinths the water washed and gurgled. Seals and penguins on magic gondolas were the silent denizens of this dreamy Venice. In the soft glamour of the midsummer midnight sun, we were possessed by a rapturous wonder—the rare thrill of unreality.

The ice closed in, and shock after shock made the ship vibrate as she struck the smaller pieces full and fair, followed by a crunching and grinding as they scraped past the sides. The dense pack had come, and hardly a square foot of space showed amongst the blocks; smaller ones packing in between the larger, until the sea was covered with a continuous armour of ice. The ominous sound arising from thousands of faces rubbing together as they gently oscillated in the swell was impressive. It spoke of a force all-powerful, in whose grip puny ships might be locked for years and the less fortunate receive their last embrace.

The pack grew heavier and the bergs more numerous, embattled in a formidable array. If an ideal picture, from our point of view it was impenetrable. No water-sky showed as a distant beacon; all over was reflected the pitiless, white glare of the ice. The *Aurora* retreated to the open sea, and headed to the west in search of a break in the ice-front. The wind blew from the south-east, and, with sails set to assist the engines, rapid progress was made.

The southern prospect was disappointing, for the heavy pack was ranged in a continuous bar. The over-arching sky invariably shone with that white effulgence known as "ice blink," indicative of continuous ice, in contrast with the dark water-sky, a sign of open water, or a mottled sky proceeding from an ice-strewn but navigable sea.

Though progress can be made in dense pack, provided it is not too heavy, advance is necessarily very slow—a few miles a day, and that at the expense of much coal. Without a well defined water-sky it would have been foolish to have entered. Further, everything pointed to heavier ice-conditions in the south and, indeed, in several places we reconnoitred, and such was proved to be the case. Large bergs were numerous, which, on account of being almost unaffected by surface currents because of their ponderous bulk and stupendous draught, helped to compact the shallow surface ice under the free influence of currents and winds. In our westerly course we were sometimes able to edge a little to the south, but were always reduced to our old position within a few hours. Long projecting tongues of pack were met at intervals, and when narrow or open, we pushed through them.

Whales were frequently seen, both rorquals and killers. On the pack, sea-leopards, and crab-eater seals sometimes appeared. At one time as many as a hundred would be counted from the bridge and at other moments not a single one could be sighted. They were not alarmed, unless the ship happened to bump against ice-masses within a short distance of them. A small sea-leopard, shot from the fo'c'sle by a well-directed bullet from Wild, was taken on board as a specimen; the meat serving as a great treat for the dogs.

On January 2, when driving through a tongue of pack, a halt was made to "ice ship." A number of men scrambled over the side on to a large piece of floe and handed up the ice. It was soon discovered, however, that the swell was too great, for masses of ice ten tons or more in weight swayed about under the stern, endangering the propeller and rudder—the vulnerable parts of the vessel. So we moved on, having secured enough fresh water ice to supply a pleasant change after the somewhat discoloured tank water then being served out. The ice still remained compact and forbidding, but each day we hoped to discover a weak spot through which we might probe to the land itself.

On the evening of January 2 we saw a high, pinnacled berg, a few miles within the edge of the pack, closely resembling a rocky peak; the transparent ice of which it was composed appeared, in the dull light, of a much darker hue than the surrounding bergs. Another adjacent block exhibited a large black patch on its northern face, the exact nature of which could not be ascertained at a distance. Examples of rock debris embedded in bergs had already been observed, and it was presumed that this was a similar case. These were all hopeful signs, for the earthy matter must, of course, have been picked up by the ice during its repose upon some adjacent land.

At the same spot, large flocks of silver-grey petrels were seen resting on the ice and skimming the water in search of food. As soon as we had entered the ice zone, most of our old companions, such as the albatross, had deserted, while a new suite of Antarctic birds had taken their place. These included the beautiful snow-petrel, the Antarctic petrel, and the small, lissome Wilson petrel—a link with the bird-life of more temperate seas.

On the evening of January 3 the wind was blowing fresh from the south-east and falling snow obscured the horizon. The pack took a decided turn to the north, which fact was particularly disappointing in view of the distance we had already traversed to the west. We were now approaching the longitude of D'Urville's landfall, and still the pack showed no signs of slackening. I was beginning to feel very anxious, and had decided not to pass that longitude without resorting to desperate measures.

The change in our fortunes occurred at five o'clock next morning, when the Chief Officer, Toucher, came down from the bridge to report that the atmosphere was clearing and that there appeared to be land-ice near by. Sure enough, on the port side, within a quarter of a mile, rose a massive barrier of ice extending far into the mist and separated from the ship by a little loose pack-ice. The problem to be solved was, whether it was the seaward face of an ice-covered continent, the ice-capping of a low island or only a flat-topped iceberg of immense proportions.

By 7 a.m. a corner was reached where the ice-wall trended southward, limned on the horizon in a series of bays and headlands. An El Dorado had opened before us, for the winds coming from the east of south had cleared the pack away from the lee of the ice-wall, so that in the distance a comparatively clear sea was visible. Into this we steered, hugging the ice-wall, and were soon in the open, speeding along in glorious sunshine, bringing new sights into view every moment.

The wall, along the northern face, was low—from thirty to seventy feet in height—but the face along which we were now progressing gradually rose in altitude to the south. It was now clear that this was a floating ice formation of great thickness, in its nature similar to that of the well-known Great Barrier (a shelf-ice* formation) of the Ross Sea described by Ross, Scott, Shackleton and others—whether it was still attached to land remained to be proved.

On pieces of broken floe Weddell seals were noted. They were the first seen on the voyage and a pure indication of land, for they are rarely met with far from the coast.

A large, low, dome-topped elevation, about one mile in diameter, was passed on the starboard side, at a distance of

* Refer to the glossary forming Appendix II.

two miles from the long ice cliff. This corresponded in shape with what Ross frequently referred to as an "ice island," uncertain whether it was a berg or ice-covered land. A sounding close by gave two hundred and eight fathoms, showing that we were on the continental shelf, and increasing the probability that the "ice island" was aground.

Birds innumerable appeared on every hand: snow-petrels, silver-grey petrels, Cape pigeons and Antarctic petrels. They fluttered in hundreds about our bow. Cape pigeons are well known in lower latitudes, and it was interesting to find them so far south. As they have chess board-like markings on the back when seen in flight, there is no mistaking them.

The ice-wall now took a turn to the south-east. At this point it had risen to a great height, about two hundred feet sheer. A fresh wind was blowing in our teeth from the south-south-east, and beyond this point would be driving us on to the cliffs. The ship was put about, therefore, and made for the lee side of the "ice island."

In isolated coveys on the inclined top of the "island" were several flocks, each containing hundreds of Antarctic petrels. At intervals they would rise into the air in clouds, shortly afterwards to settle down again on the snow.

Captain Davis moved the ship carefully against the lee wall of the "island," with a view to replenishing our water supply, but it was unscalable, and we were forced to withdraw. Crouched on a small projection near the water's edge was a seal, trying to evade the eyes of a dozen large killer whales which were playing about near our stern. These monsters appeared to be about twenty-five feet in length. They are the most formidable predaceous mammals of the Antarctic seas, and annually account for a large number of seals, penguins, and even other cetaceans. The sea-leopard is its competitor, though not nearly so ferocious as the killer, of whom it lives in terror.

The midnight hours were spent off the "ice island" while we waited for a decrease in the wind. Bars of cirrus clouds covered the whole sky—the presage of a coming storm. The wind arose, and distant objects were blotted out by driving snow. Captain Davis aimed at keeping the ship in the lee of the great ice formation, where there was some shelter. After hours of anxiety, pitching and plunging about and blindly groping our way, the calmer water close up to the ice wall was reached at a point discovered later to be some fourteen miles to the north. There we steamed up and down until the afternoon of January 5, when the weather improved. A sounding was taken and the course was once more set for the south.

The sky remained overcast, the atmosphere foggy, and a south-south-east wind was blowing as we came abreast of the "ice island," which, by the way, was discovered to have drifted several miles to the north, thus proving itself to be a free-floating berg. The ice wall on the port side took a sharp turn to the east-south-east, disappearing on the horizon. As there was no pack in sight and the water was merely littered with fragments of ice, it appeared most likely that the turn in the wall was part of a great sweeping curve ultimately joining with land or fast-ice to the south. On our south-south-east course we soon lost sight of the ice cliffs in a gathering fog.

On the afternoon of January 6 the wind abated and the fog began to clear. At 5 p.m. a line of ice confronted us and, an hour later, the *Aurora* was in calm water under another mighty ice face trending across our course. This wall was precisely similar in appearance to the one with which we had been in touch during the several preceding days, and might well have been a continuation of it. We were afterwards to learn that this was not so, but that the former ice formation was nothing more than a huge iceberg measuring forty miles in length. This was ascertained the following year when the *Aurora* came south; it was found to have disappeared, but we later re-discovered it some fifty miles to the north-west. Close to the face of the new ice formation* a mud bottom was found at a depth of three hundred and ninety-five fathoms.

* Subsequently this shelf-ice formation was found to be a floating tongue sixty miles in length, the seaward extension of a large glacier which we named the Mertz Glacier. It appears on our charts, therefore, as the Mertz Glacier Tongue.

While we were steaming in calm water to the south-west the massive front, serrated by shallow bays and capes, passed in magnificent review. Its height attained a maximum of about one hundred and thirty feet. In places the sea had eaten out enormous blue grottoes. At one spot, several of these had broken into each other to form a huge domed cavern, the roof of which hung one hundred feet above the sea. The noble portico was flanked by great pillars. A table-topped berg in the act of formation was seen, separated from the parent body of the shelf-ice by a deep fissure several yards in width.

At 11 p.m. the *Aurora* entered a bay, afterwards named Buchanan Bay, several miles wide, bounded on the east by the shelf-ice wall and on the west by a steep snow-covered promontory rising approximately two thousand feet in height, as yet seen dimly in hazy outline through the mist. No rock was visible, but the contour was clearly that of ice-capped land.

There was much jubilation among the watchers on deck at the prospect. Every available field-glass and telescope was brought to bear upon it. It was almost certainly a part of the Antarctic continent, though, at that time, its extension to the east, west and south remained to be proved. The shelf-ice was seen to be securely attached to it and, near its point of junction with the undulating land-ice, we beheld the mountains of this mysterious land haloed in ghostly mist.

While passing the extremity of the western promontory, we observed an exposure of rock, jutting out of the ice near sea-level, in the face of a scar left by an avalanche. Later when passing within half a cable's length of several berg-like masses of ice lying off the coast, rock was again visible in black relief against the water's edge, forming a pedestal for the ice-islets completely ice-capped. The ship was kept farther off shore, after this warning, for though she was designed to buffet with the ice, we had no desire to test her resistance to rock.

The bottom was very irregular, and as an extra precaution, soundings were taken every few minutes. Through a light fog all that could be seen landwards was a steep, sloping, icy surface descending from the interior, and terminating abruptly in a seaward cliff fifty to two hundred feet in height.

The ice-sheet terminating in this wall presented a more broken surface than the floating shelf-ice. It was riven and distorted by gaping crevasses; an indication of the rough bed over which it had travelled.

Towards midnight another bay was entered and many rocky islets appeared on its western side. The engines were stopped for a few hours, and the voyage was resumed in clearer weather on the following morning.

All day we threaded our way between islands and bergs. Seals and penguins swam around, the latter squawking and diving in a most amusing manner.

Cautiously we glided by an iceberg, at least one hundred and fifty feet high, rising with a faceted, perpendicular face chased with soft, snowy traceries and ornamented with stalactites. Splits and rents broke into the margin, and from each streamed the evanescent, azure vapour. Each puncture and tiny grotto was filled with it, and a sloping cap of shimmering snow spread over the summit. The profile view was an exact replica of a battle-ship, grounded astern. The bold contour of the bow was perfect, and the massive flank had been torn and shattered by shell-fire in a desperate naval battle. This berg had heeled over considerably, and the original water-line ran as a definite rim, thirty feet above the green water. From this rim shelved down a smooth and polished base, marked with fine vertical striæ.

Soundings varied from twenty to two hundred fathoms, and, accordingly, the navigation was particularly anxious work.

Extending along about fifteen miles of coast, where the inland ice came down steeply to the sea, was a marginal belt of sea, about two or three miles in width, thickly strewn with rocky islets. Of these some were flat and others peaked, but all were thickly populated by penguins, petrels and seals.

Later that night we lay off a possible landing-place for one of our bases, but, on more closely inspecting it in the morning, we decided to proceed farther west into a wide sweeping bay which opened before us. About fifty miles ahead, on the far side of Commonwealth Bay, as we named it, was a cape which roughly represented in position Cape

Découverte, the most easterly extension of Adelie Land seen by D'Urville in 1840. Though Commonwealth Bay and the land already seen had never before been sighted, all was placed under the territorial name of Adelie Land.

The land was so overwhelmed with ice that, even at sea-level, the rock was all but entirely hidden. Here was an ice-age in all earnestness; a picture of northern Europe during the Great Ice Age some fifty thousand or more years ago. It was evident that the glaciation of Adelie Land was much more severe than that in higher Antarctic latitudes, as exampled on the borders of the Ross Sea. The temperature could not be colder, so we were led to surmise that the snow-fall must be excessive. The full truth was to be ascertained by bitter experience, after spending a year on the spot.

I was now anxious to find a suitable location for our main Antarctic land base; two reasons making it an urgent matter. The first was, that as we advanced to the west we were receding from the South Magnetic Pole, and I was anxious to have our magnetographs running as near the latter as possible. Secondly, we would be daily increasing our distance from Macquarie Island, making wireless communication more uncertain.

At noon on January 8, while I was weighing the pros and cons with Captain Davis, Wild came into the Chart Room to say that there was a rocky exposure about fifteen miles off on the port side, and suggested altering our course to obtain a better view of it.

Just after 4 p.m. when the ship was about one mile from the nearest rocks, the whale-boat was lowered and manned. We rowed in with the object of making a closer investigation. From the ship's deck, even when within a mile, the outcrop had appeared to project directly from the inland ice-sheet. Now, however, we were surprised to find ourselves amongst an archipelago of islets. These were named the Mackellar Islets.

Weddell seals and Adelie penguins in thousands rested upon the rocks; the latter chiefly congregated upon a long, low, bare islet situated in the centre. This was the largest of the group, measuring about half a mile in length; others were not above twenty yards in diameter. As we came inshore, the main body of the archipelago was found to be separated by a mile and a half from the mainland. A point which struck us at the time was that the islets situated on the southern side of the group were capped by unique masses of ice; resembling iced cakes. Later we were able to see the caps in process of formation. In the violent southerly hurricanes prevalent in Adelie Land, the spray breaks right over them. Part of it is deposited and frozen, and by increments the icing of these monstrous "cakes" is built up. The amount contributed in winter makes up for loss by thawing in mid-summer. As the islets to windward shelter those in their lee, the latter are destitute of these natural canopies.

As we proceeded through the archipelago of islets soundings were taken at frequent intervals with a hand leadline. The water was on the whole shallow, varying from a few to twenty fathoms. The bottom was clothed by dense, luxuriant seaweed. This rank growth along the littoral was unexpected, for nothing of the kind exists on the Ross Sea coasts within five or six fathoms of the surface.

Advancing towards the mainland, we observed a small inlet in the rocky coast, and towards it the boat was directed. We were soon inside a beautiful, miniature harbour completely land-locked. The sun shone gloriously in a blue sky as we stepped ashore on a charming ice-quay—the first to set foot on the Antarctic continent between Cape Adare and Gaussberg, a distance of about two thousand miles.

Wild and I proceeded to make a tour of exploration. The rocky area at Cape Denison, as it was named, was found to be about one and one-third miles in length and half a mile in extreme width. Behind it rose the inland ice, ascending in a regular slope and apparently free of crevasses—an outlet for our sledging parties in the event of the sea not firmly freezing over. To right and left of this oasis, as the visitor to Adelie Land must regard the welcome rock, the ice was heavily crevassed and fell sheer to the sea in cliffs, sixty to one hundred and fifty feet in height. Two small dark patches in the distance were the only evidences of rock to relieve the white monotony of the coast.

In landing cargo on Antarctic shores, advantage is generally taken of the floe-ice adjacent to the shore, on to which the materials can be conveniently unloaded and at once sledged away to their destination on shore. Here, on the other hand, there was open water, too shallow for the *Aurora* to be moored alongside the ice-foot. The only alternative was to anchor the ship at a distance and discharge the cargo by boats running to the ideal harbour we had discovered. Close to the Boat Harbour, as we called it, was suitable ground for the erection of a hut, so that the various impedimenta would have to be carried only a short distance. For supplies of fresh meat, in the emergency of being marooned for a number of years, there were many Weddell seals at hand, and on almost all the neighbouring ridges colonies of penguins were busy rearing their young. As a station for scientific investigations, it offered a wider field than the casual observer would have imagined. So it came about that the Main Base was finally settled at Cape Denison, Commonwealth Bay.

We arrived on board at 8 p.m., taking a seal as food for the dogs. Without delay, the motor launch was dropped into the water, and both it and the whale-boat loaded with frozen carcases of mutton, cases of eggs and other perishable goods.

While some of us went ashore in the motor launch, with the whale-boat in tow, the *Aurora* steamed round the Mackellar Islets seeking for a good anchorage under the ice barrier, immediately to the west of the Boat Harbour. The day had been perfect, vibrant with summer and life, but towards evening a chill breeze off the land sprang up, and we in the motor launch had to beat against it. By the time we had reached the head of the harbour, Hoadley had several fingers frost-bitten and all were feeling the cold, for we were wearing light garments in anticipation of fine weather. The wind strengthened every minute, and showers of fine snow were soon whistling down the ice-slopes. No time was lost in landing the cargo, and, with a rising blizzard at our backs, we drove out to meet the *Aurora*. On reaching the ship a small gale was blowing and our boats were taken in tow.

The first thing to be considered was the mooring of the *Aurora* under the lee of the ice cliffs, so as to give us an opportunity of getting the boats aboard. In the meantime they were passed astern, each manned by several hands to keep them bailed out; the rest of us having scrambled up the side. Bringing the ship to anchor in such a wind in uncharted, shoal water was a difficult and hazardous operation. The sounding machine was kept running with rather dramatic results; depths jumping from five to thirty fathoms in the ship's length, and back again to the original figure in the same distance. A feeling of relief passed round when, after much manœuvring, the anchor was successfully bedded five hundred yards from the face of the cliff.

Just at this time the motor launch broke adrift. Away it swept before a wind of forty-five miles per hour. On account of the cold, and because the engine was drenched with sea-water, some difficulty was found in starting the motor. From the ship's deck we could see Bickerton busily engaged with it. The rudder had been unshipped, and there was no chance of replacing it, for the boat was bobbing about on the waves in a most extraordinary manner. However, Whetter managed to make a jury-rudder which served the purpose, while Hunter, the other occupant, was kept laboriously active with the pump.

They had drifted half a mile, and were approaching an islet on which the sea was breaking heavily. Just as everyone was becoming very apprehensive, the launch began to forge ahead, and the men soon escaped from their dangerous predicament. By the united efforts of all hands the boats were hoisted on board and everything was made as "snug" as possible.

The wind steadily increased, and it seemed impossible for the anchor to hold. The strain on the cable straightened out a steel hook two inches in diameter. This caused some embarrassment, as the hook was part of the cable attachment under the fo'c'sle-head. It is remarkable, however, that after this was adjusted, though a succession of gales swept down upon us, the ship did not lose her position up to the time of departure from Adelie Land.

Though we were so close under the shelter of a lofty wall, the waves around us were at least four feet in height, and when the wind increased to sixty-five and seventy miles per hour, their crests were cut off and the surface was hidden by a sheet of racing spindrift.

Everything was securely lashed in readiness for going to sea, in case the cable should part. Final arrangements were then made to discharge the cargo quickly as soon as the wind moderated.

Two days had elapsed before the wind showed any signs of abatement. It was 8 p.m. on January 10 when the first boat ventured off with a small cargo, but it was not till the following morning that a serious start was made. In good weather, every trip between the ship and the Boat Harbour, a distance of a mile, meant that five or six tons had been landed. It was usual for the loaded launch to tow both whale-boats heavily laden and, in addition, a raft of hut timbers or wireless masts. Some of the sailors, while engaged in building rafts alongside the ship, were capsized into the water; after that the occupation was not a popular one.

Ashore, Wild had rigged a derrick, using for its construction two of the wireless royal masts. It was thus possible to cope with the heavier packages at the landing-place.

During the ensuing days, unloading operations were very much interfered with by the recurrence of severe gales off the land. Never was landing so hampered by adverse conditions, and yet, thanks to the assiduous application of all, a great assortment of material was at length safely got ashore. Comprised among them was the following: twenty-three tons of coal briquettes, two complete living-huts, a magnetic observatory, the whole of a wireless equipment, including masts, and more than two thousand packages of general supplies containing sufficient food for two years, utensils, instruments, benzine, kerosene, lubricating oils, an air-tractor and sledges.

This work was completed on the afternoon of January 19. Then came the time for parting. There was a great field before Wild's party to the west, and it was important that they should be able to make the most of the remainder of the season. My great regret was that I could not be with them. I knew that I had men of experience and ability in Davis and Wild, and felt that the work entrusted to them was in the best possible hands.

My instructions were for Captain Davis to proceed west with the *Aurora*, and attempt to effect a landing with Wild's party to establish a Western Base station at some place not less than four hundred miles west of Commonwealth Bay.

All members of the land parties and the ship's officers met in the ward-room. There were mutual good wishes expressed all round, and then we celebrated previous Antarctic explorers, more especially D'Urville and Wilkes. The toast was drunk in excellent Madeira presented to us by Mr. J. T. Buchanan, who had carried this sample with him from Madeira round the world when a member of the celebrated *Challenger* expedition.

The motor launch was hoisted and the anchor raised. Then at 8.45 p.m. on January 19 we clambered over the side into one of the whale-boats and pushed off for Cape Denison, shouting farewells back to the *Aurora*. Several hours later she had disappeared below the north-western horizon, and we had set to work to carve out a home in Adelie Land.

CHAPTER IV

NEW LANDS

On the evening of January 19, after taking leave of myself and companions of the Main Base party, the *Aurora* set a course to round a headland visible on the north-western horizon. At midnight she came abreast at that point and continued steaming west, keeping within a distance of five miles from the coast. A break in the icy monotony came with a short tract of islets, which we named the Curzon Group, fronting a background of black, rocky coastline similar to that at Cape Denison but more extensive.

Beyond that point was the coast which d'Urville had sighted and named Adelie Land. Progressing west they found it to be an elevated ice-encased land fringed by small islets and numerous grounded bergs.

At 10 p.m. on January 20 further progress in proximity to the coast was barred by fields of berg-laden pack-ice trending to the north and north-east. This necessitated a sweeping detour. However, at 1.30 a.m. on the 23rd, they were able to stand to the south-west and make up some of the lost ground. Shortly afterwards they sailed over the charted position of d'Urville's Côte Clarie. The great ice-wall which the French ships followed in 1840 had vanished. Within the next few hours they passed over the charted position of Wilkes's Cape Carr, and thereafter were able to make well to the south.

At 5.30 p.m. more new land was sighted to the southward —snowy highlands similar to those of Adelie Land but of greater elevation.

Captain Davis's narrative at this point proceeds:
"After sounding in one hundred and fifty-six fathoms on mud, the ship stood directly towards the land until 9 p.m. The distance to the nearest point was estimated at twenty

miles; heavy floe-ice extending from our position, latitude 65° 45' S. and longitude 132° 40' E., right up to the shore. Another sounding recorded two hundred and thirty fathoms, on sand and small stones. Some open water was seen to the south-east, but an attempt to force a passage in that direction was frustrated.

"At 3 a.m. on the 24th we were about twelve miles from the nearest point of the coast, and further progress became impossible. The southern slopes were seamed with numerous crevasses, but at a distance the precise nature of the shores could not be accurately determined."

To this country, which had never before been seen, was given the name of Wilkes's Land,* to commemorate that great American Exploring Expedition.

A course was made to the west with Wilkes's Land visible to the south. At 8 p.m. on the 24th, the sky was very clear to the southward and the land could be traced to a great distance until it faded to the south-west. But the ship had come up with the solid floe-ice once more and had to give way to the north, losing touch with the land.

The next four days were a period of gales and heavy seas, which drove the ship some distance to the north. Nothing was visible through whirling clouds of snow. By noon on January 31 the weather was again clear and the ship passed south of Balleny's Sabrina Land without any indication of its existence.

At 11 a.m. the floes were found too heavy for further advance. The ship was made fast to a big one and a large quantity of ice was taken on board to replenish the fresh-water

---

* On some charts the name of Wilkes's Land has been applied to prospective Antarctic coast extending over a couple of thousand miles in length in the region visited by Wilkes. In view of the fact that d'Urville was actually the first to sight land in that sector, I propose to describe the land in general as the Antarctic Continent, but to retain the names adopted by individual discoverers for the stretches of coast actually seen by them. Though Wilkes fixed such names as Knox Land, North's High Land, etc., to coasts reported to have been seen by him, it has been left for us to commemorate his own name in like manner by attaching it to this new stretch of coast.

supply. A tank with a capacity of two hundred gallons, heated within by a steam coil from the engine-room, stood on the poop deck. Into this ice was continuously fed, flowing away as it melted into the main tanks in the bottom of the ship.

"At noon the weather was clear, but nothing could be discerned in the south except a faint blue line on the horizon. It may have been a 'lead' of water, an effect of mirage, or even land-ice—in any case we could not approach it."

The position as indicated by the noon observations placed the ship within seven miles of a portion of Totten's High Land in Wilkes's charts. As high land would have been visible at a great distance, it is clear that Totten's High Land either does not exist or is situated a considerable distance from its charted location. A sounding was made in three hundred and forty fathoms.

It was about this time that a marked improvement was noted in the compass. Ever since the first approach to Adelie Land it had been found unreliable, for, on account of the proximity to the magnetic pole, the directive force of the needle was so slight that very large local variations were experienced.

The longitude of Wilkes's Knox Land was now approaching. With the exception of Adelie Land, the account by Wilkes concerning Knox Land is more convincing than any other of his statements relating to new Antarctic land.

In laying our plans we had hoped to disembark the western land party in the vicinity of Knox Land, if not already accomplished further to the east. It was, therefore, most disappointing when impenetrable ice blocked the way before Wilkes's "farthest south" in that locality had been reached. Three determined efforts were made to find a weak spot, but each time the *Aurora* was forced to retreat, and the third time was extricated only with great difficulty. In latitude 65° 5' S. longitude 107° 20' E., a sounding of three hundred fathoms was made on a rocky bottom. In our opinion this sounding points to the probability of land within sixty miles—so far confirming Wilkes's report of land in this vicinity.

Repulsed from his attack on the pack, Captain Davis set out westward towards the charted position of Termination Land, and in following the trend of the ice was forced a long way to the north.

At 7.40 a.m., February 8, in foggy weather, the cliff face of floating shelf-ice was met. This was disposed so as to point in a north-westerly direction and it was late in the day before the ship doubled its northern end. Following the wall towards the south-south-east, it was interesting to find, at 5.30 p.m., a sounding of one hundred and ten fathoms.

On plotting the observations, it became apparent that the vessel had been hugging a prolonged tongue of floating ice six or seven hundred feet in thickness and seven miles in breadth. As it occupied the position of "Termination Land" which had appeared on some charts it was named Termination Ice-Tongue.

A blizzard sprang up, and, after it had been safely weathered in the lee of some grounded bergs, the *Aurora* moved off on the afternoon of February 11. The horizon was obscured by mist, as she pursued a tortuous track amongst bergs and scattered fragments of heavy floe. Gradually the seam became more open, and by noon on February 12 the water had deepened to two hundred and thirty-five fathoms. Good progress was made to the south; the vessel dodging icebergs and detached floes.

The discovery of a comparatively open sea southward of the main pack was a matter of some moment. As later voyages and the observations of the Western Party showed, this tract of sea is a permanent feature of the neighbourhood. I have named it the Davis Sea, after the gallant Captain of the *Aurora*, in appreciation of the fact that he placed it on the chart.

During the afternoon of February 13, when in about latitude 66° S. longitude 94° 25' E., new land was clearly defined to the south extending to east and west. This was subsequently named Queen Mary Land.

The sphere of operations of the German expedition of 1902 was at hand, for its vessel, the *Gauss,* had wintered frozen in the pack, one hundred and twenty-five miles to the west. It appeared probable that Queen Mary Land would be found to be continuous* with Kaiser Wilhelm II Land, which the Germans had reached by a sledging journey from their ship across the intervening sea-ice. On board the *Aurora* there was great disappointment shortly after sighting the land, for a white expanse of solid floe was met extending right up to the coast. Further approach was barred and there was still a distance of twenty-five miles to traverse to reach the shore.

By this time the ship's coal supply was getting rather low, and the season was coming to a close, so that the commencement of the return voyage to Hobart could not long be delayed. If a western base was to be formed at all, Wild's party would have to be landed without further delay.

At midnight when the *Aurora* set off to the east, hoping to approach nearer to the land in that direction, there was a strong swell from the north-east and the temperature went down to 13° F.

At 8.45 a.m. shelf-ice was observed from aloft trending from north to south in a long wall. At 1 p.m. the ship arrived at the junction of this shelf-ice and the unbroken floe which reached to the rising slopes of ice-mantled land visible to the south, some seventeen miles off.

The ice-shelf also joined the land and stretched far to the east. Later on it was proved to extend for at least two hundred miles from east to west, and to reach a maximum† distance from the land of one hundred and eighty-six miles—to this great ice pontoon, pushing far out into the Southern Ocean, we gave the name of the Shackleton Ice-Shelf.

After a consultation, Davis and Wild decided that, under the circumstances, this floating formation was to be considered as a possible foundation upon which to build a hut.

Wild, Harrisson and Hoadley went to examine it, walking across the floe to which the ship was anchored. The cliff stood eighty to one hundred feet in height above the sea-ice, so that

---

* Such was eventually proved to be the case.
† Measured from land to the extremity of Termination Ice-Tongue, which is apparently a prolongation of the shelf.

the formation, in total thickness, must have attained to at least as much as six hundred feet. Assisted by ramps of snow accumulated on the floe in the lee of the cliff, the ascent with ice-axes and alpine ropes was fairly easy. Two hundred yards from the brink, the shelf-ice was thrown into pressure-undulations and fissured by crevasses, but beyond that was practically sound and unbroken.

After a brief examination Wild and his party unanimously agreed to seize upon this last opportunity. As a site for a wintering station nothing so daring had been attempted before, for they were threatened with the possibility of the breaking away of part of the ice-shelf, setting them adrift on nothing more substantial than an iceberg.

The work of discharging stores was at once commenced. To raise the packages from the floe to the top of the ice-shelf, a "flying-fox" was rigged. This consisted of a wire hawser strained taut between an anchor on the floe and the extremity of a pair of sheer-legs on the brow of the cliff. The packages were sent up slung on a travelling pulley. The ship's crew "broke" stores out of the hold and sledged them three hundred yards to the foot of the "flying-fox," where they were hooked on and sent up to the top by the shore party.

As this work went ahead the floe gradually broke up and floated away. Landing operations continued for four days in all weathers. During that time thirty-six tons of stores were raised on to the shelf-ice one hundred feet above sea-level.

The parting came early on February 21, when the ship's company gave their hearty farewell cheers to Wild and his seven companions who were to build a hut and reside during the ensuing year in novel and anxious circumstances. Davis then turned the *Aurora* north and the long return journey to Hobart commenced.

Before reaching the tempestuous Southern Ocean there was to be negotiated a stretch of several hundred miles of sea thickly strewn with bergs and pack. Further, this had to be accomplished at a time of year when in that latitude navigation was menaced by several hours of darkness.

On February 21 they spent a hair-raising night, several times narrowly averting disaster, groping their way in the darkness amongst packed bergs. Fortune favoured them, for the open sea was reached without mishap.

The eventful cruise was drawing to an end and it was with great satisfaction that Davis could look back upon the achievements of the past three months—the successful landing of three shore parties at stations each separated by intervals of approximately one thousand miles, two of them on entirely new Antarctic lands.

The journey from Queen Mary Land to Tasmania was across a stretch of two thousand three hundred miles of the notoriously wild Southern Seas. So it was the end of a perilous voyage when, by dint of good seamanship, the *Aurora* arrived safely at Hobart, having only nine tons of coal left and almost nothing else to act as ballast.

On March 12 they steamed up the Derwent, passing on their way the Polar ship, *Fram*, at anchor at Sandy Bay. Flags were dipped and a hearty cheer given for Captain Amundsen and his gallant comrades just returned from the South Pole.

CHAPTER V

FIRST DAYS IN ADELIE LAND

HALF an hour after leaving the *Aurora*, on the evening of January 19, the overcrowded whale-boat deposited its human freight on the ice-quay at Cape Denison. The only shelter was a cluster of four tents and a temporary room constructed of cases containing benzine, so the first consideration was the erection of a commodious living-hut.

It was then 10 p.m., so while the majority retired to rest to be ready for a fresh burst of work on the morrow, a few of us discussed the preliminary details, and struck the first blows in the laying of the foundations.

A site for the living-hut was finally approved. This was a nearly flat piece of rocky ground of just sufficient size, partially sheltered on the southern side by a large upstanding rock. Othe~ recommend it were, proximity to the good sledging surface; the ice of the "front door" on the western side.

been said about the type of hut ic stations; those of both stations ne construction. The design chosen room with pyramidal roof. The d the walls on the three windward iich was in turn enclosed by an he veranda was to serve as a store iut warm.

isted with the details of design. were stronger than usual in a all securely bolted together. and outside, were of tongued 'e extra wind-proof by two is not expected, this roofing ~ iour windows in the roof, one on each side of the pyramid. We should thereby get light even though almost buried in snow.

On the morning of January 20 all were at work betimes. As we were securely isolated from trade-union regulations, our hours of labour ranged from 7 a.m. to 11 p.m.

Dynamite was to be used for blasting out the holes for the reception of the stumps, and so the steel rock-drills were unpacked and boring commenced. This was easier than it appeared, because the rock was much traversed by cracks. By the end of the day a good deal of damage had been done to the rock, at the expense of a few sore fingers and wrists caused by the sledge-hammers missing the drills. The work was tedious, for water introduced into the holes had a habit of freezing. The metal drills, too, tended to become brittle in the cold and required to be tempered softer than usual. Hannam operated the forge, and picks and drills were sent along for pointing; an outcrop of gneiss serving as an anvil.

Among other things it was found difficult to fire the charges, for, when frozen, dynamite is not readily exploded. This was overcome by carrying the sticks inside one's pocket until the last moment. In the absence of earth or clay, we had no tamping material until someone suggested guano from the penguin rookeries, which proved a great success.

Next day the stumps were in place; most of them being fixed by wedges and other devices. Cement was tried, but it is doubtful if any good came of it, for the low temperature did not encourage it to set properly. By the evening, the bottom plates were laid on and bolted to the tops of the stumps, and everything was ready for the superstructure.

On January 22, while some were busy with the floor-joists and wall-frames, others carried boulders from the neighbouring moraine, filling in the whole space between the stumps. These were eventually embedded in a mass of boulders, as much as three feet deep in places. By the time both huts were erected, nearly fifty tons of stones had been used in the foundations—a circumstance we did not regret at a later date.

Hodgeman was appointed clerk of works on the construction, and was kept unusually busy selecting timber,

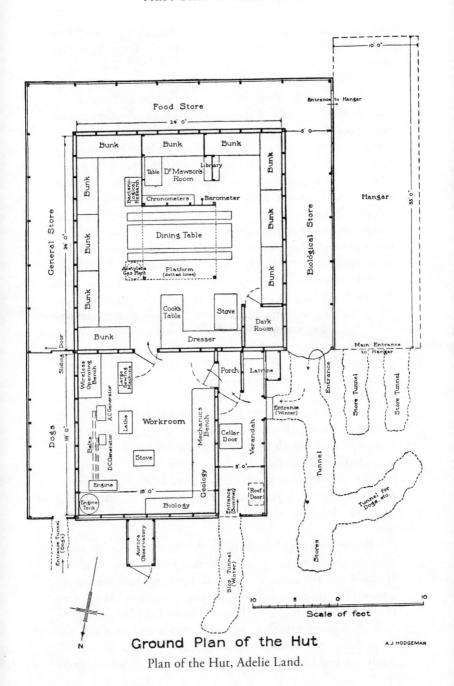

Ground Plan of the Hut

Plan of the Hut, Adelie Land.

A.J. HODGEMAN

patrolling among the workmen, and searching for his foot-rule which had an unaccountable knack of vanishing in thin air.

Hannam had various occupations, but one was to attend to the needs of the inner man, until the completion of the hut. There is no doubt that he was regarded at the time as the most important and popular member of the party, for our appetites were abnormally good. About an hour before meals he was to be seen rummaging amongst the cases of provisions, selecting tins of various brands and hues from the great confusion. However remote their source or diverse their colour, experience taught us that only one preparation would emerge from the tent-kitchen. It was stew. Its good quality was undoubted, for a few minutes after the alarm was sounded there was not a particle left. The alarm was a lusty shout from the master cook, which was re-echoed by the brawny mob who rushed madly to the Benzine Hut. Plates and mugs were seized and portions measured out, while the diners distributed themselves on odd boxes lying about on the ice. Many who were accustomed to restaurants built tables of kerosene cases and dined *al fresco*. After the limited stew, the company fared on cocoa, biscuits—"hard tack"—and jam, *ad libitum*.

On those rare summer days the sun blazed down on the blue ice; skua gulls nestled in groups on the snow; sly penguins waddled along to inspect the building operations; seals basked in torpid slumber on the shore; out on the sapphire bay the milk-white bergs floated in the swell. We can all paint our own picture of the good times round the Benzine Hut. We worked hard, ate heartily and enjoyed life.

By the evening of January 24 the floor and outside walls were finished and the roof frame was in position. Work on the roof was the coldest job of all, for now there was rarely an hour free from a cold breeze, at times reaching the velocity of a gale. This came directly down from the plateau, and to sit with exposed fingers handling hammer and nails was not an enviable job. To add to our troubles, the boards were all badly warped from being continually wet with sea-water on the voyage. However, by judicious "gadgetting," as the phrase went, they were got into place.

The windward roof was up on January 25, and several of us camped in sleeping-bags under its shelter. Already Hannam had unpacked the large range and put the parts together in the kitchen. Henceforth the cooking operations were simplified, for previously a sledging-cooker had been used.

Mention of the stove recalls a very cold episode. It happened that while our goods were being lifted from the boats to the landing-stage, a case had fallen into the harbour. When the parts of the stove were being assembled, several important items were found to be missing, and it was thought that they might compose the contents of the unknown case lying in the kelp at the bottom of the bay.

Laseron and I went on board the whale-boat one day at low water, and located the box with a pole, but though we used several devices with hooks, we were unable to get hold of it. At last I went in, and, standing on tip-toe, could just reach it and keep my head above water. It took some time to extricate it from the kelp, following which I established a new record for myself in dressing. The case turned out to be full of jam, and we had to make a new search for the missing parts. I do not think I looked very exhilarated after that bath, but strange to say, a few days later Correll tried an early morning swim which was the last voluntary dip attempted by any one.

The enthusiasm of the builders rose to its highest pitch as the roof neared completion, and we came in sight of a firm and solid habitation, secure from the winds which harassed us daily. A dozen hammers worked at once, each concentrated upon a specific job. The men inside nailing on the ceiling boards worked steadily ahead without interruption; the behaviour of those sitting on the roof busy on the outer covering was more erratic, as individuals were sometimes observed to start up suddenly and temporarily lose interest in the work.

A climax was reached when McLean, working on the steeply inclined roof, lost his footing and as a last hope, in passing, seized hold of the wire stay supporting the chimney. Alas, that was, so far, the only stay secured and so the chimney collapsed. As McLean proceeded over the end of the roof into a bank of snow below, Ninnis, within the hut, impressed by the row above and seeing the inner section of the stove-pipe performing extraordinary evolutions was convinced that nothing less than a cyclone had struck the building. Attempting at all costs to save the flue, he gallantly held on to it, hot though it was, amidst a shower of soot. A few moments later, realizing what had actually happened, he retired to the wash-tub determined in future to take things less seriously.

Everybody was in the best of spirits, and things went ahead merrily. On January 30 the main building was almost completed, and all slept under its roof. Bunks had been constructed, forming a double tier around three sides of the room. For the first time since coming ashore we retired to sleep in blankets; fur sleeping-bags had been previously used. That night the sky which had been clear for a fortnight banked up with nimbus cloud, and Murphy, who was sleeping under a gap in the roof, woke up next morning to find over him a thick counterpane of snow.

Madigan was to take charge of the meteorological observations and, assisted by Ninnis and Mertz, he erected the two screens and mounted the instruments. Special care was taken to secure the screens against violent winds. Phosphor-bronze wire stays, each with a breaking strength of one ton, were used, attached to billets of wood driven into fissures in the rock. Strong as these wires were, several breakages had to be replaced during the year.

Webb was engaged with the magnetic work. For this two huts were to be erected; the first for "absolute" determinations, the second for housing the self-recording instruments— the magnetographs. Distant sites, away from the magnetic disturbances of the living-hut, were chosen. Webb and Stillwell assisted by others were busy throughout February on these erections.

It was now necessary to institute a routine of night-watchmen, cooks and messmen. The night-watchman's duties included periodic meteorological observations, attention to the fire in the range, and other miscellaneous duties arising between the hours of 8 p.m. and 8 a.m. The cook prepared the meals, and the messmen of the day rendered any assistance necessary. A rotation was adopted, so arranged that those most actively engaged in scientific observations were least saddled with domestic duties. Thus each contributed his equivalent share of work.

The kitchen department was a very important one for in food matters, at least, a pleasant variation could be introduced into the life, relieving the monotony which is ever the bugbear of winter life in the polar zones.

Regulations were drafted governing the issue of foods to the cook, and in the matter of meals we entered upon a routine. Breakfast was henceforth to consist of porridge followed by canned fruit. Lunch was made very appetizing by a chief course selected from cold ham, fried sardines, salmon or other preserved fish. At dinner there was always soup, followed by penguin or seal in some form served with potatoes and a second preserved vegetable; finally a pudding course and a sweet dessert.

At meal times the eighteen of us were ranged round one long narrow table and the cook and messmen were kept very busy attending to all needs. No unnecessary refinements were indulged in, for example, should one desire some comestible, jam for instance, out of arm's reach it was quite *de rigueur* to call out, "Give the jam a fair wind," upon which it would commence travelling down the table in the right direction, often, however, very haltingly as it was fair game for anybody along its track who would exclaim, "on the way!"

A friendly rivalry sprang up amongst the cooks, which reflected beneficially on the fare, so that everybody was happy and well satisfied in the matter of meals.

Whilst others were occupied finishing off the interior of the hut, Whetter and Close sledged the cases of stores across from the landing-stage, classified them and stacked them against the veranda walls, as an additional breakwind. Liquids liable to freeze and burst their bottles were taken into the hut.

Already we had several times seized the opportunity of a calm hour to take out the whale-boat and assist Hunter to set traps and make a few hauls with the small dredge. Even in five fathoms, bright red and brown star-fish had been caught in the trap, as well as numerous specimens of a common Antarctic fish resembling a cod, of a species known as *Notothenia*. In ten fathoms and over the results were better, though in no case was the catch so abundant as one would expect from the amount of life in the water. The luxuriant kelp probably interfered with the proper working of the traps.

On one afternoon while building operations were still in progress Hunter, our biologist, was very unfortunate in crushing some of his fingers whilst carrying a heavy case. This accident came at a time when he had just recovered from a severe strain of the knee-joint which he suffered during our activities in the Queen's Wharf shed at Hobart. Several of us were on the point of setting out with him to visit the fish traps when it happened. Hunter's enthusiasm in his work was eloquently expressed in that even this painful accident did not quell his desire to join the boat, so we waited for him until McLean had sewn up the two fingers.

Weddell seals, and with them occasional crab-eater seals, were at this time always to be found in numbers sleeping on the ice-foot around the Boat Harbour. It appeared as if we would have plenty of meat throughout the year, so I waited until the building was completed before laying in a stock. The penguins, however, were fast diminishing in numbers and the young birds in the rookeries had grown very large and were beginning to migrate to warmer regions. Several parties, therefore, raided them and secured some hundreds for the winter.

Giant petrels and skua gulls swarmed in flocks around the carcases of seals and penguins. These scavengers demolish an incredible amount of meat and blubber in a short time. It is a diabolical sight to witness a group of birds tearing out the viscera of a seal, dancing the while with wings outspread.

During the afternoon of February 11 Webb came in with the news that a sea-elephant was making its way over the rocks near the shore. We rushed out in time to see it standing over Johnson, one of the dogs. He was a fair-sized male with a good skin, so we shot him before he had time to get back into the sea. His measurements were seventeen feet six inches in length and twelve in maximum circumference. A visit from a sea-elephant was most unexpected for they are sub-Antarctic in distribution. As far as I am aware the only other occasion on record of a sea-elephant on the shore of the Antarctic Continent was that noted by Captain Scott in McMurdo Sound.

With the temperature well below freezing point, skinning is cold work in the wind, and must be done before the animal has time to freeze stiff. A number of us set to work flaying. In order to move the mountain of flesh a couple of block-and-tackle purchases had to be rigged. It was several hours before everything was disposed of; the skin and skull for the biological collection and the meat and blubber for the dogs. Ninnis and Mertz, who were the wardens of the dogs, cut up about one ton of meat and blubber, and stored it as a winter reserve for their charges.

The dogs, ever since their arrival ashore, had been chained up on the rocks below the hut. The continuous wind worried them a good deal, but they had a substantial offset to the cold in a plentiful supply of seal-meat. On the whole, they were in a much better condition than when they left the *Aurora*. Nineteen in all, they had an odd assemblage of names, which seemed to grow into them until nothing else was so suitable: Basilisk, Betli, Caruso, Castor, Franklin, Fusilier, Gadget, George, Ginger, Ginger Bitch, Grandmother, Haldane, Jappy, John Bull, Johnson, Mary, Pavlova, Scott and Shackleton. Grandmother would have been more appropriately known as Grandfather. The head dog was Basilisk, and next to him came Shackleton.

Early in February, after having experienced nothing but a succession of gales for nearly a month, I was driven to conclude that the average local weather must be much more windy than in any other known part of Antarctica. The conditions were not at all favourable for sledging, which I had hoped to commence as soon as the main part of the hut was completed. Now that the time had arrived and the weather was still adverse, it seemed clear that our first duty was to see everything snug for the winter before making an attempt.

The timbers for a small living-hut, twenty feet square, which had formed part of the *Aurora's* freight, provided in case the prospects warranted the landing of an additional separate wintering party on Antarctic coasts, had been put ashore with our equipment. This we decided to build on the lee wall of the main hut, to be used to house the wireless gear and as a work-room. Hannam, assisted by Bickerton, Madigan and others, had laid heavy and firm foundations for the petrol-motor and generator of the wireless installation. The floor of the work-room was then built around these bed-plates, and last of all came the walls and roof. Murphy, Bage and Hodgeman were chiefly responsible for the last-named, which was practically completed by February 10. Minor additions and modifications were added after that date. Meanwhile, Hannam continued to unpack and mount the instruments of the wireless equipment. Along one wall and portion of another, in the outer hut, a bench was built for mechanical work and for scientific purposes.

Our home had attained to a stage of complex perfection. To penetrate to the inside hut, the stranger steps through a hole in the snow to the veranda, then by way of a vestibule with an inner and outer door he invades the privacy of the work-room, from which he passes by a third door into the *sanctum sanctorum*. Later, when the snow-tunnel system came into vogue, the place became another Labyrinth of Minos.

The three doors were fitted with springs to keep them shut unless they were jammed open for ventilation, which was at once obtained by opening an aperture in the cooking-range flue. A current of air would then circulate through the open doors. The roof windows were immovable and soon became more securely sealed by a thick accumulation of ice on the inside. During the winter these slabs of ice attained a thickness of five inches. An officer of public health, unacquainted with the climate of Adelie Land would be inclined to regard the absence of more adequate ventilation as a serious omission. It would enlighten him to know that much of our spare time, for a month after the completion of the

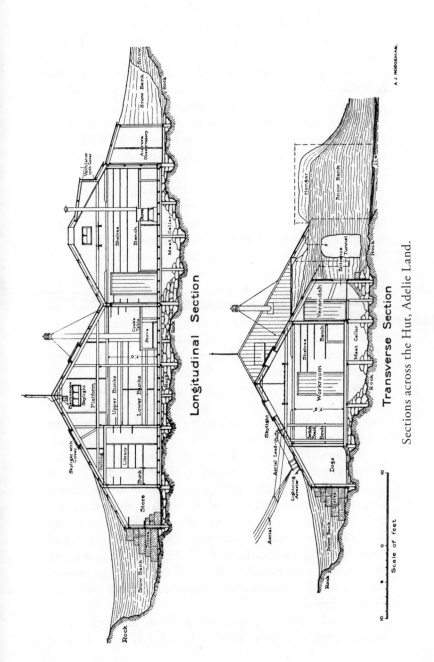

Longitudinal Section

Transverse Section

Sections across the Hut, Adelie Land.

building, was spent in plugging off samples of the blizzards without which found their way through most unexpected places, urged by a wind pressure of many pounds to the square foot.

Excepting the small portion used as an entrance-porch, the verandas were left without any better flooring than well-trodden snow. In the boarded floor of the porch was a trap-door which led down into a shallow cellar extending under the work-room. The cellar was a natural refrigerating chamber for fresh meat and contained fifteen carcases of mutton besides piles of seal meat and penguins.

On account of the limited depth of this cellar it was an awkward job getting at the meat, necessitating a scramble on hands and knees with a wary look-out for projecting joists and stumps. Murphy, the storeman, who was rather ingenious in the matter of labour-saving devices, invented the plan of pushing a dog through the trap-door to bring out the penguins when required. As the dog sprang out Murphy would seize the bird much to the disappointment of the dog. One fine day, however, the dog discovered one of the very few legs of mutton we possessed. Out he bounded and succeeded in evading Murphy who spent the greater part of an hour in pursuit. After this event the dog method was abolished.

In preparation for our contemplated sledging, masts, spars and sails were fitted to some of the sledges, rations were prepared and alterations made to harness and clothing. Soon a sledge stood packed, ready to set out on the first fine day.

For several days in succession, about the middle of February, the otherwise continuous wind fell off to a calm for several hours in the evening. On those occasions Mertz gave us some fine exhibitions of ski-ing, of which art he was a consummate master. Skis had been provided in case we should have to traverse a country where the snow lay soft and deep. From the outset, there was little chance of that being the case in wind-scoured Adelie Land. Nevertheless, most of the men seized the few opportunities we had to become prac- tised in their use.

The end of February approached. We were fully prepared for sledging, and were looking forward to it with great

Nuggets Beach looking down from cliff (*Hurley*)

Sea Leopard showing fight (*Hamilton*)

Sealers rolling barrels up the beach at the nuggets. Barrels to be filled with penguin oil (*Hamilton*)

Royal penguins on Nuggets Beach (*Hurley*)

Wireless station, Macquarie Island (*Sawyer*)

A male elephant seal, Macquarie Island

Frank Wild

Horn Bluff with organ pipe rock formation

Ninnis on board the S.Y. *Aurora* on the voyage south

Dr Xavier Mertz

Loading the ship at the wharf, Hobart (Mawson in hat) (*Gray*)

A.A.E. Main Base Party members who wintered a second year (1913) and the Macquarie Island (1913) Party returning on the S.Y. *Aurora*, January 1914 (*Hurley*)

Mawson after epic sledge journey

Mawson emerging from a make-shift tent (*Hurley*)

In Aladdin's cave—Bage cooking hoosh, Hurley
in sleeping bag (*Mertz*)

Captain John King Davis

"Huskies" hauling with a will in a fan arrangement of dogs (*Mertz*)

Laseron and Hunter with a hand cart containing
dredging gear (*Mawson*)

Mertz at land's end where the ice cliff begins

Madigan's frost-bitten face (*Hurley*)

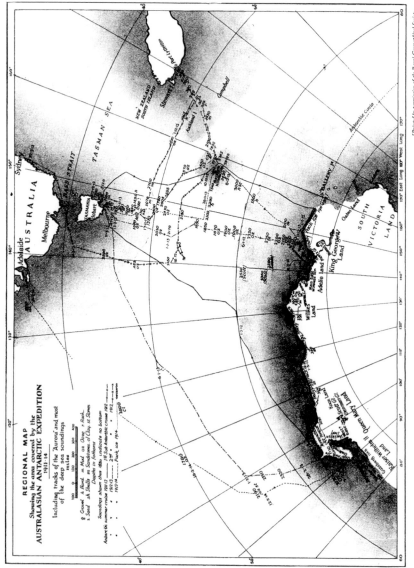

REGIONAL MAP
Showing the area covered by the
AUSTRALASIAN ANTARCTIC EXPEDITION
1911-14

Including tracks of the *Aurora* and most
of the deep sea soundings

miles

g. Gravel   h. Hard   m. Mud   oz. Ooze   r. Rock.
s. Sand   sh. Shells   vs. Sandstones of Clay   st. Stones
Depths in fathoms

Soundings shown thus ᵒᵒᵒ indicate no bottom

Antarctic summer cruise 1911-12 ————
                        1912-13 —·—·—
                        1913-14 ·······   Pack ice 1914· ✕✕✕✕

AUSTRALIA

Adelaide
Melbourne
Sydney

TASMANIA
Hobart

BASS STRAIT

TASMAN SEA

NEW ZEALAND
SOUTH ISLAND

Stewart I.

Auckland I.

Campbell I.

SOUTH
VICTORIA
LAND

Oates Land

King George V Land

Adelie Land

Wilkes Land

Kaiser Wilhelm II Land

Queen Mary Land

Termination
Land

[Printed by permission of the Royal Geographical Society.]

expectation. The wind still continued, often rising to the force of a hurricane, and was mostly accompanied by snow.

One evening, when we were all at dinner, there was a sudden noise which drowned the rush of the blizzard. It was found that several sledges had been blown away from their comparatively secure positions to the south of the hut, striking the building as they passed. They were all rescued except one, which had already reached the sea and was travelling rapidly toward Australia.

Mertz, Bage and I had taken advantage of a lull to ascend the ice-slope to the south, and to erect a flag-staff at a distance of two miles. Besides being a beacon for sledging parties, it was used for ablation measurements.

Many schemes required our attention, and there was not a spare moment for any one. Though we chafed at the delay in sledging, there was some consolation in the fact that the scientific programme was daily becoming more and more complete.

CHAPTER VI

AUTUMN PROSPECTS

As far as we could see, the inland ice was an unbroken plateau with no natural landmarks. From the hinterland, in a vast solid stream, the ice flowed with heavily crevassed downfalls near the coast. The effect of the rock mass in the vicinity of Cape Denison was to dam back the ice immediately to the south, preserving a narrow belt reasonably free from crevasses leading to the plateau. To reach the Hut in safety it would be necessary for sledging parties returning from the interior to descend by this highway. The problem was to locate the path. Determinations of latitude and longitude would guide them to the neighbourhood of Commonwealth Bay, but the coastline in the vicinity of winter quarters, with the recognizable rocks and islets, would not come into view until within two miles, as above that point the icy slopes filled the foreground up to the distant berg-studded horizon. Delays in reaching the Hut owing to the difficult descent might have serious consequences, for provisions are usually short near the conclusion of a sledging journey.

The necessity of making artificial landmarks was, therefore, most obvious. Already we had a flagstaff two miles to the south. It was now my intention to run a line of similar marks backwards to the plateau.

Bage, Madigan and I were to form a reconnoitring party to plant these flags, and to make a journey of a few days' duration into the hinterland, to ascertain its possibilities, and with a view to an extended sledging campaign to commence as soon as possible after our return. It was decided not to make use of the dogs until later in the year, when they would be in better form.

The wind continued, accompanied by more or less drift-snow. This appeared to be the settled state of the weather.

We decided to move out as soon as a moderate phase should occur.

On the afternoon of February 28 the weather cleared up for several hours, and we decided to leave on the following day. The wind resumed operations once more, but fell off late on February 29, so we made a start. We intended to get the packed sledge up the first steep slope, there to leave it until the morrow. The drift was slight and low, flowing along like a stream below our knees. Bickerton, Hurley and Mertz assisted us with the hauling. At a distance of a little more than a mile, at an elevation of five hundred feet, the sledge was anchored and we returned to the Hut for the night.

Next morning the weather cleared still more, and we left just before noon. Three miles out, a mast and flag were erected, when our companions of the day before, who had again assisted us, turned back. At five and a half miles the brow of the main rise was reached, and the gradient became much flatter beyond it. The elevation was found to be one thousand five hundred feet.

To the south nothing was visible but a great, wan, icy wilderness. To the north a headland appeared on either hand, each about twenty-five miles away, and between them lay an expanse of sea dotted with many bergs. The nearer portions of the coast, together with the Mackellar Islets, were lost to view on account of the curvature of the foreground.

During most of the day we had travelled over a surface of clear ice, marked by occasional scars where fissuring, now healed, had at some time taken place. Beyond the three-mile flag, however, the ice was gashed at frequent intervals, producing irregular crevasses, usually a few yards in length and, for the most part, choked with snow. At five and a half miles we were on the edge of a strip of snow, half a mile across, whose whiteness was thrown in dazzling contrast against the foil of transparent, dark ice.

It was dusk, and light drift commenced to scud by, so, as this was a suitable place to erect a flag, we decided to camp for the night. Some hours later I woke up to hear a blizzard blowing outside, and to find Madigan fumbling amongst some gear at the head-end of the tent. From inside my bag I called out to inquire if there was anything wrong, and received a reply that he was looking for the primus-pricker. Then he slipped back into his sleeping-bag, and all became quiet, except for the snow beating against the tent. So I presumed that he had found it. Revolving the incident in my mind, and dimly wondering what use he could have had for a primus-pricker in the middle of the night, I again fell asleep. In the morning the blizzard was still blowing, accompanied by a good deal of drift. On inquiry I found that Madigan knew nothing of his midnight search, so it must have been a case of somnambulism.

It would serve no useful purpose to go on in thick drift, for the main object of our journey was to define the best route through the crevassed zone; and that could only be done on a clear day. I decided, accordingly, that if the weather did not improve by noon to leave the sledge with the gear and walk back to the Hut, intending to make another attempt when conditions became more settled.

Whilst the others erected a flag-staff and froze into the ice the legs of a drift-proof box containing a thermometer, which was to continue recording during our absence, I made lunch and prepared for our departure. The tent was taken down and everything lashed securely on the sledge.

It was nearly 3 p.m. when we set out in thick drift, and in two hours we were at the Hut; the weather having steadily improved as we descended. On comparing notes with those at home it appeared that we, at the fifteen hundred foot level, had experienced much more wind and drift than they at sea-level.

Webb and his assistants were beginning to make quite a display at the Magnetograph House. The framework, which had already been erected once, to be demolished by the wind, was now strongly rebuilt and they went ahead covering it with boards and a lining of tarred paper. All hands then joined in piling boulders around it, to form a wall, in which some thirty tons of rock were utilized. It was so well lagged from the penetration of heat and cold that it was possible to maintain a very steady temperature within; a most desirable feature in a magnetograph house.

From the night of our return to March 8 there was a high
wind accompanied by much drift; for some hours it continued
at eighty miles per hour, the mean temperature being about
15° F., with a minimum of 5° F.

Up to this date the dogs had been kept on the chain,
on account of their depredations amongst the seals and
penguins. The severe weather now made it necessary to
release them. Thenceforth their abode for part of the day
was inside the veranda, where a section was barricaded off
for their exclusive use. Outside in heavy drift their habit
was to take up a position in the lee of some large object,
such as the Hut. In such a position they were soon
completely buried and oblivious to the outside elements.
Thus one would sometimes tread on a dog, hidden beneath
the snow; and the dog often showed less surprise than the
offending man. What the dogs detested most of all in the
drifting snow was that it filled their eyes until they were
forced to stop and frantically brush it away with their
paws. The snow driven into their coats would partly thaw
and freeze again, matting the hair together, a solid armour
of ice. Another trouble arising from such weather was that
they often became frozen down to ice surfaces; an ice-axe
would have to be used to chip them free. In high winds,
accompanied by a low temperature, they were certainly
very miserable, unless in some kind of shelter.

It was really wonderful that the dogs managed as well
as they did in such conditions. They certainly used what
brains they had to great advantage. It was often quite
interesting to study their tactics. One amusing habit was
frequently observed whilst out walking with them in
windy weather. No sooner would one halt for some purpose
or another than all the dogs would squat down in a line,
each in the lee of the other. As soon as number one realized
he was being made a screen he got up and trotted round
to the back. A moment later number two would follow
him, and so on until in sheer disgust maybe they would
break up the formation.

Several families were born at this time, but although we did
everything possible for them they all perished, except one,

Blizzard, the offspring of Gadget. Needless to say Blizzard was a great favourite.

On the night of March 7, Caruso, who had been in poor condition for some time, was found to have a gaping wound around the neck. It was a clean cut, an inch deep and almost a foot in length. The cause was never satisfactorily explained, though a piece of strong, frozen string embedded in the wound evidently made the incision. Caruso was brought inside, and, whilst Whetter administered chloroform, McLean sewed up the wound. After careful attention for some days, it healed fairly well, but as the dog's general health was worse, it was deemed advisable to shoot him.

After the calm of March 8 the wind steadily increased and became worse than ever. Madigan, who was in charge of the whale-boat, kept it moored in the Boat Harbour under shelter of the ice-foot. An excursion was made to the fish traps, buoyed half a mile off shore, on February 8, and it was found that one had been carried away in the hurricane. The other was brought in very much battered. That night it was decided at the first opportunity to haul up the boat and house it for the winter. Alas! the wind came down again too quickly, increasing in force, with dense drift. It was still in full career on the 12th, when Madigan came in with the news that the boat had disappeared. It was no fault of the rope-attachments, for they were securely made, and so we were left to conclude that a great mass of ice had broken away from the overhanging shelf and carried everything before it.

The regularity of the high-velocity winds was clearly recognized as one of the most remarkable features of Adelie Land. By itself such wind would have been bad enough, but accompanied by dense volumes of drifting snow, it effectually put a stop to most outdoor occupations.

The roof and walls of the veranda being covered only with a single layer of boards, the snow drove through every chink. Much time was spent endeavouring to make it drift-tight; but as the materials at our disposal were very limited, the result was never absolutely satisfactory. The small veranda serving as an entrance-porch was deluged with snow which drove in past the canvas doorway. The only way to get over this trouble was to shovel out the accumulations every morning.

One advantage of the deposit of snow around the Hut was that all draughts were sealed off. Before this happened it was found very difficult to keep the inside temperature up to 40° F. A temperature taken within the Hut varied according to the relative position in reference to the walls and stove. That shown by the thermometer attached to the standard barometer, which was suspended near the centre of the room, was taken as the "hut temperature." Near the floor and walls it was lower, and higher, of course, near the stove. On one occasion, in the early days, I remember the "hut temperature" being 19° F., notwithstanding the heat from the large range. Under these conditions the writing-ink and various solutions froze, and, when the night-watchman woke up the shivering community he had many clamorous demands to satisfy. The photographer produced an interesting product from the dark room, immediately at the back of the stove—a transparent cast of a developing-dish in which a photographic plate left overnight to wash was firmly set.

We arranged to maintain an inside temperature of 40° F., when it rose to 50° F. means were taken to reduce it. The cooking-range, a large one designed to burn anthracite coal, was also the warming apparatus. To raise the temperature quickly, blocks of seal-blubber, of which there was always a supply at hand, were used. The coal consumption averaged one hundred pounds a day, approximately; this being reduced at a later date to seventy-five pounds by employing a special damper for the chimney. The damper designed for ordinary climates allowed too much draught to be sucked through during the high winds which prevailed continually.

The chimney was very short and securely stayed, projecting through the lee side of the roof, where the pressure of the wind was least felt. It was fitted with a cowl which had to be specially secured to keep it in place. During heavy drifts the cowl became choked with snow and ice, notwith-standing the red-hot fire below, and the Hut would rapidly fill with smoke until someone, hurriedly donning burberrys, rushed out with an ice-axe to chip an outlet for the draught. A massive casing of ice which had to be periodically cleared away developed around and obstructed the chimney at all times but in the height of summer.

The first good display of aurora polaris was witnessed during the evening of March 12, though no doubt there had been other exhibitions obscured by the drift. As the days went by and the equinox drew near, auroral phenomena were with few exceptions visible on all clear evenings. In the majority of cases they showed up low on the northern sky.

In the midst of a torment of wind, March 15 came as a beautiful, sunny, almost calm day. I remarked in my diary that it was "typical Antarctic weather," thinking of those halcyon days which are so striking a feature of the climate I had experienced on the southern shores of the Ross Sea. In Adelie Land, we were destined to find it was hard to number more than a dozen or two in the year.

A fine day! the psychological effect was remarkable; pessimism vanished, and we argued that with the passing of the equinox there would be a marked change for the better. Not a moment was lost; some were employed in making anchorages for the wireless masts; others commenced to construct a hangar to house the air-tractor sledge.

In building the hangar, the western wall of the Hut was used for one side; empty cases formed the other sides and over all was nailed a roof of thick timber—part of the air-tractor's case. The dimensions inside were thirty-four feet by eleven feet; the height, eleven feet at the northern and six feet at the southern end. As a break-wind a crescent-shaped wall of benzine cases was built several yards to the south. As in the case of the veranda, it was very difficult to make the hangar impervious to drift; a certain quantity of snow always made its way in, and was duly shovelled out.

Seals had suddenly become very scarce, no doubt disgusted with the continuous winds. Every one that came ashore was shot for food. Unfortunately, the amount of meat necessary for the dogs throughout the winter was so great that dog-biscuits had to be used to eke it out.

Only a few penguins remained by the middle of March. They were all young ones, waiting for the completion of their second moult before taking to the sea. The old feathers hung in untidy tufts, and the birds were often in a wretched plight owing to the wind and drift snow. Many were added to the bleaching carcases which fill the crevices or lie in heaps on ancient rookeries among the rocky ridges. None were free from the encumbrance of hard cakes of snow which often covered their eyes or dangled in pendent icicles from their bodies, often giving them a very ludicrous appearance. Odd ones were met so heavily encased in ice, especially about the head, as to be rendered helpless and, but for our timely aid, must have perished.

Hurley obtained some excellent photographs of the seals and penguins, as of all other subjects. So good were they that most of us withdrew from competition. His enthusiasm and resourcefulness knew no bounds. It was soon recognized as futile to await calm days, and ways were found to secure records even in the face of freezing gales. Occasional days, during which cameras that had been maltreated by the wind were patched up, were now looked upon as inevitable.

But the taking of still-pictures in the wind was as nothing compared with the difficulties and painful frost-bites associated with cinematography under the same conditions. However, our photographer was determined not to be beaten, and eventually succeeded in filming wonderful illustrations of the blizzard itself. Many devices were improvised for screening the camera; even then, the instrument soon became clogged with drift-snow and put out of action, which meant several hours of hard work in the Hut cleaning, drying and repairing the mechanism. It was by no means easy to get about in high gales, with the awkward cinematograph camera, as was illustrated one day when it was arranged to take a picture from the lee of a rock shelter. Webb and Hurley were devoting their united efforts to the task of carrying the camera across from the Hut, when they were picked up clear of the ground and blown some yards away, resulting in sundry damages all round, more especially to the instrument.

The good conditions of the 15th lasted only a few hours, and back came the enemy as bad as ever. On the 18th the wind was only thirty miles per hour, giving us an opportunity of continuing the buildings outside. It was only by making the most of every odd hour when the weather was tolerable that our outdoor enterprises made any headway. Sometimes when it was too windy for building we were able to improve our knowledge of the neighbourhood.

A glance at Stillwell's map, on the opposite page, is instructive as to the extent and character of the rocky area. Geologically it is mainly a uniform type of gneiss crumpled and folded, showing all the signs of great antiquity. It is devoid of any forms of vegetation sufficiently prominent to meet the casual eye. Soil is lacking, for all light materials and even gravel are carried away by the winds. The bare rock rises up into miniature ridges, separated by valleys largely occupied by ice-slabs and lakelets. Snow fills all the crevices and tails away in sloping ramps on the lee side of every obstacle. The highest point of the rock is one hundred and forty feet. The seaward margin is deeply indented, and the islets off-shore tell of a continuation of the rugged, rocky surface below the sea. On the northern faces of the ridges, fronting the ice-foot, large, yellowish patches mark the sites of penguin rookeries. These are formed by a superficial deposit of guano which never becomes thick, for it blows away as fast as it accumulates. Standing on the shore, one can see kelp growing amongst the rocks even in the shallowest spots, below low-water level.

To the south, the rocks are overridden by the inland-ice which bears down upon and overwhelms them. The ice-sheet shows a definite basal moraine, which means that the lowest stratum, about forty feet in thickness, is charged with stones and earthy matter. Above this stratum the ice is free from foreign inclusions and rises steeply to several hundred feet, after which the ascending gradient is reduced.

Where the ice-sheet terminates there is a great accumulation of debris, a terminal moraine, which was in itself a veritable museum. For Stillwell this was a "happy hunting-ground," for the story of the buried land to the south is in

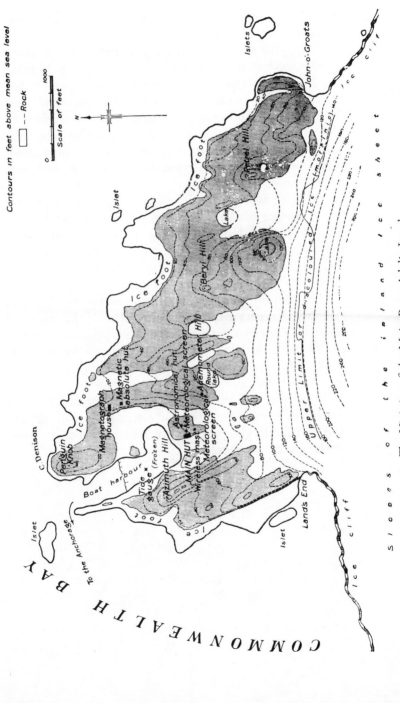

The Vicinity of the Main Base, Adelie Land.

large measure revealed in the samples brought by the ice and so conveniently dumped.

The equinox arrived, and the only indication of settled weather was a more marked regularity in the winds. Nothing like it had been reported from any part of the world. Any trace of elation we may have felt at this meteorological discovery could not compensate for the ever-present discomforts of life. Day after day the wind fluctuated between a gale and a hurricane. Overcast skies and heavy nimbus clouds were the rule and the air was continually charged with drifting snow.

Sledging was out of the question. Indeed, we recognized how fortunate we were not to have pushed farther afield in March. Had we thus advanced, it is more than likely that provisions would have been exhausted before we could have located the Hut in the sea of drift. Our hopes were now centred on midwinter calms.

Looking through my diary, I notice that on March 24 "we experienced a rise in spirits because of the improved weather." Referring to the records I find the average velocity of the wind for that day to have been forty-five miles per hour, corresponding to a "strong-gale" on the Beaufort scale. This tells its own story.

After the equinox, the temperature remained in the vicinity of zero, Fahrenheit. The penguin's took to the sea, and, save for the glimpse of an occasional petrel on the wing, the landscape was desolate.

CHAPTER VII

THE BLIZZARD

THE climate proved to be little more than one continuous blizzard the year round; a hurricane of wind roaring for weeks together, pausing for breath only at odd hours. Such pauses—lulls of a singular nature—were a welcome relief to the dreary monotony, and on such occasions the auditory sense was strangely affected. The contrast was so severe when the racking gusts of an abating wind suddenly gave way to intense, eerie silence that the habitual droning of many weeks would still reverberate in the ears. At night one would involuntarily wake up if the wind died away and be loth to sleep "for the hunger of a sound." In the open air the stillness conveyed to the brain an impression of audibility, interpreted as a vibratory murmur.

During these pauses the sequence of events could almost be predicted; indeed, they would often occur at the same time on several succeeding days.

The first well-marked lull of this kind, intervening at the height of a gale, occurred on March 19. On that day the wind, which had been blowing with great force during the morning, commenced to subside rapidly just after noon. Towards evening, the air about the Hut was quite still except for gusts from the north and rather frequent "whirlies"—whirlwinds of a few yards to a hundred yards or more in diameter. Beyond a strange stillness of the immediate vicinity, broken occasionally by the tumult of a passing, wandering whirlie, an incessant, seething roar could be heard. One could not be certain from whence it came, but it seemed to proceed either from the south or overhead. Away on the icy promontories to the east and west, where the slopes were visible mounting to an altitude of several thousand feet, clouds of drifting snow blotted out the details of the surface above a level of about six hundred feet; evidence that the gale still continued above that level. It certainly appeared as if the gale, for some reason, had lifted and was still raging overhead. At 7.30 p.m. the sound we had heard, like the distant lashing of ocean waves, became louder. Soon gusts swept the tops of the rocky ridges, gradually descending to throw up the snow at a lower level. Then a volley raked the Hut, and within a few minutes we were once more enveloped in a sea of drifting snow, and the wind blew stronger than ever.

The duration of the lulls was found to range from a few minutes to several hours; that just described was longer than usual.

In the course of time, after repeated observations, much of the mystery connected with these lulls was cleared up. For instance, on one occasion, a party ascending the ice-slopes to the south met the wind blowing as hard as ever at and above an elevation of four hundred feet. At the same time snow could be seen pouring over the ice cliffs to the west of the winter quarters, and across a foaming turmoil of water. This was evidently the main cause of the seething roar, but it was mingled with an under note of deeper tone from the upland plateau—like the wind in a million tree-tops.

Again early in the spring, while we were transporting provisions to the south, frequent journeys were made to higher elevations. It was then established that even when whole days of calm prevailed at the Hut, the wind, even without exception, continued to blow as usual above a level of one thousand feet. On such occasions it appeared that the gale was impelled to blow straight out from the plateau slopes over a lower stratum of dead air.

So we came to realize that when a calm fell upon the Hut, the wind had merely retired to higher elevations and hung over us like the sword of Damocles, ready to descend at any moment.

Reverting to the subject of the whirlies. Similar disturbances are known elsewhere but seldom so conspicuous and constant a phenomenon as in the coastal region of Adelie Land. On such occasions as just described the whirlies tracked about in a most irregular manner and woe betide any light object that came in their path. The velocity of the wind in the rotating column being very great, a corresponding lifting power was imparted to it. As an illustration of this force, it may be mentioned that the lid of the air-tractor case had been left lying on the snow near the Hut. It weighed more than three hundredweights, yet it was whisked vertically into the air one morning and dropped fifty yards in a north-easterly direction. An hour afterwards it was picked up again and returned near its original position, this time striking the rocks with such force that it was shattered.

The radius of activity of the whirlies was strictly limited; objects directly in their path only being disturbed. For instance, Laseron one day was skinning at one end of a seal and remained in perfect calm, while McLean, at the other extremity, was on the edge of a furious vortex.

Travelling over the sea the whirlies displayed fresh capabilities. Columns of brash-ice, frozen spray and water-vapour were frequently seen lifted to heights of from two hundred to four hundred feet, simulating water-spouts. On the land one might observe several wandering about the landscape simultaneously, outlined by snow dust sucked up a great height. They were altogether an uncanny proposition.

During one hour on March 22 it blew eighty-six miles. On the morning of that day there was not much snow in the air to limit vision and the raging sea was a fearful sight. Even the nearest of the islands, little more than a hundred yards off the land, was partially hidden in the clouds of spray. What an impossible coast this would be for the wintering of a ship.

Everybody knows that the pressures exerted by wind against objects in its path mount up in much greater proportion than do the corresponding velocities; this fact is illustrated by the figures quoted in the table below. Thus may be realized the stupendous force of the winds of Adelie Land in comparison with those of half the velocity which fall within one's ordinary experience. As this subject was ever before us, the following figures quoted from a work of reference will be instructive. The classification of winds, here stated, is that known as the "Beaufort scale." The corresponding velocities in each case are those measured by the "Robinson patent" anemometer; our instrument being of a similar pattern.

No.	Beaufort scale.	Velocities in miles per hour.	Pressures in lb. per square ft. of area.	Apparent effect.
0	Calm	2	0.02	May cause smoke to move from the vertical.
1	Light air	4	0.06	Moves the leaves of trees.
2	Light breeze	7	0.19	Moves small branches of trees and blows up dust.
3	Gentle breeze	10	0.37	
4	Moderate breeze	14	0.67	
5	Fresh breeze	19	1.16	Good sailing breeze and
6	Strong breeze	25	1.90	makes white caps.
7	Moderate gale	31	2.81	Sways trees and breaks
8	Fresh gale	37	3.87	small branches.
9	Strong gale	44	5.27	Dangerous for sailing
10	Whole gale	53	7.40	vessels.
11	Storm	64	10.40	Prostrates exposed trees
12	Hurricane	77	14.40	and frail houses.

Beyond the limits of this scale, the pressures exerted rise very rapidly. A wind recorded as blowing at the rate of a hundred miles per hour exerts a pressure of about twenty-three pounds per square foot of surface exposed to it.

The mileages registered by our anemometer were the mean for a whole hour, having no special regard for individual gusts, whose velocity much exceeded the average and which were always the potent factors in destructive work.

Obviously the greatest care had to be taken to secure everything. Still, articles of value were occasionally missed. They were usually recovered, caught in crevices of rock or amongst the broken ice. Northward from the Hut there was a trail of miscellaneous objects scattered among the hummocks and pressure-ridges out towards Penguin Hill on the eastern side of the Boat Harbour: tins of all kinds and sizes, timber in small scraps, cases and boards, paper, ashes, dirt, worn-out finnesko, ragged mitts and all the other details of a rubbish heap. Boxes in which Whetter used to carry ice for domestic requirements were as a rule short-lived. His problem was to fill the boxes without losing hold of them, and the wind often gained the ascendancy before a sufficient ballast had been added. We sometimes wondered whether any of the flotsam thus cast upon the waters ever reached the civilized world.

Whatever has been said relative to the wind-pressure exerted on inanimate objects, the same applied, with even more point, to our persons; so that progression in a hurricane became a fine art. The first difficulty to be encountered was a smooth, slippery surface offering no grip for the feet. Stepping out of the shelter of the Hut, one was apt to be immediately hurled at full length down wind. No amount of exertion was of any avail unless a firm foothold had been secured. The strongest man, stepping on to ice or hard snow in plain leather or fur boots, would start sliding away with gradually increasing velocity; in the space of a few seconds or earlier exchanging the vertical for the horizontal position. He would then either stop suddenly against a jutting point of ice, or glide along for twenty or thirty yards till he reached a patch of rocks or some rough sastrugi.

Of course we soon learned never to go about without crampons on the feet. Many experiments in the manufacture of crampons were tried with the limited materials at our disposal. Those designed for normal Antarctic conditions had been found unserviceable. A few detachable pairs made of wrought iron with spikes about one and a half inches in length, purchased in Switzerland, gave a secure foothold. Some of the men covered the soles of their boots with long, bristling spikes and these served their purpose well. Spikes of less than an inch in length were inadequate in hurricanes. Nothing devised by us gave the grip of the Swiss crampons, but, unfortunately they could not be worn in conjunction with fur boots, being designed for use with leather boots which are a cold proposition at low temperatures. Further the crampon lashings required to be secured very tightly round the boots, compressing the feet and increasing the liability to frost-bite.

Shod with good spikes, in a steady wind, one had only to push hard to keep a sure footing. It would not be true to say "to keep erect," for equilibrium was maintained by leaning against the wind. In course of time, those whose duties habitually took them out of doors became thorough masters of the art of walking in hurricanes—an accomplishment comparable to skating or ski-ing. Ensconced in the lee of a substantial break-wind, one could leisurely observe the unnatural appearance of others walking about, apparently in imminent peril of falling on their faces.

Experiments were tried in the steady winds; firmly planting the feet on the ground, keeping the body rigid and leaning over on the invisible support. This "lying on the wind," at equilibrium, was a unique experience. As a rule the velocity remained uniform; when it fluctuated in a series of gusts, all our experience was likely to fail, for no sooner had the correct angle for the maximum velocity been assumed than a lull intervened—with the obvious result.

Before the art of "hurricane-walking" was learnt, and in the primitive days of ice-nails and finnesko, progression in high winds degenerated into crawling on hands and knees. Many of the more conservative persisted in this method, and, as a compensation, became the first exponents of the popular "board-sliding." A small piece of board, a wide ice-flat and a hurricane were the three essentials for this new sport.

Conversation in the ordinary way was out of the question for the words were cut off at the mouth and drowned by the howl of the wind. So communication, other than by signs, could be conducted only by placing the heads right close together and shouting as loud as possible.

Wind alone would not have been so bad; drift snow accompanied it in overwhelming amount. In the autumn overcast weather with heavy falls of snow prevailed, with the result that the air for several months was seldom free from drift. Indeed, during that time, there were not many days when objects a hundred yards away could be seen distinctly. Whatever else happened, the wind never abated, and so, even when the snow had ceased falling and the sky was clear, the drift continued until all the loose accumulations on the hinterland, for hundreds of miles back, had been swept out to sea. Day after day deluges of drift streamed past the Hut, at times so dense as to totally obscure objects three feet away, until it seemed as if the atmosphere were almost solid snow.

Picture drift so dense that daylight comes through dully, though, maybe, the sun shines in a cloudless sky; the drift is hurled, screaming through space, at a hundred miles an hour, and the temperature is below zero, Fahrenheit.* You have then the bare, rough facts concerning the worst blizzards of Adelie Land. The actual experience of them is another thing.

Shroud the infuriated elements in the darkness of a polar night, and the blizzard is presented in a severer aspect. A plunge into the writhing storm-whirl stamps upon the senses an indelible and awful impression seldom equalled in the whole gamut of natural experience. The world a void, grisly, fierce and appalling. We stumble and struggle through the Stygian gloom; the merciless blast—an incubus of vengeance—stabs, buffets and freezes; the stinging drift blinds and chokes.

In its ruthless grip we realized that we are, as Henley says, but

"poor windlestraws
On the great, sullen, roaring pool of Time."

It may well be imagined that none of us went out on these occasions for the pleasure of it. The scientific work required all too frequent journeys to the instruments at a distance from the Hut, and, in addition, supplies of ice and stores had to be brought in, while the dogs needed constant attention.

Every morning, Madigan visited all the meteorological instruments and changed the daily charts; at times having to

* Temperatures as low as −28° F. (60° below freezing point) were experienced in hurricane winds, which blew at a velocity occasionally exceeding one hundred miles per hour. Still air and low temperatures, or high winds and moderate temperatures, are well enough; but the combination of high winds and low temperatures is difficult to bear.

feel his way from one place to the other. Attending to the exposed instruments in a high wind with low temperature was bad enough, but with suffocating drift difficulties were increased tenfold.

Around the Hut there was a small fraternity who chose the outside veranda as a rendezvous. Here the latest gossip was exchanged, and the weather invariably discussed in forcible terms. There was Whetter, who replenished the water-supply from the unfailing fountain-head of the glacier. For cooking, washing clothes and for photographic and other purposes, eighteen men consumed a good deal of water, and, to keep up with the demand, Whetter piled up many hardly-won boxes of ice in the veranda. Close unearthed coal briquettes from the heap outside, shovelled tons of snow from the veranda and made himself useful and amiable to every one. Murphy, our stand-by in small talk, travel, history, literature and what not, was the versatile storeman. The store in the veranda was continually invaded by similar snow to that which covered the provision boxes outside. To keep the veranda cleared, renew the supplies and satisfy the demands of the kitchen required no other than Murphy. Ninnis and Mertz completed the "Veranda Club," to which honorary members from within the Hut were constantly being added.

The meteorological instruments, carefully nursed and housed though they were, were bound to suffer in such a climate. Correll, who was well fitted out with a lathe and all the requirements for instrument-making, attended to repairs, doing splendid service.

It was a fortunate thing that no one was lost through failing to discover the Hut during the denser drifts. Hodgeman on one occasion caused everyone a good deal of anxiety. Among other things, he regularly assisted Madigan by relieving him of outdoor duties on the day after his night-watch, when the chief meteorologist was due for a "watch below." It was in the early autumn—few of us, then, were adepts at finding our way by instinct—that Hodgeman and Madigan set out, one morning, for the anemometer. Leaving the door of the Hut, they lost sight of each other at once, but anticipated meeting at the instrument. Madigan reached his destination, changed the records, waited for a while and then returned, expecting to see his companion at the Hut. He did not appear, so, after a reasonable interval, search-parties set off in different directions.

The wind was blowing at eighty miles per hour, making it tedious work-groping about and hallooing in the drift. The sea was close at hand and we realized that, as the wind was directly off shore, a man without crampons was in a dangerous situation. Two men, therefore, roped together and carefully searched round the head of the Boat Harbour; one anchoring himself with an ice-axe, whilst the other, at the end of the rope, worked along the edge of the sea. Meanwhile Hodgeman returned to the Hut, unaided, having spent a very unpleasant two hours struggling from one landmark to another, his outer garments filled with snow.

The fact that the wind came steadily from the same direction made it possible to steer, otherwise outdoor occupations would not have been conducted so successfully. For instance, Webb, who visited the Magnetograph House, a quarter of a mile distant, at least once a day, made his way between various "beacons" by preserving a definite bearing on the wind. His journeys were rendered all the more difficult because they were frequently undertaken at night.

In struggling along through very dense drifts one would be inclined to think that the presence of the sun was an affair of small concern. As a matter of fact there was, during the day, a good deal of reflected white light and dark objects loomed up within a yard or two. In darkness there was nothing to recognize. So Webb would often run by dead reckoning on to the roof of the Hut, and would then feel his way round it till he caught the glimmer of a hurricane lantern coming through the veranda entrance.

I have the greatest admiration for the unfailing manner in which those responsible for the tidal, magnetic and meteorological work carried out their duties under such difficult conditions.

As a measure of the enormous amount of drift, we set about constructing a gauge, which, it was hoped, would give us a rough estimate of the quantity passing the Hut in a year. Hannam, following the approved design, produced a very satisfactory contrivance, which continued to be used with success during the succeeding two years.

In thick drifts, one's face became rapidly packed with snow, which, by the warmth of the skin and breath, was converted into a mask of ice. This adhered firmly to the helmet and to the beard and face; though not particularly comfortable, it was actually a protection against the wind. The mask became so complete that one had continually to break it away in order to breathe and to clear away obstructions from the eyes. Outside in the wind, at really low temperatures, it was scarcely possible to remove the casing of ice, and such attempts were liable to lead to painful scratches on the cornea by ice adhering to the eyelids. An experienced man, once inside the Hut, would first see that the ice was broken away from the helmet; otherwise, when it came to be hastily dragged off, the hairs of the beard would follow as well. As soon as the helmet was off the head, the ice casing the beard, eyelashes and skin was gradually thawed by the warmth of the fingers and removed.

It frequently happened that the face was superficially frost-bitten beneath the mask, areas of hard white flesh showing up as the ice was removed. In the absence of a toilet mirror such patches, being devoid of feeling, were easily mistaken by the individual for an obstinate remnant of the ice mask. Thus it was that Madigan was once observed by an amused audience toying with a lifeless cheek endeavouring to remove it under the impression that it was ice.

The abrasion effects produced by the impact of the snow particles were astonishing. Pillars of ice were cut through in a few days, rope was frayed, wood etched and metal polished. Some rusty dog-chains were exposed to it, and, in a few days they had a definite sheen. A deal box, facing the wind, lost all its painted bands and in a fortnight was handsomely marked; the hard knotty fibres being only slightly attacked, whilst the softer, pithy laminæ were corroded to a depth of one-eighth of an inch.

The effect of constant abrasion upon a compact snow, névé or even ice surface is to carve ridges known as sastrugi. Of these much will be said when recounting our sledging adventures, because they increase so much the difficulties of travelling. Both névé and ice surfaces receive a wind-polish which makes them very slippery; a most undesirable feature in a land of the fur boot.

In regard to the drift, a point which struck me was the enormous amount of cold communicated to the sea by billions of tons of low-temperature snow thrown upon its surface. The effect upon the water, already at freezing-point, would be to congeal the surface at once. Whilst the wind continued, however, there was no opportunity for a crust to form, the uppermost layers becoming of a pea-soup-like consistency and streaming away to the north.

A description of the blizzards of Adelie Land would not be complete without mentioning the startling electrical effects which were sometimes observed. The first record of these was made by McLean, when on night-watch on March 22. While taking the observations at midnight, he noticed St. Elmo's fire, a "brush discharge" of electricity, on the points of the nephoscope. As the weather became colder this curious phenomenon increased in intensity. At any time in the drift, an electroscope exposed outside became rapidly charged. A spark gap in a vacuum, connected with a free end of wire, gave a continuous discharge. At times, when the effects were strong, the night-watchman would find the edges and wire stays of the screen outlined in a fashion reminiscent of a pyro-technic display or an electric street advertisement. The corners of boxes and points of rock glowed with a pale blue light. The same appeared over points on the clothing, on the mitts and round the funnel of the helmet. No sensation was transmitted to the body from these points of fire, at least nothing suffi-ciently acute to be felt, with the drift and wind lashing on the body outside. However, the anemograph several times discharged a continuous stream of sparks into Madigan's fingers while he was changing the records. Once these sparks reached half an inch in length, and, as his fingers were bared for the work, there was no mistaking the feeling.

For regular observations on the subject, Correll fixed a pointed collector—a miniature lightning-conductor—above the flagpole on the summit of the roof. A wire was led through an insulator, so that the stream of electricity could be subjected to experiment in the Hut. Here a "brush" of blue light radiated outwards to a distance of one inch, and the air was pervaded with a strong smell of ozone. When a conductor was held close to it, a rattling volley of sparks immediately crossed the interval. Of course sparks were not always being emitted by the collector, and it was important to determine the periods of activity. To ensure this, Hurley devised an automatic arrangement, so that an electric bell was set ringing whenever a current was passing; the night-watchman would then note the fact in the log-book. However, the bell responded so often and so vigorously that it was soon dismantled for the benefit of sleepers.

We dwelt on the fringe of an unspanned continent, where the chill breath of a vast, polar wilderness, quickening to the rushing might of eternal blizzards, surged to the northern seas. We had discovered an accursed country. We had found the Home of the Blizzard.

CHAPTER VIII

TROGLODYTES

THE snow continued to descend in torrents and, but for the wind, the Hut would have been quite lost to sight. The packed drifts rose higher and higher round the walls, and back eddies brought the snow past the canvas flap at the entrance, though situated on the lee side, until the veranda became choked. Frequent shovelling was necessary to maintain freedom of exit.

Eventually, during the early morning hours of April 7, it reached such a pass that Close, who was night-watchman, had the greatest difficulty in getting outside to attend to his duties. To dig his way through the entrance, reach the instruments adjacent to the Hut and to return occupied a whole hour; a performance which had to be repeated at regular intervals.

We were inundated with snow, even a considerable portion of the roof was buried, so the situation required immediate attention.

By a fortunate accident, an out-draught had established itself at the north-western end of the store-veranda, preserving a vertical funnel-like opening in the snow always free for entrance or exit. So it was decided to make a tunnel connecting this veranda with the buried entrance-veranda which contained the vestibule of the Hut itself.

A second tunnel, over twenty feet in length, was driven out from the original entrance with a view to reaching the surface at a point beyond the lee of the Hut. It was thought that the scouring effect of the wind there would keep the opening free of drift; but when completed, as it failed in this respect, it came to be used as a dump for slop-water. While the fever for excavation was at its height, Whetter drove, as an offshoot to the first, another tunnel which was eventually utilized as a nursery for the pups. Other drives were made from the Hangar to serve as stores for timber. So it came about that within a short space of time a subterranean labyrinth was developed which was sometimes referred to as the Catacombs.

At this stage to leave our submerged abode starting from the living-room, it was necessary for us to pass through the door into the workshop, then by the double-doored vestibule into the original entrance-veranda, now sealed; the way then led through a trap-door in the wall opening into the snow tunnel connecting with the store-veranda; finally one climbed through a man-hole in the snow to the elements without. As an additional convenience, a trap-door was made in the roof of the original entrance veranda to be used in spells of clear weather or in light drift.

The old landmarks became smothered in snow, making the Hut's position a matter of greater uncertainty. A journey by night to the magnetic huts was an outing with a spice of adventure.

Climbing out of the veranda, one was immediately swallowed in the choas of hurtling drift, the darkness sinister and menacing. The shrill wind fled by—

> ". . . the noise of a drive of the Dead,
> Striving before the irresistible will
> Through the strange dusk of this, the Debatable land
> Between their place and ours."

Unseen wizard hands clutched with insane fury, hacked and harried. It was "the raw-ribbed Wild that abhors all life, the Wild that would crush and rend."

Cowering blindly, pushing fiercely through the turmoil, one strove to keep a course to reach the rocks in which the Hut was hidden—such and such a bearing on the wind—so far. When the locality of the rocks was attained the position of the final destination was only deduced by recognizing, mainly by sense of touch, a few surrounding objects.

On the return journey, the vicinity of the Hut would be heralded by such accidents as tripping over some protruding portion of the "wireless" ground wires or kicking against a box or other object that had survived the deluge. These clues, properly followed up, would lead to the Hut itself, or at least to its shelving roof. In very thick drifts one might stand on snow-covered portions of the roof without any notion of the fact, hearing nothing of the noise below however boisterous, oblivious to the proximity of refuge and even despairing of ever reaching it. Fossicking about, one kept on the alert for the feel of woodwork. When found and proved to be too extensive to be a partially buried box, it might safely be concluded to be some part of the roof, and only required to be skirted in order to reach the vertical entrance. The home-comer often discovered this pitfall by dropping suddenly through into the veranda.

At the inner extremity of the entrance tunnel, the roar of the tempest died away to a rumble, the trap-door opened and perhaps the strains of the gramophone would come in a kind of flippant defiance from the interior. Passing through the vestibule and workshop one beheld a scene in utter contrast to the outer hell. Here were warm bunks, rest, food, light and companionship—for the time being—heaven!

From the crude and naked elements of that primitive and desolate land, whose ice bosom knows but the throb of the surging blizzard gusts, we ever sought the cheery shelter of our cave-hut, as did our ancestors, the troglodytes of the primeval past.

The night-watchman's duty of taking the meteorological observations at the screen adjacent to the Hut was comparatively a small matter. First of all, it was necessary for him to don a complete outfit of protective clothing. This dressing and undressing was tedious, and absorbed a good deal of time. At the screen, he would spend a lively few minutes wrestling in order to hold his ground, forcing the door back against the pressure of the wind, endeavouring to make the light shine on the instruments, and, finally, clearing them of snow and reading the figures. For illumination a hurricane lantern wrapped in a calico wind-shield was first used, to be displaced later by an electrical signalling-lamp and, while the batteries lasted, by a light permanently fixed in the screen itself. To assist in finding the entrance on his return, the night-watchman was in the habit of leaving a light burning in the outer veranda, from whence rays shone up through the man-hole.

I remember waking up early one morning to find the Hut unusually cold. On rising, I discovered Hurley also awake, busy lighting the fire which had died out. There was no sign of Correll, the night-watchman, and we found that the last entry in the log-book had been made several hours previously. Hurley dressed in windproofs and went out to make a search, in which he was soon successful.

It appeared that Correll, running short of coal during the early morning hours, had gone out to procure some from the stack. While he was returning to the entrance, the wind rolled him over a few times, causing him to lose his bearings. It was blowing a hurricane, the temperature was some 40° below freezing point and the drift snow was so thick as to be wall-like in opacity. He abandoned his load of coal, and, after scrambling about fruitlessly for some time in the darkness, decided to wait for dawn. Hurley found him about twenty yards from the back of the Hut.

The suppression of outdoor occupations reacted in an outburst of indoor work. The smaller room had been well fitted up as a workshop, and all kinds of schemes were in progress for adapting our sledging-gear and instruments to the severe conditions. Correll worked long hours to keep up with the demands made upon him. Nobody was idle during the day, for, when there was nothing else to be done, there always remained the manufacture and alteration of garments and crampons.

As soon as the wind abated to a reasonable velocity, there was a rush to the outside jobs. Lulls would come unexpect- edly, activity inside ceased, and the Hut, as seen by a spec- tator, resembled an ants' nest upon which a strange foot had trodden: eighteen men swarming through the manhole in rapid succession, hurrying hither and thither.

The neighbouring sea still remained free from an ice crust. This, of course, did not mean that freezing was not going on continuously. On the contrary, the chilling was no doubt accelerated, but the bulk of the ice was carried off to the north as fast as it was formed. Quantities, however, remained as ground-ice, anchored to the kelp and stones on the bottom. Gazing down through the clear waters one saw a white, mammillated sheath covering the jungle of giant seaweed, recalling a forest after a heavy snowfall. The ice, instead of being a dead weight bearing down the branches, tended to float, and, when accumulated in large masses, sometimes succeeded in rising to the surface, uprooting and lifting great lengths of seaweed with it. One branching stem, found floating in the harbour, measured eighteen feet in length.

Whenever a temporary calm intervened, a skin of ice quickly appeared over the whole surface of the water. In the early stages, this formation consisted of loose, blade-like crystals, previously floating freely below the surface and rising by their own buoyancy. At the surface, if undisturbed, they soon became cemented together. For example, during a calm interval on April 6, within the interval of an hour, an even crust, one inch thick, covered the sea. But the wind returned before the ice was sufficiently strong to resist it, and it all broke up and drifted away to the north, except a piece which remained wedged firmly between the sides of the Boat Harbour.

In the calm weather, abundant free-swimming marine worms, jelly-fish, pteropods and small fish were observed. Traps were lowered along the edge of the ice and dredgings were made whenever possible. The bulk of the biological collecting was effected under circumstances in which Hunter and Laseron might well have given up in disgust. There was considerable danger in such work, conducted, as it frequently was, in strong off-shore winds along the slippery edge of the bay-ice.

During April the head of the Boat Harbour froze over permanently, the ice reaching a thickness of eighteen inches in ten days. By that time it was strong enough to be suitable for the accommodation of a tide-gauge. This was one of Bage's charges, destined to take him out for many months in the foulest of weather.

There were several occasions in April when the velocity of the wind exceeded ninety miles an hour. On the evening of the 26th, the wind slackened, and for part of the 27th had almost fallen to a calm. This brought the optimists to the fore, once again, with the theory that the worst was over. The prediction was far from being fulfilled, for, as the days passed, the average velocity steadily rose. On May 11 the average for the twenty-four hours was eighty miles per hour. By that time the Hut had been further protected by a crescent of cases, erected behind the first break-wind. In height this erection stood above the hangar, and, when the snow became piled in a solid ramp on the leeward side, it was more compact than ever. Inside the Hut extra struts were introduced, stiffening the principal rafters on the southern side. It was reassuring to know that these precautions had been taken, for, on May 15, the wind blew at an average velocity of ninety miles per hour throughout the whole twenty-four hours.

Having failed to demolish us by dogged persistence, the hurricane tried new tactics on the evening of May 24, in the form of a terrific series of Herculean gusts. As we learned afterwards from the puffometer, an instrument for deter-mining the velocity of the gusts, the momentary velocity of these was of the order of two hundred miles per hour. At 11.30 p.m. the situation was cheerfully discussed, though everyone was tuned up to a nervous pitch as the hut creaked and shuddered under successive blows. It seemed very doubtful whether the roof would resist the onslaught, and the feasibility of the meat cellar as a last haven of refuge was discussed. After the passage of each gust, the barometer dropped, rising again immediately afterwards. Similar pulsa-tions of the barometer were observed many times later in the year. The maximum sudden movement noted was one-fifth inch. Had the interior of the Hut been more freely in commu-nication with the outside air, instead of resembling a hermeti-cally sealed box, the "kicks" would undoubtedly have been much greater.

Cyclonic gusts were repeated a few days after, when the upper tiers of heavy boxes composing the break-wind were thrown down and pebbles from the moraine were hurled on the roof. The average velocity of the wind for each of the three autumn months was as follows: March, 49 miles per hour; April, 51.5 miles per hour, and May, 60.7 miles per hour.

On May 1 the temperatures became lower, so that it was difficult to move about in the gales without the face getting frost-bitten. Our usual remedy when this occurred was to hold a mitt over the part affected; thus sheltered, its circulation of blood was soon re-established, unless the cold was very intense. In the extremities—the fingers and toes—warmth was not so easily restored.

Returning from attending the instruments at noon on May 22, Madigan discovered that his face under the ice mask was extensively frost-bitten. Frost-bites that day were excusable enough, for the wind was blowing between ninety-five and one hundred miles per hour, there was dense drifting snow and a temperature of −28° F. Already and for long months we were beneath "frost-fettered Winter's frown."

CHAPTER IX

DOMESTIC LIFE

OUR hearth and home was the living-hut and its focus was the stove. Kitchen and stove were indissolubly linked, and beyond their pale was a wilderness of hanging clothes, boots, finnesko, mitts and what not, bounded by tiers of bunks and blankets, more hanging clothes and dim photographs between the frost-rimed cracks of the wooden walls.

One might see as much in the first flicker of the acetylene through a maze of hurrying figures, but as the eyes grew accustomed to the light, a multitude of detail would be revealed: books, orderly and disorderly, on bracketed shelves, cameras great and small in motley confusion, guns and a gramophone-horn, serpentine yards of gas-tubing, sewing machines, a microscope, rows of pint-mugs, until—thud! one has obstructed a wild-eyed messman staggering into the kitchen with a box of ice.

The wilderness was always inhabited, so much so that it often became a bear-garden in which raucous good humour prevailed over everything.

Noise was a necessary evil, and it commenced at 7.30 a.m., with the subdued melodies of the gramophone, mingled with the stirring of the porridge-pot and the clang of plates deposited none too gently on the table. At 7.50 a.m. came the stentorian: "Rise and shine!" of the night-watchman, and a curious assortment of cat-calls, beating on pots and pans and fragmentary chaff. At the background, so to speak, of all these sounds was the swishing rush of the wind and the creaking strain of the roof, but these had become neglected. In fact, if there were a calm, everyone was restless and uneasy.

The seasoned sleeper who survived the ten-minute bombardment before 8 o'clock was an unusual person, and he was often the "astronomer royal." This dignitary possessed a wrist-watch, and there was never a movement in his mountain of blankets until 7.59 a.m., unless the jocular night-watchman chose to make a heap of them on the floor. To calls such as "Breakfast all ready!" "Porridge on the table getting cold!" seventeen persons in varying stages of wakefulness responded. No one was guilty of an elaborate toilet, water being a scarce commodity. There were adherents to the snow-wash theory, but these belonged to the summer epoch of our history.

For downright, tantalizing cheerfulness there was no one to equal the night-watchman. While others strove to collect their befuddled senses, this individual prated of "wind eighty miles per hour with moderate drift," and "brilliant St. Elmo's fire." He boasted of the number of garments he had washed, expanded vigorously on bread making—his brown, appetising specimens in full public view—told of the latest escapade among the dogs, spoke of the fitful gleams of the aurora between 1.30 and 2 a.m., of his many adventures on the way to the meteorological screen and so forth; until from being a mere night-watchman he had raised himself to the status of a public hero. For a time he was most objectionable, but under the solid influence of porridge, tinned fruit, fresh bread, butter and tea others began to assert themselves. Meanwhile the night-watchman commenced to show signs of abating energy after his lengthy vigil. Soon some wag had caught him having a private nap, whispered signal was passed round and the unfortunate hero was startled into life again with a rousing "Rise and shine!" in which all past scores were paid off.

Everyone was at last awake, and the day began in earnest. The first hint of this came from the messman and cook who commenced to make a clean sweep of the mugs and plates. The former began deferentially to scrape the plates, the master-cook presiding over a tub of boiling water in which he vigorously scoured knives, forks and spoons, transferring them in dripping handfuls to the cleanest part of the kitchen table. Cooks of lyric inclination would enliven the company with the score of the latest gramophone opera, and the messman and company would often feel impelled to join in the choruses.

The night-watchman had sunk into log-like slumber, and the meteorologist and other members of the out-door brigade were making preparations to go abroad. The rest subdivided themselves between the living-room at about 45° F. and the work-shop well below freezing-point, taking up their endless series of jobs.

The out-door brigade began to make an organized raid on the kitchen. Around and above the stove hung oddments like fur mitts, finnesko, socks, stockings and helmets, which had passed from icy rigidity through sodden limpness to a state of parchment dryness. Those in charge of the culinary affairs viewed with great disfavour the surreptitious hanging of garments over the range, for these had a habit of dripping into the tea-water as they thawed, or of falling into the soup with a strong probability of imparting an undesirable bouquet of dog and blubber. So the problem was to recover one's own property and at the same time to avoid the cook engaged in scraping the porridge-saucepan and the messman scrubbing the table.

The urbane storeman saved the situation by inquiring of the cook: "What will you have for lunch?" Then followed a heated colloquy. The argument finally crystallized down to lambs' tongues and beetroot, through herrings in tomato sauce, fresh herrings, kippered herrings, sardines and corned beef.

The second question was a preliminary to more serious business: "What would you like for dinner?"

Although much trouble might have been saved by refer-ence to the regulation programme posted on the wall composed to provide variety in diet and to eliminate any remote chance of scurvy, most cooks adopted an attitude of surly independ-ence, counting it no mean thing to have wheedled from the storeman a few more ounces of glaxo, another tin of peas or an extra ration of penguin meat. All this chaffering took place in the open market place, so to speak, and there was no lack of frank criticism from bystanders, onlookers and distant eavesdroppers. In case the cook was worsted, the messman sturdily upheld his opinions, and in case the weight of public opinion was too much for the storeman, he slipped on his felt mitts, shouldered an empty box and made for the tunnel which led to the store.

He reaches an overhead vent admitting a cool torrent of snow, and with the inseparable box plunges ahead into darkness. An hour later his ruddy face reappears in the hut, and a load of frosted tins is soon unceremoniously dumped on to the kitchen table. The cook in a swift survey notes the absence of penguin meat. "That'll take two hours to dig out!" is the storeman's rejoinder, and to make good his word, proceeds to pull off blouse and helmet. By careful inquiry in the outer hut he finds an ice-axe, crow-bar and hurricane lantern. The next move is to the outer veranda where the trap-door is removed, and the storeman, with a light twist, is out of sight.

We have passed the tools down and, following the storeman, painfully squeezed into a fairyland of starry snow and scintil-lating crystals of ice, through which project a few boulders and several carcases of mutton. The storeman rummages in the snow and discloses a pile of penguins, for the most part bedded in a homogeneous slab of ice. Dislodging a couple of penguins appears an easy proposition, but we are soon disillusioned. The storeman seizes the head of one bird, wrenches hard, and off it breaks as brittle as a stalactite. The same distracting thing happens to both legs, and the only remedy is to chip laboriously an icy channel around it. In a crouching or lying posture, within a confined space, this means the expenditure of much patience, not to mention the exhaustion of all invective. A crow-bar decides the question. One part of the channel is undermined, into this the end of the crow-bar is thrust and the penguin shoots up and hits the floor of the hut.

The storeman, plastered with snow, reappears hot and triumphant before the cook, but this dignitary is awkwardly kneading the dough of wholemeal scones, and the messman is feeding the fire with seal blubber to ensure a "quick" oven. Everyone is too busy to notice the storeman, for, like the night-watchman, his day is over and he must find another job.

Jobs in the hut were the elixir of life, and a day's cooking was no exception to the rule. It began at 7 a.m., and, with a brief intermission for lunch and afternoon tea, continued strenuously till 8.30 p.m. Cooks were broadly classified as "Crook Cooks" and "Unconventional Cooks" by the eating public. Such flattering titles as "Assistant Grand Past Master of the Crook Cooks' Association" or "Associate of the Society of Muddling Messmen" were not empty inanities; they were founded on solid fact—on actual achievement. If there were no constitutional affiliation, strong sympathy undoubtedly existed between the "Crook Cooks' Association" and the "Society of Muddling Messmen." Both contained members who had committed "championships."

"Championship" was a term evolved from the local dialect, applying to a slight mishap, careless accident or unintentional disaster in any department of hut life. The fall of a dozen plates from the shelf to the floor, the fracture of a table-knife in frozen honey, the burning of the porridge or the explosion of a tin thawing in the oven brought down on the unfortunate cook a storm of derisive applause and shouts of "Championship! Championship!"

Thawing-out tinned foods by the heroic aid of a red-hot stove, though frowned at in the best circles, was a common practice. One day a tin of baked beans was shattered in the "port" oven, the fragments of dried beans were visible on the walls and door for weeks. Our military cook would often facetiously refer to "platoon firing in the starboard oven."

One junior member of the "Crook Cooks' Association" had the hardihood to omit baking-powder in a loaf of soda-bread, trusting that prolonged baking would repair the omission. The result was a "championship" of a very superior order. Being somewhat modest and fancying himself unobserved, he seized an opportunity in the dead of the night to commit it through the trap-door to the mercy of the winds, and retired to bed with a load off his mind thinking to have seen the last of it. However, that was merely the beginning of its history. For a time it was lost in the drift amongst the straggling rubbish which tailed away to the north. Even the prowling dogs in their wolfish hunger could not overcome a certain prejudice. Of course someone found it, and the public hailed the discovery with delight and mounted it in a prominent place as a warning to future cooks. An inquiry led to no confession, but in a very short time a guilty conscience cast it out once more into the drift. The dogs now joined in the joke and triumphantly returned it to the veranda. And thus it went on, the loaf disappearing for short intervals but, like the proverbial bad penny, certain to turn up again. When the catacombs were being excavated it was unearthed. In the early summer following, when the aeroplane was dug out of the hangar, that loaf appeared once more, and almost the last thing we saw when abandoning the Hut, nearly two years later, was this same petrifaction defying the blizzard on an icy pedestal near the Boat Harbour. Doubtless it will remain a permanent landmark at Cape Denison.

No one ever forgot the roly-poly pudding made without the chief ingredient, suet. By this oversight the author accidentally discovered a recipe for synthetic rubber. Table knives could make no headway with it and so it arrived in the dog-bucket. But alas! our canine friends turned it down and this also remained one of our fixed associations.

One day a certain cook, overloaded with theory and deficient in practice, came on the scene determined to make a mark by serving a hot luncheon in place of the usual cold meal. Canned salmon was the order of the day and so, after consideration, he decided to produce a dish defined in the cookery-book as "fish-kedgeree." Unfortunately there was a slight omission in the punctuation, for the book read: ". . . add 2 oz. of butter pepper and salt." It certainly was a *hot* luncheon—too hot for all but three individuals whose devotion to salmon caused them to persevere, with large beads of perspiration dripping from the faces, though the Hut temperature was little above freezing-point. An investigation, made in response to clamorous appeals, revealed that the cook had employed the greatest precision in weighing out the full two ounces of pepper.

The muddling messman who put into the melting-pots for drinking-water the briny sea-ice specimens from the laboratory, where they were stored for examination, could only be surpassed by his absent-minded colleague who sat in a dish of prime penguin-egg batter waiting its turn for the oven.

Cooking, under the inspiration of Mrs. Beeton's comprehensive work, became a fine art. On birthdays and other auspicious occasions dishes appeared which would tempt a gourmet. Puff-pastry, steam-puddings, jellies and blancmanges, original *potages* and *consommés,* seal curried and spiced, penguin delicately fried, vegetables reflavoured, trimmed and adorned were received without comment as the culinary standard rose.

Birthdays were always greeted with special enthusiasm. Speeches were made, toasts were drunk, the supple boards of the table creaked with good things, cook and messman vied with each other in lavish hospitality. The Hut was ornate with flags, every man was spruce in his snowiest cardigan and neckcloth, the gramophone sang of music-hall days, the wind roared its appreciation through the stove-pipe, and rollicking merriment was supreme. On such occasions the photographer and the biologist made a genial combination.

The dark-room was the nursery of the topical song. There, by candle-stump or lantern, wit Rabelaisian, Aristophanic or Antarctic was cradled into rhyme. From there, behind the scenes, the comedian in full dress could step before the footlights into salvoes of savage applause, "A pair of Unconventional Cooks are we, are we," and the famous refrain, "There he is, that's him," were long unrivalled in our musical annals.

Celebrations were carried on into the night, but no one forgot the cook and the messman. The table was cleared by many willing hands, some brought in ice or coal or swept the floor, others scraped plates or rinsed out mugs and bowls. Soon everything had passed through the cauldron of water, soap and soda to the drying-towels and on to the shelves. The majority then repaired with pipes and cigars to "Hyde Park Corner," where the storeman, our *raconteur par excellence,* entertained the smokers' club. A mixed concert brought the evening to the grand finale—"Auld Lang Syne."

After events of this character, the higher shelves of the kitchen, in the interstices between thermographs, photographic plates, ink bottles, and Russian stout, abounded with titbits of pie crust, blancmange, jelly, Vienna rusks, preserved figs, and other "perks." Such "perks," or perquisites, were the property of the presiding cook or night-watchman and rarely survived for more than a day.

The mania for celebration became so great that in search of memorable occasions reference was frequently made to an almanac of notable events. So it happened that during one featureless interval, the anniversary of the "First Lighting of London by Gas" was observed with extraordinary *éclat*.

The great medium of monetary exchange was chocolate. A ration of one cake totalling thirty squares was distributed by the storeman every Saturday night, and for purposes of betting, games of chance, "Calcutta sweeps" on the monthly wind-velocity and general barter, chocolate held the premier place.

At the "sweeps," the meteorologist stood with a wooden hammer behind the table, and the gaming public swarmed on the other side. Numbers ranging from "low field" and forty-five to sixty-five and "high field" were sold by auction to the highest bidder. Excitement was intense while the cartographer in clerical glasses worked out the unknown number.

As a consequence of wild speculation, there were several cases of bankruptcy, which was redeemed in the ordinary way by a sale of the debtor's effects.

Two financiers, indifferent to the charms of chocolate, established a corner or "bank" in the commodity. "The Bank," by barter and usurious methods, amassed a great heap of well-thumbed squares, and, when accused of rapacity, invented a scheme for the common good known as "Huntoylette." This was a game of chance similar to roulette, and for a while it completely gulled the trusting public. In the reaction which followed, there was a rush on "The Bank," and the concern was wound up, but the promoters escaped with a large profit in candles and chocolate.

Throughout the winter months, work went on steadily even after dinner. For those who found periods of leisure the hours were easy to fill; some wrote up their diaries, smoked and yarned, or read. The Mackellar Library was a boon to all, and the literature of polar exploration was keenly followed and discussed.

The whole world is asleep except the night-watchman, and he, having made the bread, washed a tubful of clothes, kept the fire going, observed and made notes on the aurora every fifteen minutes and the weather every half-hour, and, finally, having had a bath, indulges in buttered toast and a cup of coffee.

The Hut is dark, and a shaded burner hangs by a canvas chair in the kitchen. The wind is booming in gusts, the dogs howl occasionally in the veranda, but the night-watchman and his pipe are at peace with all men. He has discarded a heavy folio for a light romance, while the hours scud by, broken only by the observations. The romance is closed, and he steals to his bunk with a hurricane lamp and finds a bundle of letters. He knows them well, but he reads them—again!

Pearly light rises in the north-east through the lessening drift, and another day has come.

CHAPTER X

WINTER ACTIVITIES

DURING the winter months work outside had a chequered career. When a few calm hours intervened in the blizzard routine a general rush was made to continue some long-standing job. Often all that could be done was to clear the field for action, that is, dig away large accumulations of snow. Then the furies would break loose again, and once more we would play the waiting game, meanwhile concerning ourselves with more sedentary occupations.

There was a familiar cry when, for some meteorological reason, the wind would relapse into fierce gusts and then suddenly stop, to be succeeded by intense stillness. "Dead calm, up with the wireless masts!" Everyone hastily dashed for his burberrys, and soon a crowd of muffled figures would emerge through the veranda exit, dragging ropes, blocks, picks and shovels. There was no time to be lost.

So the erection of the wireless masts began in earnest on April 4 and continued for some months during every favourable occasion. The first thing to do was to establish good anchorage. Then the oregon masts, section by section, were erected and securely stayed by stout steel-wire cables. This was a much more difficult piece of work than anyone in a genial climate is likely to imagine.

Fumbling with bulky mitts, handling hammers and spanners, and manipulating knots and bolts with bare hands, while suspended in a boatswain's chair in the wind, the man up the mast had a difficult and miserable task. Bickerton was the hero of all such endeavours. His work was all the more remarkable because much of it was accomplished in considerable wind. Frost-bites were common. Attempting to climb to a block on the topgallant mast one day, McLean had all his fingers painfully frost-bitten.

It was not until early in October that a height likely to be effective was reached; the aerial was then about ninety feet above the ground. Hannam began to send out messages, some of which were caught by Sawyer at Macquarie Island. However, before there was time to perfect the working, a hurricane on October 13 completely wrecked one of the masts. It was a different story the following year when the wireless did us splendid service.

While messages were being sent, induction effects were noted in metallic objects around the Hut. A cook at the stove was the first to discover this phenomenon, and was startled to find that he drew sparks every time that he handled his pans. Others received reminders accidentally brushing their heads against one of the numerous coils of flexible metal gas-piping festooned about the place.

It fell to the lot of most of the staff that they developed an interest in terrestrial magnetism; for in this work Webb was assisted from time to time by various members acting as recorders in connection with his determinations. Three hours sitting writing figures in a temperature of forty-seven degrees of frost is no joke. The magnetician is as badly off, because, though he is moving about, he often has to stop and warm his fingers, handling the cold metal.

Webb's time was further occupied with the-self-recording instruments in the magnetograph house. Later on a special set of magnetic determinations was made in a fine cavern hewn in the ice of the glacier three-quarters of a mile south of the Hut.

While the wind rushed by at a maddening pace and stars flashed like jewels in a black sky, a glow of pale yellow light overspread the north-east horizon—the aurora polaris. A streak of dark cloud was often visible below the light which brightened and diffused till it curved as a low arc across the sky. It was eerie to watch the contour of the arc break, die away into a delicate pallor and re-illumine in a travelling riband. Soon a long ray, as from a searchlight, flashed above one end, and then a row of vertical streamers ran out from the arc, probing upwards into the outer darkness. The streamers waxed and waned, died away to be replaced, and then faded into the starlight. The arc lost its radiance, divided in patchy fragments, and all was dark once more.

This would be repeated again in a few hours and regularly throughout the dark hours. By the observer, who wrote down his exact observations in the meteorological log, this was called a "quiet night."

At times the light was nimble, flinging itself about in rich waves, warming to dazzling yellow-green and rose. These were the nights when "curtains" hung festooned in the heavens, alive, rippling, dancing to the lilt of lightning music. Up from the horizon they would mount, forming a vortex overhead, soundless within the silence of the ether.

A "brilliant display," we would say, and the observer would be kept busy following the track of the evanescent rays.

Powerless, one was in the spell of an all-enfolding wonder. The vast, solitary snow-land, cold-white under the sparkling star-gems; lustrous in the rays of the southern lights; furrowed beneath the sweep of the wind. We had come to probe its mystery, we had hoped to reduce it to terms of science, but there was always the "indefinable" which held aloof, yet riveted our souls.

An occupation which helped to introduce variety in our life was the digging of ice-shafts. For the purpose of making observations upon its structure and temperature various excavations were made in the sea-ice, in the ice of the glacier, and in that of the freshwater lakes. The work was always popular. Even a whole day's labour with a pick and shovel at the bottom of an ice-hole never seemed laborious. It was all so novel.

A calm morning in June, the sky is clear and the north ablaze with the colours of sunrise—or is it sunset? The air is delicious and a cool waft comes down the glacier. A deep ultramarine, shading up into a soft purple hue, blends in a colour-scheme with the lilac plateau. Two men crunch along in spiked boots over snow mounds and polished sastrugi to the harbour-ice. The sea to the north is glazed with freezing spicules, and over it sweep the petrels—our only living companions of the winter. It is all an inspiration; while hewing out chunks of ice and shovelling them away is the acute pleasure of movement, exercise.

In contrast with sea-ice, which is tough, sticky and merely translucent, the ice of a glacier is a marvel of prismatic colours and glassy brilliance. This is more noticeable near the surface when the sun is shining. Deep down in a shaft, or in an ice cavern, the sapphire reflection gives to the human face quite a ghastly pallor.

During the high winds it was easy to dispose of the fragments of ice in the earlier stages of sinking a shaft. To be rid of them, all that was necessary was to throw a shovelful vertically upwards towards the lee side of the hole, the wind then did the rest. Away the chips would scatter, tinkling over the surface of the glacier. Of course, when two men were at work, each took it in turns to go below, and the one above, to keep warm, would impatiently pace up and down. Nevertheless, so cold would he become at times that a heated colloquy would arise between them on the subject of working overtime. When the shaft had attained depth, both were kept busy. The man at the pit's mouth lowered a bucket on a rope to receive the ice and, in hauling it up, handicapped with clumsy mitts, he had to be careful not to drop it on his companion's head.

A popular subject commanding general interest, apart from the devoted attention of specialists, was zoological collecting. Seals and birds were made the prey of everyone, and dredging through the sea-ice in winter and spring was always a possible diversion, weather permitting.

It was a splendid sight to watch the birds sailing in the high winds of Adelie Land. In winds of fifty to sixty miles per hour, when with good crampons one had to stagger warily along the ice-foot, the snow-petrels and Antarctic petrels were in their element. Wheeling, swinging, sinking, planing and soaring, they were radiant with life—the wild spirits of the tempest. Even in moderate drift, when through swirling snow the vistas of sea whitened under the flail of the wind, one suddenly caught the silver flash of wings and a snow petrel glided past.

But most memorable of all were certain winter mornings of unexpected calm, when ruddy clouds tessellated the northern sky, and were mirrored in the freezing sea. Then the petrels would be *en fête*, flying over from the east following the line of the Barrier, winding round the icy coves, and darting across the jutting points.

Numbers of birds were secured for our collection, keeping Laseron, who was an artist at skinning, busy for several months.

During the winter for a long period, no seals ventured ashore, though a few were seen swimming in the bay. The force of the wind was so formidable that even a heavy seal, exposed in the open, broadside-on, would be literally blown into the water. This fact was actually observed out on the harbour-ice. A Weddell seal made twelve attempts to land on a low projecting shelf—an easy feat under ordinary circumstances. The wind was in the region of eighty-five miles per hour, and every time the clumsy, ponderous creature secured its first hold, back it would be tumbled. Once it managed to raise itself on to the flat surface, and, after a breathing spell, commenced to shuffle towards the shelter of some pinnacles on one side of the harbour. Immediately its broad flank was turned to the wind it was rolled over, hung for a few seconds on the brink, and then splashed into the sea. On the other hand, during the spring, a few seals, more ambitious, won their way ashore in high winds; but they did not remain long in the piercing cold, moving uneasily from place to place in search of protecting hummocks and finally taking to the water in despair. Often a few hours of calm weather was the signal for half a dozen of them to land. The wind sooner or later sprang up and drove them back to their warmer element.

Under the generic name, seal, are included the true or half-seals and the sea-bears or fur-seals. Of these the fur-seals are sub-polar in distribution and are not met with amongst the ice. Ours were the hair-seals, of which there are several species. In these a layer of blubber, several inches in thickness, invests the body beneath the skin and acts as a conserver of warmth.

The sea-leopard, the only predaceous member of the seal family, has an elongated agile body and a large head with massive jaws. Early in April, Hurley and McLean actually observed one of these brutes tearing off and swallowing great pieces of flesh and blubber from the carcase of a Weddell seal.

The main part of the biological work lay in the marine collections. Hunter with his small hand-dredge brought up abundant samples of life from depths ranging to fifty fathoms. On land only the meagre mosses and lichens, and specialized forms of insect life which live amongst them, can exist.

Searching for "fleas" amongst the feathers of birds and the hair of seals or examining the viscera for "worms" is not a pleasant occupation. To be really successful, the enthusiasm of the specialist is necessary. Hunter allowed no opportunities to pass, and secured a fine collection of parasites.

Among societies privileged to see the daily paper and to whom diversity and change are the breath of life, the weather is apt to be tabooed as a subject of conversation. But even the most versatile may suddenly find themselves stripped of ideas, ignominiously reduced to the obvious topic. To us, instead of being a mere prelude to more serious matters, or the last resort of a feeble intellect, it was the all-engrossing theme. The man with the latest hair-brained theory of the causation of the wind was accorded a full hearing. The lightning calculator who estimated the annual tonnage of drift-snow sweeping off Adelie Land was received as a futurist and thinker. Discussion was always free, and the subject was never thrashed out. Evidence on the great topic accumulated day by day and month by month; yet there was no one without an innate hope that winter would bring calm weather or that spring-time, at least, must be propitious.

Meanwhile the meteorologist accepted things as he found them, and performed miracles in supplying without fail the daily figures of wind-mileage and direction, amount of drift, temperature and so forth, which were immediately seized by more vivacious minds and made the basis of daring speculations.

The steadiness of the temperature was a subject for debate. The stronger the wind blew, the less variation did the thermometer show. Over a period of several days there might be a range of only four or five degrees. The uniform conditions experienced during steady high winds were not only expressed by the slight variation in the temperature, but often in a remarkably even barometric curve. Thus on July 11 the wind-velocity for twenty-four hours was, throughout, seventy miles per hour; the temperature remaining within a few degrees of −21° F., and the barometric curve did not show as much range as one-twentieth of an inch.

The most chronic sufferer throughout the vicissitudes of temperature was the clock belonging to Bage's tide-gauge. Every sleeper in the Hut who was sensitive to ticking knew and reviled that clock. So often was it subjected to warm curative treatment in various resting-places that it was hunted from pillar to post.

Midwinter's Day! For once, the weather rose to the occasion and calmed during the few hours of the twilight-day. It was a jovial occasion, and we celebrated it with the uproarious delight of a community of young men unfettered by small conventions. The sun was returning, and we were glad of it. Already we were dreaming of spring and sledging, of the ship and home. Away in the north, the liquid globe of the sun had departed, and its glory still remained. Down from the zenith his colours descended through greenish-blue, yellowish-green, straw-yellow, light terra-cotta to a diffuse brick-red; each reflected on the sheen of freezing sea. Out on the far horizon floated ice bergs in a mirage of mobile gold. The barrier curving to east and west is a wall of delicate pink overlaid with a wondrous mauve—the rising plateau.

While others in delight roamed over the whole extent of our small rocky oasis, Hannam and Bickerton shouldered the domestic responsibilities. Their *menu de dîner* to us was a marvel of gorgeous delicacies. After the toasts and speeches came a musical and dramatic programme, punctuated by choice choruses. The washing-up was completed by all hands at midnight. Outside, the wind was not to be outdone; it surpassed itself with an unusual burst of ninety-five miles per hour.

Throughout the winter, the preparation of sledging equipment was a standing job in which all participated as opportunity offered. The world of fashion insists on its minute vagaries in dress not always with an eye to utility, and an explorer in the polar regions is a very fastidious person, expending a vast amount of care on his attire, but with the sole idea of comfort, warmth and usefulness. The clothes he wears are many and often cumbersome, but they have gradually been perfected to meet the demands of the local weather conditions.

The main features of our clothing equipment have been already outlined. There remains to be mentioned only the fact that under the extremely severe conditions of Adelie Land much ingenuity was applied to make us masters of the climate. This principally consisted in strengthening the outer garments, and in additional lashings to secure things and prevent drift snow from penetrating within. Lamp-wick, the universal polar "cord," was used in larger or smaller size wherever possible for lashings on account of its width, softness, comparative warmth, and easy manipulation in cold weather. Like every other movable thing, mitts had to be made fast to prevent them blowing away. So they were slung round the neck by a yoke of lamp-wick.

The fur-boots, or finnesko, made of reindeer skin are worn with the hair outside. They are soft and warm on the feet and made amply large to receive, within, a warmth-retaining sole-pad and stuffing of dried grass. The padding used was Lapland sennaegrass which is particularly absorbent of any moisture. Each pair lasts a distance of several hundreds of miles unless, as is unfortunately frequently the case, the fur suddenly commences to moult and the soles become bald.

As with every other part of the equipment the tents had to be modified to face the winds. We were provided with

Willesden-drill tents of the well-known circular pattern, fitted below with a broad flounce, suggestive of the brim to a hat, designed to receive blocks of snow which anchor to the tent. To facilitate their erection in the perpetual winds we made the important innovation of sewing the cover permanently on to the five bamboo poles of the frame, instead of throwing the cover over the latter previously set in position. Thus the tents opened like large conical umbrellas.

Three poles were placed to windward and two formed the supports on the lee side, between the latter was situated the funnel shaped entrance. A raw hide loop was fixed on the inside one-third of the way up the centre, windward leg to facilitate the work of erection in a wind.

The following is the procedure adopted in raising such a tent in a high wind. A suitable spot having been selected, the approximate floor-space to be occupied is marked out. Then chunks of hard snow or ice, quarried with the shovel or pick, are stacked round in a circle on the windward side, just beyond the limits of the tent-site, where they are at hand for use in anchoring.

The tent, still folded up, is brought with its peak pointing up-wind. All three men catch hold, one crawling half into it, gripping hard the leather loop on the windward leg. The others each grip an up-wind side leg. Then, at a given order, up goes the peak and amidst the roar and the flap each man struggles to step his particular pole into a notch prepared for it in the surface; the leeward legs are automatically blown more or less into position and take a great deal of the weight. The man inside, upon whom falls most of the strain, looks after the centre leg and exerts himself to the utmost to maintain it in position, throwing all his weight on to the leather loop. The others are busy outside each holding down a windward pole and freeing, as soon as it is safe, one hand with which to pull blocks of snow on to the skirt. Once a fair weight of snow is on the latter, it is safe for the man inside to let go; the rest is simple. The leeward legs are pushed out into their correct position; the skirt is pulled out taut and the load upon it increased; finally all necessary measures are taken to reduce to a minimum flapping and consequent wear on the material. After repeated experience we could usually erect the tent in such weather in from twenty to forty minutes, depending upon the strength of the wind.

Besides the Willesden-drill tents we were provided with others of japara sail-cloth fitted with Willesden-canvas flounces. These were specially suitable for heavy weather, giving one a feeling of greater security and were almost wind-proof, but unfortunately twice as heavy as the others.

A floor-cloth of light Willesden-canvas covered the surface of snow or ice in the interior of the tent; performing when sledging the alternative office of a sail.

In order to cut snow, névé or ice to pile on the flounce, a pick and spade had to be included in the sledging equipment. As a rule, a strong, pointed shovel weighing about six pounds answers very well; but in Adelie Land, the surface was so often wind-swept ice, or polished porcelain-like névé, that a pick was necessary to make any impression upon it. It was found that a four-pound spade, carefully handled, and a four-pound miner's pick provided against all emergencies.

Our sledges were similar to those of other British Antarctic expeditions; of eleven- and twelve-foot lengths. The best were Norwegian, made of ash and hickory. Others built in Sydney, of Australian woods, were admirably suited for special work. A decking of bamboo slats secured by copper wire to the crossbars was usually employed.

A light bamboo mast and spar were fitted to each sledge. Immediately in front of the mast came the "cooker-box," containing in respective compartments the primus and bottle of spirit for lighting it, as well as spare prickers, openers and fillers for the kerosene tins, repair outfits and other odd articles. The cooker-boxes were of three-ply board, with hinged lids secured by chocks and overlapped by japara to exclude as much drift-snow as possible. An instrument-box was secured to the sledge near the rear and just forward of a tray made of three-ply wood or aluminium on which the kerosene, contained in a number of one-gallon tins, was carried. Rearmost of all was the sledge-meter, attached, through a universal joint, to a crossbar at the tail end of the sledge. The middle section of the sledge, between the cooker-box and the instrument-box, was occupied by sleeping-bags, food-bags, tent and other items, held firmly in position by buckled straps passing over the load from side to side.

Sledging harness for both men and dogs was constructed of canvas. In the former case, a wide belt of triple thickness encircled the body at the hips, sewn to braces of narrower strips passing over the shoulders, while hauling-rope was attached to the belt behind. The strength of the whole depended on the care bestowed in sewing parts together, and since his life might depend upon it, no one made anything else but a thorough job of his harness.

Ninnis and Mertz ran a tailoring business for the dogs, who were brought one by one into the outer Hut to be measured for harness. After many lengths had been cut with scissors the canvas bands were sewn together on the large sewing-machine and then each dog was fitted and the final alterations were made. The huskies looked quite smart in their "suits."

Upon the primus heater, alone, did we rely for cooking the meals on sledging journeys.

In the Nansen Cooker, used in conjunction with the primus heater, a maximum result is secured from the heat available. The cooker is constructed throughout of aluminium so, though somewhat bulky, it is still light. The hot gases from the combustion of the kerosene vapour in the primus, before they escape into the outer air, are made to circulate along a tortuous path, passing from the hot interior to the cold exterior compartments, all the time transferring their heat to the cooker itself. Thus a hot hoosh is preparing in the central vessel side by side with the melting of snow for cocoa or tea in the annulus. Used in this way one gallon of kerosene oil properly husbanded is easily made to last for twelve days in the preparation of the ordinary ration for three men.

The subject of food is one which requires particular consideration and study.

Speaking generally, while living for months in an Antarctic hut, it is a splendid thing to have more than the mere neces-saries of life. Luxuries are good in moderation, and mainly for their psychological effect. With due regard for variety during the monotonous winter months, there is a corresponding rise in the "tide of life" and the ennui of the same task, in the same place, in the same *wind*, is not so noticeable.

In the matter of sledging foods, it is of prime importance to reduce as far as possible the weight of food taken upon any journey. To this end only highly concentrated foods

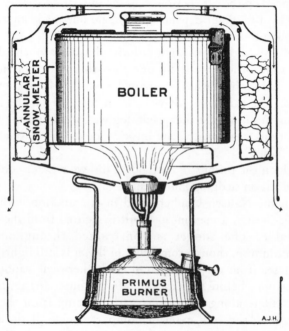

Section through a Nansen Sledging Cooker, mounted on the Primus.

are admissible, and further, the daily ration must be limited to the smallest quantity that will sustain the energies necessary for the undertaking.

In calculating the relative nutrient merits of foods each is reduced to energy equivalents by a calculation based on its chemical composition. Here it suffices to add that fat has more than twice the concentration of other concentrated foods. Fat, however, would be quite unsuitable as an exclusive ration, for other substances of a meaty, sugary and starchy nature are necessary in order to fill all the requirements of the body.

Our allowance was made up as follows, the relative amounts in the daily sledging ration for one man being stated: plasmon biscuit, 12 oz.; pemmican, 8 oz.; butter, 2 oz.; chocolate, 2 oz.; glaxo (dried milk), 5 oz.; sugar, 4 oz.; cocoa, 1 oz.; tea, .25 oz.; a total of 34.25 oz. It will be instructive to make a short note on each item.

The plasmon biscuits were large, about 2.25 oz. each, also tough to resist rough handling when sledging. They consisted of wholemeal flour with the addition of 30 per cent. of Plasmon. This latter is a trade name for the casein (albuminous content) of milk.

The pemmican we used was specially prepared for us by the Bovril Company. It consisted of powdered dried beef with an addition of 50 per cent. of beef fat.

Glaxo is a proprietary food preparation of dried milk manufactured in New Zealand. The value of milk as an all-round food is well known. In this form, with practically all the water removed, it was taken in the most concentrated form.

Butter, being a fat, is a food of high heat value, and is certainly very much appreciated by anyone on short rations.

Sugar is one of the best of foods for work and heat. It is concentrated, it is quickly assimilated, and within a few minutes of taking imparts fresh energy for muscular exertion.

Cocoa and tea were the two sledging beverages. Normally cocoa was used for the first and the last meals of the day, and the tea for lunch. Besides the stimulating substances both contain, there is also in the case of the cocoa considerable nutritive value.

The chocolate was partly Messrs. Cadbury's Bournville chocolate and partly a variety containing 10 per cent. of Plasmon.

As food for the dogs, there was nothing better than dried seal-steaks with the addition of a little blubber. Ordinary pemmican is readily eaten, but not appreciated by the dogs in the same way as seal meat. The meat was dried over the stove without heating sufficiently to cook it. By this measure, almost 50 per cent. was saved in the weight to be dragged on the sledges.

The hut was agog with movement and bustle on the days when rations were being made up and packed. The foods were taken out of tins, weighed out into weekly rations and prepared as far as possible to save operations while sledging.

There was the hoosh-compound, a mixture of chopped up pemmican and crushed plasmon biscuit; the cocoa-compound consisting of cocoa, glaxo and sugar thoroughly mixed together in the right proportions; also a glaxo and sugar mixture to be used with the tea. The tea, in rations for a single brew, was sewn up in small muslin bags ready to be dropped into the cooker.

Weekly allowances for each of three men of each of the items were put up in calico bags; these in turn were packed in larger bags made of strong waterproof material, some holding all the items of a week's ration for a party, others accommodating a fortnight's supplies.

Meanwhile, other occupations were in full swing. An amateur cobbler, his crampon on a last, studded its spiked surface with clouts, hammering away in complete disregard of the night-watchman's uneasy slumbers. The big sewing-machine raced at top speed round the flounce of a tent, and in odd corners among the bunks were groups mending mitts, strengthening sleeping-bags and patching burberrys.

If the "winter calms" were a delusion, there were at least several beautifully clear, moderately calm days in June. The expectation of colder weather had been realized, and by the end of the month it was a perceptible fact that the sun had definitely turned, describing a longer arc when skimming the distant fleets of bergs along the northern horizon. Thus on June 28 the refracted image of the sun rose into visibility about eleven o'clock, heralded by a striking green sky and damask cloud and by one o'clock had disappeared.

There was much expected of July, but the wind soughed on and the temperature decreased. Just to demonstrate its resource, the wind maintained ninety-seven miles per hour for six hours on July 19, while the puffanemometer indicated several "breaks" of one hundred and fifty miles per hour.

July 21 was cold, calm and clear. For the first time after many weeks the sun was mildly warm, and all felt with a spring of optimism that a new era had begun. The sea which had been kept open by the wind was immediately overspread with thin, dark ice, which in a few hours was dotted with many ice-flowers—rosette-like aggregates of fern-like, sprouting fronds. Soon the surface had whitened and by next morning was firm enough to hold a man out beyond the nearest island. The wind did not allow this state of affairs to last for long, for by lunch-time it had hurried away the floe-ice and raged across a foaming sea.

We still considered the question of sledging, and I decided that if there were the slightest prospect of accomplishing anything, several of us would start before the end of July on a short journey. The month, however, closed with nothing to commend it. So our hopes were centred on the spring.

CHAPTER XI

SPRING EXPLOITS

It was not until August 8 that there was any indication of improvement in the weather. That day opened with a steady barometer and bright sunshine, the wind fell to forty miles an hour and a fine radiant of cirrus clouds spread out fanwise from the north, the first from that direction for many months.

Accordingly on August 9, accompanied by Ninnis and Madigan, I set off with a team of dogs against a forty-mile wind in an attempt to push to the south. The start was made after lunch and darkness arrived as we groped our way up to the bamboo pole marking a point three and a quarter miles south of the Hut; so camp was pitched there.

Continuing in a strong steady wind the following day, we were fortunate in finding intact the sledge which had been abandoned in the autumn, five and a half miles from the Hut; it was partly buried in a bank of hard névé, and was much bleached and abraded. The aluminium cooker had become brightly polished on the windward side due to the scour of dry snow impelled by furious winds. The remains of Madigan's plum-pudding of the autumn were unearthed and found to be in splendid condition. That evening it was thawed over the primus and demolished.

At that spot the steeper grades of the ascent to the plateau are left behind, and it appealed to us as a strategic point from which to extend sledging efforts to east, south and west. So it was decided to locate a depot there, five and a half miles from the Hut. Further, we determined to excavate a cavern in the ice under the surface of the glacier, for such a refuge from the hurricane would be of great service to all future sledging parties. The work was commenced forthwith and we were installed therein on the evening of the following day.

The entrance to the cavern was by way of an almost vertical shaft situated to one side and sealed by spreading over it, as a temporary measure, the tent-cover, to be replaced later on by a specially designed canvas flap.

It was a great relief to be in a strong room, with solid walls of ice, in place of the cramped tent flapping violently in the wind. Inside, the silence was profound, the blizzard was banished. Aladdin's Cave it was henceforth called—a truly magical world of glassy facets and scintillating crystals.

Shelves for primus stove, spirit bottle, matches, kerosene and other oddments were chipped out at a moment's notice. In one wall a small hole was cut to communicate with a narrow crevasse fissure which provided ventilation without allowing the entrance of drifting snow. Another fissure crossing

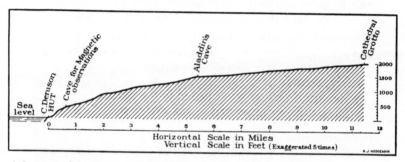

A Section of the Coastal Slope of the Land Ice-sheet Island from Cape Denison

the floor at one corner was a natural receptacle for rubbish. Whatever daylight there was filtered through the roof and walls without hindrance. The purest ice for cooking could be immediately hacked out from the walls without the inconvenience of having to don one's burberrys and go outside for it. Finally one neatly disposed of spare clothes by moistening the corner of each garment and pressing it against the wall for a few seconds, where it would freeze on and remain hanging until required. The place, in fact, was simply replete with conveniences. We thoroughly enjoyed the night's rest in Aladdin's Cave, notwithstanding alarming cracks proceeding occasionally from the crevasses around.

Madigan and Ninnis dug a shelter for the dogs, who spent their time curled up so as to expose as little surface as possible to the biting wind.

On August 13 the advance to the south was continued. The dogs hated to face the strong wind, but, on the whole, did better than expected. In the afternoon, when only three miles had been accomplished and having attained an altitude of two thousand feet, dark and lowering clouds formed overhead portending thick, drifting weather, during which, in the crevassed ice of that vicinity it would not be advisable to travel. Therefore, as there were provisions for a few days only, I decided that we should be wise to turn back to the Hut without delay. The return was down-hill over slippery ice surface intersected by small crevasses and with a stiff wind behind. The dogs had to be set loose for they only added to our difficulties. Capsizes were frequent and darkness descended upon us, so that it was with some relief that we saw the sledge and flag-pole left at Aladdin's Cave suddenly loom up in front. The sleeping-bags and other gear were passed down into the Cave and the dogs, who had all turned up safely, were fed.

When the doorway was opened in the morning, a blizzard with dense drifting snow was in full progress. As it was not possible to see any distance, we decided to await an improvement on the morrow.

On the 15th, though the weather was no better, we set off for the Hut. The sledge having been dug out, one man went in front to keep the course and the others brought up the rear, holding back the load. In dense drift it was no simple matter to steer a correct course for the Hut, at the same time it was essential not to deviate far therefrom as the rocky foreshore extended only for a mile, on either side abutting on vertical ice cliffs. With a compelling force like a hurricane at our backs, it was not a nice thing to contemplate finding ourselves on the slippery, sloping brink of a precipice.

The wind, however, was steady and we knew at what angle to steer to keep a fair course; also we were helped by the existence of a number of small crevasse fissures which we were aware trended approximately north and south.

Half a mile had been covered before we remarked the absence of the dogs who had been left to follow. We had taken for granted that they would follow us, and were so fully occupied after starting that their absence had passed unnoticed. It would be difficult to locate them if we returned; the weather would improve in a few days; if they felt hungry they would come down of their own accord. So we decided to go on without them.

At two miles from the Hut the drift thinned out and the wind became more gusty. Between the gusts the view opened out for a considerable distance, and the rocks showed black below the last steep fall.

Back at the Hut it was arranged that if the dogs did not return in a reasonable time, Bage, Mertz and Hurley should go up to Aladdin's Cave in search of them.

They made a great effort to get away next morning. The sledge was hauled for one thousand one hundred yards up to Webb's Cave against a bitter torrent of air rushing by at eighty-two miles an hour. From there they retreated exhausted.

On the 17th the wind was gauged at eighty-four miles an hour, and nothing could be done. Dense drift and ferocious wind continued until the morning of August 21, and still none of the dogs had come home. The dog-relief party took advantage of a slight lull to start off at 6.30 a.m. and were absent for four days, during which time thick drift and a high wind continued. They returned at 2 p.m. on the 25th bringing all the dogs except Grandmother, who had died of exhaustion. The party related that Aladdin's Cave had been difficult to find in the driving snow, which had thickened after the first few miles. They actually passed close to it when Mertz, between the gusts, sighted Castor jumping about, fully alive to the approaching relief. The dogs were found curled up in the snow, in a listless, apathetic state; apparently in the same position when left seven days before. They had made no attempt to break into several bags of provisions lying close at hand, preferring to starve rather than expose their faces to the pelting drift. All were frozen down except Basilisk and Castor. Grandmother was in the worst condition, and, despite all efforts at revival, died four hours after.

ιe poor brutes were very weak after their long fast and ɪ̣sure, they were taken into the Cave and fed on warm hoosh. Everything possible was done for them, and in return the party passed a very miserable time cramped in such a small space with six dogs.

Five days of calm weather! It could scarcely be credited, yet September came with such a spell. These gave us great opportunities, and, for once, a vision of what perfect Antarctic days might be. The sea speedily froze over and extended our territory to the north.

Every day we dredged through cracks in the floe, until Hunter and Laseron had material enough to sort and bottle to occupy them for many days. Whilst engaged upon this work I was treated on two occasions to an involuntary sea bath, for the floe was quite thin and gave way occasionally. Others fared similarly; amongst them was Hurley, whose wanderings in search of subjects for his whole-plate camera were thus brought to an abrupt conclusion—a sad affair for the camera.

Here and there Weddell seals scrambled out of cracks to bask on the floe. We were so glad to see them after their long absence that it seemed a pity to kill them; but as we were badly in need of fresh meat both for ourselves and the dogs, there was no other course but to replenish out supplies of seal steaks and blubber.

The behaviour of Weddell seals on first acquaintance with man is really very remarkable. Lying asleep on the ice, the seal takes very little notice until one is within a few yards' distance. Even then it is loath to wake, contenting itself for several moments with sniffing the air, until realizing that there is really something unusual in the wind. Then suddenly, its large calf-like eyes are opened wide in amazement at the sight of what appears to be an apparition; but after one intense and anxious gaze they are closed and screwed up tightly, doubtless seeking for reassurance that it is all a dream. The next move is invariably a sudden opening and somewhat terrified dilation of the eyes. Apparently not sufficiently convinced, this performance is repeated several times until, finding that there has been no deception and overcome by emotion at the discovery that such an animal as man exists, large tears well up in its eyes. This performance, however, does not last long, for if one holds one's ground, not approaching closer to the animal, it will shortly forget all about the incident, turn over and go to sleep again.

The opportunity of this fine weather was taken to transport several big loads of foodstuffs to the depot at Aladdin's Cave. On these occasions, the dogs, who were set loose at the Cave, showed great reluctance to return to the Hut, preferring to camp at the Cave. On return one day Scott and Franklin were not present at "roll-call." Three days later Franklin was found sleeping on the glacier; there was no sign of Scott. Nor did we ever see him again, so were left to conclude that he lost his life in a crevasse.

Parties visiting the Cave all met with wind and drift above an elevation of one thousand feet, though calm conditions prevailed at sea-level.

At 4 p.m. on September 5, while a number of the men were still dredging out on the floe, whirlies with great columns of drift came steadily down the glacier, pouring over the seaward cliffs. In a few minutes the clouds of snow were round the Hut and the wind was not long in working up to eighty miles per hour. It was all so sudden that the dredging party had a narrow escape. The sea-ice soon vanished to the north. Thus ended one of the most remarkable periods of fine weather experienced by us in Adelie Land, only to be excelled in the height of summer.

The possibility of such a spell being repeated fired us with the hope that after all a reasonable amount of sledging could be accomplished in the spring. Three parties were chosen to reconnoitre in different directions and to test the sledging gear. As we were far from being confident of the weather, I made it clear that no party should penetrate farther than fifty miles from the Hut, nor remain away longer than a fortnight. They were all to drag their own sledges, for the use of dogs was scarcely possible in such weather.

Webb, McLean and Stillwell were to reconnoitre to the south. They set out on September 7 in the face of a wind of fifty-six miles per hour. Though they were poorly off for crampons, there being a shortage of the long-spiked Swiss variety, the steep ice slopes to Aladdin's Cave were negotiated in five hours. A couple of days later they reached a point eleven and three-quarter miles south of the Hut. The wind rose to the eighties during that night, so in view of inadequate crampons further progress was impossible. For shelter a cave was hewn in the glacier, subsequently known as Cathedral Grotto.

Webb took a full set of magnetic observations behind a breakwind of ice blocks, it having been found that the instrument could not be used in the Grotto, for there it became rapidly coated with ice crystals, interfering with the mechanism.

The return to the Hut was a furious race with a seventy-five mile wind in the rear.

A second party comprised Ninnis, Mertz and Murphy, who went to the south-east, leaving on September 11. For two days they proceeded in a wind of about fifty miles per hour. On the third day the wind was blowing sixty-five miles per hour and the temperature standing at –17° F.

By the evening of the 14th they had reached a point eighteen miles south-east of the Hut. The next day the wind had increased still further and they could not move. With the tent split above them, the night was passed in the three-man sleeping-bag, fully dressed, shod with crampons and with ice-axes in hand, expecting to be hurled away down the ice slopes.

When daylight came the conditions moderated somewhat, and with a furious wind abeam, a break was made for Aladdin's Cave. They were fortunate to get back safely, for on the way the sledge was blown sideways on to the lids of many wide crevasses, and accidents were narrowly averted.

From the realistic reports of the two parties which had returned it was evident that Madigan and his companions, Close and Whetter, who had set out on the 12th to reconnoitre to the west, were having a bad time. But it was not until the 23rd, after a week of clear skies, low temperatures and unceasing drift-free wind that we began to feel apprehensive about them.

At the Hut September 24 and 25 were punctuated by several intervals of calm during which it was judged the party would have been able to travel.

On the morning of September 26 Ninnis and Mertz, with a team of dogs, set off up the hill to Aladdin's Cave to deposit some provisions and to scan the horizon for any sign of the sledgers. On the way they fell in with them descending the slopes, very worn and frost-bitten.

They had a thrilling story to tell, and, when it was known that the party had reached fifty miles to the west, everybody crowded round to listen.

The wind average at the Hut during their fortnight of absence was fifty-eight miles per hour, implying worse conditions on the plateau. Madigan gave the facts:

"After leaving Aladdin's Cave on the 12th we continued due south, lunching at 2 p.m. on the site of Webb's first camp. Our troubles had already begun, the wind averaged sixty miles an hour all day with a temperature at noon of $-14°$ F.

"A few tears appeared in the tent during the night. Crouched in the lee of the sledge a lunch was made of frozen butter, biscuit and chocolate.

"We sewed up the rents in the tent during the halt, having to use bare fingers in the open. About four stitches at a time were as much as one man could manage, and then the other two took their turns.

"The next day was the only comparatively calm period of the two weeks of travelling. The wind was in the vicinity of thirty miles per hour, and, going west, by nightfall we reached a spot twenty miles 'out.'

"All day on the 15th a steady seventy-five mile wind accompanied by thick, low drift blew at right angles to our course. The surface was partially consolidated snow, very hard and smooth. Sometimes the sledge would grip and we could pull straight ahead. Then, suddenly, it would slide away sideways down wind and often pull us off our feet with a sudden vicious jerk. Most of the time we were dragging in a south-westerly direction to make the sledge run west, stumbling through the drift with the sledge now behind us, now sliding away to leeward, often capsizing and requiring to be laboriously righted and sometimes repacked.

"After many experiments, we found the best device was to have two men on the bow-rope, about twenty feet long, and one with about ten feet of rope attached to the rear of the sledge. The man on the tail-rope, usually Whetter, found it very difficult to keep his feet, and, after a score of falls in stinging drift with incidental frost-bites on fingers and cheeks, he did not feel exactly cheerful.

"By 4 p.m. on the 25th we had reached twenty-five miles and were exhausted. We pitched camp at an early hour, partly influenced by the fact that it was a special occasion—Close's birthday! Some port wine had been slipped in to provide against that 'emergency.' On taking the precious bottle from the instrument-box, I found that the cork was out, and for one awful moment thought the bottle was empty. Then I realized that the wine had frozen solid and had pushed the cork out by its expansion on solidification.

"At last, the tent safely pitched and hoosh and cocoa finished, the moment came to drink to Close's health and happiness. The bottle had stood on the top of the cooker while the meal was being prepared, but the wine was still as solid as ever. After being shaken and held over the primus for a good half-hour it began to issue in lumps. Once the lumps were secured in mugs the rest of the thawing was easy.

"During September 16 my right eyelid became frost-bitten. Noticing that it was hard and refused to shut I rubbed vigorously to bring it round. However, it swelled and blistered badly and the eye remained quite closed for two days.

"From twenty to fifty miles 'out,' the surface was névé with areas of sastrugi up to three feet in height. No crevasses were noticed. At twenty miles 'out,' we lost sight of the sea, and at forty miles an altitude of four thousand five hundred feet was reached.

"We turned out at 6 a.m. every morning, but the difficulties of carrying on under the weather conditions were so great that it was 9 a.m. before we were on the move. We never camped before 6 p.m. and were obliged to consider five miles a good day's run. Pitching camp took nearly an hour.

"At almost every camp there was some sewing necessary in order to keep the tent in repair, and it was not long before everyone's fingers were in a bad state. After repeated frost-bites they became, especially near the tip, as hard as wood and devoid of sensation. Manipulating toggles and buttons on one's clothing gave an immense amount of trouble and it always seemed an interminable time before we got away in the morning. Our lowest temperature was −35° F., early on September 18.

"We were fifty miles 'out' on September 19 on a white, featureless plain. A bamboo pole with a black flag was raised, a mound was built, and a week's provisions for three men and two gallons of kerosene were cached.

"In the morning there was a howling eighty-mile blizzard with dense drift, and our hopes of an early start homeward were dispelled. We feared for the safety of the tent, knowing that if it had gone out at that time, our hopes of getting back to the Hut would have been small.

"The wind continued all day and the next night, but, to our joy, abated on the 21st to fifty miles an hour, permitting us to travel.

"Through a seventy-five-miler on the 22nd and a quieter day on the 23rd, we picked up our half-way mound at Birthday Camp on September 24. On the same night the long-suffering sledge-meter, much battered, gave up recording.

"At 3 a.m. I was awakened by something striking me on the head. I looked out of the sleeping bag and found that the tent had collapsed. The extra stays run out up the wind from the apex had carried away and the poles were down on top of us. The cap was gone, and one side of the tent was split from top to bottom. Fortunately the barricade of névé around the flounce prevented what remained of it from blowing away. I awakened the others and Whetter and I got out, leaving Close inside to hold on to the bag. Luckily we had kept on our burberrys in case of accidents. For once the entrance had not to be unfastened, as there was a ready-made exit. The poles were roughly bound together with a rope and anchored to a pick on the windward side. It was blowing about eighty miles an hour, but fortunately there was no drift. When daylight came the tent was found to be hopelessly ruined, and to light the primus was impossible, though the wind had abated to thirty-five miles an hour.

"We ate some frozen food and pushed on, hoping to find Aladdin's Cave before dark, so that we should not have to spend a night without a tent. After a struggle of thirteen miles over rough ice we arrived there, footsore and worn out. Close's feet were badly blistered and both my big toes had become frost-bitten at the fifty-mile camp, giving me a good deal of trouble on the way back.

"Never was the Cave a more luxurious place. The cooker was kept busy far into the night, while we drank and smoked and felt happy."

The successful conclusion of this journey in the face of the most adverse weather conditions was something upon which Madigan, Whetter and Close could well feel proud, for in its way it must be a record in the sledging world. They were indeed badly frost-bitten; Madigan's great toes had suffered most of all and he was fortunate in not losing them altogether. Whetter's chief injury was a wound under the chin occasioned by a pair of scissors handled by Madigan to free Whetter's helmet on an occasion when it was so firmly frozen to his face that it was necessary to adopt drastic measures for its removal in order that he could partake of food.

October came with a deluge of snow and transient hours of bright sunlight, during which the seals would make a temporary landing and retire again to the water when their endurance was exhausted. Snow-petrels flew in great numbers about the rocks in the evening, seeking out their old nest-crevices. Seeing these signs of returning life, everyone was in great expectation of the arrival of the penguins.

On the night of the 11th, Hurley, Laseron, Hunter and Correll made an innovation by presenting a small farce to an audience which had been starved of dramatic entertainments for a long time, and consequently showed tremendous appreciation.

The first penguin came waddling up the ice-foot against a seventy-mile wind late on the afternoon of October 12. McLean brought the bird back to the Hut and the newcomer received a great ovation. Stimulated by their success on the previous night and the appearance of the first penguin, the theatrical party added to their number, and, dispensing with a rehearsal, produced an opera, "The Washerwoman's Secret," composed by Laseron. Part of the Hut was curtained off as a combined green-room and dressing-room; the kitchen was the stage, footlights twinkled on the floor; the acetylene beamed down from the rafters, while the audience crowded on a form behind the dining-table, making tactless remarks and steadily eating chocolate. The entertainment proved an immense success, and at midnight we all retired wearied with laughter.

By the middle of October the weather showed but meagre signs of improvement, but the penguins came up in great numbers. They were in groups all along the ice-foot in the lee of rocks and icy pinnacles. They climbed up to their old resorts, and in a few days commenced to build nests of small pebbles. Skua gulls mysteriously appeared, snow-petrels hovered along the rocky ridges and odd seals landed on the wind-raked harbour ice. Silver-grey and Antarctic petrels flew along the shore with occasional Cape pigeons. If the weather was indifferent to the fact, the birds did not forget that spring had come.

A Weddell seal calved on the floe in the Boat Harbour on October 18. For a week the calf had a miserable time in winds ranging mostly about the seventies, with the temperature below zero Fahrenheit. At last it became so weak that having thawed a hole in the soft, sludgy ice it could not extricate itself. Both it and the mother were killed and skinned for the biological collection.

The hangar was dug out and the air-tractor brought out for Bickerton to experiment with and improve.

On October 21 there was a marked thaw inside the Hut. The thick cakes of ice on the roof windows dripped continually, coming away in lumps at lunch-time and falling among the diners at both ends of the table. Every available bucket and tub was in use to catch the drip and that evening we retired to bed with our umbrellas up, so to speak.

Stillwell came in during the afternoon bearing an albino Adelie penguin with a prettily mottled head; a curious freak of which the biologists immediately took possession. The penguins now swarmed along the foreshores, those not settling down in the rookeries wandered about in small crowds, occasionally visiting the Hut and exploring among the rocks or up the slippery glacier. Murphy was heard at this time to advance a theory accounting for the fact that Adelie penguins never made their nests on a scale more elaborate than a collection of stones. He submitted that anything else would be blown away. Further, he held that close observation would reveal that the penguins of Adelie Land, immediately the egg is laid, place a stone on top to weigh it down. The biologists kept a dignified silence during the discussion.

The penguins were a never failing source of interest and amusement; it was quite an entertainment to spend half an hour amongst them in one of the many rookeries near by. These droll little fellows, pugnacious to a degree and altogether ignorant of man, have no fear but, on the contrary, approach resolutely pecking in a friendly way at one's legs or else, ignoring one entirely, go about their business undisturbed.

When they first come ashore, about the middle of October, they are wonderfully clean, sleek and fat. The first few days are spent lazying about on the ice-foot, then they begin to take a greater interest in the adjoining deserted rookeries. Several days later, all are feverishly busy making nests of small pebbles which they search for and bring in their beaks from many yards away, not omitting to steal from the nests of others in the absence of the proprietors. Partners are selected and the pairs, united in matrimonial bliss, settle down for a short honeymoon at their nests. During several weeks at this time they do not return to the water for food, but exist on the fat stored up in their tissues during the winter. Early in November two eggs are laid which are defended from the depredations of marauding skua gulls throughout the succeeding weeks, as the hatching proceeds in blizzard and in sunshine.

At this time a new light comes into their eyes and with the greatest persistence they gallantly assail anybody venturing amongst them in the rookeries, pecking viciously and raining showers of blows with their hard and muscular flippers. When collecting the eggs for culinary purposes we found that by approaching the nests quietly, then stroking the back of the bird, meanwhile taking several pecks on a thickly mittened fist, a hand could be slipped under the bird, extracting the eggs without further opposition. After a momentary uproar on realizing that the eggs have gone she settles herself down and continues to sit on, resolved not to be influenced by any such untoward event.

The downy young have voracious appetites, ever clamouring for more food, in search of which the parents make daily journeys to the sea, returning a few hours later with crops gorged with a small red shrimp which constitutes their chief diet. So rapidly do the chicks mature, that in six weeks' time they are almost as large as their parents which, by the way, are then in very poor condition as a result of the arduous period just passed. A few more weeks and the young have passed through a double moult and they are almost undistinguishable from their parents. Autumn has arrived and they all disappear in the sea, migrating during the winter to the northern limits of the pack-ice.

On October 21 an Emperor penguin landed on the ice in the Boat Harbour, and, early in November, several more were captured. As these were the only ones to come ashore at Cape Denison during the year, it is clear that they are infrequent visitors to the shores of Adelie Land. As the coast is otherwise eminently suitable for the establishment of Emperor penguin rookeries their absence is doubtless solely owing to the impossible winds prevailing during the winter. No degree of mere cold appears to inconvenience them, for, as evidenced elsewhere on the Antarctic coast in localities favoured with less wind where their rookeries have been discovered, they actually choose the winter months as their hatching season. There, in the bitterest weather of the year, at temperatures reaching even below ninety degrees of frost they are known to spend weeks standing in snow-drifts or on bare ice keeping their single large egg out of harm's way on top of their thick muscular feet, with no further protection against the weather for that delicate object than a fold of feathers and skin which falls over it. The wonder is that any of the eggs hatch out at all for, presumably, if by chance one rolls off the parent's feet and is left on the ice for a few moments it is irrevocably frozen.

October closed with an average wind velocity of 56.9 miles per hour. Yet the possibility of summer sledging was no longer remote. The sun was high, spells of calm were longer and more frequent, and, with the certain knowledge that we should be on the plateau in November, the sledging parties were chosen, schemes of exploration were discussed, and the last details for an extensive campaign completed.

The investigation by sledging journeys of the coastline to the eastward was regarded as of prime importance, for our experience in the *Aurora*, when in those longitudes during the previous year, was such as to give little promise of its ever being accomplished from the sea.

Westward the coast, at least for some distance, was accessible from the sea. The field in that direction was therefore not so promising as that to the east.

The following is a list of the parties which had been arranged and which, now fully equipped, were on the tiptoe of expectation to depart.

1. A Southern Party composed of Bage (leader), Webb and Hurley. The special feature of their work was to be magnetic observations.

2. A Southern Supporting Party, including Murphy (leader), Hunter and Laseron, who were to accompany the Southern Party as far as possible, returning to Winter Quarters by the end of November.

3. A Western Party of three men—Bickerton (leader), Hodgeman and Whetter—who were to traverse the coastal highlands west of the Hut. Their intention was to make use of the air-tractor sledge, of somewhat doubtful utility. As it was obvious that the engine could be operated only in moderately good weather, the departure of the party was postponed until early November.

4. Stillwell, in charge of a Near-Eastern Party, was to map the coast-line between Cape Denison and the Mertz Glacier Tongue, dividing the work into two stages. In the first

instance, Close and Hodgeman were to assist him; all three acting partly as supports to the other eastern parties working further afield. After returning to the Hut at the end of November for a further supply of stores, he was to set out again with Close and Laseron in order to complete the work.

5. An Eastern Coastal Party composed of Madigan (leader), McLean and Correll was to start in early November with the object of investigating the coast-line beyond the Mertz Glacier Tongue.

6. Finally, a Far-Eastern Party, assisted by the dogs, was to push out rapidly overland to the southward of Madigan's party, mapping more distant sections of the coast-line beyond the limit to which the latter party would be likely to reach.

As the plans for the execution of such a journey had of necessity to be more provisional than in the case of the others, I determined to undertake it myself, accompanied by Ninnis and Mertz, both of whom had so ably acquitted themselves throughout the Expedition and, moreover, had always been in charge of the dogs.

CHAPTER XII

ACROSS KING GEORGE LAND

"We yearned beyond the sky-line."—KIPLING.

NOVEMBER opened with more moderate weather, auguring still better conditions for midsummer. Accordingly, November 6 was fixed as the date of final departure for several of the parties. Everybody was on the tiptoe of expectation.

The evening of November 5 was made a special occasion: a farewell dinner, into which everybody entered very heartily. However, on the morning of the 6th we found a strong blizzard raging and the landscape blotted out by drift-snow, which did not clear until the afternoon of the following day.

At the first opportunity, Murphy's party got away, but found the wind so strong at a level of one thousand feet on the glacier that they anchored their sledge and returned to the Hut for the night. The next morning saw them off finally, and, later in the day, Stillwell's and Madigan's parties got under way, though there was still considerable wind.

My own party was to leave on the 9th for, assisted by the dogs, we could easily catch up to the other eastern parties, and it was our intention not to part company with them until all were some distance out on the road together.

The wind increased on the 9th and the air became charged with drift, so we felt sure that those who preceded us would still be camped at Aladdin's Cave, and that the best course was to wait.

At this date the penguin rookeries were full of new-laid eggs, and the popular taste inclined towards omelettes, in the production of which we found Mertz was a past master. I can recall the clamouring throng that pressed round for the final omelette as Mertz officiated at the stove just before we left on the 10th.

It was a beautiful calm afternoon as the sledge mounted up the long icy slopes. Bage's party was a short distance in advance, but by the help of the dogs we were soon abreast of them. Then Bickerton, who had given a hand to pull their sledge as far as the three-mile post, bade us good-bye and returned to the Hut, where he was to remain in charge with Whetter and Hannam until the return of Murphy's party.

At Aladdin's Cave, while some prepared supper, others selected tanks of food from the depot and packed the sledges. After the meal, Bage's party bade us farewell and set off at a rapid rate, intending to overtake their supporting party on the same evening at the Cathedral Grotto. Many finishing touches had to be put to our three sledges and two teams of dogs, so that the departure was delayed till next morning.

We were up betimes and a good start was made before anything came of the overcast sky which had formed during the night. The rendezvous appointed for meeting the others, in case we had not previously caught them up, was eighteen miles south-east of Aladdin's Cave. But with a view to avoiding crevasses as much as possible, a southerly course was followed for several miles, after which it was directed well to the east. In the meantime the wind had arisen and snow commenced to fall soon after noon. In such weather it was impossible to locate the other parties, so after having covered eight miles we decided to camp and await a clearance in the weather.

Operations connected with camping at the end of a day's march developed into a set routine. First the sledges are drawn across the wind where they serve as a break-wind to shelter the dogs. Then the straps round the load are loosened carefully; the shovel, pick and tent withdrawn, and the straps retightened, the latter precaution to prevent articles from being carried off by the wind. Snow blocks are broken out ready and then the tent itself is erected and made snug against the onslaught of the weather.

Whilst two of the party tether and feed the dogs, the cook of the occasion takes the food into the tent and prepares the meal. The primus is started and over it is placed the cooker with annulus and boiler both filled with snow. Very soon that in the inner vessel is melted and into it is dumped a measured quantity of hoosh-compound. A few minutes more and it has reached the boil. Meanwhile the other two have settled with the dogs and arrive in time to receive a steaming hut mug of hoosh, which is none the less welcome on account of such adventitious ingredients as reindeer-hairs. This ubiquitous constituent of all food preparations on sledging-journeys is transferred in some mysterious way from moulting sleeping-bags.

The boiler is roughly scraped after the hoosh has been poured out and is then refilled with cold water from the annulus and to it the ration of cocoa-compound is added. By the time the hoosh has been consumed the cocoa has arrived at the boil; the primus is extinguished and the warm water in the annulus is added to the boiling cocoa, reducing it to a bearable temperature. The fact that the cocoa contains a certain amount of hoosh from the sides of the pot does not lessen its palatability, so keen is the appetite. The ration of biscuit is eaten with the cocoa and presently the meal is over.

The cooker, primus and food-bag, as there is no room in the tent, are taken out and strapped on the sledge; the sleeping-bags and spare-clothing bag are passed inside and the entrance-tunnel securely tied up for the night.

Then commences a general clean up with the object of removing all loose snow from the gear in the tent; for this we included in the equipment a small clothes-brush. After brushing one's burberrys they are taken off and rolled up to serve as a pillow. Attention is next turned to fur mitts, finnesko, sleeping-bags and finally the floor-cloth itself.

After this there is little left to do, for on sledging journeys one does not indulge in elaborate toilet arrangements, nor did we ever undress. However, before slipping down into the bag a complete change of footgear is made, donning warm dry sleeping socks and special finnesko kept for the purpose. If the articles of day-wear, always damp and sometimes sodden, are retained during sleeping hours, the feet are likely to become frost-bitten.

The absorbent sennaegrass (dried grass from Lapland) padding the finnesko becomes quite wet in a day's march and has to be dried before again being used. It is teased out and put into an airy muslin bag where it dries in the course of a few days, fresh material taking its place in the meantime. The damp socks are pushed under one's jacket where the heat of the body is relied upon to dry them by the morning. The more or less sodden finnesko are usually quite limp as they are removed from the feet but soon freeze stiff, so rigid that they cannot be drawn on to the feet in the morning unless care has been taken that in the freezing they retain the proper shape of the foot. This is best insured by stuffing them when limp with spare sennaegrass and then hanging them up by string from the peak of the tent.

The time occupied between the halt and the writing of diaries whilst sitting up in the bags preparatory to going off to sleep depends entirely upon the weather. It might be as little as an hour and a half, but in heavy drifts with clothes and gear loaded with snow three hours would be easily consumed.

Returning to events of November 11: Five days of wind and drift followed, and for the next two days we remained in camp. Then, on the afternoon of the 13th, the drift became less dense, enabling us to move forward on an approximate course to what was judged to be the vicinity of the rendezvous, where we camped again for three days.

As a penalty for travelling in such weather our mitts and finnesko had become saturated with drift, promising us a cold time when donning them next at break of camp. Felt mitts are the worst drift absorbers, and the ice resulting permeates the whole fabric, leaving them as uninviting, hard and untractable as mail.

On such occasions, when weather-bound in our sleeping-bags, we made it a practice to eat very little food, saving what we could for future emergencies. Outside the dogs had a very unpleasant time, but fortunately they were soon buried in snow which sheltered them from the stinging wind.

The monotony and disappointment of delay were just becoming acute when the wind fell off, and the afternoon of November 16 turned out gloriously fine.

The vicinity was reconnoitred in search of the other parties but without success. At length it occurred to us that something serious might have happened, so we left our loads and started back at a gallop for Aladdin's Cave with two empty sledges, Mertz careering ahead on skis over the sastrugi field.

We had not gone far, however, before two black specks were seen away in the north; a glance with the binoculars leaving no doubt as to the identity of the parties. We returned and picked up our loads and then made a course to the east to intercept them.

It was a happy camp that evening with the three tents pitched together, while we compared our experiences of the previous six days and made plans for the outward journey.

Our sledge-meter had already suffered through bumping over rough ice and sastrugi, so an exchange was made with the stronger one on Stillwell's sledge. A quantity of food was also taken over from him and the loads were finally adjusted.

The details and weights of the three sledges and their loads comprising the equipment of my party, being illustrative of the outfit for a sledging journey, are sufficiently interesting to be set out at length. Most of the items were included in the impedimenta of all our patties, but slight variations were necessary to meet particular circumstances or to satisfy the whim of an individual.

Total Load

	lb.	oz.
The Principal Sledge and Fittings: The bare sledge (11 ft. long), 45 lb.; instrument-box, 7 lb. 5 oz.; cooker-box, 7 lb. 6 oz.; kerosene-tray, 3 lb. mast-attachment, 2 lb. 8 oz.; mast, 1 lb. 15 oz.; spar, 1 lb. 8 oz.; decking (canvas and bamboo), 3 lb. 5 oz.; rigging, 7.5 oz.; 5 leather straps, 5 lb.	77	6.5
The Second Sledge: Sledge 11 ft. long decked with Venesta boarding and fitted with straps	55	0
The Third Sledge: Sledge 12 ft. long, and strong rope lashings (spare spars mentioned elsewhere acting as decking)	60	0
Tent: Drill tent strengthened and attached to poles, also floor-cloth, 33 lb.; spare drill cover, 11 lb. 8 oz. .	44	8

	lb.	oz.

Sleeping-bags: 3 one-man bags . . . . . — 30 0

Cooking Gear: Nansen cooker, 11 lb. 3 oz.; 3 mugs, 1 lb. 8 oz.; 2 tins, 10 oz.; scales, 0.5 oz.; 3 spoons, 1.5 oz.; matches, 13.5 oz.; and damp-proof tin to hold same, 3.7 oz.; primus heater, full, 3 lb. 10 oz.; primus prickers, 2.5 oz.; primus repair outfit, 2 oz.; kerosene tin openers and pourers, 4.5 oz.; spirit for primus in tin, 5 lb. 14 oz.; also a ready bottle, full, 1 lb. 5 oz. . . . — 25 14.2

Repair Outfit: Spare copper wire, rivets, needles, thread, etc., 1 lb. 14.5 oz.; set of 12 tools, 15.5 oz.; requirements for repairing dog-harness and medically treating the dogs, 3 lb. 8 oz. . . . . — 6 6

Medical Outfit: 6 Burroughs & Wellcome first field dressings; absorbent cotton wool; boric wool; pleated lint; pleated bandages; roll bandages; adhesive tape; liquid collodion; "tabloid" ophthalmic drugs for treating snow-blindness; an assortment of "tabloid" drugs for general treatment; canvas case containing scissors, forceps, artery-forceps, scalpel, surgical needles and silk, etc. . — 2 12.3

Photographic Outfit: A $\frac{1}{4}$-plate, long extension-camera in a case, with special stiffening board and 36 packets each containing 12 cut films, 4 lb. 4.5 oz.; adaptor to accommodate camera to theodolite legs, 2 oz.; a water-tight tin with 14 packets, each containing 12 cut films, 3 lb. 10 oz. — 8 0.5

Surveying Requirements: A 3 in. transit theodolite in case, 5 lb. 14 oz.; legs for same, 3 lb. 6 oz.; sledge-meter, 8 lb.; Tables from Nautical Almanack and book of Logarithmic Tables, 1 lb. 3 oz.; 2 note books, 1 lb. 6 oz.; angle-books, 5 oz.; map-tube, 10 oz.; maps, 6.5 oz.; pencils, 1.5 oz.; dividers and rubber, 1.5 oz.; protractor and set-square, 0.5 oz.; prismatic compass and clinometer, 8.5 oz.; sun-compass (Bage's), 1.5 oz. . . . . . . — 22 0

Other Instruments: Prism binoculars, 12 powers, 1 lb. 13.5 oz.; hypsometer, 2 lb. 1 oz.; 2 ordinary and 2 small minimum thermometers, 10 oz.; specimen labels, 1 oz. . — 4 9.5

Sporting items: 22-bore rifle, with cover and cleaner, 3 lb. 3.7 oz.; ammunition, 1 lb. 0.5 oz.; sheath knife, 5.5 oz.; sharpening stone, 1.5 oz.; fishing line and hooks, 3.5 oz. . . . . — 4 14.7

Waterproof Clothes-bag and Contents: Waterproof bag, 4 lb. 8 oz.; 9 pairs of finnesko stuffed with sennaegrass, 21 lb.; extra sennaegrass, 3 lb.; 3 private kit-bags containing spare clothing, etc., 39 lb.; 4 extra rolls of lamp wick for lashings, 1 lb. 3.5 oz. . . . . . — 64 3.5

Odd Gear: Pick, 4 lb. 5 oz.; 2 spades, 8 lb. 4 oz.; ice-axe, 2 lb. 4 oz.; alpine rope (20 metres), 3 lb.; skis (1 pair), 11 lb.; ski-stick, 1 lb. 1 oz.; ski-boots (2 pairs),

	lb.	oz.
6 lb.; attachable crampons for the same, 4 lb.; finnesko-crampons (3 pairs), 9 lb.; 3 man-harnesses, 6 lb. 8 oz.; man-hauling tow-rope, 1 lb. 1 oz.; flags, 9.5 oz.; a water-proof bag to hold oddments, 4 lb. 8 oz. . . .	61	8.5
Beacons: A depot-flag and bamboo pole, 5 lb.; a special metal depot-beacon, mast, flag and stays, 16 lb.; 2 damp-proof tins for depositing records at depots, 7.5 oz. .	21	7.5
Fuel: Kerosene, 6 gallons in one-gallon tins	60	0
Man Food: 9 weeks' supplies for 3 men on the ration scale; also 25 lb. weight of special foods—"perks" .	475	0
Dog Food: Dried seal meat, blubber and pemmican, also the weight of the tin and bag-containers . . .	700	0
Total	1723	11.3

Madigan's and Stillwell's parties broke trail to the east on the morning of the 17th, while we were still attending to the sledges and dogs preparatory to departure. It was decided that Gadget, a rather miserable animal, who had shown herself useless as a puller thus far, should be killed, The following dogs then remained: Basilisk, Shackleton. Ginger Bitch, Franklin, John Bull, Mary, Haldane, Pavlova, Fusilier, Jappy, Ginger, George, Johnson, Castor, Betli, and Blizzard.

We then went in pursuit of the other six men over a surface of rough sastrugi. The dogs, who were in fine fettle, barking with joy, rushed the sledges along, making frantic efforts to catch up to the parties ahead, who showed as black specks across the white undulating plain.

At noon all lunched together, after which we parted, shaking hands warmly all round and interchanging the sledgers' "Good luck!" Our dogs drew away rapidly to the east, travelling on a slight down grade; the other two parties with their man-hauled sledges following in the same direction.

The surface was splendid and the weather conditions were ideal. The pace, if anything, was too rapid, for capsizes, notwithstanding our utmost endeavours to avoid them, were apt to occur in racing over high sastrugi. Any doubts as to the capability of the dogs to pull the loads were dispelled;

in fact, on this and on many occasions when the sledges were running easily, two of us were able to ride, while the third broke trail ahead. In sledging with dogs over wide, monotonous wastes without tracks or landmarks, especially in wind and drift, it is necessary to have a fore-runner, that is somebody to go ahead for the dogs to follow. We each took turns as fore-runner changing over at intervals of about an hour.

If the weather is reasonably good and food is ample, the dogs enjoy the work. Their desire to pull is doubtless inborn, implanted in a long line of ancestors who have faithfully served the Esquimaux. We found that they were glad to get their harnesses on and to be led away to the sledge. Indeed, it was often a case of the dog leading the man, for, as soon as the harness was in place, the impatient animal strained to drag whatever might be attached to the other end of the rope. Before harnessing up a team of dogs therefore, it was necessary to anchor the sledge firmly, otherwise in their ardour they would make off with it before everything was ready.

There can be no question as to the supreme value of dogs as a means of traction in the polar regions. It is only in such special circumstances as when travelling continuously over very rugged country, over heavily crevassed areas, or during unusually bad weather that man-hauling is to be preferred. Further, in an enterprise where human life is always at stake, it is only fair to put forward the consideration that the dogs represent a reserve of food in cases of extreme emergency.

At an altitude of two thousand six hundred feet we continued due eastwards until five o'clock on the afternoon of the 17th. Then arriving on the crest of a ridge which bore away in distinct outline, on our right, a fine panorama of coastal scenery was visible, including glimpses of the cliff face of the Mertz Glacier Tongue.

As the information conveyed by this view bore directly upon the programme ahead I decided to communicate to the parties following up behind my intentions which had now become more definite; and, in the meantime, we halted and treated ourselves to afternoon tea. This innovation in the ordinary routine was extended to a custom of saving a portion of the lunch ration for a "snack" at 5 p.m. on all days when the weather was moderately good. As latitude sights were required at midday and longitude shots at 5 p.m., the arrangement was very convenient, for, while one of us made tea, the other two took the observations.

About 6 p.m. the two man-hauled sledges caught up to us, our plans for the future were reviewed and the final instructions were given. We then bade the other parties adieu once more and, turning to the south—east, descended quickly down a long slope leading into the valley. The sky was overcast and it was almost impossible to see the irregularities of the surface. Only a dull-white glare met the eyes, and the first indication of a hillock was to stub one's toes against it, or of a depression to fall into it—this we came to refer to as a "snow-blind" light. We pulled up the dogs at 7.30 p.m., after covering thirteen and a quarter miles in the day.

At 9.45 a.m. on November 18 everything was ready for a fresh start. The parties behind could be seen rapidly bearing down on us under full sail, but our willing teams had soon dragged the sledges over an eminence and we saw no more of Madigan's and Stillwell's parties.

It was a lovely day; almost like a dream after so many months of harassing blizzards. To the north-west, behind us, a projecting ridge of rock—Madigan Nunatak—came into sight. From the camp of the previous-evening it had evidently been hidden from view by an undulation in the surface.

Here the direction of the sastrugi was found to be at variance with that usually pertaining, owing to a slight local swing in the direction of the prevailing wind. The irregularities in the coastline account" for this: the wind tending to flow down to sea-level by the nearest route.

A venturesome skua gull appeared at lunch time, but, fortunately for him, by the time Ninnis had unpacked the rifle he had flown away. During the afternoon a stretch of very deeply furrowed surface was encountered, the troughs between the sastrugi being commonly three feet in depth. As these ridges were hard, polished, marble-like ice we had plenty of falls and frequent capsizes with the sledge. However, as it was slightly downhill and our course lay almost directly across them, the pace did not suffer and we were able to move along at a jog-trot. The sledge-meter suffered, and to save it from further destruction, it had to be temporarily thrown out of action and taken on board.

At 5.30 p.m. a dark object rose above the snowy skyline on the right. We changed course so as to approach it, and pressed on eager and excited. At nine o'clock it resolved itself into the summit of an imposing peak rising from the depths of a deep glacier valley ahead. The name, Aurora Peak, applied to it by Madigan's party, was subsequently adopted for this prominent landmark, which was to remain in view for several days to come.

All were ready to be on the move at 8.45 a.m. on November 19. While Mertz and Ninnis built a cairn of snow, I wrote a note to be left on it in a tin, containing instructions to Stillwell in case he should happen on the locality.

The weather was good and the temperatures were high, ranging at this time (one month from midsummer) between zero and 18° F. When we camped for lunch the air was quite calm and the sun's rays proved extremely warm.

The surface became softer and smoother as the afternoon lengthened until Mertz was tempted to put on his skis. On account of their doubtful value under the Adelie Land conditions we had not felt inclined to load ourselves up with the extra weight of skis. However, as Mertz was exceptionally expert with them, it had been agreed that one pair should be included in the equipment. On occasions such as the present when the surface was suitable, Mertz would don his skis and relieve Ninnis and myself in the van.

Owing to the steeper down grade, the sledges were now commencing to run more freely and improvised brakes were tried, all of which were ineffectual in restraining the dogs. The pace became so hot that a small obstacle would capsize the sledge, causing it to roll over and over down the slope. The dogs, frantically pulling in various directions to keep ahead of the load, became hopelessly entangled in their traces and were dragged along unresistingly until the sledge stopped of its own accord or was arrested by one of us. At length, most of the dogs were allowed to run loose, and, with a man holding on behind and a couple of dogs pulling ahead, the loads were piloted down quite a steep slope for several miles.

The evening camp was situated immediately above the last and steepest fall of a tributary valley which enters the main depression of the Mertz Glacier at the foot of the Aurora Peak. Above us to the west stood a line of riven ice bluffs and behind our track, clearly defined, could be traced with the eye winding back up the valley, carefully avoiding crevassed areas on either hand.

Ninnis developed a touch of snow-blindness which, however, rapidly improved under treatment. The stock cure for this very irritating and painful affliction is to place tiny tabloids of zinc sulphate and cocaine hydrochloride under the eyelids where they quickly dissolve in the tears, alleviating the smarting, gritty sensation. This operation is usually effected when retiring to the sleeping-bag, then the sufferer has an opportunity of keeping his eyes closed for some hours. In acute cases the eyes are bandaged. In certain lights, unless coloured glasses are worn, one is sure to be attacked more or less severely. Unfortunately, the wearing of glass before the eyes is sometimes impracticable on account of the moisture from the breath covering it with an icy film or owing to snow, driven by the wind, clogging and obscuring the view. For such contingencies slits of various shapes are cut in discs of wood or other opaque substance which take the place of the glass in ordinary goggles. The amount of light reaching the eye can thus be immensely reduced, still admitting of moderately clear vision.

The morning of the 20th broke with wind and drift which persisted until after noon. Already everything had been packed up, but, as there was a steep fall in front and crevasses close by, we decided not to start until there was a clear outlook.

When at last a move was possible, it was clear that the descent ahead was altogether too steep to negotiate with the dogs harnessed to the sledges. So they were left tethered while we lowered the sledges one by one. Lengths of rope were coiled around to act as brakes and by exercising other ingenuities also, we were able to get them down in safety. This occupied several hours, then came the dogs who were most impatient.

The descent brought us almost to the bed of the main body of the Mertz Glacier. Rapid travelling now commenced over a perfectly smooth, gently sloping surface. Mertz donned his skis and shot ahead. Our column of dogs and sledges followed quickly in his trail.

Having made several readjustments during preceding days we had now settled down to a definite order of march. Behind the forerunner came the first team of dogs dragging two sledges which were joined together by a short length of rope. Bringing up the rear were the rest of the dogs harnessed to the third sledge. Each team pulled approximately equal weights; the front load being divided between two sledges. The rear sledge, owing to its heavy load, was severely taxed but, in a corresponding degree, relieved the wear and tear on the other sledges which were expected to be still in good condition in the later stages of the journey, by which time we had planned to have abandoned the worn one. Except when taking my turn ahead, 1 looked after the leading team; Ninnis or Mertz, as the case might be, driving the one behind.

Aurora Peak which rose above us to a height of about seventeen hundred feet was skirted on its south-west side and we emerged into the wide depression of the Mertz Glacier. Far ahead to the east the dim outline of uprising ice slopes was visible, though at the time we could not be certain as to their precise nature.

It was all smooth travelling that afternoon and over such a surface we expected to cover a long distance before halting for the day. Blizzard and Ginger Bitch were out of harness trotting alongside with their brushes in the air. The former had injured one of her paws and Ginger Bitch was allowed to go free because she was daily expected to give birth to pups. As she was such a good sledge dog we could not have afforded to leave her behind at the Hut, and she actually turned out the best puller and strongest of the pack.

Suddenly without any warning the leading dogs of my team dropped out of sight, swinging on their harness ropes in a crevasse. The next moment I realized that the sledges were on a bridge covering a crevasse, twenty-five feet wide, the dogs having broken through on one edge. We spent some anxious moments before they were all hauled to the daylight and the sledges rested on solid ground.

There were other crevasses about and almost immediately afterwards Ginger Bitch and Blizzard had broken through into a fissure and were frantically struggling to maintain their hold on the edge. They were speedily rescued; following which, Ginger gave birth to the first of a large litter of pups. After this second adventure and discovering traces of wide crevasses on every hand we decided to camp.

The next morning opened with a chill wind blowing drift-snow down the glacier bed. Travelling was rather miserable, especially as crevasses lurked beneath the crust, some of them gaping wide open.

Toward noon the light improved and a nunatak was observed rising from the glacier fifteen miles or more away to the south—this came to be called the Correll Nunatak. Ahead, there was a glittering line of broken ice stretching directly across our path.

As we proceeded across a fairly level plain of hard snow, immense cauldrons, ensconced in big mounds to resemble small craters, were passed at intervals. These were observed to be associated with old crevasses where the wind, striking the gaping mouth of an abyss, was caused to eddy in some special way.

The crust of compact snow dwindled and the ice began to show up, bringing more crevasses to light. Occasionally some of the dogs broke through, but without mishap.

Camp was pitched for lunch in the vicinity of many gaping holes leading down into darkness, places where the bridges over large crevasses had fallen. Mertz prepared the lunch and Ninnis and I went to photograph a blue abyss near by. Returning, we diverged on reaching the back of the tent, he passing round on one side and I on the other. The next instant I heard a bang on the ice and, swinging round, could see nothing of my companion but his head and arms.

He had broken through the lid of a crevasse fifteen feet wide and was hanging on to its edge close to where the camera lay damaged on the ice. After hauling him out I investigated the fissure and found nought but black space below; a close shave for Ninnis.

As the tent was discovered to encroach partly on the same crevasse, it may be imagined that we did not dally long over the meal.

In the afternoon the weather cleared but, as if to offset this, the broken surface became hopelessly shattered and tossed about. The region was one of the sérac where the glacier was puckered up, folded and crushed. After several repulses in what had seemed to be promising directions, we were finally forced to camp, having ten miles to our credit.

Whilst Mertz fed the dogs and prepared hoosh, Ninnis and I roped up and went off to search for a passage.

All around, the glacier was pressed up into great folds, two hundred feet in height and between one-quarter and a third of a mile from crest to crest. The ridges of the folds were either domes or open rifts partly choked with snow. Precipitous ice-falls and deep cauldrons were encountered everywhere. To the north the glacier was observed to flatten out; to the south it was more rugged.

In this chaos we wandered for some miles, until what appeared to be a favourable line of advance had been discovered for the march on the following day.

The first three miles, on the 22nd, were over a piece of very dangerous country, after which the prospect improved and we came to the border of a level plain.

There Mertz slipped on his skis, went ahead and kept a good pace. Although the sky had become overcast and snow fell fitfully, progress was rapid towards the rising slopes of the land on the eastern side of the glacier. Over the last three miles of the day's journey the surface was raised in large irregular, beehive-shaped masses and crossed by wide fissures. Into one of these fissures, bridged by snow, Ninnis's sledge fell, but fortunately jammed itself just below the surface. As it was, we had a long job getting it up again, first having to unpack the sledge until it was light enough to be easily manipulated. Despite the delay, the day's run was sixteen and a half miles.

At 8 p.m. on the 23rd everything was in readiness for a fresh start. Moderate wind and drift descended from the hills. There were yet three miles of hidden perils to be passed. With the object of making the advance less dangerous, various devices were employed.

First of all the hindermost of the sledges was secured by a length of rope to the rear of number two; thus all three were linked together. This arrangement had to be abandoned because the dogs of Ninnis's team persisted in entangling themselves and working independently of the dogs in front. Then we tried with all the sledges joined together and with all the dogs pulling in front. The procession was then so long that it was quite unmanageable on account of the tortuous nature of our track through the labyrinth. In the long run, it was decided that the original method was the best, provided that special precautions were taken over the more hazardous crossings.

On arriving at a crevasse the man in advance selected the best crossing, testing it with a ski-stick. The sledges were then brought up to the spot and one of us went over the snow bridge and took up a position on the other side, sufficiently far away to allow the first team to cross to him and to clear the crevasse. Then the second team was piloted to safety before any further move forward was attempted.

This precaution was very necessary, for otherwise the dogs in the rear would make a course direct for wherever the front dogs happened to be, cutting across corners and most probably dragging their sledge sideways into a crevasse; the likeliest way to lose it altogether.

Proceeding that morning the dogs broke through the snow bridges on a number of occasions, but only once were matters serious, when Ninnis's sledge, doubtless on account of its extra weight, again went through and was securely jammed in a crevasse just below the surface.

On this occasion we were in a serious predicament, for the sledge was in such a position that an unskilful movement would have sent it hurtling into the chasm below. So the unpacking of the load was a tedious and delicate operation. The freight consisted chiefly of large, soldered tins, packed tightly with dried seal meat. Each of these weighed about ninety pounds and all were most securely roped to the sledge. Eventually the sledge was got up and reloaded without the loss of a single tin, and once more we breathed freely.

From the bed of the glacier on its eastern side, a course upwards to the plateau was chosen by way of a shallow valley fortunately almost free of crevasses. We threw in our weight, hauling with the dogs and had a long, steep drag over furrowed névé, pitching the tent after a run of twelve miles.

On waking up on November 24 I found that my watch had stopped. I had been so tired on the previous evening that I had fallen asleep without remembering to wind it. The penalty of this accident was paid in my being forced to take an extra set of observations in order to start the watch again at correct time relative to the Hut.

Besides the observations for position, necessary for navigation, sets of angles were taken from time to time to fix the positions of objects of interest appearing within the field of view, while the magnetic variation was obtained at intervals. In this work Ninnis always assisted me. Mertz boiled the hypsometer when necessary to ascertain our elevation above sea-level. The meteorological conditions were carefully noted several times each day for future comparison with those of other parties and of winter quarters.

The day's work on November 24 brought us high up on the slopes. Away to the north-west, Aurora Peak was still visible, standing up like a mighty beacon pointing the way back to the Hut. Below lay the Mertz Glacier extending out to sea on a floating tongue beyond the horizon. Inland, some twenty miles to the south-west, the Mertz Glacier mounted up in seamed and riven "cataracts" to a smooth, broad and shallow groove which indented the ice-cap for many miles beyond. Ahead, on our south-east course, the ground still rose, but to the north-east the ice-sheet fell away in long wide valleys, along which, on the far horizon, what we took to be icebergs occasionally came into view, reminding us that the sea existed in that direction.

The tent was raised at 10 p.m. in a forty-mile wind with light drift; temperature 10° F. The altitude of this camp was two thousand three hundred and fifty feet.

One of the worst features of drift overnight is that sledges and dogs become buried in snow and have to be dug out in the morning. Thus on the 25th, on account of such delay, it was 10 a.m. before we got away. The march that day was across endless fields of sastrugi, in face of a strong wind and flying snow.

The dogs detested the wind, and with their heads so near the ground they must have found the incessant stream of thick drift most irritating. The snow became caked over their eyes so that every few minutes they had to scrape it away with their paws or rub their faces on the ground.

We stopped at 6 p.m. after a wearing day, but had the satisfaction of having covered sixteen miles.

November 26 broke overcast. The wind was still strong and the light bad for travelling. Nevertheless we set out at 10 a.m. through falling snow.

As the day progressed the wind subsided and the surface commenced to slope gradually to the east. The light was diffused uniformly over the irregularities of snow and ice so that depressions only a few feet away were invisible. Black objects, on the other hand, stood out with startling distinctness, and our attention was soon arrested by a hazy, dark patch which appeared in front. At first there was much doubt as to its nature, but it was soon clear that it must be a patch of rocks, apparently situated at a considerable distance. The rocky exposure was subsequently found to be sixty miles away (Organ Pipe Cliffs, near Cape Blake).

Presently our course ended abruptly at the edge of a precipitous crevassed fall. We skirted round this for a while, but were ultimately forced to camp owing to the uncertainty of the light.

At 11 p.m. the sky cleared and a better idea could be gained of what lay ahead. In a line between our elevated position and the distant rocky outcrop far away to the east, the ice fell in a steep descent to a broad valley, undulating and in places traversed by torn masses of sérac-ice. After examining the prospect carefully with a view to selecting a track for the journey next day, we finally resolved to pass to the south of a large ice-capped island—Dixson Island—which was only about ten miles to the north-east. The immense glacier flowing down this valley and pushing north-ward to the sea was subsequently named the Ninnis Glacier.

The next morning, the 27th, Mertz and I roped up, reconnoitred for a while and returned to the sledges. We then spent several hours in advancing a mile over badly broken ground, arriving at a slope covered with sastrugi and descending steeply for one thousand feet into the bed of the glacier.

In order the more safely to negotiate this, the dogs were all let loose, excepting two in each sledge. Even then the sledges were often uncontrollable, rolling over and over many times before the bottom was reached.

When the dogs were reharnessed it was found that Betli was missing and was not to be seen when we scanned the slopes in our rear with binoculars. It was expected that unless she had fallen into a crevasse she would turn up at the camp that night. However, she did not appear, and we saw no more of her. An end had already been put to two of the dogs, Jappy and Fusilier, as neither was of any use as a puller. Blizzard, who had been always a great favourite with us, had to be shot next day.

Having accomplished the descent, our path lay over a snow-covered ice-sheet rising and falling in a succession of billows two hundred and fifty feet in height. There it is slow-moving ice, forming a western margin of the Ninnis Glacier which had become buckled by compression against Dixson Island. Still, the "caravan" made considerable progress, ending with a day's journey of sixteen miles.

During the small hours of November 28 the wind rose to a velocity of sixty miles per hour, but gradually diminished to a twenty-mile breeze as the day advanced. Light snow fell from a sky which was densely clouded.

We still pursued a devious track amid the rolling waves of the glacier, encountering beds of soft snow through which the sledges moved but slowly. By 6 p.m. pinnacles and hummocks stood around on every side, and the light was inadequate for safely dodging crevasses. We had to camp and be satisfied with seven miles "to the good." By this time the dogs had used up all their superfluous fat and grew noticeably ravenous. In the evening, before they were properly tethered, Shackleton seized a one-week provision bag, ripped it open and ate a block of butter weighing more than two and a half pounds. This was a sorely-felt loss to us, as butter was held in high esteem.

The sun was shining brightly next day and it was at once evident that we were in a zone of tumbled and disrupted ice. For many hours a way was won through a mighty turmoil of sérac and over innumerable crevasses. Just before lunch my two sledges were nearly lost through the dogs swinging sharply to one side before the second sledge had cleared a rather rotten snow bridge. I was up with the dogs at the time, and the first intimation of an accident was observing the dogs and front sledge being dragged backwards; the rear sledge was hanging vertically in a crevasse. Exerting all my strength I held back the front sledge, and in a few moments was joined by Ninnis and Mertz, who soon drove a pick and ice-axe down between the runners and ran out an anchoring rope.

It was a ticklish business recovering the sledge. It could not be lifted vertically as its bow was caught in a V-shaped offshoot from the main fissure. To add to our troubles the ground all about the place was precarious and unsafe.

After some unsuccessful efforts to salve it, Ninnis and Mertz lowered me down to where a rope could be attached to the tail end of the sledge. The bow-rope and tail-rope were then manipulated alternately, until the bow of the sledge was manœuvred slowly through the gaping hole in the snow lid and finally its whole length was hoisted into safety. No more remarkable test of the efficiency of the sledge straps and the compactness of the load could have been made.

After lunch Mertz ascended a high ridge and was able to trace out a route which conducted us in a few hours to a better surface.

We were now at an elevation of from four hundred to five hundred feet above sea-level. An unpleasant wind which descended the glacier catching us on the beam increased during the afternoon. After a run of ten and one-third miles camp was pitched in a rising blizzard.

The wind blew up to seventy miles an hour during the night, but eased in strength early in the morning. At 10 a.m. we tried to make a start, but the dogs refused to face the drift. On the wind falling off to a succession of gusts in the afternoon, it was once more possible to travel, and we set out.

Dense drift was still to be seen pouring over the highlands, to the south-east. Across the glacier, on every hand, revolving columns of snow "stalked about" in their wayward courses.

The sledges ran through a sea of crevassed, blue ice, over ridges and past open chasms, necessitating much reconnoitring to discover a passable track. Seven miles brought us to the foot of the rising land slopes on the eastern border of the wide depression occupied by the Ninnis Glacier. There we pitched camp.

The first day of December was still and hot, with brilliant sunshine. The shade temperature reached 34° F. and the snow became so sticky that it was as much as we and the dogs could do to move the sledges up the slopes. As the evening lengthened and the sun sank lower the surface froze hard and our toil was lightened. At midnight we reached an altitude of nine hundred feet.

December 2 was another warm, bright day. The surface was atrociously bad; hard, marble-like or blue ice carved into sharp sastrugi which were never less than two feet high and in many instances three feet six inches from crest to trough. The dogs were not able to exert a united pull for, as they scrambled over the ridges, there were never more than half of them in action at a time. So we went on for hours tugging at the sledges which invariably capsized every few moments.

Once more we were at a comparatively high altitude and a fine view presented itself to the north. One could look back to the mainland slopes descending on the far western side of the Ninnis Glacier. Then the glacier, tumultuous and broken, was seen to extend far out into the ice-strewn sea and, sweeping round to the north-east, the eye ranged over a great expanse of floe dotted with bergs. Some twenty miles or more to the east there was a precipitous coast-line of dark rock which, for a while, we thought of visiting. But then it seemed likely that Madigan's party would reach as far east, so we set our faces once more to the rising plateau in the south-east.

At midnight the sun was peering over the southern skyline, and we halted at an elevation of one thousand five hundred and fifty feet, having covered eight and a half miles in the day. The temperature was 5° F.

We were not long on the way on December 3 before the sky became overcast and light snow fell. The rising gradient was becoming flatter. Camp was pitched at 11 p.m. after eleven and two-third miles.

December 4 was another day of bad light, but the surface improved and good headway was made on an easterly course at an elevation of between two thousand and two thousand eight hundred feet. The crevasses that had haunted the march on preceding days were practically past, allowing of a good run of fifteen miles.

December 5 was a disappointing day; overcast, snowing and a gale of wind from the east-south-east. However, we plugged on blindly into it until 7.30 p.m. and then camped, having done eleven and a half miles.

During the three days that followed a dense blizzard raged, the wind reaching seventy miles per hour. Snow descended in a deluge and there was nothing to do but lie in our bags and think out plans for the future. Each morning Ninnis and Mertz took it in turns to go out and feed their charges, who were snugly buried in the deep snow.

One day in the sleeping-bag does not come amiss after long marches, but three days on end is enough to bore anyone thoroughly.

Ninnis was not so badly off with a volume of Thackeray, but already, long ago, Mertz had come to the end of his particular literary diversion, a small edition of "Sherlock Holmes," and he contented himself with reciting passages from memory for our mutual benefit. It should be added that the very strict regulations limiting the weights allowable on sledging journeys reduce such luxuries as reading matter to the most meagre proportions.

Just at this time both Ninnis and myself were suffering from troublesome inflammations; in his case it affected two fingers, while I happened to have it in the face. This was evidently an expression of fatigue as the march up to this point, though not of long duration, had been strenuous, having continued without a break in all weathers and at times over well-nigh impassable surfaces. Under the influence of the rest while thus weather-bound my trouble subsided, but Ninnis's case was more obstinate.

Confined to the tent, we took the opportunity to reduce the food ration. This caused us to have more than ordinarily vivid dreams. I happened to be awake one night when Ninnis was sledging in imagination, vociferously shouting to the dogs.

Despite considerable wind and drift we got away at 8 a.m. on December 9. The sky was overcast and there was nothing to be seen except a soft carpet of newly fallen snow into which we sank half-way to the knees. The sledges ran deeply and heavily so that the dogs had to be assisted. Ahead, Mertz glided along triumphant on his skis, the value of which was never more apparent.

During the day a snow-petrel circled above us for a while and then returned to the north.

The course was due east at an elevation of two thousand three hundred feet, and the total distance we threw behind during the day was sixteen and a half miles.

On the 10th light wind and low drift were the order of things. Our spirits rose when the sky cleared and a slight down grade commenced.

During the morning, Ninnis was the first to catch sight of what appeared to be small ice-capped islets fringing the coast to the north, but the distance was too great for us to be sure of their exact nature. Out near the verge of the horizon a tract of ice-covered sea with scattered bergs could be seen.

Next day more features were distinguishable. The coast was seen to run in a north-easterly direction as a long penin- sula ending in a sharp cape which we named Cape Freshfield.

The north appeared to be filled with frozen sea, though we could not be certain that it was not dense pack-ice. Little did we know that Madigan's party, about a week later, would be in that vicinity, marching over the frozen sea towards Cape Freshfield.

At 10 p.m. on the 11th, at an altitude of one thousand eight hundred feet, the highland we were traversing fell away rapidly in front of us and an ice-covered sea opened up ahead. The coast near by took a turn to the south and then ran away in an unbroken line to the east. There the ice-cap descended in steep broken slopes to the sea terminating in a high cliff, off the seaward face of which large, tabular bergs were grouped within environing floe.

Throughout December 12 a somewhat irregular course was made to the south-east and south with a view to skirting the appalling shattered slopes ahead.

For some days Ninnis, without complaining, had been enduring a throbbing pain in his inflamed fingers, so bad indeed that he had scarcely slept. Nevertheless, he had continued to do his share of the work and bore up splendidly under the ordeal. On several occasions I had waked up at night to find him sitting up in his sleeping-bag, puffing away at a pipe or reading. After breakfast on the 13th I lanced one of his offending fingers, and during the day he had much relief.

While Ninnis rested before we made a start, Mertz and I re-arranged the sledges and their loads. A third sledge was no longer necessary, so the rear one which by now was much damaged, was discarded and all the gear was divided between the other two sledges in nearly equal amounts. When the work was completed, the rear sledge carried an extra weight of fifty pounds. As, however, food for both men and dogs were to be drawn from it, this super-added load would soon diminish.

After covering several miles of an undulating surface in the forenoon, we commenced ascending a long steep slope well sprinkled with dangerous crevasses. Some of the latter were as much as one hundred feet in width, but, as is generally the case with such wide fissures, these were well packed with snow. At times great gaping holes were passed which kept us mindful of the dangers lurking elsewhere beneath the snowy cover.

From the leeward edge of some of the larger crevasses, high ramps of névé with bluff faces on the windward side stood up like monoliths, reaching twenty-five feet in maximum height. By evening the crest of the slope was reached and an undulating surface of hard snow and pie-crust, apparently free from crevasses, lay ahead.

Presently a dull booming sound like the noise of far-distant cannon was heard. This was evidently connected with the subsidence of large areas of the surface crust disturbed by our passage.

The sun appeared late in the day and, as it was almost calm, the last few hours of marching were very pleasant. At midnight we camped at an altitude of one thousand nine hundred feet, an elevation of about one thousand feet above that of the preceding camp.

A light east-south-east wind was blowing as the sledges started away eastward on the morning of December 14. The weather was sunny and the temperature registered 21° F. Ninnis had slept well and was feeling much relieved.

We were a happy party that morning as we revelled in the sunshine and laid plans for a final dash eastwards before turning our faces homewards.

Mertz who was well in the lead, the conditions being both suitable and agreeable for employment of skis, was in high spirits as was evident from the snatches of song wafted back from time to time. Shortly after noon while travelling thus light-heartedly, a terrible catastrophe happened.

I noticed Mertz halt for a moment and hold up his ski-stick—this was a signal that something unusual was afoot. Approaching the vicinity with the foremost sledge a few minutes later, I kept a look-out for crevasses or other explanation of his action. As a matter of fact crevasses were not expected, since we were on a smooth even surface inland from the obviously broken coastal slopes.

Failing to observe any cause for the signal, I jumped on the sledge, got out the book of tables and commenced to figure out the latitude observation taken a few minutes previously. A moment later the faint indication of a crevasse passed beneath the sledge but it had no appearance of being in any degree specially dangerous. However, as had come to be the custom I called out a warning to Ninnis. The latter, who was close behind walking along by the side of his sledge, heard the warning, for in my backward glance I noticed that he immediately swung the leading dogs so as to cross the crevasse squarely instead of diagonally as my sledge had done. I then resumed my work and dismissed the matter from my thoughts.

There was no sound from behind except a faint, plaintive whine from one of the dogs which I imagined was in reply to a touch from Ninnis's whip. I remember addressing myself to George, the laziest dog in my own team, saying, "You will be getting a little of that, too, George, if you are not careful."

When next I looked back, it was in response to the anxious gaze of Mertz who had turned round and halted in his tracks. Behind me nothing met the eye except my own sledge tracks running back in the distance. Where were Ninnis and his sledge?

I hastened back along the trail thinking that a rise in the ground obscured the view. There was no such good fortune, however, for I came to a gaping hole in the surface about eleven feet wide. The lid of the crevasse that had caused me so little thought had broken in; two sledge tracks led up to it on the far side—only one continued beyond.

Frantically waving to Mertz to bring up my sledge, upon which there was some alpine rope, I leaned over and shouted into the dark depths below. No sound came back but the moaning of a dog, caught on a shelf just visible one hundred and fifty feet below. The poor creature appeared to have a broken back, for it was attempting to sit up with the front part of its body, while the hinder portion lay limp. Another dog lay motionless by its side. Close by was what appeared in the gloom to be the remains of the tent and a canvas food-tank containing a fortnight's supply.

We broke back the edge of the hard snow lid and, secured by a rope, took turns leaning over, calling into the darkness in the hope that our companion might be still alive. For

Greenland sledging dogs—"Basilisk" and "Ginger"—
at Winter Quarters, Cape Denison (*Mertz*)

Madigan paying attention to the wind recording instrument
at the Cape Denison Station (*Hurley*)

Picking ice in the wind (*Hurley*)

The S.Y. *Aurora*—photograph taken when off
Queen Mary Land (*Hurley*)

"Blizzard" (*Hurley*)

Steaming along the wall of the Mertz glacier tongue

A dredge-haul of life from the floor of the ocean,
dumped on the deck

Shovelling ice from the *Aurora*'s deck during a lull
in a blizzard (*Hurley*)

Landing equipment at the Boat Harbour (*Hurley*)

Mertz emerging from Aladdin's cave (*Hurley*)

An Adelie Penguin couple demonstrating at the nest (*Hurley*)

Rorquals (*Hurley*)

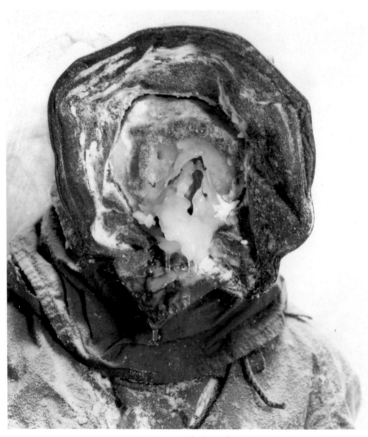

An ice mask (*Hurley*)

Blubbering an elephant (*Hamilton*)

Adelie penguins, Cape Denison (*Hurley*)

Building the workshop on the living hut (*Hurley*)

The fire brigade in action after the Main Base hut
caught alight (*Hurley*)

Interior of the hangar with the entrance blocked
by drift snow (*Hurley*)

Close looking at the sledging rations ready for the trek.
The supply would probably be for three men
for three months (*Hurley*)

Barber scene in hut—Hurley trims Hunter's beard (*Hurley*)

Peering into an abyss where the lid of a crevasse has collapsed (*Watson*)

Enjoying a rest on a sledging trip (*Watson*)

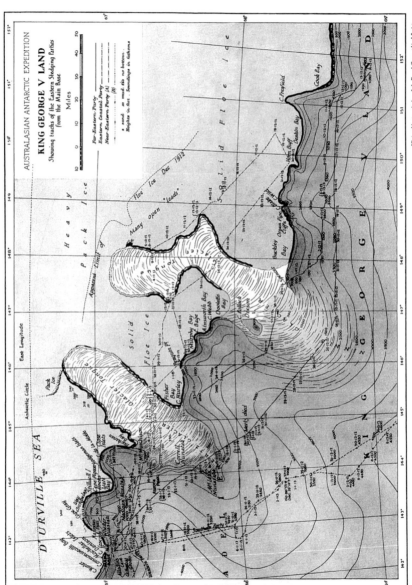

AUSTRALASIAN ANTARCTIC EXPEDITION

KING GEORGE V LAND

Showing tracks of the Eastern Sledging Parties
from the Main Base

Miles

Far-Eastern Party
Eastern Coastal Party
Near-Eastern Party (A)
Near-Eastern Party (B)

s sand: as mud: bio no bottom:
Brighter in feet. Soundings in fathoms.

three hours we called unceasingly but no answering sound came back. The dog had ceased to moan and lay without a movement. A chill draught rose out of the abyss. We felt that there was no hope.

It was difficult to realize that Ninnis, who was a young giant in build, so jovial and so real but a few minutes before, should thus have vanished without even a sound. It seemed so incredible that we half expected, on turning round, to find him standing there.

Why had the first sledge escaped? It seemed that I had been fortunate, as my sledge had crossed diagonally, with a greater chance of breaking the lid. The sledges were within thirty pounds of the same weight. The explanation appeared to be that Ninnis had walked by the side of his sledge, whereas I had crossed it sitting on the sledge. The whole weight of a man's body bearing on his foot is a formidable load, and no doubt was sufficient to smash the arch of the roof.

By means of a fishing line we ascertained that it was one hundred and fifty feet sheer to the ledge upon which the remains were seen; on either side the crevasse descended into blackness. It seemed so very far down there and the dogs looked so small that we got out the field-glass to complete the scrutiny of the depths.

All our available rope was tied together but the total length was insufficient to reach the ledge, and any idea of going below to investigate and to secure some of the food had to be abandoned.

Stunned by the unexpectedness of it all and having exhausted the few appliances we carried for such a contingency, we felt hopeless. In such moments action is the only tolerable thing, and if there had been any expedient however hazardous which might have been taken, we should have taken all and more than all the risk.

Later in the afternoon Mertz and I went on to a higher point in order to obtain a better view of our surroundings and to see if anything helpful lay ahead. In that direction, however, the prospect of reaching the sea, where lay chances of obtaining seal and penguin meat, was hopeless on account of the appalling manner in which the coastal slopes were shattered. At a point two thousand four hundred feet above sea-level and three hundred and fifteen and three-quarter miles eastward from the Hut, a complete set of observations was taken.

We returned to the crevasse to consider what was to be done and prepare for the future. At regular intervals we called down into those dark depths in case our companion might not have been killed outright, and, in the meantime, have become unconscious. There was no reply.

A weight was lowered on the fishing line as far as the dog which had earlier shown some signs of life, but there was no response. All were dead, swallowed up in an instant.

When comrades tramp the road to anywhere through a lonely blizzard-ridden land in hunger, want and weariness the interests, ties and fates of each are interwoven in a wondrous fabric of friendship and affection. The shock of Ninnis's death struck home and deeply stirred us.

Associated with the Expedition from its earliest stages he had been one of the most ardent members, keen and thorough to a degree, never sparing himself when the enterprise was at stake. Throughout the year at Cape Denison one and all of us had developed a real admiration for Ninnis, and the sadness of this catastrophe was to be heartfelt by everyone. He was a fine fellow and a born soldier—and the end:

> "Life—give me life until the end,
>   That at the very top of being,
>   The battle spirit shouting in my blood,
>   Out of every reddest hell of the fight
>   I may be snatched and flung
>   Into the everlasting lull,
>   The Immortal, Incommunicable Dream."

At 9 p.m. we stood by the side of the crevasse and I read the burial service. Then Mertz shook me by the hand with a short "Thank you!" and we turned away to harness up the dogs.

CHAPTER XIII

TOIL AND TRIBULATION

"But to fight and to fight when hope's out of sight—
Why, that's the best game of them all."—SERVICE.

THE homeward track! A few days ago—only a few hours ago—our hearts had beaten hopefully at the prospect and there was no hint of this, the overwhelming tragedy. Our companion, comrade, chum, in a woeful instant, buried in the bowels of the awful glacier. We tried to drive the nightmare from our thoughts; we strove to forget it in the necessity of work, but we knew that the truth would assuredly enter our souls even more poignantly in the dismal days to come. It was to be a fight with Death and the great Providence would decide the issue.

On the outward journey we had left no depots of provisions en route, for it was our bad fortune to meet such impossible country that we had decided to make a circuit on our return to winter quarters sufficiently far inland to avoid the coastal crevassed zones. As a matter of fact, on the very day of the calamity, preparations had been made to cache most of the food within twenty-four hours, as during the last few days of the journey we were to make a dash to a "farthest east" point. In this wise by the way, we had expected to link up with the new land some two years previously sighted by members of the Scott Expedition on board the *Terra Nova* and by them named Oates Land. Such had been the plans, and now we were ranged against unexpected odds.

With regard to the dogs, there were but six very miserable ones left. The best animals had been drafted into the rear team, as it was expected that if an accident were to happen through the collapse of a crevasse lid the first sledge would in all probability be the sufferer. For the same reason most of the food and other indispensable articles had been carried on the rear sledge.

All the dogs which had perished were big and powerful; Basilisk, Ginger Bitch, Shackleton, Castor, Franklin and John Bull. We had fully anticipated that those at least would come back alive, at the expense of the six dogs in poorer condition which we grouped to form the team of the leading sledge.

The whole of the dog food had been lost and there remained but a bare one and a half week's man-food. In addition, the tent with its floor-cloth and poles, the spade, ice-axe, mugs and spoons, and Mertz's burberry trousers were numbered among the missing. Fortunately the spare tent-cover happened to have been on the first sledge and needed only some sort of a frame over which to spread it. The best substitute to replace Mertz's burberry trousers was a pair of thick woollen under-trousers which happened to be amongst the spare clothing. Thus handicapped with the loss of these articles our return to the Hut, a journey of over three hundred miles, was made so much more difficult.

We had carefully sorted over what gear remained and discarded everything unnecessary so as to reduce the weight of the load. All we could afford ourselves for dinner was a thin soup made by boiling up all the empty food bags prepar-atory to throwing them away. The product was not very sustaining, but we were glad of it to quench our thirst. There was, of course, nothing for the dogs but we tossed them some worn out fur mitts, finnesko, and several spare raw hide straps all of which they devoured.

A silent farewell!—and we started back, aiming to reach our camping ground of December 12, where several things had been discarded which should be of use in our straitened circumstances. All speed was necessary before snow should fall and obliterate the track which alone served to locate the goal; so the journey that night was a desperate affair across steeply undulating country so badly crevassed in places that even on the outward journey, when it had been negotiated methodically and at leisure, it had caused us some anxiety. Mertz donned his skis and went ahead as forerunner. The hours went by as we plodded slowly up the hills and dashed recklessly down them. One of these icy descents was seven miles long, barred from beginning to end with white scars, sunken snow lids covering crevasses, frequently only mere gutters but as often wide, depressed roads stretching away far on either hand. Mertz was on ahead shooting across patches of rough ice and névé, swerving along the brinks of crevasses, on the alert for a promising crossing which when perceived would cause him to turn like a flash and stake all in a plunge across the roof of the hidden abyss—never faltering or stumbling but ever gliding swiftly onwards in one grand sweep—a consummate master of skis.

It was an inspiration to watch him, but I had little opportunity to do so, for the dogs flew after him and I had to throw myself upon the sledge, twist my arms into the lashings and hold on for dear life. It was a wild race as we careered along, the dogs cutting across the crevasses anyhow with the one idea of catching up to the black figure whirling on ahead. We plunged on to the lids of crevasses and thundered across the sunken ways, crashed into hummocks of ice, sidled on the steep grades and frequently enough capsized and rolled over and over, dogs and sledge and myself, for yards at a stretch. Twice I was wrenched from the sledge as it shot over the brink on to old deeply sunken crevasse lids; three times, portions of the gear broke away from the sledge straps. On every such occasion it was with the greatest possible difficulty that I could secure and hold the dogs to make amends, for the poor animals were almost frenzied with the mad speed, the jarring and rattle of the cooker on the sledge. After all, it was only the pace that saved us. Many of these crevasses were dangerous enough in all conscience, but we plunged across with a tense heart and a grim sense of unreality—such was the effect of the day's tragedy upon us.

At half past two in the early morning of December 15, the relics discarded at our camps of three days previous came into sight. Projecting from the snow were the remains of the damaged sledge and the broken spade. Soon afterwards Mertz set to work to construct a makeshift frame to support the spare tent-cover. The very unwieldy frame produced was composed of two half-lengths of sledge-runner and Mertz's two skis, all lashed together at the apex. This answered very well, though it only reached a maximum height of four feet from the ground. Inside there was just room for two one-man sleeping-bags on the floor; but, unfortunately, only one could move about at a time and neither of us could ever rise above a sitting posture. Still, it was shelter and protection from the elements without, and, with plenty of snow blocks piled around it, was wonderfully resistant to the wind.

When we retired to rest it was about five o'clock and the warmth of the sun was very pleasant as we lay in our bags. Though we had passed a very strenuous twenty-four hours since last resting, including as one item only the crossing of twenty-seven miles of dangerous country, we were in no mood to sleep. The hours went by as the events of the day passed in review—tragic and sad. As there was no retrieving the past we tried to concentrate our thoughts on the solution of the future which loomed up sinister before us. In a few hours we were to rise with plans for the homeward race finally crystallized.

It was obvious that a descent to the frozen sea would be accompanied by difficulties and dangers on account of the heavily crevassed nature of the falling ice-sheet, delay would undoubtedly be caused and our distance from the Hut would be increased. To decide definitely for the sea-ice would be to take other risks as well, since, from the altitude and distance inland at which we were placed, we could not be sure of the nature of the sheet of floe which appeared to cover the sea; we decided that in all probability at that season of the year it would be much shattered and so quite unsuitable as a travelling surface. On the other hand, there was on the sea-ice a chance of obtaining seals for food.

After due consideration we decided to follow the shorter route, returning inland over the plateau, for it was reckoned that, if the weather were reasonable, we could win through to winter quarters with the one and a half weeks' rations of man-food which still remained, provided we ate the dogs to help matters.

We were up at two o'clock in the afternoon busily engaged improvising and packing items of equipment ready for the trail. Two pannikins were produced, cut out of tins in which cartridges and matches had been packed; wooden spoons were carved out of the frame of the broken sledge. The broken spade was now gladly reclaimed and Mertz made it once more useful by the application of splints and lashings. Then the food was carefully gone over, tallied and subdivided.

George, who was in very poor condition, was killed to provide food for the other dogs and to amplify our own supply. Though some of the best meat was reserved for ourselves it was a very poor sample, chiefly sinews with a very undesirable taste. We tried frizzling it on the aluminium lid of the cooker, thinking thereby to cook it sufficiently without undue expenditure of kerosene. As there was no fat in which to fry it and none in the meat itself, this resulted in little more than scorching the surface. At that first repast on starved-dog we got little satisfaction for, prepared in this way, the meat proved so stringy as to tax our powers of mastication to their utmost. It was a happy relief when the liver appeared which, even if little else could be said in its favour, was easily chewed and demolished.

There was no breeze that afternoon and a bright sun shone in the sky making the air quite sultry in the hollow where the camp lay. We had already decided to march during the evening hours when the surface would be crisp, offering the best conditions for sledging. Camp was, therefore, not finally broken until 6 p.m. when the long and painful journey to the Hut commenced.

We plodded on hour after hour while the sun sank lower in the southern sky. For fourteen miles the way led up rising snow slopes until an elevation of two thousand five hundred feet had been reached, after that, undulating and flatter country was encountered. Though the sledge was light the dogs required helping and progress was correspondingly slow.

Soon after the sun, from skimming the southern horizon, commenced to rise upwards to the advent of a new day, the

16th, fleecy clouds formed and the sky rapidly became overcast and light snow began to fall. The snowy sky merged into the snowy land to trap us, as it seemed. There were no shadows to create contrasts; it was impossible to distinguish the detail of the surface, even that directly underfoot. So, with gaze straining forward for a hint as to direction, we stumbled onwards over unseen sastrugi.

We banished thought of food as completely as possible, knowing well that nothing of the kind could be afforded to provide a welcome break in the day's march. Our daily work in future promised to be long and tedious with no prospect of refreshment until the final halt. We would have much appreciated a drink of water at half time, but the erection of the makeshift tent in which to light the primus was such a long operation, in any but good weather, so that we had to get along as best we could without. However, that morning at about 2 a.m. the air being quite still we went so far as to melt a little snow, lighting the primus in the lee of the sledge. To the water, a few drops of primus alcohol were added which communicated to it a degree of substantiality very much appreciated at the time.

At 6 a.m. having covered a distance of twenty miles and ascended about one thousand six hundred feet we pitched camp. The dogs were thoroughly exhausted and we, ourselves, were glad enough to rest. The strain and glare of the overcast sky had visited me with an unusually bad attack of snow-blindness. I had very little sleep from the smarting of it and had to get Mertz to treat both eyes at intervals with zinc sulphate and cocaine.

Preparations for "turning in" and for "getting under way" from each camp were seriously hindered by the wretchedly limited proportions of the tent. Only one could move about at a time. Thus, although we rose before six o'clock that evening, December 16, the start was not made until 8.30 p.m., notwithstanding the fact that the meal was of the "sketchiest" character.

Ours was a mournful procession as we moved off that evening; the sky thickly clouded, snow falling, I with one eye bandaged and Johnson, whom we found too exhausted to walk, strapped on top of the load on the sledge. A snow-hush brooded over the scene. Beyond the dismal whining of Johnson, into whose body the frost was swiftly penetrating, there was scarcely a sound; only the rustle of the thick, soft snow as we pushed on, weary but full of hope.

The dogs dumbly pressed forward in their harness, forlorn but eager to follow. Their weight now told little upon the sledge, the work mainly falling upon ourselves. Mertz was tempted to try hauling on skis, but came to the conclusion that it did not pay, and thenceforth never again used them.

We were making about due west and it was a most difficult task in overcast calm weather to keep anything like a proper course. The magnetic compass was quite useless and without the sun we had to rely for direction upon the trend of the old, hard, winter sastrugi which we knew to be channelled out approximately from south to north. In the snow-blind light of an overcast day, the strain on the eyes to delineate the trend of the sastrugi would have been trying enough, but with all the surface markings blanketed in a shroud of soft, newly fallen snow, the task was rendered still more difficult and the only recourse was to feel about under the snow cover with the feet for the outline of the ridges. Under these conditions our progress degenerated into a sort of shuffling march; pushing one's finnesko-covered feet through the soft snow, sliding them along the old hard surface, ever on the alert to correct direction of march by hints from the irregularities underfoot. This was very exhausting work, so by 2 a.m. on the 17th, though only eleven miles had been covered, a halt was called.

Poor Johnson was too weak to stand up or even to eat his ration of meat, so after he had fumbled about with it and licked it for some time we decided to finish him off, as it was quite certain that he would not ever again be strong enough to march. Johnson had always been a very faithful hardworking and willing beast, with rather droll ways of his own, and we were very sorry that his end should come so soon. He could never be accused of being a handsome dog, in fact he was generally disreputable and dirty, curiously enough these latter qualities seemed reflected even in the qualities of his meat, for it was permeated with a unique and unusually disagreeable flavour. This we subsequently referred to as "Johnsonian." In the days that followed one's fortune was "in" or "out" according as, in drawing one's ration from the meat bag, one happened to miss or to light upon a relic of our faithful old Johnson.

All the dogs were thin and miserable when they reached the stage of extreme exhaustion. Their meat was tough, stringy and without a vestige of fat. For a change we sometimes chopped it up finely, mixed it with a little pemmican, and brought it all to the boil in a large pot of water. We were exceedingly hungry, and the ration went but a short way to satisfy our cravings. The daily ration was only about six ounces of ordinary sledging food making up with about eight to ten ounces of dog meat. Even in the case of this latter article we were strictly limited, for all the dogs were small in stature and so emaciated that each animal yielded very little indeed beyond skin and bones. The major part of each carcase was rationed out to the surviving dogs. They crunched the bones and ate the skin until nothing remained.

A fresh start was made at 7.30 p.m. and a wretched, trying night it proved, marching under adverse conditions without a break for twelve and a half hours. Overhead there was a dense pall of nimbus from which snow fell at intervals. None of the dogs except Ginger was equal to giving any help with the load, and Mary was so worn out that she had to be carried on the sledge. Poor Mary had been a splendid dog, but we had to put an end to her at camping time, which was at 8 a.m., after a run of eighteen and a half miles.

At 5.30 p.m. a light south-easterly wind was blowing and snow falling from a completely overcast sky. Shortly after the start was made, we began to descend slightly and arrived at a locality that had been swept by wind recently, for the surface was bare of new soft snow. The sastrugi were high and hard; over them we bumped, slipping and falling unceasingly in the uncertain light. That kind of surface could not be endured for long, so shortly after midnight we resolved to camp, intending to continue when the day had advanced further and the light become stronger.

To meet a combination of bad surface and unsuitable weather was most disappointing, but we retired to rest hopeful for improved conditions. I could not have wished for a better companion in such adversity than Mertz. He was always full of life and vigour and his good spirits helped to make those trying days pass as cheerfully as possible. Each mile ticked off by the sledgemeter we recorded by a pencil mark on the tail-board of the sledge, and in this there was a very keen interest, not only because each mile marked down meant one less between us and the Hut, but for the reason that it was agreed that the amount of the ration doled out for each day was to depend very much upon the number of miles covered. The disappointments of a bad day's work were therefore correspondingly accentuated by the scantiness of the meal to follow.

We were up again at noon that same day, December 19, and tried a few more miles in the snow-glare. Later in the afternoon the sky began to break and we picked our way with less difficulty. At 5 p.m. we camped once more to await a further clearance of the sky in order to obtain more definite bearings, for there was a strong suspicion that the trend of the sastrugi thereabouts was abnormal.

At 8 p.m. the sun shone out and we were off once more on a due westerly course, soon dropping several hundred feet crossing rough, slippery fields of high sastrugi.

In the early morning hours that followed the surface changed from marble-like névé to ice and occasional crevasses appeared. It was clear that we had arrived at the head of the Ninnis Glacier above the zone of sérac we had traversed on the outward journey. It was very satisfactory to know this, to have some tangible proof that we really were where we thought we were.

Soon after this discovery we came near losing Haldane, the big grey wolf, in a crevasse. Miserably thin from starvation the wretched dogs no longer filled their harness. As we hoisted Haldane, after he had broken into a deep sheer-walled crevasse, his harness slipped off just as he reached the top.

Fortunately I was just able to grab a fold of his skin at the same instant, otherwise many days' rations would have been lost. Haldane took to the harness once more, but soon became uncertain in his footsteps, staggered along and then tottered and fell.

Poor brutes! That was the way they all finished up; from putting little or no weight into the harness they relapsed into an uncertain "groggy" pace with a slack trace; a few miles more and they would commence to totter and stumble, soon to rise no more.

The tent was pitched at 4 a.m., thinking that a short rest would revive Haldane. Inside the tent some snow was thawed and we had a drink of water flavoured with an addition of a little primus spirit. A temperature reading showed –1° F. Outside, the hungry huskies moaned unceasingly until we could no longer bear to hear them. The tent was struck and we set off once more.

Haldane was strapped on the sledge for he was unable to walk. He had not consumed the food doled out to him, for his jaws were too weak to eat, and he had been contented to nurse the meat between his paws and lick it.

The day's march was completed at 10.30 a.m. and a further fourteen and a half miles lay behind.

Great care had to be taken in tethering the dogs at each camp, in order to keep them away from valuable articles, for they were seized with a morbid desire to gnaw everything within reach, including the straps and even the wood of the sledges. After a rest at each camp and ever as we prepared for a fresh start, they seemed momentarily to regain their old strength, for they struggled and fought to seize any scraps left on the ground, however useless or loathsome. The most repugnant refuse was greedily devoured and dog ate dog so completely that the wonder was how the sledge-load and the team came to diminish in bulk.

At 11.20 p.m. we were out again under a clear sky, but to our sorrow there was a rising wind which soon increased to thirty miles an hour. This with low flying drift and a temperature of about zero Fahrenheit was distinctly unpleasant to us in our declining condition. So I recorded that the night's march was a miserable one. There was one incident, however, which helped to relieve it, namely that Dixson Island stood out in the north for a moment, miraged up above the horizon. We felt that we had met an old friend, which means a lot in that icy desolation. After traversing eleven miles of a surface furrowed by hard, sharp sastrugi, camp was pitched at 9 a.m. There Haldane was dispatched.

At 9 p.m. that evening, December 21, the march was resumed in the face of a strong and chilly south-south-east wind accompanied by low drift. The undulating hard polished sastrugi surface, more slippery than glass, continued, resulting in repeated falls. Camp was pitched at 6.40 a.m. in a forty-mile wind with low drift. The distance marched was somewhat under thirteen miles, a poor result for the effort expended, but our strength was waning and neither the surface nor the weather was what had been hoped for at the height of summer.

After a little refreshment and before turning into the sleeping-bags sundry repairs were effected. Amongst other things Mertz re-lashed the handle of the shovel which had broken apart and I busied myself with mending the sledge-meter. The mechanism of the latter had frozen stiff, encased in ice, at our last camp and, on starting, the main axle had broken off sharp at the screw-nut on one side. There was little prospect of making a satisfactory job of it, but after a long and tedious operation, tapping at the frozen end with a mini-ature (bonza) hammer, it was sufficiently riveted-over to hold.

When we got under way that evening there was a moderate breeze blowing and light snow falling from an overcast sky. Winsome Pavlova, who had already collapsed during the march of the previous day, was in very little better condition after the rest and soon had to be hoisted on to the sledge. It was an uphill march rendered particularly heavy on account of deep fallen snow.

Suddenly gaping crevasses appeared dimly through the falling snow. There was nothing to do but camp, though it was only 4.30 a.m. and scarcely six miles had been covered. At the last camp we had reluctantly thrown away the rifle to lighten the burden and now were reduced to finishing off Pavlova with a knife—a revolting and depressing operation.

The outlook was darkening, for the days brought us more than a reasonable share of bad weather; this combined with crevassed and awkward surfaces landed us in most undesirable circumstances. Of the dogs there was only Ginger left; the pack had gone down in a way never to have been foreseen. Though little in the way of pulling had been hoped for from them, it was expected that they would at least have been able to trot along with us much further towards the Hut than actually happened. This all showed how little nutriment there can have been in the carcases of their stricken fellows. Our own experience also bore this out, for our strength was decreasing in a way that indicated that the dog-meat was more filling than nutritious. However, about this time we discovered that we could afford to be more lavish with the kerosene and in future boiled the meat and bones in the cooker with much more satisfactory results. So it came about at that camp of December 23 we treated ourselves to what we deemed a delicious soup made from some of Pavlova's bones cracked open with the spade.

Confined to camp until the weather cleared, we set to work to boil a supply of meat sufficient to last for several days. By long boiling the sinews and gristle were reduced to the consistency of jelly. The paws took longest to cook, but, treated to a lengthy stewing, even they became quite digestible.

When we lay down to sleep it was only to doze for, with hunger gnawing at one, such hours of repose were never more than a half-waking dream wherein, in a tumult of longings, our minds carried us off to the feasts of "the land of plenty" which we had forsaken for the desolation of the Antarctic plateau. Even by day, as we tramped along through the snow, these food questions took possession of us; we racked our brains thinking how to make the most of the meagre quantity of food available.

At about 8 a.m. on December 24 the sun commenced to gleam through the clouds and we got under way as cheerily as possible. The light was still bad, however, and snow fell as we zigzagged about among many crevasses. Suddenly the sun burst forth and beating down upon the deep soft snow made it so sticky that the load would hardly move. After four miles we were driven to halting until the evening, when it was expected that the surface would harden.

A small sea-bird, apparently a prion, visited us for a brief moment as we pitched camp. We were then more than one hundred miles distant from the sea. As the bird flew away, we watched it until it disappeared in the north, wishing that we too had wings to cross the interminable ice ridges.

With this fresh disappointment the outlook was less promising and we decided to economize still further on the rations and to overhaul all the gear with a view to making a further reduction in the load. The frame for the tent was made lighter by discarding the two heavier sledge-runner sections and replacing them by two poles built up of sections of the telescopic theodolite legs which were dismantled for the purpose. The theodolite itself was retained as it would be necessary to obtain observations for position and could be used in a rough way standing directly on the cooker box. All other instruments were abandoned including the camera, all unexposed and many packets of exposed films, the hypsometer, thermometers, etc.

Lying in the sleeping-bag that day I dozed off into the land of food once more. This time it was a confectioner's shop, decidedly grandiose and apparently opulent. From amidst the ruck of other customers crowding the counter, I commanded the attention of no less than the proprietor himself who courteously led me by a winding stairway to the roof where, he explained, his primest productions were stocked. There to my amazed gaze were exposed two long rows of gigantic cakes, each about four feet in diameter. Never before had I ever imagined anything so glorious—for a brief space at least I was in Heaven. My delight was increased to a still further degree when it was explained that they were no ordinary cakes but that each was fitted with a fuse to be lighted just before serving, when the whole of the ingredients would react chemically (after the manner of thermit) completing the cooking and delivering a steaming hot article. In rapture

I ordered one, feeling disappointed that I could not carry more, and hurried down to the counter to settle for it. I remember paying the money over, but my next consciousness was the realization, as I walked down the street, of having omitted to carry off the prize itself. With all haste I returned to the shop only to be disappointed and mocked by discovering the door shut and on it the placard "early closing."

At other times the scene of such dreams was commonly enough a seductive restaurant, but, whatever the theme, something almost invariably happened to interrupt the course of events before one managed to set one's teeth into the food, so to speak, and get satisfaction from it. On those rare occasions when the deception of the dream carried through even to the realization of the food itself and the communication of a feeling of repletion, the relating, in the morning, of one's good fortune invariably raised some feeling of disappointment in the other fellow who had not been so fortunate.

We were up at 11 p.m., but so much time was absorbed in making a special stew for Christmas from some of the bones that it was not until 2.30 a.m. that we got under way. To make the spread more exceptional I produced two scraps of biscuit which I had saved up, stowed away in my spare kit-bag, as relic of the good days before the accident. It was certainly a cheerless Christmas; I remember we wished each other happier anniversaries in the future, drinking the toast in dog soup.

The course henceforth was to the north-east and the southerly wind helped the sledge along. The surface was a moderately good one, undulating, hard, but seamed with fairly rough sastrugi. The sun shone brightly and only for the wind and low drift we might have felt comfortable enough. As we sat in the lee of the sledge occasionally for a rest the drift swirled up in our faces like fine sand. On our right, down within the shallow depression of the Ninnis Glacier, the low outline of Dixson Island, forty miles to the north, could be seen miraged up on the horizon.

After a run of eleven miles we commenced to raise the tent at 9.30 a.m. I took observations for position, computing the distance in an air-line to the Hut to be one hundred and sixty miles. At the meal an ounce each of butter was served out from our small stock to give a festive touch to the stew. There never was a trace of fat associated with any of our dog preparations and we positively longed for it.

The next morning, December 26, we got under way at 2 a.m. The sun shone, but there was a strong, penetrating, chill wind reaching forty miles per hour and raising low drift. We found the march very trying and by noon, when camp was pitched, had covered little over ten miles. This brought us to the west of the Ninnis Glacier Valley.

Though up at 11 p.m., we were not on the move till 4 a.m., the five hours being consumed in the preparation of stew and experiments in the matter of a sail to lighten the labour up the rising slopes ahead. The only material available for the sail was the tent-cover itself, so the apex was attached to the top of one ski lashed vertically as a mast and secured below to another ski, lashed across the sledge as a boom. The excessive amount of lashing and unlashing connected with this arrangement when starting and camping, all of which had to be done with bare fingers in a biting wind, was a great drawback, but could not be avoided. How we longed for the beautiful sail, spar and mast that had been swallowed up in the crevasse!

The surface proved moderately soft and combined with the ascent made the work more than usually laborious, notwithstanding the help from the sail under the influence of a thirty-mile wind. Bright sunlight helped to counteract the depressing effect of low drift and kept up our spirits. Whenever a halt was called for a few minutes' spell the conversation invariably turned on the subject of food and we laid plans for a celebration on arrival on board the *Aurora*.

At noon the wind fell off and we decided to camp, though the sledge-meter showed that under ten miles had been covered.

There was one great drawback in the prolonged running of the primus in our very confined tent, necessary to render the dog sinews digestible, and that was that a thawing temperature was often reached. This often resulted in a drip from the walls where snow-drift or falling snow lodged, and worse still the snow floor itself started thawing. As we were without a waterproof floorcloth, that valuable article having been numbered amongst our losses, the moisture soaked into the sleeping-bags which soon became wet outside and soggy inside. As soon as such cooking bouts finished the tent cooled off and the wet walls froze, becoming stiff and heavy with adhering cakes of ice.

At this time the ration was mainly composed of dog meat to which was added one or two ounces of chocolate or raisins, three or four ounces of a mixture of pemmican and biscuit, and, as a beverage, very dilute cocoa. In all the total weight of solid food consumed by each of us per day was about fourteen ounces. Comparison with our normal sledging-ration of over two pounds of unconcentrated rich food illustrates how inadequate, to maintain our strength, was this diminished ration. The small supply of butter and glaxo was saved for emergency, while a few tea bags that remained were each boiled over and over again.

On December 28 the march commenced at 3 a.m. in a thirty-mile wind and light drift. Overhead there was a wild sky which augured badly for ensuing days. Stepping the jury mast and rigging the sail was cold work and we were glad to be marching. Presently our devoted Ginger could walk no longer and was strapped on the sledge. She was the last of the team and had been some sort of help until a few days before.

On account of the steep up grade, the surface rising in successive terraces, we camped at 7.15 a.m. after completing less than five miles. There the very unpleasant duty of despatching our faithful retainer had to be faced.

As we worked on a system which aimed at using up the bony parts of the carcase first, it happened that Ginger's skull figured as the dish for the next meal. As there was no instrument capable of dividing it, the skull was boiled whole and a line drawn round it marking it into right and left halves. These were drawn for in the old and well-established sledging practice of "shut-eye," after which, passing the skull from one to the other, we took turns about in eating our respective shares. The brain was certainly the most appreciated and nutritious section, Mertz, I remember well, remarking specially upon it.

In explanation of the term "shut-eye" it should be stated that on sledging journeys it is usual to divide all food in as nearly even portions as possible. Then one man turns away and another, pointing to a share, and addressing the former asks, "Whose?" The reply is "Yours" or "Mine." In this way an impartial and satisfactory division is made.

Before retiring to the sleeping-bag, I spent another four hours cracking and boiling down bones with the object of extracting the nutriment for future use and at the same time ridding the load of a lot of useless weight in the form of inert bone. Those hours which we spent from time to time boiling the meat are never to be forgotten for the operation had to be conducted sitting in a very squat and cramped position flat on the floor. With the cooker in operation, the tent was too small to allow us either to lie down or to sit comfortably on a rolled-up sleeping bag.

Mertz rose early that evening and took his turn at the cooking. We were away at 2.30 a.m., December 29, in a thirty-mile wind and light drift. The sail helped us nicely up a series of terraces, the rises being from fifty to one hundred and fifty feet in height and occurring at distances of about one and a half miles apart. We camped after six hours' marching, having covered but little over seven miles.

The following day the ascent was continued in the same biting wind. After several hours' work we were cheered to find that we had overtopped the last terrace and reached a flat surface. Our spirits rose and the prospects for the future had more promise than for many days past. On the level ground we strode along at a good pace and by 9 a.m. had accomplished a splendid march of fifteen miles. Fortune was beginning to smile upon us at last, but, alas! trouble of a new order was brewing.

The first intimation of this came to me in the latter part of the march, when I realized that my companion was not as cheerful as usual. As he had always been so bright and energetic it was clear that there was some good reason for this change, but he gave no hint upon the subject and I was loath to speak to him directly about it as it would likely pass off.

At 10.15 p.m. we woke to find the sky overcast, snow falling and a strong wind blowing, and so decided to wait for better conditions. At 5.30 next morning, the 31st, the wind fell off somewhat and so preparations for a start were made.

On talking things over with Mertz, I found that, though he had said little on the subject in the past, he had found the dog meat very disagreeable and felt that he was getting little nutriment from it. He suggested that we should abstain for a time from eating any further of this meat and draw solely upon the ordinary food of which we still had some days' supply carefully husbanded. This plan was adopted as it was expected to act beneficially on our health. I will always remember the wonderful taste that the food had in those days. Acute hunger enhances the taste and smell of food beyond all ordinary conception. The flavour of food under such conditions is a miracle altogether unsuspected by the millions of mortals who daily eat their fill. Cocoa was almost intoxicating and even plain beef suet, such as we had in fragments in our hoosh mixture, had acquired a sweet and aromatic taste scarcely to be described, but by contrast with the suet of our days of repletion it was certainly as different as chalk is from the richest chocolate cream.

The march that morning, the last day in the year, was under wretched conditions, for the light was atrocious and the surface slippery and ridged. The wind, tending to blow the sledge along sideways, only added to our troubles and assisted to bring us to "earth" at frequent intervals. After stumbling along for two and a half miles we were obliged to give up and camp.

At 9.30 p.m. the sun appeared for a brief space gleaming through a pall of clouds, but was lost a moment afterwards. It was sufficient, however, to give us a bearing and as the wind subsided another stage was attempted. It was a costly performance, however, for on the polished surface in snow-blind light we literally staggered along, continually falling over unseen sastrugi. Of the latter, two sets crossing one another soon appeared confounding the only means of maintaining a course to march on, so camp was pitched after five miles.

Snow continued to fall all day long throughout New Year's day and the light remained as bad as ever. We waited anxiously for a glimpse of the sun to give us direction, in the meantime we decided not to attempt a move as Mertz was not up to his usual form and the rest might recuperate him. He had not been himself since the early morning hours of the 30th and had not responded to the change of diet. On the other hand, it was difficult to discover exactly what was the matter beyond exhaustion and the depressing effect of our continued bad fortune in the matter of weather. He did not complain, but endeavoured to be as cheerful as possible. I found that, like myself, he had from time to time a dull painful gnawing sensation in the abdomen; it may well have been that his was more acute than in my case. I had discovered that the pain was greatly relieved by frequently changing position as one rested. My theory, at the time, was that the gastric secretions, especially under the influence of food dreams, were so active in search of food as actually to attack the wall of the stomach itself. By turning over at intervals the damage would be distributed and less severe.

Later in the day I had another surprise finding that Mertz had lost appreciation of the biscuit; it was then that I first began to realize that something really serious was the matter and that his condition was worse than my own. As he expressed a desire for glaxo our small stock was made over to him, a larger proportion of biscuit and dog-meat falling to my share.

The wretched conditions persisted on January 2. It was decided that the few odd miles that might be covered were not worth attempting for the expenditure entailed would be out of all proportion to the result. In the first place we could not expect to make satisfactory course unless the sun were visible at least at intervals, for we had already found that thereabouts the trend of the sastrugi and the direction of the prevailing wind were considerably influenced locally by the depression ahead forming the upper part of the Mertz Glacier Valley. This confusion as to the direction of the sastrugi left us with only a rough notion of the bearing of the Hut. Secondly, owing to our reduced state and the awkwardness of the makeshift gear, an undue time was absorbed on every occasion when we got under way or pitched camp. Thus for the paltry gain of several miles we sometimes worked hours breaking and making camp, getting our clothes loaded with snow into the bargain. We longed for a good fine day when we could tramp on by the hour and appreciably lessen the distance ahead. While we lay in the bags weather-bound we felt constrained to eat less than ever.

At length in the evening of January 3 the clouds broke and the sun peered through for a time. We were not long in packing and getting on the way. It was an exceptionally cold night and the wind pierced our emaciated frames like a knife. Alas, before five miles were covered we were again in camp for Mertz had suddenly developed dysentery. To make matters worse his fingers had been badly frost-bitten, which for a moment he himself could scarcely believe, for so resistant to cold was he that he had never before suffered in this way. To convince himself he bit a considerable piece of the fleshy part off the end of one of them.

Though the wind howled and the drift flew past unceasingly throughout January 4, the sun shone brightly in the sky. We had intended rising at 10 a.m. to push on once more, but the condition of my companion called for a rest. I spent the day improving some of the gear, mending Mertz's and my own clothing and cooking a quantity of meat.

The day following was most depressing, for instead of improving the weather had relapsed. All day long in a gale of wind, falling snow lashed against the tent. The question of marching was referred to Mertz and he decided that we should remain in camp.

I busied myself cooking more meat and making appetizing broths which, however, my companion did not appreciate as I had hoped, furnishing additional evidence of the weakness of his digestive arrangements. Then followed wretched hours lying in the wet sleeping-bags—how we longed to get them properly dry!

January 6 was a great improvement on its predecessors, but the sky still remained overcast. Mertz agreed to try another stage. The grade was slightly downhill and the wind well behind, but these advantages were offset by an extremely slippery surface and awkward sastrugi ridges. Falls were frequent and they soon told severely upon my companion in his weak condition. At last, after consistently demurring, he consented to ride on the sledge. With a wind blowing from behind, it required no great exertion to bring the load along, though it would often pull up suddenly against sastrugi. After we had covered two and a half miles, Mertz became so chilled through inaction in the wind that, though otherwise all was going smoothly, there was nothing to do but pitch the tent.

Mertz was depressed and, after a little refreshment, sank back into his bag without saying much. He was troubled from time to time with recurrences of dysentery and had no power to hold in his stomach the broth which he was prevailed upon to swallow at intervals. Occasionally, during the day, I would ask him how he felt, or we would return to the old subject of food. Even then the conversation often led to the discussion of what we would do on arrival on board the *Aurora*, though I doubt if either of us at that time really expected to get through. I recollect that it was agreed that once on board the ship Mertz was to spend the day making penguin-egg omelettes, for the excellence of those he had made just prior to leaving the Hut had not been forgotten.

Starvation combined with superficial frost-bite, alternating with the damp conditions in the sleeping-bags, had by this time resulted in a wholesale peeling of the skin all over our bodies; in its place only a very poor unnourished substitute appeared which readily rubbed raw in many places. As a result of this, the chafing of the march had already developed large raw patches in just those places where they were most troublesome. As we never took off our clothes, the peelings of hair and skin from our bodies worked down into our under-trousers and socks, and regular clearances were made from the latter.

Our hair and beards, where exposed to the weather, were now bleached to a light sandy colour. A curious effect which, however, is noticed in greater or less degree by all sledging parties.

The night of the 6th was long and wearisome as I tossed about sleeplessly, mindful that for both of us our chances of reaching succour were now slipping silently and relentlessly away. I was aching to get on, but there could be no question of abandoning my companion whose condition now set the pace.

The morning of January 7th opened with better weather, for there was little wind and no snow falling; even the sun appeared gleaming through the clouds.

In view of the seriousness of the position it had been agreed overnight that at all costs we would go on in the morning, sledge-sailing with Mertz in his bag strapped on the sledge. It was therefore a doubly sad blow that morning to find that my companion was again touched with dysentery and so weak as to be quite helpless. After tucking him into the bag again, I slid into my own in order to kill time and keep warm, for the cold had a new sting about it in those days of want.

At 10 a.m. hearing a rustle from my companion's bag I rose to find him in a fit. Shortly afterwards he became normal and exchanged a few words, but did not appear to realize that anything out of the way had happened.

The information that this incident conveyed fell upon me like a thunderbolt, for it was certain that my companion was in a very serious state with little hope of any alleviation, for he was already unable to assimilate the meagre foods available.

There was no prospect of proceeding so I settled myself to stand by my stricken comrade and ease his sufferings as far as possible. It would require a miracle to bring him round to a fit travelling condition, but I prayed that it might be granted.

After noon he improved and drank some thick cocoa and soup.

Later in the afternoon he had several more fits and then, becoming delirious, talked incoherently until midnight. Most of that time his strength returned and he struggled to climb out of the sleeping-bag, keeping me very busy tucking him in again. About midnight he appeared to doze off to sleep and with a feeling of relief I slid down into my own bag, not to sleep, though weary enough, but to get warm again and to think matters over. After a couple of hours, having felt no movement, I stretched out my arm and found that my comrade was stiff in death. He had been accepted into "the peace that passeth all understanding."

It was unutterably sad that he should have perished thus, after the splendid work he had accomplished not only on that particular sledging journey but throughout the expedition. No one could have done better. Favoured with a generous and lovable character, he had been a general favourite amongst all the members of the expedition. Now all was over, he had done his duty and passed on. All that remained was his mortal frame which, toggled up in his sleeping-bag, still offered some sense of companionship as I threw myself down for the remainder of the night, revolving in my mind all that lay behind and the chances of the future.

CHAPTER XIV

ALONE

"Then on the shore of the wide world I stand alone."—Keats.

Outside the bowl of chaos was brimming with drift-snow and as I lay in the sleeping-bag beside my dead companion I wondered how, in such conditions, I would manage to break and pitch camp single-handed. There appeared to be little hope of reaching the Hut, still one hundred miles away. It was easy to sleep in the bag, and the weather was cruel outside. But inaction is hard to bear and I braced myself together determined to put up a good fight.

Failing to reach the Hut it would be something done if I managed to get to some prominent point likely to catch the eye of a search-party, where a cairn might be erected and our diaries cached. So I commenced to modify the sledge and camping gear to meet fresh requirements.

The sky remained clouded, but the wind fell off to a calm which lasted several hours. I took the opportunity to set to work on the sledge, sawing it in halves with a pocket tool and discarding the rear section. A mast was made out of one of the rails no longer required, and a spar was cut from the other. Finally, the load was cut down to a minimum by the elimination of all but the barest necessities, the abandoned articles including, sad to relate, all that remained of the exposed photographic films.

Late that evening, the 8th, I took the body of Mertz, still toggled up in his bag, outside the tent, piled snow blocks around it and raised a rough cross made of the two discarded halves of the sledge runners.

On January 9 the weather was overcast and fairly thick drift was flying in a gale of wind, reaching about fifty miles an hour. As certain matters still required attention and my chances of re-erecting the tent were rather doubtful, if I decided to move on, the start was delayed.

Part of the time that day was occupied with cutting up a waterproof clothes-bag and Mertz's burberry jacket and sewing them together to form a sail. Before retiring to rest in the evening I read through the burial service and put the finishing touches on the grave.

January 10 arrived in a turmoil of wind and thick drift. The start was still further delayed. I spent part of the time in reckoning up the food remaining and in cooking the rest of the dog meat, this latter operation serving the good object of lightening the load, in that the kerosene for the purpose was consumed there and then and had not to be dragged forward for subsequent use. Late in the afternoon the wind fell and the sun peered amongst the clouds just as I was in the middle of a long job riveting and lashing the broken shovel.

The next day, January 11, a beautiful, calm day of sunshine, I set out over a good surface with a slight down grade.

From the start my feet felt curiously lumpy and sore. They had become so painful after a mile of walking that I decided to examine them on the spot, sitting in the lee of the sledge in brilliant sunshine. I had not had my socks off for some days for, while lying in camp, it had not seemed necessary. On taking off the third and inner pair of socks the sight of my feet gave me quite a shock, for the thickened skin of the soles had separated in each case as a complete layer, and abundant watery fluid had escaped saturating the sock. The new skin beneath was very much abraded and raw. Several of my toes had commenced to blacken and fester near the tips and the nails were puffed and loose.

I began to wonder if there was ever to be a day without some special disappointment. However, there was nothing to be done but make the best of it. I smeared the new skin and the raw surfaces with lanoline, of which there was fortunately a good store, and then with the aid of bandages bound the old skin casts back in place, for these were comfortable and soft in contact with the abraded surface. Over the bandages were slipped six pairs of thick woollen socks, then fur boots and finally crampon over-shoes. The latter, having large stiff soles, spread the weight nicely and saved my feet from the jagged ice encountered shortly afterwards.

So glorious was it to feel the sun on one's skin after being without it for so long that I next removed most of my clothing and bathed my body in the rays until my flesh fairly tingled— a wonderful sensation which spread throughout my whole person, and made me feel stronger and happier.

Then on I went, treading rather like a cat on wet ground endeavouring to save my feet from pain. By 5.30 p.m. I was quite worn out—nerve-worn—though having covered but six and a quarter miles. Had it not been a delightful evening I should not have found strength to erect the tent.

The day following passed in a howling blizzard and I could do nothing but attend to my feet and other raw patches, festering finger-nails and inflamed frost-bitten nose. Fortunately there was a good supply of bandages and antiseptic. The tent, spread about with dressings and the meagre surgical appliances at hand, was suggestive of a casualty hospital.

Towards noon the following day, January 13, the wind subsided and the snow cleared off. It turned out a beautifully fine afternoon. Soon after I had got moving the slope increased, unfolding a fine view of the Mertz Glacier ahead. My heart leapt with joy, for all was like a map before me and I knew that over the hazy blue ice ridge in the far distance lay the Hut. I was heading to traverse the depression of the glacier ahead at a point many miles above our crossing of the outward journey and some few miles below gigantic ice cascades. My first impulse was to turn away to the west and avoid crossing the fifteen miles of hideously broken ice that choked the valley before me, but on second thought, in view of the very limited quantity of food left, the right thing seemed to be to make an air-line for the Hut and chance what lay between. Accordingly, having taken an observation of the sun for position and selected what appeared to be the clearest route across the valley, I started downhill. The névé gave way to rough blue ice and even wide crevasses made their appearance. The rough ice jarred my feet terribly and altogether it was a most painful march.

So unendurable did it become that, finding a bridged crevasse extending my way, I decided to march along the snow bridge and risk an accident. It was from fifteen to twenty feet wide and well packed with winter snow. The march continued along it down slopes for over a mile with great satisfaction as far as my feet were concerned. Eventually it became irregular and broke up, but others took its place and served as well; in this way the march was made possible. At 8 p.m. after covering a distance of nearly six miles a final halt for the day was made.

About 11 p.m. as the sun skimmed behind the ice slopes to the south I was startled by loud reports like heavy gun shots. They commenced up the valley to the south and trailed away down the southern side of the glacier towards the sea. The fusillade of shots rang out without interruption for about half an hour, then all was silent. It was hard to believe it was not caused by some human agency, but I learnt that it was due to the cracking of the glacier ice.

A high wind which blew on the morning of the 14th diminished in strength by noon and allowed me to get away. The sun came out so warm that the rough ice surface underfoot was covered with a film of water and in some places small trickles ran away to disappear into crevasses.

Though the course was downhill, the sledge required a good deal of pulling owing to the wet runners. At 9 p.m., after travelling five miles, I pitched camp in the bed of the glacier. From about 9.30 p.m. until 11 p.m. "cannonading" continued like that heard the previous evening.

January 15—the date on which all the sledging parties were due at the Hut! It was overcast and snowing early in the day, but in a few hours the sun broke out and shone warmly. The travelling was so heavy over a soft snowy surface, partly melting, that I gave up, after one mile, and camped.

At 7 p.m. the surface had not improved, the sky was thickly obscured and snow fell. At 10 p.m. a heavy snowstorm was in progress, and, since there were many crevasses in the vicinity, I resolved to wait.

On the 16th at 2 a.m. the snow was falling as thick as ever, but at 5 a.m. the atmosphere lightened and the sun appeared. Camp was broken without delay. A favourable breeze sprang up, and with sail set I managed to proceed in short stages through the deep newly-fallen blanket of snow. It clung in lumps to the runners, which had to be scraped frequently. Riven ice ridges as much as eighty feet in height passed on either hand. Occasionally I got a start as a foot or a leg sank through into space, but, on the whole, all went unexpectedly well for several miles. Then the sun disappeared and the disabilities of a snow-blind light had to be faced.

After laboriously toiling up one long slope, I had just taken a few paces over the crest, with the sledge running freely behind, when it dawned on me that the surface fell away unusually steeply. A glance ahead, even in that uncertain light, flashed the truth upon me—I was on a snow cornice, rimming the brink of a great blue chasm like a quarry, the yawning mouth of an immense and partly filled crevasse. Already the sledge was gaining speed as it slid past me towards the gaping hole below. Mechanically, I bedded my feet firmly in the snow and, exerting every effort, was just able to take the weight and hold up the sledge as it reached the very brink of the abyss. There must have been an interval of quite a minute during which I held my ground without being able to make it budge. It seemed an interminable time; I found myself reckoning the odds as to who would win, the sledge or I. Then it slowly came my way, and the imminent danger was passed.

The day's march was an extremely heavy five miles; so before turning in I treated myself to an extra supper of jelly soup made from dog sinews. I thought at the time that the acute enjoyment of eating compensated in some measure for the sufferings of starvation.

January 17 was another day of overcast sky and steady falling snow. Everything from below one's feet to the sky above was one uniform ghostly glare. The irregularities in the surfaces not obliterated by the deep soft snow blended harmoniously in colour and in the absence of shadows faded into invisibility. These were most unsuitable conditions for the crossing of such a dangerous crevassed valley, but delay meant a reduction of the ration and that was out of the question, so nothing remained but to go on.

A start was made at 8 a.m. and the pulling proved more easy than on the previous day. Some two miles had been negotiated in safety when an event occurred which, but for a miracle, would have terminated the story then and there. Never have I come so near to an end; never has anyone more miraculously escaped.

I was hauling the sledge through deep snow up a fairly steep sloop when my feet broke through into a crevasse. Fortunately as I fell I caught my weight with my arms on the edge and did not plunge in further than the thighs. The outline of the crevasse did not show through the blanket of snow on the surface, but an idea of the trend was obtained with a stick. I decided to try a crossing about fifty yards further along, hoping that there it would be better bridged. Alas! it took an unexpected turn catching me unawares. This time I shot through the centre of the bridge in a flash, but the latter part of the fall was decelerated by the friction of the harness ropes which, as the sledge ran up, sawed back into the thick compact snow forming the margin of the lid. Having seen my comrades perish in diverse ways and having lost hope of ever reaching the Hut, I had already many times speculated on what the end would be like. So it happened that as I fell through into the crevasse the thought "so this is the end" blazed up in my mind, for it was to be expected that the next moment the sledge would follow through, crash on my head and all go to the unseen bottom. But the unexpected happened and the sledge held, the deep snow acting as a brake.

In the moment that elapsed before the rope ceased to descend, delaying the issue, a great regret swept through my mind, namely; that after having stinted myself so assiduously in order to save food, I should pass on now to eternity without the satisfaction of what remained—to such an extent does food take possession of one under such circumstances. Realizing that the sledge was holding I began to look around. The crevasse was somewhat over six feet wide and sheer walled, descending into blue depths below. My clothes, which, with a view to ventilation, had been but loosely secured were now stuffed with snow broken from the roof, and very chilly it was. Above at the other end of the fourteen-foot rope, was the daylight seen through the hole in the lid.

In my weak condition, the prospect of climbing out seemed very poor indeed, but in a few moments the struggle was begun. A great effort brought a knot in the rope within my grasp, and, after a moment's rest, I was able to draw myself up and reach another, and, at length, hauled my body on to the overhanging snow-lid. Then, when all appeared to be well and before I could get to quite solid ground, a further section of the lid gave way, precipitating me once more to the full length of the rope.

There, exhausted, weak and chilled, hanging freely in space and slowly turning round as the rope twisted one way and the other, I felt that I had done my utmost and failed, that I had no more strength to try again and that all was over except the passing. It was to be a miserable and slow end and I reflected with disappointment that there was in my pocket no antidote to speed matters; but there always remained the alternative of slipping from the harness. There on the brink of the great Beyond I well remember how I looked forward to the peace of the great release—how almost excited I was at the prospect of the unknown to be unveiled. From those flights of mind I came back to earth, and remembering how Providence had miraculously brought me so far, felt that nothing was impossible and determined to act up to Service's lines:

> "Just have one more try—it's dead easy to die,
> It's the keeping-on-living that's hard."

My strength was fast ebbing; in a few minutes it would be too late. It was the occasion for a supreme attempt. Fired by the passion that burns the blood in the act of strife, new power seemed to come as I applied myself to one last tremendous effort. The struggle occupied some time, but I slowly worked upward to the surface. This time emerging feet first, still clinging to the rope, I pushed myself out extended at full length on the lid and then shuffled safely on to the solid ground at the side. Then came the reaction from the great nerve strain and lying there alongside the sledge my mind faded into a blank.

When consciousness returned it was a full hour or two later, for I was partly covered with newly fallen snow and numb with the cold. I took at least three hours to erect the tent, get things snugly inside and clear the snow from my clothes. Between each movement, almost, I had to rest. Then reclining in luxury in the sleeping-bag I ate a little food and thought matters over. It was a time when the mood of the Persian philosopher appealed to me:

"Unborn To-morrow and dead Yesterday,
   Why fret about them if To-day be sweet?"

I was confronted with this problem: whether it was better to enjoy life for a few days, sleeping and eating my fill until the provisions gave out, or to "plug on" again in hunger with the prospect of plunging at any moment into eternity without the supreme satisfaction and pleasure of the food. While thus cogitating an idea presented itself which greatly improved the prospects and clinched the decision to go ahead. It was to construct a ladder from a length of alpine rope that remained; one end was to be secured to the bow of the sledge and the other carried over my left shoulder and loosely attached to the sledge harness. Thus if I fell into a crevasse again, provided the sledge was not also engulfed, it would be easy for me, even though weakened by starvation, to scramble out by the ladder.

Notwithstanding the possibilities of the rope-ladder, I could not sleep properly, for my nerves had been overtaxed. All night long considerable wind and drift continued.

On the 19th it was overcast and light snow falling; very dispiriting conditions after the experience of the day before, but I resolved to go ahead and leave the rest to Providence.

My feet and legs, as they wallowed through the deep snow, occasionally broke through into space. Then I went right under, but the sledge held up and the ladder proved "trumps." A few minutes later I was down again, but emerged once more without much exertion, though half-smothered with snow. Faintness overcame me and I stopped to camp, though only a short distance had been covered.

All around there was a leaden glare and the prospect was most unpromising. The sun had not shown up for several days and I was eager for it, not only that it might illuminate the landscape, but for its cheerful influence and life-giving energy. A few days previously my condition had been improving, but now it was relapsing.

During the night of the 18th loud booming noises, sharp cracks and muffled growls issued from the neighbouring crevasses and kept waking me up. At times one could feel a vibration accompanying the growling sounds, and I concluded that the ice was in rapid motion.

The sun at last appeared on the 19th, and the march was resumed by 8.30 a.m. The whole surface, now effectively lighted up, was seen to be a network of ice-rifts and crevasses, some of the latter very wide. Along one after another of these, I dragged the sledge in search of a spot where the snow bridge appeared to be firm. Then I would plunge across at a run risking the consequences.

After a march of three hours safer ground was reached. On ahead, leading to the rising slopes on the far side of the glacier, was a nearly level ice plain dotted over with beehive-shaped eminences usually not more than a few feet in height. Once on this comparatively safe wind-swept surface I became over-reliant and in consequence sank several times into narrow fissures.

At length the glacier was crossed and the tent pitched on a snowy slope under beetling, crevassed crags which rose sheer from the valley-level some five hundred feet. I had never dared expect to get so far and now that it was an accomplished fact I was intoxicated with joy. Somewhat to the right could be traced out a good path, apparently free from pitfalls, leading upwards to the plateau which still remained to be crossed. This entailed a rise of some three thousand feet and led me to reconsider the lightening of the load on the sledge. The length of alpine rope was abandoned as also were finnesko-crampons and sundry pairs of worn finnesko and socks. The sledge was overhauled and sundry repairs effected, finishing up by treating the runners to a coat of water-proofing composition to cause them to glide more freely on moist snow.

January 20 was a wretched overcast day and not at all improved by considerable wind and light drift. In desperation a start was made at 2 p.m. and, though nothing was visible beyond a few yards distant, I kept a steady course uphill and, assisted by the wind, covered two and a half miles as the day's work.

The next day, though windy, was sunny and a stretch of three miles of steep rise was negotiated. All that night and until noon on the 22nd wind and drift prevailed, but the afternoon came gloriously sunny. Away to the north beyond Aurora Peak was a splendid view of the sea at Buchanan Bay. It was like meeting an old friend and I longed to be down near it. That evening six more miles had been covered, but I felt very weak and weary. My feet were now much improved and the old skin-casts after shrivelling up a good deal had been thrown away. However, prolonged starvation aided by the unwholesomeness of the dog meat was taking the toll in other ways. My nails still continued to fester and numerous boils on my face and body required daily attention. The personal overhaul necessary each day on camping and before starting consumed much valuable time.

During the early hours of the 23rd the sun was visible, but about 8 a.m. the clouds sagged low, the wind rose and everything became blotted out in a swirl of drifting snow.

I wandered through it for several hours, the sledge capsizing at times owing to the strength of the wind. It was not possible to keep an accurate course, for even the wind changed direction as the day wore on. Underfoot there was soft snow which I found comfortable for my sore feet, but which made the sledge drag heavily at times.

When a halt was made at 4 p.m. to pitch camp I reckoned that the distance covered in a straight line was but three and a half miles. Then followed a long and difficult task erecting the tent in the wind. It proved a protracted operation.

When the outside was finished off satisfactorily the inside was discovered to be filled with drift snow and had to be dug out. Everything was stuffed with soft damp snow including the sleeping-bag, and it took a rare time to put things right.

By this time I was doing a good deal of "thinking out aloud" which, by the way, seemed to give some sort of consolation.

High wind and dense driving snow persisted throughout the 24th and a good five and a half miles were made. I was able to sit on the sledge much of the time and the wind and the good sail did the work. I was quite done up when at last the tent was up and everything snug for the night.

Torrents of snow fell throughout the 25th and it sizzled and rattled against the tent under the influence of a gale of wind. After the trying experience of the previous two days I did not feel well enough to go on. As the hours went by the snow piled higher, bulging in the sides of the small, odd-shaped tent until it weighed down upon the sleeping-bag and left practically no room at all. The threshing of the seething drift was no longer audible. I was buried indeed! The coffin shape of the bag lent a more realistic touch to the circum-stances. With such a weight above there was no certainty that I would be able to get out when the time came to move. So, though the weather was just as bad on the 26th, I determined to struggle out and try another stage. It was a long and labo-rious work reaching the daylight from beneath the flattened tent and digging everything free. Then some hot food was prepared of which I was much in need. Only four or five pounds of food remained now and there was no guarantee that the weather would clear in the near future, so the position was most anxious. At that time the skin was coming off my hands which were the last parts of my body to peel. A moulting of the hair followed the peeling of the skin. Irregular tufts of beard came out and there was a general shedding of hair from my head, so much so that at each camp thereabouts the snowy floor of the tent was noticeably darkened.

There was no need of a sail on the 26th. The wind, blowing from behind, caught the sledge and drove it along so that, though over a soft surface of snow, the travelling was rapid. The snow came down in the form of large pellets and rattled as it struck the sledge. For one in so poor a condition it was a very trying day, blindly struggling through the whirl of the seething snow; after covering nine miles and erecting the tent I was thoroughly done up. The night was far spent before I had cleared the snow out of my clothes, sleeping-bag, etc.: cooked some food and given myself the necessary medical attention.

As the 27th was just such another day as the 26th I decided to rest further to recuperate from the exertions of the previous day.

By the morning of January 28 the wind had moderated considerably, but the sky remained overcast and snow continued to fall. It was a difficult matter getting out of the tent and a long job excavating it, for the packed snow had piled up within a few inches of the peak. There was no sign of the sledge which with the harness and spars had all to be prospected for and dug out. It appeared that since pitching the tent the whole level of the country had been raised a uniform three feet by a stratum of snow packed so densely that in walking over it but little impression was left.

Soon after the start the sun gleamed out and the weather improved. The three-thousand-foot crest of the plateau had been crossed and I was bearing down rapidly on Commonwealth Bay, the vicinity of which was indicated by a dark water-sky on the north-west horizon.

The evening turned out beautifully fine and my spirits rose to a high pitch, for I felt for the first time that there was a really good chance of making the Hut. To increase the excitement Madigan Nunatak showed up a black speck away to the right front. Eight good miles were covered that afternoon. The change in the weather had come most opportunely, for there now remained only about twenty small chips of cooked dog meat in addition to half a pound of raisins and a few ounces of chocolate which I had kept carefully guarded for emergencies.

However, the wind and drift got up in the night and the start next morning was made in disappointing weather. When five miles on the way another miracle happened.

I was travelling along on an even down grade and was wondering how long the two pounds of food which remained would last, when something dark loomed through the haze of the drift a short distance away to the right. All sorts of possibilities raced through my mind as I headed the sledge for it. The unexpected had happened—in thick weather I had run fairly into a cairn of snow blocks erected by McLean, Hodgeman and Hurley, who had been out searching for my party. On the top of the mound, outlined in black bunting was a bag of food, left on the chance that it might be picked up by us. In a tin was a note stating the bearing and distance of the mound from Aladdin's Cave (E. 30° S., distance twenty-three miles), and mentioning that the ship had arrived at the Hut and was waiting, and had brought the news that Amundsen had reached the Pole, and that Scott was remaining another year in Antarctica.

It certainly was remarkably good fortune that I had come upon the depot of food; a few hundred yards to either side and it would have been lost to sight in the drift. On reading the note carefully I found that I had just missed by six hours what would have been crowning good luck, for it appeared that the search party had left the mound at 8 a.m. that very day (January 29). It was about 2 p.m. when I reached it. Thus, during the night of the 28th our camps had been only some five miles apart.

Hauling down the bag of food I tore it open in the lee of the cairn and in my greed scattered the contents about on the ground. Having partaken heartily of frozen pemmican, I stuffed my pocket, bundled the rest into a bag on the sledge and started off in high glee, stimulated in body and mind. As I left the depot there appeared to be nothing on earth that could prevent me reaching the Hut within a couple of days, but a fresh obstacle with which I had not reckoned was to arise and cause further delay, leading to far-reaching results.

It happened that after several hours' march the surface changed from snow to polished névé and then to slippery ice. I could scarcely keep on my feet at all, falling every few moments and bruising my emaciated self until I expected to see my bones burst through the clothes. How I regretted having abandoned those crampons after crossing the Mertz Glacier; shod with them, all would be easy.

With nothing but finnesko on the feet, to walk over such a sloping surface would have been difficult enough in the wind without any other hindrance; with the sledge sidling down the slope and tugging at one, it was quite impossible. I found that I had made too far to the east and to reach Aladdin's Cave had unfortunately to strike across the wind.

Before giving up, I even tried crawling on my hands and knees.

However, the day's run, fourteen miles, was by no means a poor one.

Having erected the tent I set to work to improvise crampons. With this object in view the theodolite case was cut up, providing two flat pieces of wood into which were stuck as many screws and nails as could be procured by dismantling the sledgemeter and the theodolite itself. In the repair-bag there were still a few ice-nails which at this time were of great use.

Late the next day, the wind which had risen in the night fell off and a start was made westwards over the ice slopes with the pieces of nail-studded wood lashed to my feet. A glorious expanse of sea lay to the north and several recognizable points on the coast were clearly in view to east and west.

The crampons were not a complete success for they gradually broke up, lasting only a distance of six miles. Then the wind increased and I got into difficulties by the sledge sidling into a narrow crevasse. It was held up by the boom at the foot of the mast. It took some time to extract and the wind continued to rise, so there was nothing for it but to pitch camp.

Further attempts at making crampons were more handicapped than ever, for the best materials available had been utilized already. However, from the remnants of the first pair and anything else that could be pressed into the service, a second pair was evolved of the nature of wooden-soled finnesko with spikes. This work took an interminable time, for the tools and appliances available were almost all contained in a small pocket knife that had belonged to Mertz. Besides a blade it was furnished with a spike, a gimlet and a screw-driver.

A blizzard was in full career on January 31 and I spent all day and most of the night on the crampons. On February 1 the wind and drift had subsided late in the afternoon, and I got under way expecting great things from the new crampons. The beacon marking Aladdin's Cave was clearly visible as a black dot on the ice slopes to the west.

At 7 p.m. that haven within the ice was attained. It took but a few moments to dig away the snow and throw back the canvas flap sealing the entrance. A moment later I slid down inside, arriving amidst familiar surroundings. Something unusual in one corner caught the eye—three oranges and a pineapple—circumstantial evidence of the arrival of the *Aurora*.

The improvised crampons had given way and were squeezing my feet painfully. I rummaged about amongst a pile of food-bags hoping to find some crampons or leather boots, but was disappointed, so there was nothing left but to repair the damaged ones. That done and a drink of hot milk having been prepared I packed up to make a start for the Hut. On climbing out of the cave imagine my disappointment at finding a strong wind and drift had risen. To have attempted the descent of the five and a half miles of steep ice slope to the Hut with such inadequate and fragile crampons, weak as I still was, would have been only as a last resort. So I camped in the comfortable cave and hoped for better weather next day.

But the blizzard droned on night and day for over a week with never a break. Think, of my feelings as I sat within the cave, so near and yet so far from the Hut, impatient and anxious, ready to spring out and take the trail at a moment's notice. Improvements to the crampons kept me busy for a time; then, as there was a couple of old boxes lying about, I set to work and constructed a second emergency pair in case the others should break up during the descent. I tried the makeshift crampons on the ice outside, but was disappointed to find that they had not sufficient grip to face the wind, so had to abandon the idea of attempting the descent during the continuance of the blizzard. Nevertheless, by February 8 my anxiety as to what was happening at the Hut reached such a pitch that I resolved to try the passage in spite of everything, having worked out a plan whereby I was to sit on the sledge and sail down as far as possible.

Whilst these preparations were in progress the wind slackened. At last the longed for event was to be realized. I snatched a hasty meal and set off. Before a couple of miles had been covered the wind had fallen off altogether, and after that it was gloriously calm and clear.

I had reached within one and a half miles of the Hut and there was no sign of the *Aurora* lying in the offing. I was comforted with the thought that she might still be at the anchorage and have swung inshore so as to be hidden under the ice cliffs. But even as I gazed about seeking for a clue, a speck on the north-west horizon caught my eye and my hopes went down. It looked like a distant ship—Was it the *Aurora?* Well, what matter! the long journey was at an end—a terrible chapter of my life was concluded!

Then the rocks around winter quarters began to come into view; part of the basin of the Boat Harbour appeared, and lo! there were human figures! They almost seemed unreal—was it all a dream? No, indeed, for after a brief moment one of them observed me and waved an arm—I replied—there was a commotion and they all ran towards the Hut. Then they were lost, hidden by the crest of the first steep slope. It almost seemed to me that they had run away to hide.

Minutes passed as I slowly descended trailing the sledge. Then a head rose over the brow of the hill and there was Bickerton, breathless after a long run uphill. I expect for a while he wondered which of us it was. Soon we had shaken hands and he knew all in a few brief words, I for my part learning that the ship had left earlier that very day. Madigan, McLean, Bage and Hodgeman arrived, and then a newcomer, Jeffryes. Five men had remained behind to make a search for our party, and Jeffryes was a new wireless operator landed from the *Aurora*.

My heart was deeply touched by the devotion of these men who thus faced a second year of the rigours and extreme discomfort of the Adelie Land blizzard.

For myself that wonderful occasion was robbed of complete joy by the absence of my two gallant companions, and as we descended to the Hut there were moist eyes amongst the little party as they learnt of the fate of Ninnis and Mertz.

We were soon at the Hut, where I found that full preparations had been made for wintering a second year. The weather was calm and the ship was not more than eighty miles away, so I decided to recall her by wireless. The masts at the Hut had been re-erected during the summer, and on board the *Aurora* Hannam was provided with a wireless receiving set. Jeffryes had arranged with Hannam to call up at 8, 9 and 10 p.m. for several evenings while the *Aurora* was within wireless range, in case there were any news of my party. A message recalling the ship was therefore sent off and repeated at frequent intervals till past midnight.

Next morning there was a forty mile wind, but the *Aurora* was in view away across Commonwealth Bay to the west. She had returned in response to the call and was steaming up and down, waiting for the wind to moderate.

We immediately set to work getting all the records, instruments and personal gear ready to be taken down to the Boat Harbour in anticipation of calm weather during the day.

The wind chose to continue and towards evening was in the sixties, while the barometer fell. The sea was so heavy that the motor-boat could never have lived through it.

That evening Jeffryes sent out another message, which we learned afterwards was not received, in which the alternative course was offered to Captain Davis of either remaining until calm weather supervened or of leaving at once for the Western Base. I felt that the decision should be left to him, as he could appreciate exactly the situation of the Western Base and what the ship could be expected to do amid the ice at that season of the year.

The wintering of Wild's party on the floating ice through a second year would be fraught with such danger for their safety that it was to be avoided at all costs.

On the morning of the 10th there was no sign of the ship and evidently Captain Davis had decided to wait no longer, knowing that further delay would endanger the chances of picking up the eight men on the shelf ice far away to the west. At such a critical moment determination, fearless and swift, was necessary, and, in coming to his momentous decision Captain Davis acted well and for the best interests of the Expedition.

A long voyage lay before the *Aurora*, through fifteen hundred miles of ice-strewn sea, swept by intermittent blizzards and shrouded now at midnight in darkness. Indeed, it was by no means certain that it would be possible to reach them, for the pack-ice off Queen Mary Land was known to be exceptionally heavy.

The long Antarctic winter was fast approaching and we turned to meet it with resolution, knowing that the early summer of the same year would bring relief.

CHAPTER XV

SOUTHWARD OVER THE PLATEAU

From Bage's Narrative

IT will be remembered that to Bage, Webb and Hurley had been entrusted the execution of a southern journey, inland over the plateau. An exploit which experience had taught us would be fraught with the most adverse weather conditions. They were to set their backs to the coast and traverse an icy desolation, an unbroken wilderness of sastrugi.

By going due south, the party would approach very close to the South Magnetic Pole. Hence frequent determinations of the magnetic elements were to be a special feature of their work.

Orders were given to Bage, as leader of the party, to march towards the South Magnetic Pole provided that the compass continued to indicate that it lay not far due south from winter quarters. In the event of the needle diverging much from due south, as they continued the march, it was left to their discretion as to whether they should continue to the true South or towards the Magnetic South.

Had Adelie Land been favoured with reasonable weather, I had intended making, as a special feature, a journey to the Magnetic Pole and there securing magnetic observations extending over many days. As it was, starting out in November in the face of disappointing weather, and with orders to report again at the Hut on January 15, there was opportunity only for a rapid dash inland as far as the time would allow.

However, our Southern Party accomplished even more than I had anticipated, though naturally much was expected

SOUTHWARD OVER THE PLATEAU

from such an admirable combination. The following short story of their adventure is culled from Bage's report.*

After bidding farewell to Mertz, Ninnis and myself at Aladdin's Cave at 7 p.m. on November 10, they pushed on south reaching Cathedral Grotto at 11.30 p.m. There they found Murphy, Hunter and Laseron, their Supporting Party. The last five miles of the way was over a crevassed surface, and as it was negotiated in the dusk and in the face of a forty-five mile wind they were well satisfied with the first day's work.

Next day both parties struck camp and started south up the ice slopes in fairly thick drift. Under the conditions little headway was made. The succeeding days of high wind and dense drift allowed small opportunity to proceed. The morning of the 16th broke and found them only nineteen miles away from the Hut. The drift could still be heard hissing against the tent, but diminished as the morning advanced. Accordingly, after making a depot of a few items that could be spared, they got under way once again.

Later in the day it fell calm and when evening arrived camp was pitched at a point twenty-four and a half miles out and at an elevation of three thousand two hundred feet. Bage's narrative proceeds:

"We were making good headway against a strong breeze next day, when it was noticed that two gallons of kerosene were missing from the Supporters' sledge. While Murphy and Laseron went back two miles to recover them, Webb secured a magnetic declination and I took sun observations for time and azimuth.

"We were off early on the 18th and for the first time were able to appreciate the 'scenery.' Glorious sunshine overhead and all around snow—gorgeous light and shadow in the sunshine, very different from the smooth, soft, white mantle usually attributed to the surface of Antarctica by those in the

---

* The full text of Bage's report, as well as the reports of other leaders of parties, will be published *in extenso* in the series of volumes of Scientific Results of the Expedition now commencing to appear. These reports in an abbreviated and popular form have already appeared in the large edition of this work.

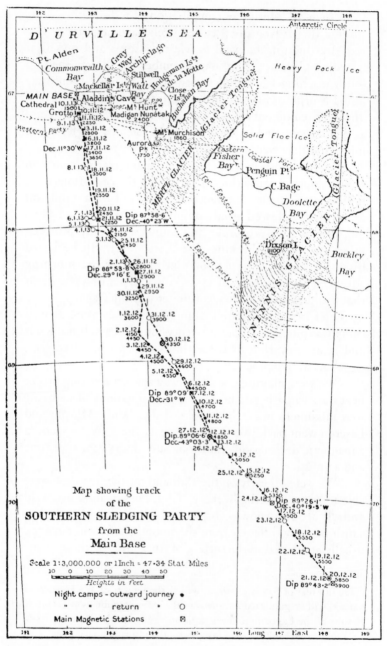

Map showing the Track of the Southern Sledging Party from the
Main Base.

homeland. Here and there, indeed, were smooth patches which we called bowling-greens, but hard and slippery as polished marble, with much the same translucent appearance. Practically all the country, however, was a jumbled mass of small, hard sastrugi, averaging about a foot in height, with an occasional gnarled old veteran twice as high. To either side the snow rolled away for miles. In front, we made our first acquaintance with the accursed next ridge, which is always ahead of you on the plateau. Generally we passed from one ridge to another so gradually that we could never say for certain just when we had topped one; still the next ridge was always there.

"The weather had lately been colder with the increased altitude. The temperature in daily range varied from −10° F. to 9° F. On the 18th we had lunch in the shadow of the tent, as it was too hot inside with the strong sun beating down.

"As we went on after lunch the country changed in a wonderful manner, the sastrugi gradually becoming smaller and finally disappearing. The surface was soft enough to push a bamboo in anywhere for about a foot. Evidently it was fairly old and laid down in calm weather, for excavations showed that it became more compact without any hard windswept layers marking successive falls of snow.

"It proved later that we were commencing a gradual descent of one thousand five hundred feet down the north side of a valley feeding the Mertz Glacier. In order to explain the surface, smooth and unruffled by any wind, the question arose as to whether it is possible that there is a cushion of dead air more or less permanently over the north side of this depression.

"On the soft surface we were able to march without crampons. Hitherto, it had been impossible to haul into a head wind over a slippery surface in finnesko. Now we felt as light as air. A run of twelve miles for the day brought us to forty-two miles from winter quarters.

"Another splendid day on the 19th. We had lunch in a curious cup-shaped hollow, estimated to be two miles wide and one hundred and fifty feet deep. Webb obtained here an approximate dip of 88° 44′,* a very promising increase from the Hut (87° 27′).

"Snow-blindness had now begun to make itself felt for the first time.

"The afternoon was very hot. The thermometer stood at 10° F. at 4 p.m., but the dead calm made it almost unbearable. By the time we had hauled up out of the basin, our attire would hardly have passed muster on a surf beach.

"Before halting, we sighted a dark, distant ridge, thirty miles away, and the course was corrected by its bearing. Our extravagant hopes of finding a permanently calm region had been dwindling for the last few miles, as a hard bottom, a few inches under the surface, had become evident. They were finally dispelled by a south-west wind springing up during the night.

"The hard work was now beginning to tell so we decided to have an easy march next day and build our main depot. We had hoped, of course, to be much further out before the Supporting Party left us, but the weather had settled the question.

"On the 21st, taking things as easily as a thirty-five mile wind would permit, we pulled on, up and down small undulations till 4 p.m. when we found ourselves on a small rise, with the next ridge a considerable distance ahead. It was decided to build the depot here."

During the evening a splendid beacon was erected on bamboo poles standing sixteen feet above the ground. Alongside, a cairn ten feet high and ten feet in diameter was constructed of snow blocks. The sledge loads were rearranged and a bag of provisions cached at the cairn to be picked up on the return journey.

It was 7 p.m. on the 22nd when the parting came and Bage, Webb and Hurley bade good-bye to their supporters. A moment later they were standing alone watching three black specks disappearing in the drift; a stiff wind helping Murphy's Party along in great style.

---

* At the South Magnetic Pole the dip is, of course, 90°.

The same night it blew a hurricane, and only dropped to sixty miles per hour during the 23rd, compelling them to remain in camp. Not an ideal birthday for Webb, but they made the most of it as far as their limited resources would allow.

The load on the sledge was an exceptionally heavy one including, in addition to the usual necessities, special requirements to meet the fiendish weather of the zone; also a magnetic dip circle which was to yield the most important results of the journey. Complete sets of observations including those for position, magnetic declination and inclination were taken daily whenever possible. This entailed an immense amount of labour and fortitude on the part of the observers. In every case a break-wind had to be built to secure some degree of shelter, and the operations were unusually protracted owing to the difficulties of manipulating the instruments in such cold and windy circumstances.

From winter quarters to about sixty miles south of it, the declination had proved fairly constant, but now at the Southern Cross Depot, as they had christened the sixty-seven-mile camp, the compass from pointing a little to the east of south had travelled 40° east of true south, so that it became obvious that there was a considerable magnetic disturbance in the country over which they were travelling. Whether they went south or south-east seemed unlikely to affect the value of geographical and other information they might gather, while Webb was of the opinion that the best magnetic results would be obtained by marching directly towards the Magnetic Pole, particularly if there were disturbances over the intervening area. For these reasons the course was maintained magnetic south.

At 11 a.m. on November 24 they moved off to the south-east in a wind of fifty miles per hour. The light was bad and marching difficult. The surface continued to grow worse till it was nothing but sastrugi eighteen to thirty inches high and very close together. The sledge was continually blown sideways, making considerable lee-way. By 8.30 p.m. it was blowing sixty miles per hour, so they halted, thoroughly tired out, having hauled their one-third of a ton eight and three-quarter miles. It was long afterwards, however, ere the tent was erected in the face of the gale and everything made snug for the night.

In calm weather, pitching camp was a very different thing. On such occasions, half an hour after the halt would usually find them carefully scraping the last of the hoosh out of their pannikins ready for the cocoa.

Next morning the wind was too strong for travelling. Whilst outside the tent, they suddenly observed two snow-petrels. It was hard to realize that these birds had actually flown seventy-six miles inland to a height of two thousand four hundred and fifty feet. Bage writes:

"I dashed inside for the fishing-line, while Hurley got out the camera. They were a beautiful sight, hovering with outspread wings just above the snow, tipping it with their feet now and then, so that they were kept stationary without a movement of their wings in a sixty-five-mile gale. Hurley secured a couple of 'snaps' at the expense of badly frost-bitten hands. Just as I arrived with the fishing-line hooked and baited, the birds flew away to the north-east; our visions of fresh meat went with them."

Towards evening the wind dropped suddenly to twenty miles per hour and the drift cleared. A good view was obtained of the country behind and to the north-east. That camp was on the southern side of the great valley depression they had encountered on the 18th. This deepened to the north-east, where it became differentiated from the general expanse of the inland ice to form the Mertz Glacier Valley. Of course, at the time, Bage's party was not aware of this. All they could identify was the ridge crossed seven days previously, seen blue and dim, forty miles away to the north; also the appearance of greater depression and crevassed bluffs twenty-five miles off to the north-east.

The wind did not rise again much until 10 p.m., when they had moved on seven and a half miles, rising about three hundred feet over ridges and practically losing their view to the north.

The march continued day after day in weather such as, in the case of explorations in more normal polar climates, has been regarded as impossible for travel. Not only had they a heavily laden sledge to drag, but every mile of advance had to be fought out against a relentless gale. At each evening camp a substantial break-wind of névé blocks had to be constructed round the tent; and each day at lunch a hole was dug five feet square and two feet deep with the excavated material piled high around it. This latter served three purposes. First, it gave a good shelter for a longitude observation; secondly, roofed with the floor-cloth thrown over the mast and yard it was converted into a shelter snug enough to house the primus and to lunch comfortably; and thirdly, a mound was left as a landmark to be picked up on the return journey.

Under these conditions progress was slow. For example, on November 27 in the face of a sixty-mile wind, after taking four hours to do three and three-quarter miles, they were all thoroughly exhausted. Again on the 30th, after plodding for four hours against a wind from fifty to sixty miles per hour, they succeeded in covering four miles, but they were nearly played out.

About this time Bage seized an opportunity to sink a shaft eight feet deep in the névé, taking temperatures every foot. From these thermometer records it would appear that the mean annual temperature of that locality is approximately −16° F.

The magnetic declination and dip varied along the route, from day to day, in a most erratic manner. The region traversed on November 28 was exceptionally "disturbed" for the declination actually changed 80° in a march of ten miles. The ordinary compass now responded so weakly as to be almost useless and the direction, when marching, was kept henceforth by means of Bage's sun compass. A course was set for the approximate mean position of the Magnetic Pole..

Referring to the evening of November 30, Bage continues:

"While we were lying half-toggled into the sleeping-bags, writing our diaries, Hurley spent some time alternately imprecating the wind and invoking it for a calm next day.

As he said, once behind a break-wind one could safely defy it, but on the march one is much more humble.

"Whether it was in honour of Queen Alexandra's birthday, or whether Hurley's pious efforts of the evening before had taken effect, December 1 proved a good day. By noon, the wind had dropped sufficiently for us to hoist the Union Jack and Commonwealth Ensign for the occasion.

"After four miles we saw a distinct ridge, ten miles to the west and south—quite the most definitely rising ground observed since leaving the coast. In one place was a patch of immense crevasses, easily visible to the naked eye. On the same ridge, almost due south from us, were black shadows and towards these we headed.

"At a point more than one hundred and twenty-five miles from the sea, a skua gull paid an afternoon call, alighting a few yards from the track. I immediately commenced to stalk it with a fishing-line, this time all ready and baited with pemmican. However, it was quite contemptuous, flying off to the south-south-east as far as we could follow it. Was it taking a short cut to the Ross Sea?

"December 2 saw us through 'Dead-beat Gully.' Late in the evening as we topped a ridge the shadows towards which we had been steering suddenly appeared two miles away, a weird sight—like the edge of the moon seen through a large telescope. The shadows were due to large mounds of snow on the south side of a steep escarpment. There were three main mounds cross-connected with regular lines of smaller prominences, giving the impression of a subdivided town-site. The low evening sun threw everything up in the most wonderful relief.

"On the morning of the 3rd we found that we were in a valley running roughly west-north-west and east-south-east. The southern side rose steeply and from it projected three large mounds, about two hundred feet above the bottom of the valley, into which they fell just like tailings-heaps from a mine. They were christened 'The Nodules.'

"Going due south uphill over névé we found ourselves in a regular network of crevasses. They were about ten feet wide and fairly well bridged. Most noticeable were 'hedges' of ice up to six feet in height on either side of the crevasses which ran southward. It was now nearly calm and in every crack and chink in the snow bridges beautiful fern-like ice crystals were seen. These must have been just forming, as a very light puff of wind would destroy them.

"We spent three hours exploring the locality. On nearing the top of the ridge, roped together, we found that the crevasses were becoming much wider, while the 'hedges' were disappearing. The centre 'nodule' was ascertained to be immediately north or to the leeward of the intersection of two crevasses, each about forty feet wide. The bridge of one crevasse had dropped some thirty feet for a length of eighty yards. Doubtless, an eddy from this hole accounts for the deposits of snow and, by accretions, for the building up of the 'nodules.' Webb went down at the end of the alpine rope and found the bridge below quite solid.

"For about half a mile the summit of the ridge was practically level, three hundred feet above the bed of the valley. The surface was still of névé, intersected by canals forty, sixty and eighty feet wide, in which the snow bridge was generally four or five feet from the top.

"On the south-west horizon, perhaps twenty miles away, was a prominent crest streaked by three dark vertical bars; evidently another crevassed area.

"Returning to the sledge, we toggled on and worked it up over the top of the ridge, much regretting that time would not allow us to examine the other two large 'nodules.' Hurley was in the lead, and had lengthened his line by thirty feet of alpine rope, but even then all three of us and the sledge were often on the lid of a crevasse. Luckily, they were fairly sound, and none of us went in beyond the waist. Finally, the trail emerged on to firm ground once more, where a halt was made for lunch. We were all glad to have seen the place, but I think none of us want to see another like it.

"That night, after following the magnetic needle towards the south-east, we camped at one hundred and forty miles, with an altitude of four thousand four hundred feet."

As they proceeded, endless expanses of very hard, razor-backed sastrugi, generally about two feet high, added to their troubles. The sledge and sledge-meter both had a very rough passage.

The wind veered to the south-east on December 5 and snow drifted in long ramps diagonally across the sastrugi. In two and a half hours they covered two and a quarter miles, blindly blundering in an uncertain light among crests and troughs and through piles of soft, new snow.

Several days of dense snow-fall and drift followed, in which it was impossible to proceed. But the time was not lost, for it was seized upon by these super-men as an opportunity for obtaining a twenty-four hours' continuous record of the vagaries of the needle—actually a "quick-run" on the plateau in close proximity to the Magnetic Pole. To carry out this piece of work they excavated in the névé a shelter seven feet deep and seven feet square at the base, and roofed the opening with the mast, yard and sail. This observatory proved to be thoroughly satisfactory, though apparently not over comfortable, for the walls still retained and radiated the cold of the previous winter.

The journey was continued over a surface veneered with the recently fallen snow which hardened to form a very tiring "piecrust" surface through which they crashed from four inches to a foot.

The time was approaching when it was intended to form a second depot. On the evening of December 11 Bage continues:

"That night I decided that one more day must see us at our depot. Allowing three days' grace for contingencies, there were thirty-one days for us to attain our furthest point and back to the Hut.

"We planned to get our depot two hundred miles out and by 11.30 p.m. on the 12th came on a fine site at one hundred and ninety-nine and three-quarter miles; altitude four thousand eight hundred and fifty feet, latitude 69° 33′ south; longitude 140° 20′ east. Everything possible was left behind. A pile, including ten days' food and one gallon of kerosene, was placed on a small mound to prevent it being drifted over. A few yards distant rose a solid nine-foot cairn surmounted by a black canvas-and-wire flag, six feet higher, well stayed with steel wire.

"I took on food for seventeen days, three days more than I intended to be out, partly so that we could keep on longer if we found we could make a very fast time, and also as a safeguard against thick weather when returning to the depot."

After thus lightening the load progress was more rapid. To improve matters still further, several days of fine weather intervened.

"December 16 was a glorious day; only a fifteen-mile wind, and for ten miles an improved surface. There was no drift, and for the second time since we left we were able to turn our sleeping-bags inside out. They needed it, too. The upper parts were not so bad, as they had been opened occasionally, but the lower halves were simply solid ice. For the first time for weeks we did not wear burberrys, which was a great relief. At 11 p.m. we were fourteen miles to the good.

"All three of us were having trouble with snow-blindness; the 'zinc and cocaine' tabloids being in great demand.

"At two hundred and fifty-six miles out the altitude was five thousand five hundred feet.

"The temperature was getting lower; the minimum being −21° F. on the night of the 17th, the maximum for the same day being 3° F.

"There was dead calm and a regular heat wave on December 19. As the sun rose higher and higher, the tent became absolutely oppressive. The rime coating the walls inside thawed and water actually trickled into our finnesko. Usually we awoke to find them frozen stiff, just as we had shaped them on the previous night, but on this particular morning they were hanging limp and wet. The temperature inside the tent was 66° F., heated, of course, by the sun's rays which showed 105° F. on our black bulb thermometer. As the air temperature was 3° F. some idea can be obtained of the heating effect of the sun when there is absolutely no wind.

"Once into harness, we too began to feel it. By degrees we got rid of our clothing, but unfortunately soon came to bed-rock in that respect, as the underclothing was sewn on and immovable. At lunch time, with the thermometer at −2° F. in the shade, we reluctantly dressed knowing how soon we would cool off when halted. About 9 p.m. clouds moved over rapidly from the south-east and the landscape faded into the blank, shadowless nothing of an overcast day. The camp was pitched at two hundred and eighty-three miles amidst a jumble of ramps and sastrugi. The dip, to our satisfaction, had risen to 89° 35′.

"On December 21 the load on the sledge was stripped down to tent, dip-circle, theodolite, cooker and a little food. For two and a half miles we went south-east over rising ground until the sledge-meter showed three hundred and one miles.

"While Hurley and I pitched the tent, Webb built a break-wind for his instrument fifty yards away. Then followed a long set of observations.

"Magnetic work under these conditions is an extremely uncomfortable operation. Even a light wind will eddy round the break-wind, and it is wind which makes low temperatures formidable. Nearly all the work has to be done with bare fingers or thin instrument gloves, and the time taken is far greater than in temperate climates, owing to the fingers constantly 'going' and because of the necessity of continually freeing the instrument from frozen moisture condensed from fingers and body. Considering that the temperature was −12° F. when he had finished his four hours' work, it may be imagined that Webb was ready for his hot tea. The dip proved to be 89° 43.5′, that is, sixteen and a half minutes from the vertical. The altitude was just over five thousand nine hundred feet, in latitude 70° 36.5′ south and longitude 148° 10′ east.

"After lunch the Union Jack and the Commonwealth Ensign were hoisted and three cheers given for the King— willing but rather lonesome away out there! We searched the horizon with glasses, but could see nothing save snow, undulating and sastrugi-covered. To the south-east the horizon was limited by our old enemy, 'the next ridge,' some two miles away. We wondered what could be beyond, although we knew it was only the same featureless repetition, since one hundred and seventy-five miles on the same course would bring us to the spot where David, Mawson and Mackay had stood in 1909.

"After Hurley had taken a photograph of the camp, the tent was struck and the sledge repacked. Then sail was rigged and after a final glance round we turned on the homeward trail.

"That night the minimum thermometer registered −25° F., our lowest temperature for the journey. It was December 21 and Midsummer Day, so we concluded that the spot would be a very chilly one in the winter."

On the return march full use was made of the sail and progress was correspondingly rapid. For several days the outgoing tracks were frequently met in patches of snow left during a previous snowfall.

Unfortunately the sledge-meter developed a serious malady contracted by severe bumping over hard sastrugi. Spoke after spoke had parted. Henceforth for some time it was packed on the sledge in order to preserve it for a later stage of the march, when it would be required to supply dead-reckoning over a stretch of seventy miles where a short cut was contemplated to eliminate the detour to "The Nodules." In the interval, the mounds marking old camps were frequently picked up and served to check distances.

Webb continued to make occasional full sets of magnetic observations, and Hurley secured excellent photographs of the surface passed over.

Christmas Day arrived but, as the food store was low, it was decided to postpone the festal meal until arrival at the two-hundred mile depot. However, the nature of the celebration was all mapped out, and matured in its finer details during several days on the march.

At that period of their journey the wind blew steadily about thirty miles per hour, and a good deal of effort was consumed in dodging big ramps, overturning on sastrugi, or dragging upwind on the course to save lee-way.

On December 27 Bage writes: "With a thirty-five mile wind and a good deal of drift, we did not see the two-hundred-

and-three-mile mound until we almost ran into it. By three o'clock the great event occurred—the depot was found! We determined to hold the Christmas feast. After a cup of tea and a bit of biscuit, the rest of the lunch ration was put aside.

"Webb set up his instrument in the lee of the big mound and commenced a set of observations; I sorted out gear and rearranged the sledge load; Hurley was busy in the tent concocting all kinds of dishes. As the table-ware was limited to three mugs and the Nansen cooker, we had to come in to deal with each course the moment it was ready. Aiming at a really high-class meal, Hurley had started by actually cleaning out the cooker.

"The absence of reindeer-hair and other oddments made everything taste quite strange, though made from the same old ration with a few remaining 'perks.' After the 'raisin gliders,' soup and a good stiff hoosh, Webb finished his observations while I recorded for him. It is wonderful what sledging does for the appetite. For the first week of the journey, the unaccustomed ration was too much for us; but now when Hurley announced 'Pudding!' we were all still ravenous. It was a fine example of 'ye goode olde English plum-pudding' made from grated biscuit, fat picked out of the pemmican, raisins and glaxo-and-sugar, all boiled in an old food-bag.

"This pudding was so filling that we could hardly struggle through a savoury, 'Angels on runners' and cocoa. There was a general recovery when the 'wine' was produced, made from stewed raisins and primus alcohol; and The King was toasted with much gusto. At the first sip, to say the least, we were disappointed. The rule of 'no heel taps' nearly settled us, and quite a long interval and cigars, saved up for the occasion by Webb, were necessary before we could get courage enough to drink to the Other Sledging Parties and Our Supporting Party.

"The sun was low in the south when, cigars out and conversation lagging, we finally toggled in for the finest sleep of the whole journey.

"For the first ten miles on the afternoon of the 28th, the sail was reefed down to prevent the sledge overrunning us on smooth patches. Not far past the one-hundred-and-ninety-mile mound which was missed in the drift, we picked up some of our outward tracks—a bas-relief of three footsteps and a yard of sledge-meter track, all raised half an inch and undercut by the wind. It was not very much but quite a comfort when one is navigating in 'blind' weather.

"At 11.30 p.m. we had covered twenty-one miles, and both light and surface were improving, so I proposed making a long run of it. Hurley and Webb eagerly agreed, and we had a preparatory hoosh. Ten miles scudded by monotonously without a sign of the mounds around the one-hundred-and-seventy-mile camp. As we were in the vicinity of a point where we had determined to diverge from our outward track, a course was laid direct for the one-hundred-and-thirteen-mile mark. The sledge-meter, which had been affixed, made its presence evident from time to time by ringing like a cash-register, as still another spoke broke and struck the forks. We would halt for a moment and extract the remains. Out of the original thirty-six wire spokes, only twelve wire and one wooden one remained. At 11.30 a.m. on December 29, a halt was called and the sledge-meter was then lying over on its side with a helpless expression. It indicated twenty-two miles, making, so we thought, a total of forty-three miles in the twenty-two and a quarter hours since leaving the depot. Observations next day for a position proved that in its dying effort it had exaggerated the truth; the total run being 41.6 miles."

This constitutes a record for man-haul sledging between camp and camp.

The sledge-meter was cut away and left standing forlornly in the snow with a pair of worn-out finnesko hanging over it.

Bage discovered a novel way of repairing rents in the tent, dispensing with the unpleasant job of handling a needle in the thin wind. This consisted in using patches of "adhesive tape" from the medical kit. Heated over the primus or a fusee and pressed hard down between the bottom of mugs, held outside and inside the tent, it adhered well and made a permanent job.

Overcast days with falling snow followed and each member of the party became snow-blind in turn. Bage himself was attacked so severely that progress over the sastrugi-ribbed surface was impossible for him during part of two days. The state of the larder would not allow of a halt, so, assisted by the wind, Webb and Hurley pressed forward bringing Bage along on the sledge.

The continuance of bad weather raised doubts as to the chances of finding Southern Cross Depot, sixty-seven miles from the Hut; so the ration was reduced to eke out the food that remained.

On January 4 the neighbourhood of the depot was reached and the 5th, 6th and 7th were spent searching for it in falling snow and thick drift. They longed for a clearance, if only for a brief space, so that a view of the surrounding country might be obtained, for undoubtedly the cache was near at hand.

Their luck was out, for the morning of the 8th broke and there was still no clearance. Only a handful of food remained, notwithstanding the short ration upon which they had subsisted during previous days. They were indeed in perilous circumstances, but succeeded in extricating themselves by a masterly effort. Of this Bage writes:

"There was only one thing for it now, and that was to make a break for the coast. Of food, there was one full day's ration with enough pemmican for half a hoosh, six lumps of sugar and nine raisins, rather the worse for wear, oil for two days, and, last but not least, a pint of alcohol. After four days on half-rations we felt perfectly fit, thanks no doubt to the good meals of the previous week.

"There were sixty-seven miles to go, and as we could not hope to find the narrow descent to the Hut in thick weather, we decided to make the food spin out for five days. Everything unessential was stripped off the sledge, including dip-circle, thermometers, hypsometer, camera, spare clothing and most of the medical and repair kit.

"At 7 a.m. we set off on the final stage of the journey. The sky was densely overcast and snow was falling, but there was a strong wind almost behind. We would march for an hour by my wrist-watch, halt for five minutes, and on again till all agreed that we had covered ten miles; when it was lunch time. Each man's share of this consisted of one-third of a biscuit, one-third of an ounce of butter and a drink made of a spoonful of glaxo-and-sugar and one of absolute alcohol, mixed in a mug of lukewarm water. We could not afford oil enough to do much more than thaw the water, but the alcohol warmed us splendidly, enabling us to get a good rest.

"After an hour's spell we started again, luckily seeing just enough of the sun to check the course. The wind grew stronger in the afternoon and several times dense fog-banks drove down on us. Meeting one steep rise, we sidled round it for what seemed hours, but my chief memory of that afternoon was of the clouds of the northern horizon. They were a deep bluish-grey colour—a typical water-sky—but I have never seen clouds moving so fast. When all were satisfied that twenty miles had been covered we camped.

"Dinner consisted of a very watery hoosh, followed by a mug of alcohol and water. We were all very thankful for the forethought of Dr. Mawson in providing absolute alcohol for lighting the primus instead of methylated spirit.

"Breakfast on the 9th was of about the same consistency as dinner the night before, except that cocoa replaced the alcohol. In fact, breakfast was possibly even more watery, as I was in charge of the food-bag and surreptitiously decided to make the rations last six days instead of five.

"This was the worst day's march of the journey. The wind was booming along at sixty miles per hour with dense drift and falling snow. What made it worse was that it had veered to the south-east, and we had to pull partly across it. I was the upwind wheeler and had to hitch on to the side of the sledge to reduce the lee-way as much as possible. The sledge was being continually jammed into big, old, invisible sastrugi and we fell about in the wind until crampons became absolutely necessary.

"At 4 p.m. we were disgusted to find that the wind had veered to south-by-east. So, for possibly several hours, we had been doing Heaven-only-knows how many times the amount of work necessary, and for any time up to four hours might have been marching three points off our course. Being blown straight down-wind, the sledge made rapid progress, and about 6 p.m. a halt was called for lunch. This was over almost as soon as it was begun, but we had a good rest, sheltering ourselves with the floor-cloth from the wind which blew through the tent.

"Off again, we 'plugged' away until midnight, when we were much surprised to find the usual snow surface merging into blue ice. The tent was pitched on the latter, snow being procured from the bridge of a crevasse, as we had no ice-axe to break ice.

"Turning out on the morning of the 10th, we were delighted to find the sky clearing and the wind moderating. And then, far away on the horizon a beautiful line of blue sea dotted with bergs.

"We now officially considered ourselves to be twenty-seven miles from the Hut. As we should not have met blue ice on the proper course till we were within thirteen miles of the Hut, it was thought that we had edged a long way to the east the day before. When a start was made we manœuvred to the west in looking for a crossing-place at each crevasse.

"It was not long before the bergs on the horizon were noticeably enlarging, and at last we realized that in reality it was only a few miles to them. Suddenly the grade increased, the ice becoming much lacerated; and we had some trouble getting the sledge along. Hurley was snow-blind and had one eye covered. He looked very comical feeling his way over the crevasses, but he probably did not feel over-humorous.

"I was in the lead, and suddenly coming over a ridge above a steep ice-fall, I caught sight of the Mackeller Islets and the old 'Piano' berg. Just at the same instant the spur of ice on which I was standing collapsed and down I went into a crevasse. The others quickly had me out, and, as soon as I was on top, I gave them the news: 'There are the Islands!' Being twenty feet further back on the rope they had not yet seen them.

"We were now able to place ourselves about three miles west of Aladdin's Cave. The last camp must have been thirteen miles from the Hut, and we had really done twenty-seven miles each day instead of our conservative twenty.

"We tried to work along to the east, but the ice was too much broken, so the camp was made on a patch of snow. In view of our good fortune, I produced that evening's ration of hoosh in addition to our usual lunch. Even this meagre spree went against Hurley's feelings, for, being snow-blind, he had not been able to see the islands and positively would not believe that we were nearly home.

"After lunch it was necessary to retrace our way upwind to get out of the rough country. About midnight, Webb recognized Aladdin's Cave. Hurley and I had a competition as to who should see it first, for I was also getting a little blind again. We had a dead-heat at one hundred and fifty yards.

"The first thing to arrest our attention was a tin of dog biscuits. These kept things going until we dug out a food-tank from which was rapidly extracted a week's supply of chocolate. After that we proceeded in a happier frame of mind to open up the cave and have a meal.

"The journey of more than six hundred miles was now practically over. After a carousal lasting till 5 p.m. on the 11th, we went down the hill, arriving just after dinner and finding all well.

"We three had never thought the Hut quite such a fine place, nor have we ever since."

Bage, Webb and Hurley were certainly to be congratulated on their great effort and the thorough manner in which it was conducted under such cheerless and adverse circumstances. The information brought back proved that Adelie Land is continuous with South Victoria Land and part of the great Antarctic Continent.

CHAPTER XVI

EASTWARD OVER THE SEA-ICE

From Madigan's Narrative

MADIGAN, McLean and Correll had set out to delineate the coast line beyond a point sixty miles east of the Hut. Stillwell, Close and Hodgeman supported them for the first forty-six miles, and returned to winter quarters along a route which gave opportunity of charting part of the nearer sixty miles of the coast.

As already chronicled Madigan's and Stillwell's Parties took leave of Mertz, Ninnis and myself on the afternoon of November 17 at a point some twenty-five miles on their way. For their story from that time on, I have recourse to Madigan's extended narrative frequently quoting his own words.

All day long on the 18th they continued on a course due east, diverging to the north of the route followed by my own party. Rapid progress was made considering the heavy loads they were dragging. Madigan Nunatak was passed on the left and a vista of Watt Bay sprang into view. The next day the Supporting Party bade them adieu, turning off towards Mount Hunt.

At about fifty miles out, a wonderful panorama of Buchanan Bay and the Mertz Glacier Tongue opened up before them. "The sea lay just below, sweeping as a narrow gulf into the great, flat plain of debouching glacier-tongue which ebbed away north into the foggy horizon. A small ice-capped island was set like a pearl in the amethyst water." To the east, the glacier surface was lost in the horizon. Southward the view was limited by the steeply rising snow slopes of Mount Murchison.

The charting of the topography was commenced forthwith. This included the erection of a cairn as a back-sight for reference as they continued the march, laboriously toiling up the slopes to the south. Capsizes over high sastrugi were frequent; and to extricate the heavy sledge from some of the deep furrows it was necessary to unload the food-bags.

It was a long laborious day to gain a few miles, but the view that met their gaze from the domed summit of Mount Murchison was ample reward. The bold rocky outcrop of Aurora Peak, five miles to the south, was the first object to arrest attention. For the rest, a magnificent view into the far distance was opened out from that point of vantage. "The wind had subsided, the sky was clear and the sun stood low in the south-west. Our view had widened to a noble outlook. The sea, a delicate turquoise-blue, lay in the foreground of the low, white, northern ice-cliffs. Away to the east was the dim suggestion of land across the bed of the glacier, about which circled the southerly highlands of the plateau, buried at times in the haze of distance. Due south, twenty miles away, projecting from the glacier, was another island of rock—Correll Nunatak."

They were all worn with the stiff uphill climb. Correll had strained his back during the day as a result of over exertion and he was troubled also with a bleeding nose. Acute sunburn and snow-blindness were telling on Madigan and McLean. So it was decided that November 21 was to be a day in camp on the summit at an altitude of one thousand eight hundred and sixty feet. The day was spent erecting a cairn and making magnetic and topographical observations. Madigan was provided with a dip circle and at intervals throughout their journey made valuable determinations of the magnetic declination and dip.

The next day was devoted to an excursion to Aurora Peak. The weather remained quite clear and calm. With camera, food-bag, cooker and other paraphernalia for a day's tour secured on their backs, they set off down a deep descent to a ridge six hundred and seventy feet below. From thence there was a stiff climb to the summit, by a rocky shoulder and then up an arête of ice and névé. Roped together they worked upwards with the aid of ice-axes. The last ten steps were cut in an almost vertical face which gave a somewhat precarious foothold.

At 11.30 a.m. the summit was reached, an altitude of seventeen hundred and fifty feet. The top of the ridge was quite a knife-edge, with barely space for standing. The rock exposed on the face below proved to be a variety of gneiss, in the chinks of which moss and lichen flourished.

They had scarcely taken in the view when clouds rapidly spread across the sky, covering the sun and resulting in a "snow-blind" light. This development was rather alarming, for the climb had been difficult enough under a clear sky, and the descent entailed even more hazards than the ascent. Madigan writes:

"McLean started off first down the steps and was out of sight in a few moments. Then the rope tightened, Correll followed him and then I came last. It was very ticklish work feeling for the steps below with one's feet, and, as we signalled to one another in turn after moving a step, it took more than an hour to reach a safe position on the rocks. With every step I drove my axe into the ice, so that if the others had fallen there would still have been a last chance.

"There was no time to be wasted; light snow was falling with the prospect of becoming thicker. In the gully the snowfall became heavy, limiting the view to within a few hundred yards. We advanced up the hill in what seemed to be the steepest direction, but circled half-way round it before finding out that the course was wrong. Vainly trying to place the broad, flat summit I came across tracks in the snow, which were then carefully followed and led us to the tent. The wind was rising outside and the hoosh in steaming mugs was eaten with extra relish in our snug retreat."

On the morrow, after depositing a bag of food and certain dispensable articles, the eastern march was resumed. In the steep descent to the valley of the Mertz Glacier, a serious accident was narrowly averted. Correll and McLean were hitched on behind the sledge, braking its progress. Madigan remained harnessed in front to keep the direction. After proceeding downhill for two miles at a running pace, the slope became suddenly steeper and the sledge began to overtake the leader, who records:

"I had expected crevasses, in view of which I did not like all the loose rope behind me. Looking round, I shouted to the others to hold back the sledge, advancing a few steps while doing so. The bow of the sledge was almost at my feet, when—whiz! I was dropping down through space. The length of the hauling-rope was twenty-four feet, and I was at the end of it. I cannot say that 'my past life flashed before me.' I just had time to think 'Now for the jerk—will my harness hold?' when there was a wrench, and I was hanging breathless over the blue depth. Then the most anxious moment came—I continued to descend. A glance showed me that the crevasse was only four feet wide, so the sledge could not follow me, and I knew with a thankful heart that I was safe. I only descended about two feet more, and then stopped. I knew my companions had pulled up the sledge and would be anchoring it with the ice-axe.

"I had a few moments in which to take in my surroundings. Opposite to me was a vertical wall of ice, and below a beautiful blue, darkening to black in that unseen chasm. On either hand the rift of the crevasse extended, and above was the small hole in the snow bridge through which I had shot.

"Soon I heard McLean calling, 'Are you all right?' And I answered in what he and Correll thought an alarmingly distant voice. They started enlarging the hole to pull me out, until lumps of snow began to fall and I had to yell for mercy. Then I felt they were hauling, and slowly I rose to daylight."

Eventually, without further mishap, the bottom of the valley debouching on to the surface of the glacier below was reached at a point just over sixty miles from winter quarters. Above them, forming the northern scarp of the valley, stood the great riven ice wall from which avalanches had tumbled shattered blocks on to the snow slopes at its foot.

Soon after breaking camp on November 24, a lofty wall of rock peering out of the ice slopes was visited and found to be similar to that of Aurora Peak.

The track then lay across the surface of the glacier, and they were soon threading their way through terribly crevassed ground. "The blue ice was riven in every direction by gaping quarries and rose smooth and slippery on the ridges which broke the surface into long waves. Shod with crampons, the rear of the sledge secured by a tail-rope, we had a trying afternoon guiding the load along the narrow ridges of ice with precipices on either hand.

"We pushed on to find a place in which to camp, as there was scarcely safe standing-room for a primus stove. At seventy miles the broken ice gave way to a level expanse of hard sastrugi dotted all over with small mounds of ice about four feet high. After hoosh, a friendly little Wilson petrel came flying to our tent from the open sea to the north. We considered it to be a good omen.

"Next day the icy mounds disappeared, to be replaced by a fine, flat surface, and the day's march amounted to eleven and a quarter miles.

"At 11 a.m. four snow petrels visited us, circling round in great curiosity. It is a cheerful thing to see these birds amid the lone inhospitable ice.

"Occasionally there were areas of rubbly snow, blue ice and crevasses completely filled with snow; the latter of prodigious dimensions, two hundred to three hundred yards wide and running as far as the eye could travel. The snow filling them was perfectly firm, but, almost always along the windward edge, probing with an ice-axe would disclose a fissure. This part of the Mertz Glacier was apparently afloat.

"The lucky Wilson petrel came again that evening. At this stage the daily temperatures ranged from 10° F. to near freezing-point."

During November 26 the surface traversed developed into a series of shallow valleys running eastwards, and very soon the march came to an abrupt termination on the brow of a bluff, a bastion of the ice wall which forms the southern edge of the Mertz Glacier Tongue.

"In front lay a perfectly flat snow-covered plain—the frozen sea. In point of fact we had arrived at the far side of the Mertz Glacier at a point about fifteen miles north of the nearest part of the coast. Old floes, deeply covered in snow, lay ahead for miles, and the hazy, blue coast sank below the horizon in the south-east, running for a time parallel to the course we were about to take It was some time before we realized all this, but at noon the following day there came the first reminder of the proximity of sea-water.

"An Adelie penguin, ski-ing on its breast from the north, surprisedus suddenly by a loud squawk at the rear of the sledge. As astonished as we were, it stopped and stared, and then in sudden terror made off. But before starting on its long trek to the land, it had to be captured and photographed.

"To the south the coast was marked by two faces of rock and a short, dark spur protruding from beneath the ice-cap. As our friendly penguin had made off in that direction, we elected to call the place Penguin Point, intending to touch there on the return journey. During the afternoon, magnetic dips and a round of angles to the prominences of the mainland were taken.

"The next evidence of the sea-ice question came in the shape of a line of broken slabs of ice to the north, sticking out of the snow like the ruins of an ancient graveyard. At one hundred and fifteen miles the line was so close that we left the sledge to investigate it, finding a depression ten feet deep, through which wound a glistening riband of sea-water."

Away to the north a strong water-sky indicated open sea. To the east, across the floe, a glinting line on the far horizon caught the eye; at the time its meaning remained in doubt. Beyond was an unmistakable ice-blink.

It seemed advisable to continue on an easterly course approximately parallel with the coast. By the evening of December 2 the mysterious line, limned on the horizon two days previously, was reached. It proved to be the western edge of another great floating mass of land-ice projecting from the coast—the Ninnis Glacier Tongue. Of course, its exact nature was not fully ascertained at the moment, and remained to be made known by the developments of ensuing days.

From the sea-ice on to the surface of the ice-tongue there was a gentle rise of one hundred and seventy feet to the summit of a prominent knoll. There, at a distance of one hundred and fifty-two miles from the Hut, a bag of food was deposited under a snow mound.

With four weeks' food on the sledge they resumed the march on December 3. The course was changed to 30° north of east in order to investigate the land appearing in that direction on the charts based on Wilkes's reports. Eager for the revelations of the morrow, they were spurred on from day to day full of hope and expectation. Madigan chronicles:

"Across rolling downs of soft, billowy snow we floundered for twenty-four miles, on the two following days. Not a wind-ripple could be seen. We appeared to be in a region of comparative calms, which was a remarkable thing, considering that the windiest spot in the world was less than two hundred miles away.

"On December 5, at the top of a rise, we were suddenly confronted with a new vision—'Thalassa!' was our cry, 'the sea!' but a very different sea from that which brought such joy to the wandering Greeks. Unfolding to the horizon was a plain of floe-ice, thickly studded with bergs and intersected by black leads of open water. In the north-east was a patch of open sea and above it, round to the north, lowering banks of steel-blue cloud. We had come to the eastern side of Ninnis Glacier Tongue.

The excitement of exploring this new realm was to be deferred. Even as we raised the tent, the wind commenced to whistle and the air became surcharged with snow. Three skua gulls squatted a few yards away, squawking at our approach, and a few snow-petrels sailed by in the gathering blizzard."

It was now clear that land did not exist to the north or to the east. As a matter of fact, though unaware of it at the time, they were seventy miles out to sea from the nearest land to the south of them.

The blizzard continued for the greater part of four days and it was not until the 10th that the tent was struck. A course was set to the south-east in which direction they expected to fall in with the coast.

"The next six days out on the broken sea-ice were full of incident. The weather was gloriously sunny till the 13th, during which time the sledge had to be dragged through a forest of pinnacles and over areas of soft, sticky slush which made the runners execrable for hours. Ponds of open water, by which basked a few Weddell seals, became a familiar sight."

During a blow on the 13th the unstable condition of the sea-ice, indicated by the presence of numerous leads of open water, caused them many hours of anxiety.

The section of the floe first traversed was of the nature of consolidated pack-ice, rendered more irregular still by the presence of occasional pressure-ridges. By dint of hard toil a near-shore belt of smooth bay-ice was reached. Even then, as was subsequently discovered, they were still forty-five miles off the coast.

"It was a fine flat surface on which the sledge ran, and the miles commenced to fly by, comparatively speaking. Except for an occasional deep rift, whose bottom plumbed to the sea-water, the going was excellent. Each day the broken ice on our left receded, the land to the south grew closer and traces of rock became discernible in the low, fractured cliffs."

On December 17 a well defined cape—Cape Freshfield— lay ahead, and to the south was visible a striking rocky promontory—the Horn Bluff.

"The Bluff was a place worth exploring. At a distance of more than fifteen miles, the spot suggested all kinds of possibilities, and in council we argued that it was useless to go much farther east, as to touch at the land would mean a detour on the homeward track and time would have to be allowed for that.

"As we neared Horn Bluff, on the first stage of our homeward march, the upper layer of snow was observed to disappear, and the underlying sea-ice became thinner in corrugated sapphire plains with blue reaches of sparkling water. McLean and I both soaked our feet and once I was immersed to the thighs, having to stop and put on dry socks and finnesko. It was a chilly process allowing the trousers to dry on me."

The great rock wall towered up higher and higher as the sledge approached its foot. When still more than a mile away, the warm sunshine was left and they entered a great shadow cast on the ice. The mammoth cliff reared its head almost sheer from the sea one thousand feet into the skies. The vertical face extended for five miles as a magnificent series of gigantic organ-pipes of columnar lava—a dolerite rock, to be specific, above a pedestal of stratified rocks of sedimentary origin, for the most part buried in rubble fallen from above. "The columns, roughly hexagonal and weathered to a dull-red, stood above in sheer perpendicular lines of six hundred and sixty feet in altitude.

"Far up the face of the cliff snow-petrels fluttered like white butterflies. It was stirring to think that these majestic heights had gazed out across the wastes of snow and ice for countless ages, and never before had the voices of human beings echoed in the great stillness nor human eyes surveyed the wondrous scene.

"From the base of the organ-pipes sloped a mass of debris; broken blocks of rock of every size tumbling steeply to the splintered hummocks of the sea-ice.

"Standing out from the top of this talus-slope were several white 'beacons' up to which we scrambled when the tent was pitched. This was a tedious task as the stones were ready to slide down at the least touch, and often we were carried down several yards by a general movement. Wearing soft finnesko, we ran the risk of getting a crushed foot amongst the large boulders. Amongst the rubble were beds of clay shale, and streams of thaw-water trickled down to the surface of a frozen lake.

"The beacons proved to be the projections of sandstone with occasional layers of coal,* and carbonized plant remains.

"That night we had a small celebration on raisins, chocolate and apple rings,† besides the ordinary fare of hoosh, biscuit and cocoa. Several times we were awakened

---

* A notable discovery. Apparently a continuation of the coal formation discovered in the Ross Sea region by the Scott and Shackleton expeditions. A remarkable sheet of coal extending in a north and south direction, more or less unbroken for over 1200 miles, to within 280 miles of the geographic pole.
† Dried sliced apples.

by the crash of falling stones. Snow-petrels had been seen coming home to their nests in the beacons, which were weathered out into small caves and crannies. From the camp we could hear their harsh cries."

The following day Madigan and Correll were chiefly occupied in preparing a rough survey and further investigating the rock formations. McLean took photographs and collected samples of lichens, algæ, moss, etc.

After lunch on December 21 the homeward trail was begun. By keeping nearer in shore than on the outward march, the floe proved less broken and progress was rapid. For three days the march continued in a moderate following wind, under full sail, through a mist of driving snow. They pushed on blindly knowing nothing of what was passing on either side; occasionally happening upon insurmountable obstacles, such as icebergs held in the floe, necessitating a detour.

Christmas was celebrated in good style at a camp on the Ninnis Glacier Tongue. McLean was chef for the occasion, and seized the opportunity to introduce fresh penguin into the menu; evidently with excellent results for Madigan records that they subsequently retired to their bags feeling very comfortable inside.

December 26 found them on the western side of the Ninnis Glacier Tongue, where they descended one hundred and eighty feet on to the floe. The depot hill to the northwest could be recognized, twenty miles away, across a wide bay. This was reached the following evening and the food recovered.

Penguin Point, thirty miles away, was the next objective; a survey of the coast was plotted *en route*. At the Point a rock wall three hundred feet high formed the sea-face, jutting out from beneath the ice slopes of the buried land. Camp was pitched and a full day devoted to investigating the locality.

"I had noticed a continuous rustling sound for some time and found at length that it was caused by little streams of ice crystals running down the steep slopes in cascades, finally pouring out in piles on the sea-ice. The partial thaw in the sunlight causes the glacier-ice to break up into separate grains. Sometimes whole areas of the surface, in delicate equilibrium, would suddenly flow rapidly away.

"During the afternoon, on the summit of the Point, it was found that an uneven rocky area, about a quarter of a mile wide, ran backwards to the ice-falls of the plateau. The surface was very broken and weathered, covered in patches by abundant lichens and mosses. Fossicking round in the gravel, Correll happened on some tiny insect-like mites living amongst the moss or on the moist underside of slabs of stone.

"At 8.30 a.m. on New Year's Eve we set off for another line of rocks about four miles away to the west. There were two masses forming an angle in the ice-front and consisting of two main ridges rising to a height of two hundred and fifty feet, running back into the ice-cap for a mile, and divided by a small glacier.

"This region was soon found to be a perfect menagerie of life. Seals lay about dozing peacefully by the narrow lanes of water. Adelie penguins strutted in procession up and down the little glacier. To reach his rookery from a water-lead at the ice-foot, a penguin would leap four feet on to a ledge, painfully pad up the glassy slope and then awkwardly scale the rocks to an elevation of one hundred and fifty feet. There he took over the care of a chick or an egg, while the other bird went to fish. Skua gulls flew about, continually molesting the rookeries. One area of the rocks was covered by a luxuriant growth of green moss flourishing on guano and littered skeletons—the site of a deserted rookery.

"Correll and I went up to where the ridges converged, selecting numerous specimens of rock and mineral and finding thousands of small red mites in the moist gravel. Down on the southern ridge we happened on a Wilson petrel with feathered nestlings. At this point McLean came along from the west with the news of silver-grey petrels, and Cape pigeons nesting in hundreds. He had secured two of each species and several eggs. This was indeed a discovery, as the eggs of the former birds had never before been found. Quite close to us were many snow-petrels in all kinds of unexpected crevices."

Having secured a small store of penguin meat to replenish the larder, a start was made for the depot on Mount Murchison. Unsettled weather commenced and then followed days of wind and falling snow. Progress was reduced correspondingly.

The crossing of the Mertz Glacier Tongue in such snow-blind weather was beset with hazards. Grim dangers lurked beneath a covering blanket of snow. It was a frequent occurrence for one of them to pitch forward with his feet down a crevasse, at times going through to the waist. The travelling was most nerve-racking. The only thing to do was to go ahead and trust to Providence. They came very near to losing their lives before reaching the Mount Murchison depot. Madigan writes:

"At last we landed the sledge on a narrow ridge of hard snow, surrounded by blue, gaping pits in a pallid eternity of white. It was only when the tent was pitched that a wide quarry was noticed a few yards away from the door.

"It was now fourteen miles to the top of Mount Murchison and we had only two more days' rations and one and a half pounds of penguin-meat.

"On January 7th the light was worse than ever and snow fell. It was only six miles across the broken country between us and the gully between Mount Murchison and Aurora Peak, where one could travel with some surety. A sharp look-out was kept, and towards 11 p.m. a rim of clear sky overtopped the southern horizon. We knew the sun would curve round into it at midnight, so all was made ready for marching.

"When the sun's disc emerged into the rift there was light; but dim, cold and fleeting. The smallest irregularity on the surface threw a shadow hundreds of yards long. The plain around was a bluish-grey chequer-board of light and shade; ahead, sharp and clear against the leaden sky, stood beautiful Aurora Peak, swathed in lustrous gold—the chariot of the goddess herself. The awful splendour of the scene tended to depress one and make the task more trying. I had never felt more nervous than I did in that ghostly light in the tense silence, surrounded by the hidden horror of fathomless depths. All was covered with a uniform layer of snow, growing heavier and deeper at every step. I was ahead and went through eight times in about four miles. The danger lay in getting the sledge and one, two, or all of us on a weak snow bridge at the same time. As long as the sledge did not go down we were comparatively safe.

"By 5.30 a.m. we breathed freely on *terra firma*, even though one sunk through a foot of snow to feel it. It had taken six hours to do the last five and three-quarter miles, and, being tired out with the strain on muscles and nerves, we raised the tent, had a meal, and then slept till noon on the 8th. It was eight miles to the depot, five miles up the gully and three miles to the summit of Mount Murchison; and no one doubted for a moment that it could be done in a single day's march.

"Advancing up the gully after lunch, we found that the surface became softer, and we were soon sinking to the knees at every step. The runners, too, sank till the decking rested on the snow, and it was as much as we could do to shift the sledge, with a series of jerks at every step. At 6 p.m. matters became desperate. We resolved to make a depot of everything unnecessary, and to relay it up the mountain afterwards.

"The sledge-meter, clogged with snow and almost submerged, was taken off and stood up on end to mark a depot, whilst a pile was made of the dip-circle, theodolite and tripod, pick, alpine rope, ice-axe, all the mineral and biological specimens and excess clothing.

"Even thus lightened, we could scarcely move the sledge, struggling on, sinking to the thighs in the flocculent deluge. Snow now began to fall so thickly that it was impossible to see ahead.

"At 7 p.m. we finished up the last scraps of pemmican and cocoa. Biscuit, sugar and glaxo had given out at the noon meal. There still remained one and a half pounds of penguin-meat, several infusions of tea and plenty of kerosene for the primus.

"We staggered on till 10.30 p.m., when the weather became so dense that the sides of the gully were invisible. Tired out, we camped and had some tea. In eight hours we had only made four and a half miles, and there was still the worst part to come.

"In our exhausted state we slept till 11 p.m. of January 9, awakening to find the sky densely overcast and a light fog in the air. During a rift which opened for a few minutes there was a short glimpse of the rock on Aurora Peak. Shreading half the penguin-meat, we boiled it up and found the stew and broth excellent.

"At 1.30 a.m. we started to struggle up the gully once more, wading along in a most helpless fashion, with breathing spells every ten yards or less. Snow began to fall in such volume that at last it was impossible to keep our direction with any certainty. The only thing to do was to throw up the tent as a shelter and wait. This we did till 4.30 a.m.; but there must have been a cloud-burst, for the heavy flakes toppled on to the tent like tropical rain. We got into sleeping-bags, and tried to be patient and to forget that we were hungry.

"It was evident that without any more food, through this bottomless, yielding snow, we could never haul the sledge up to the depot, a rise of one thousand two hundred feet in three miles. One of us must go up and bring food back, and I decided to do so as soon as the weather cleared.

"We found the wait for clearer weather long and trying with empty stomachs. As the supply of tobacco still held out, McLean and I found great solace in our pipes. All through the rest of the day and till 5 p.m. of the next, January 10, there was not a rift in the opaque wall of flakes. Then to our intense relief the snow stopped, the clouds rolled to the north, and, in swift transformation—a cloudless sky with bright sunshine! With the rest of the penguin-meat—a bare half-pound—we had another thin broth. Somewhat fortified I took the food-bag and shovel, and left the tent at 5.30 a.m.

"Often sinking to the thighs, I felt faint at the first exertion. The tent scarcely seemed to recede as I toiled onwards towards the first steep slope. The heavy mantle of snow had so altered the contours of the side of the gully that I was not sure of the direction of the top of the mountain.

"Resting every hundred yards, I floundered on hour after hour, until, arriving at a high point, I saw a little shining mound standing up on a higher point, a good mile to the east.

After seven hours' wading I reached it and found that it was the depot.

"Two feet of the original eight-foot mound projected above the surface, with the bamboo pole and a wire-and-canvas flag rising another eighteen inches. On this, a high isolated mountain summit, six feet of snow had actually accumulated. How thankful I was that I had brought a shovel!

"At seven feet I 'bottomed' on the hard snow, without result. Then, running a tunnel in the most probable direction I struck with the shovel the kerosene tin which was on top of the food-bag. On opening the bag, the first items to appear were sugar, butter and biscuits; the next quarter of an hour I shall not forget.

"I made a swag of five days' provisions, and, taking a direct route, attacked the three miles downhill in lengths of one hundred and fifty yards. Coming in sight of the tent, I called to my companions to thaw some water for a drink. So slow was progress that I could speak to them a quarter of an hour before reaching the tent. I had been away eleven and a half hours, covering about seven miles in all.

"McLean and Correll were getting anxious about me. They said that they had felt the cold and were unable to sleep. Soon I had produced the pemmican and biscuit, and a scalding hoosh was made. The other two had had only a mug of penguin broth each in three days, and I had only broken my fast a few hours before them."

Madigan's splendid effort had saved the situation, but only just in time, for a blizzard lasting three days followed, effectually blotting out the landscape.

Eventually a start for home was made on the 14th, and the fifty-three miles melted away in pleasurable anticipation. Winter quarters was reached three days later, and thus was concluded a highly successful enterprise, rich in results. Madigan's chart of the land seen, the discovery of a coal-bearing formation, and information accumulated regarding the character of the off-shore ice were all most valuable contributions.

CHAPTER XVII

ACROSS ADELIE LAND—TO EAST AND WEST

From Stillwell's and Bickerton's Reports

LEAVING Madigan's Party on November 19, Stillwell, Hodgeman and Close diverged towards the snow dome of Mount Hunt. On arrival at the summit, it was found to be the top of a well-defined promontory. A wide seascape dotted with bergs was unfolded to the north. To the west the coast extended in a sweeping curve—Watt Bay—passing out of sight amidst a chaos of bergs and islets on the far horizon. To the north-east was the flat-topped expanse of the Mertz Glacier Tongue with sheer-faced, jutting headlands succeeding one another into the distance.

Madigan Nunatak was the next point of interest visited. This curious black pinnacle, rearing its head above the icy wilderness, was an object of keen speculation. It proved to be a jagged crest of rock one hundred and sixty yards long and thirty yards wide, placed at an altitude of two thousand four hundred feet above sea-level; an excellent landmark, so a quantity of food was depoted there for future use.

The party reached winter quarters on November 27, where noticeable changes had taken place during their absence. The flow-ice had broken back a long distance towards the head of the Boat Harbour, and what remained was rotten and ready to blow out under the influence of the first strong wind; marked thawing had occurred everywhere and many islands of rock emerged from the snow; the ice-foot was diminishing; penguins, seals and flying birds made the place, for once, alive and busy.

Bickerton, Whetter and Hannam carried on the routine of work; Whetter as meteorologist and Hannam as magnetician, while Bickerton was busied with the air-tractor and in preparation for sledging. Thousands of penguins eggs had been gathered for the return voyage of the *Aurora*, or in case of detention for a second winter.

Murphy, Hunter and Laseron arrived from the south on the same day as Stillwell, Hodgeman and Close came in from the east. The former party had plodded for sixty-seven miles through a dense haze of drift, keeping a course roughly by the wind and the direction of sastrugi. The unvarying white light of thick overcast days had been so severe that all were suffering from snow-blindness. When, at length, they passed over the endless billows of snow on to the downfalls near the coast, the weather cleared and they were relieved to see once more the Mecca of all sledging parties—Aladdin's Cave.

A redistribution of parties and duties was made. Hodgeman joined Whetter and Bickerton in preparation for the air-tractor trip to the west, Hunter acted as meteorologist as well as devoting as much time as possible to biological investigations amongst the immigrant life of summer. Hannam continued to act as magnetician and general handy man. Murphy, who was also to be in charge at the Hut during the summer, was busy making preparations for departure.

In pursuance of a plan to examine in detail the coast immediately east of Commonwealth Bay, Stillwell set out with Laseron and Close on December 9. The weather was threatening at the start, and they had a struggle with wind and drift to reach Aladdin's Cave.

Next morning owing to inadequate ventilation, the whole party was overcome quite unexpectedly during breakfast. Hoosh was cooked and about to be served, when Stillwell, who was in charge of the primus, suddenly collapsed without any warning. Laseron went down at the same moment. Close, seeing his companions sink to the floor unconscious, realized what was happening not a moment too soon; he was just able to stand up and thrust the point of an ice-axe through the packed snow choking the entrance, when he also fell forward overcome. An hour and a half later—so it was reckoned—the party revived. The hole made by the ice-axe had been sufficient to save their lives. For a day they were too weak and exhausted to travel, so the tent was pitched and the night spent outside the cave.

During the weeks following till January 5, 1913, when they again reached the Hut, this Near-East Party, as it was called, worked assiduously charting and otherwise investigating the land north of Madigan Nunatak.

Along that coast, within a length of twenty-four miles, their chart shows one hundred and fifty small islands—the Way Archipelago. Such remarkable fringes of islets are a feature of portions of the coast of Adelie Land. It was evident that, during the winter, the islets of the Way Archipelago were linked up by a thick sheet of sea-ice; for Stillwell's party was just in time to observe the broken remnants of floe, as immense rectangular blocks, floating away to the north.

Several rock exposures on the sea-front were accessible to them. A great discovery was made on December 29. On the abrupt, northern face of some rocks connected to the ice-cap of the mainland by a causeway of ice, a large colony of sea-birds had nested. Cape penguins, the rare silver-grey and snow-petrels were all present. Amongst these Laseron made a collection of rare eggs and skins, and secured some instructive photographs.

They returned to the Hut well stocked with data and specimens, having successfully accomplished the survey allotted to them.

Returning to the fortunes of the air-tractor sledge and Bickerton's Party who were to start west early in December. Ours was not the first experiment in the application of mechanical transport to Antarctic land exploration. Shackleton had tried a motor car and Scott had set out with caterpillar-tractor sledges. Though useful to a certain degree, both had failed to be of any very great service. We had decided to try an air-tractor.

A suitable mechanism of the kind was most readily acquired by modifying an aeroplane, relieving it of its wings

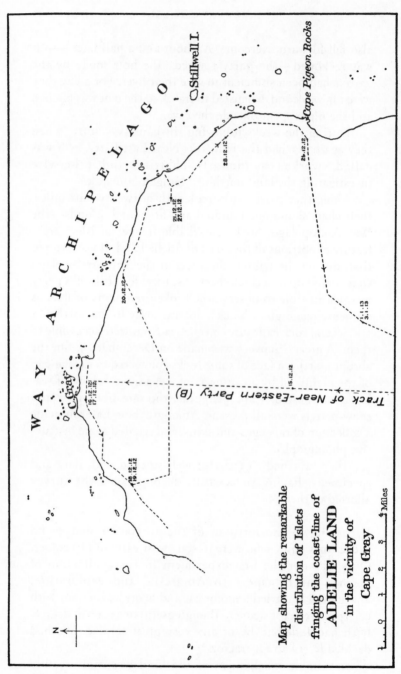

Map showing the remarkable distribution of Islets fringing the Coast-line of Adelie Land in the vicinity of Cape Gray.

and replacing the lower part of the under-carriage with long sledge runners fitted with brakes. The advantages expected from this type of machine were speed, steering control and comparative safety from crevasses owing to the great length of the runners.

Had Adelie Land been favoured with a normal Antarctic climate or a surface to travel over comparable with the Ross Barrier, where its rivals had been put to the test, there would have been a very different tale to tell.

As it was, owing to the continuous winds it had spent almost the whole year helpless and drift-bound in the hangar. During those months, Bickerton had expended a great amount of energy upon it, introducing brilliant ideas of his own into the mechanism to adapt it to local requirements. Only on November 15 was the first trial possible.

Shortly afterwards several successful trips were made up the ice slopes to Aladdin's Cave where a cargo of petrol was depoted. In the execution of this work a speed of twenty miles per hour was attained up ice slopes of one in fifteen, in the face of a wind of fifteen miles per hour. Bickerton had reason to feel highly elated with its success.

During a calm spell on the afternoon of December 3, Bickerton, Whetter and Hodgeman set out on what was to be a journey across the coastal highlands of Adelie Land. The following story is an outline of Bickerton's narrative.

An hour after leaving the camp Aladdin's Cave was passed. The three men with the air-tractor towing a chain of four loaded sledges continued on towards Cathedral Grotto. Very soon the engine developed an internal disorder which Bickerton was at a loss to diagnose or remedy. This necessitated pitching camp for the night before the Grotto was reached. At 4 p.m. next day, after drifting snow had subsided, the engine was started once more. Its behaviour, however, indicated that something was the matter with one or more of the cylinders. Bickerton was on the point of deciding to take the engine to pieces, when his thoughts were brought to a sudden close by the engine, without any warning, pulling up with such a jerk that the propeller was smashed. A moment's examination showed that even more irremediable damage* had occurred inside the engine, so there was nothing left but to abandon the air-tractor and continue on the journey man-hauling their sledge.

All but absolute necessities were cached and they moved off with one sledge carrying six weeks' provisions. To avoid the crevasses which infest the coastal slopes they steered first of all to the south-west to bring them far enough inland to be free from such dangers.

The morning of December 5 was bright and clear. After six miles' tramping the sastrugi became hard and compact and the course was changed to due west. Shortly afterwards a black object seen on the surface ahead aroused their interest; this proved to be a meteorite measuring approximately five inches by three inches by three and a half inches. When camp was pitched that evening at an elevation of three thousand feet the view of the sea was lost.

The following day it was drifting hard and part of the morning was spent theorizing on their prospects in an optimistic vein. The humour gradually wore off as the thick drift continued with a fifty-mile wind for three days. Eventually on the 8th the march was resumed in bad weather. Under such conditions every mile over the rough sastrugi surface was a struggle; but the difficulties imposed by the weather were not the only troubles. The jarring over hard sastrugi soon shook the sledge-meter to pieces and henceforth they were without that valuable guide to dead-reckoning.

The days went by as they floundered on in the drift under reefed sail with a wind on their after quarter; one man behind holding up the rear by means of a tail-rope to prevent the sledge swinging round broadside on.

No sooner was Friday, December 13, ushered in than a catastrophe overtook them. The leader, who was breaking the load up-wind, slipped and fell at a critical moment allowing the sledge to collide with a large sastruga. The bow

---

* At a later date Bickerton succeeded in bringing the air-tractor back to the Hut where it was opened up and examined. It appeared that several of the pistons had seized and were broken.

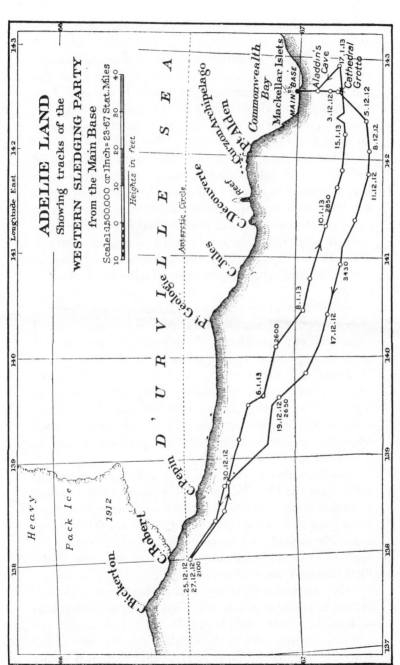

Map showing the Tracks of the Western Sledging Party from the Main Base.

struck the marble-like névé with such force that it was smashed.

The next day Bickerton and Hodgeman ingeniously manufactured a new bow from a spare, solid bamboo that had been carried for use as a depot pole. It was split, bent into position and then lashed with raw hide. The makeshift proved a great success and in spite of severe treatment stood for the rest of the journey.

Whilst on the march on December 16 the wind dropped and the drift ceased for the first time since December 5. The next morning they were visited by a Wilson petrel whose inquisitiveness had brought it thirty miles inland to an elevation of three thousand five hundred feet to investigate the dark speck in the snow-field which their camp assumed. The next four days passed in excellent weather. Making up for lost time a distance of ninety-seven miles was covered in five days.

On December 19 camp was pitched at 1 a.m. before a glorious view; an horizon of sea from west to north-east and white fields of massive bergs. The following day the route lay along ice slopes skirting a great bay.

From December 21 there was a four days' hurricane, the wind attaining a velocity of eighty miles per hour. Sleeping-bags and floor-cloth were in a wretched state. Under these conditions, in cramped quarters, the tent having encroached upon the occupants owing to snow packing around it, Christmas was not very enjoyable.

On December 26 at a point one hundred and fifty-eight miles from the Hut the limit of the journey was reached. From that camp at an altitude of over two thousand feet there was a good view to the north-west along about fifty miles of coast. Northward pack-ice was seen extending beyond the limit of vision. Hodgeman sketched in the view whilst Bickerton took observations for position.

They had learnt that though the season was meteorologically to be regarded as summer, it was hardly recognizable as such on the Adelie Land plateau. There was little prospect of any real improvement in the weather, and the state of the larder, as well as the short interval that remained before they were due at the Hut, warned them that the time to turn back had arrived.

By December 30 they had reoccupied the camp of the 20th. Whilst Bickerton took observations for time and magnetic declination, Hodgeman and Whetter went to investigate two odd-looking prominences about five miles away. These turned out to be high snow ramps, two hundred yards long, on the lee side of open crevasses. The next day, an expedition planned to visit a rock outcrop visible at sea-level on the coast had to be abandoned owing to adverse weather.

Experience taught them that the winds fell off considerably, with great regularity, in the late afternoon and early evening.* Of this they were not slow to take advantage, so night marches became the rule. Neither on the outward nor on the return journey did they catch sight of the depot made by Madigan's Party in the spring; but it was not to be expected considering the strict limitation of visibility owing to drift.

Aladdin's Cave was reached on January 17, concluding an adventure which by reason of atrocious weather conditions remains a nightmare to the participants. But the results were amply worth the sacrifice, for they have furnished concrete account of the hinterland of that stretch of coast which Dumont d'Urville sighted from the sea and to which he gave the name of Adelie Land.

---

* A land- and sea-breeze effect superimposed upon the normal conditions.

CHAPTER XVIII

THE SHIP'S STORY

From Captain Davis's Narrative

On return from his extended Antarctic voyage in March 1912, after calling at Hobart, Captain J. K. Davis proceeded with the *Aurora* to Sydney. There she was refitted at the Cockatoo Island dockyard, in preparation for sub-Antarctic cruises in which deep-sea soundings and dredgings were to form part of the programme.

The Lucas deep-sea sounding machine, designed for ascertaining depths up to six thousand fathoms, was mounted on the port side of the fo'c'sle head. In this machine a fine strand of steel wire, as it is paid out weighted heavily at the end, is made to pass over a wheel which measures and records the number of fathoms. The action of the sinker striking the bottom causes a spring brake to stop the reel of wire from further unwinding; at the same time the sinker automatically disengages, for it is more economical to use a fresh piece of cast-iron each time than laboriously to haul the weight from the bottom of the sea.

When, in addition to ascertaining the depth, samples of the bottom are required, other devices, which automatically secure specimens of the mud or rock as they strike the bottom, are attached to the end of the wire.

A second Lucas machine was installed on the starboard bow, available in case of emergency. There was also a larger mechanism operating with five-ply wire designed for obtaining serial temperatures and water samples. So there were, altogether, three sounding machines fitted on the *Aurora*, besides the small Kelvin instrument astern which was used mainly for purposes of navigation. The arduous work of winding in the wire after each sounding was eliminated by the application of a small steam-driven engine, which had been specially designed for the *Scotia* and was kindly lent to us by Dr. W. S. Bruce.

The form of trawl used on the *Aurora* for deep-water operations is known as a Mongasque trawl. For this work, a special winch and an immense drum of stout steel wire cable were installed, the latter set up on the main deck well forward on the starboard side.

During the winter and early summer of 1912, two cruises were undertaken in the seas south of Tasmania and New Zealand, calling on each occasion at Macquarie Island and the Auckland Islands. On the first occasion the *Aurora* started from Sydney on May 18, and with her, as biologist, went Mr. E. R. Waite, curator of the Canterbury Museum, Christchurch. At the conclusion of the cruise a call was made at Lyttelton, New Zealand, where Mr. J. J. Kinsey, well known in connection with various British Antarctic expeditions, gave them every assistance during their stay.

For the second cruise, the ship departed from Melbourne early in November, having on board as biologist Professor T. Flynn of Hobart University.

Nowhere in the wide ocean are the seas more tempestuous and less suited to sounding and dredging operations than in this area; so the winter programme was beset with difficulties. Nevertheless, the ship's company was successful in adding considerably to the trophies of the Expedition; in accumulating valuable data, and in making several important discoveries.

Three hundred miles to the south of Hobart, Captain Davis located a submerged "island" comparable in size to Tasmania. The Mill Rise, as it was named, mounts from depths of more than two thousand fathoms to within five hundred and forty fathoms of the surface.

Macquarie Island was found to be isolated from the sub-Antarctic islands of New Zealand by a deep trough. Davis, in his report writes: "Some idea of the steepness of the submarine mountain of which Macquarie forms the crest may be gathered from a sounding, taken ten and a half miles east of the island, which gave two thousand seven hundred and

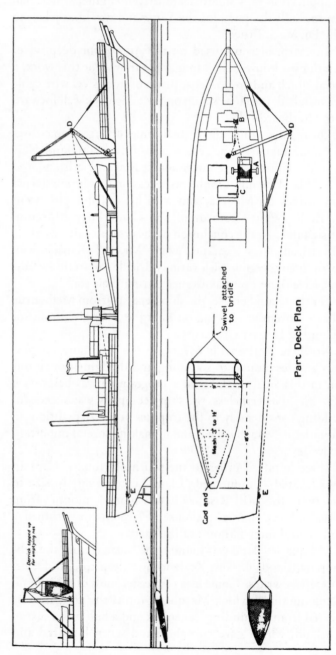

Part Deck Plan

Swivel attached to bridle

Cod end

Mesh 3" to 4"

Derrick topped up for emptying net

Plan illustrating the arrangements for Deep-Sea Trawling on board the *Aurora*.

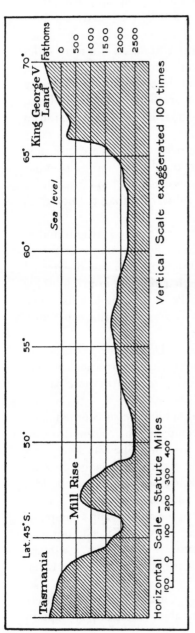

A Section of the Floor of the Southern Ocean between Tasmania and King George V Land.

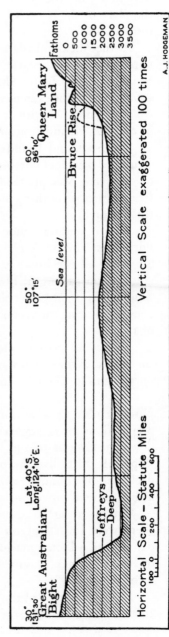

A Section of the Floor of the Southern Ocean between Western Australia and Queen Mary Land.

forty-five fathoms and no bottom. In other words, if the sea were to dry up, there would be a lofty mountain rising from the plain of the ocean's bed to a height of nearly eighteen thousand feet."

At the Auckland Islands, three hundred and forty miles north-east of Macquarie Island, dredgings were made in several of the harbours. Skins of the abundant bird life were secured, including examples of a rare flightless duck. Sea-lions, which are not met with at Macquarie Island, were found to be everywhere numerous here.

The Auckland Islands are overgrown by a dense, low scrub the principal component of which is rata, a peculiar dwarfed tree. Macquarie Island is evidently too far south for trees to exist, as nothing more substantial than tussock grass thrives there.

A short stay was made both at Carnley Harbour and at Port Ross. The brick pier erected by the magneticians of Sir James Clarke Ross's expedition of 1840 was discovered amongst the undergrowth after having been lost sight of for so many years. At Observation Point they found a flat stone commemorating the visit of the German scientific expedition of 1874.

The *Aurora* arrived at Hobart on December 14, concluding the second of the sub-Antarctic cruises. Preparations were at once begun for the relieving voyage to the Antarctic bases.

On December 24, after working at high pressure for ten days, preparations for sailing were complete. The *Aurora* dropped down the river at 10 a.m. on the 26th. She was a very full ship with thirty-five sheep and twenty-one sledge dogs on deck, and five hundred and twenty-one tons of coal besides a large store of provisions and equipment below.

On this voyage in addition to the regular ship's company, there were four supernumeraries: van Waterschoot van der Gracht, a Dutch marine artist; S. N. Jeffryes, a wireless operator; James Davis, whaling master; C. C. Eitel, secretary.

In the early part of the voyage heavy westerly gales were encountered, but under the very able seamanship of Captain

J. K. Davis the *Aurora* came through without serious damage. On one occasion a sea swept over everything and flooded the cabins. Part of the rail of the fo'c'sle head was carried away on the morning of the 31st. At that time they were in the vicinity of the reputed position of the Royal Company Islands. A sounding was taken under most difficult circumstances, finding two thousand and twenty fathoms and a mud bottom. Thus was the possibility of the existence of those islands finally disposed of, for Davis had spent some time during the winter voyage cruising about in that neighbourhood without meeting anything.

The first ice was reached at 6 p.m. on January 10 in about latitude 64° 30' S. The pack-ice zone was traversed during the 11th and 12th, and at 2 a.m. on the 13th anchor was dropped at Cape Denison. At that date there were only nine men at the Hut, for three of the sledging parties were still absent. Captain Davis writes: "At 2.30 p.m. the launch was hoisted over and the mail taken ashore, with sundry specimens of Australian fruit as refreshment for the shore party. The Boat Harbour was reached before anyone ashore had seen the *Aurora*. At the landing-place we were greeted most warmly by nine wild-looking men; some with beards bleached by the weather. As they danced about in joyous excitement, they all looked healthy and in very fair condition, after the severe winter."

Murphy handed Davis a letter from me, stating that I had planned for all sledge parties to be back at the Hut not later than January 15; in the event of the failure of my own party to return by that date Captain J. K. Davis was to take charge.

By the 18th Madigan's and Bickerton's parties had both arrived, it only remained for Mertz, Ninnis and myself to turn up and all would be well. As the days went by and brought no sign of us their anxiety increased. Davis called Bage and Madigan to a consultation; plans were laid to operate in the event of my not returning before the *Aurora* would be forced to depart. In that event a small party was to be left at the Hut for a second year, whose duty it would be to search for and to ascertain as far as practicable the fate of the missing men.

In the meantime the necessary coal and stores were brought ashore and the wireless mast re-erected in preparation for a second year's occupation should the worst happen. Three parties went out beyond Aladdin's Cave to bring back good news, but were disappointed.

Davis decided to wait at Commonwealth Bay, if necessary until January 30; to remain later would, he believed, seriously jeopardize the chances of relief for the West Base Party.

The landing of stores was greatly hampered by squalls off the land. Indeed southerly and south-easterly gales continued for days together, and the ship's party began to realize that if this were summer there must be some truth in the stories that came from the Hut of really atrocious weather conditions at other times of the year. It is only necessary to quote Davis's report to give an idea of the conditions under which the Ship's Party maintained themselves during those days. Already the main anchor and chain had gone by the board: "On the 25th there was a hard south-east gale blowing until the afternoon, when it moderated sufficiently to send off the launch with the thirteen bags of coal, Gillies being in charge. The Boat Harbour was reached in safety, the wind freshening to a gale before 6 p.m.

"Terrific gusts followed in rapid succession and without warning the cable parted sixty fathoms from the anchor at 9 p.m. Having cleared the reefs to leeward, we managed to get in the rest of the chain and then stood along the coast to the north-west. By keeping about three miles from the shore, we seemed to be beyond the reach of the more violent gusts, but a short sea holding the ship broadside on to the wind during the squalls rendered it difficult to maintain a fixed course.

"With reefs and bergs around, the increasing darkness about midnight made our position unpleasant. The engines had to be stopped and the ship allowed to drift with the wind, owing to a bearing becoming hot, but in a quarter of an hour they were moving once more.

"Early on January 26 the *Aurora* was half-way between winter quarters and the western point of Commonwealth Bay, when the wind suddenly ceased, and then came away light from the north-west. We could see that a south-east gale was still raging close in-shore. Over the sea, towards the north, dark clouds were scudding with great rapidity along the horizon; the scene of a violent disturbance.

"We returned towards our late anchorage. On reaching it, the south-east wind had moderated considerably and we let go our spare anchor and what had been saved of the chain.

"To the north, violent gusts appeared to be travelling in various directions, but, to our astonishment, these gusts, after approaching our position at a great rate, appeared to curve upwards; the water close to the ship was disturbed, and nothing else. This curious phenomenon lasted about an hour and then the wind came with a rush from the southeast, testing the anchor-chain in the more furious squalls.

"The gale was in its third day on the 27th, and there was a 'hurricane sky' during the morning. The wind would die away, only to blow more fiercely than before. The suddenness with which the changes occurred is a matter for remark. For instance, at 6 a.m. on the 27th a whole gale was blowing from the south-east. At 9 a.m. the wind had dropped to light airs from the north to east, and the sea calm enough for the launch to proceed ashore. At 11 a.m. the last cargo of coal had just left the ship when the wind freshened from the south-east. The launch had just got inside the Boat Harbour when a terrific gust struck the vessel and our chain parted. We were blown out to sea while heaving in thirty fathoms of chain which remained. At 4 p.m. the wind died away once more."

On the morning of January 29 the *Aurora* steamed off east to search the coast-line for any trace of the missing party. Careful watch was kept in the hope of sighting a flag or other signal from the shore. In Buchanan Bay and along the face of the Mertz Glacier Tongue rockets were fired and a big kite flown at a height of about five hundred feet. But all to no purpose for on the morning of the 31st, having reached 146° 19' E. longitude, they very disappointedly turned the bow towards Cape Denison.

It was now clear that something serious had happened; furthermore, it was high time for the *Aurora* to depart for the West Base. So Captain Davis decided to pick up those of the shore party who were returning and hasten to the relief of Wild and his companions. On arrival at Commonwealth Bay, however, the wind had risen and they had to stand off, steaming up and down, waiting for a favourable opportunity to communicate with the shore.

"A week's gale in Commonwealth Bay! The seven days which followed I do not think any of us will forget. From the 1st to the 7th of February it blew a continuous heavy gale, interrupted only when the wind increased to a full hurricane.*

"We endeavoured to maintain a position under the cliffs where the sea had not room to become heavy. This entailed a constant struggle, as, with a full head of steam during the squalls, the vessel drove steadily seaward where the rising waves broke on board and rendered steering more difficult. Then, when it had moderated to a mere 'howl,' we could crawl back, only to be driven out again by the next squall. The blinding spray which was swept out in front of the squalls froze solidly on board encasing the blocks and tackle and so lending additional difficulty to the operation of 'wearing ship.'

"It was on this occasion that we realized what a fine old vessel the *Aurora* was, and as we slowly moved back to shelter, could appreciate how efficiently the members of our engine-room staff under Gillies were carrying out their duties. The ordinary steaming speed was six knots, yet for the whole of this week, without a hitch, the ship was being driven at an equivalent of ten knots. The fact of having this reserve power undoubtedly saved us from disaster.

"A typical entry from my diary reads:

"'*February* 6. Just as the sun was showing over the ice slopes this morning (4 a.m.) the wind became very violent with the most terrific squalls I have ever experienced. Vessel absolutely unmanageable, driving out to sea. I was expecting the masts to go overboard every minute. This was the worst, I think, lasting about two hours. At 6 a.m., still

---

* The maximum wind velocity recorded at this time by the anemometer on shore was approximately eighty miles an hour.

Conveying supplies using the flying fox, Shackleton Ice Shelf

Wild's party making slow progress on the lower
Denman Glacier (*Watson*)

Mother and father King penguins hatching an egg

"Finding Father" after many days buried in the snow

A gargantuan ice mushroom

A keep of the ice solitudes: a turreted berg 210-feet high (*Hurley*)

Sledging on Adelie Land plateau, west of Aurora Peak
(Madigan in lead) (*Mawson*)

Madigan attending to the anemometer with
"Blizzard" the pup. (*Hurley*)

Wild and Noyes slay a Weddell Seal, West Base (*Wild*)

Madigan Nunatak—Close and Laseron standing by the sledge

The S.Y. *Aurora* alongside part of the ice shelf

Madigan and Correll in harness sledging over floe ice,
King George Land. (*McLean*)

Under reefed sail—Southern Party 290 miles S.S.E. of Winter Quarters,
Adelie Land (*Hurley*)

Helping sledges along the trough - the broken zone of
the lower Denman Glacier (*Watson*)

Frank Hurley in sledging costume—note the finnesko, burberry trousers and jacket. The thick woollen helmet illustrated was worn whenever possible without the funnelled over-helmet made of burberry gaberdine (*Hurley*)

Southern supporting party—Hunter, Murphy
and Laseron (*Hurley*)

Pitching the tent for lunch on coastal slopes south of
Winter Quarters, Adelie Land (*Hurley*)

Murphy emerging from the roof trapdoor of the
Cape Denison hut (*Hurley*)

In open pack-ice (*Hurley*)

A morning in the workshop (*Hurley*)

The slate formation at Cape Hunter (*Hurley*)

Correll on the edge of a ravine (*Hurley*)

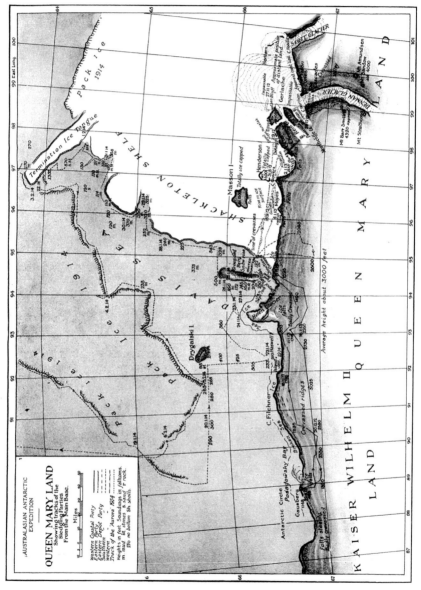

blowing very hard but squalls less violent, gradually made shelter during the morning. . . .'

"On February 8 the weather improved at 1 a.m. The gusts were less violent and the lulls were of longer duration. At 9 a.m. there was only a gentle breeze. We steamed in towards the Boat Harbour and signalled for the launch to come off with the ten returning members of the shore party. The latter had been instructed to remain at the Hut until tie vessel was ready to sail. Here, while the gale had been in full career, they had helped to secure enough seal and penguin meat to keep the Relief Party and their dogs for another year."

Madigan was to be in charge of the party remaining in Adelie Land; this included Bage, McLean, Bickerton, Hodgeman and Jeffryes, the latter a wireless operator whose enthusiasm for Antarctic adventure led to his transference from the ship.

The good-byes were brief and at 11.30 a.m. the *Aurora* steamed out of the Bay. The weather had calmed and there were light airs and a smooth sea. At that same time, at Aladdin's Cave, high up on the ice slopes, five and a half miles to the south, the drift was still whirling as I anxiously awaited an opportunity to proceed to the Hut. A notorious and memorable instance exemplifying what we ascertained to be a rule, namely, that the winds always abated first at sea-level, the calm conditions then gradually rising to higher altitudes.

The *Aurora* had just reached the pack-ice at 8.30 p.m. that evening when Hannam received the wireless message to the effect that I had arrived at the Hut.

How they returned to Commonwealth Bay and how, owing to unfavourable weather, they had eventually to abandon the idea of relieving us that year has already been told in these pages.

They departed for the second time at 6.30 p.m. on February 9. By the 11th the open sea to the north of the pack-ice was reached.

For a week they went due west most of the time in thick weather, under full sail, driving before an easterly gale. By good fortune they were spared colliding with icebergs and on the 18th the weather cleared, but none too soon for a line of heavy ice was met, crossing the course. For four days they wrestled with the pack-ice.

Late on February 22, during a blizzard, they narrowly escaped destruction; they were threading their way between ice masses in the "sea of bergs" where navigation had proved so dangerous the previous year. Captain Davis wrote in his journal: "At 8 p.m. the driving snow and growing darkness made it impossible to see any distance ahead. The next seven hours were the most anxious I have ever spent at sea. Although the wind blew hard from the south-east, we passed through the sea of bergs without mishap, guided and protected by a Higher Power."

Next day the Shackleton Shelf was sighted and by noon the floe near the Western Base hut was reached. Wild and his seven companions had sighted the ship long before and were waiting excitedly at the water's edge.

It took but a few hours to sledge the personal baggage and collections down from the hut and to "ice ship." As they turned north that evening, with Wild's Party safely on board, Davis felt that a tremendous weight of anxiety had fallen from his shoulders.

Any hope they may have had of steaming to the east with the object of attempting to relieve the seven men at Adelie Land had to be definitely abandoned, on account of the small amount of coal which remained.

Three days later they were safely out of the ice and bowling along on a two thousand-mile run to Tasmania, reaching Port Esperance on March 14.

The ship's company deserved every congratulation for the admirable and unfailing manner in which they had acquitted themselves throughout. Not only had they spent two summers facing unflinchingly the harassing gales off the Adelie Land coast and traversing immense stretches of ocean strewn with pack-ice and bergs, but the winter also had found them conducting investigations on the bosom of the heavy sub-Antarctic ocean.

The ship's officers and crew, every one of them, will ever be able to recall with pride those deeds so loyally undertaken and so cheerfully carried out.

CHAPTER XIX

A HOME ON THE FLOATING PACK-ICE

Frank Wild's Narrative

AT 7 a.m. on February 21, 1912, the *Aurora* steamed away to the north leaving us on the Shackleton Ice-Shelf, while cheers and hearty good wishes were exchanged with the ship's company. On the sea-ice that day, there stood with me my comrades—the Western Party: G. Dovers, C. T. Harrisson, C. A. Hoadley, S. E. Jones, A. L. Kennedy, M. H. Moyes and A. D. Watson.

We proceeded to the top of the cliff, where the remainder of the stores and gear was hauled up. Tents were then erected and the work of hut-building at once commenced. The site selected for our home was six hundred and forty yards inland from the spot where the stores were landed, and, as the edge of the glacier was very badly broken, I was anxious to get a supply of food, clothing and fuel moved back from the edge to safety as soon as possible.

Harrisson, Hoadley, Kennedy and Jones "turned the first sod" in the foundations of the hut, while Dovers, Moyes, Watson and I sledged along supplies of timber and stores. Inward from the brink of the precipice, which was one hundred feet in height, the surface was fairly good for sledges, but, owing to crevasses and pressure-ridges, the course was devious and mostly uphill.

Fortunately the weather was propitious during the seven days, when the carpenters and joiners ruled the situation; the temperature ranging from −12° F. to 25° F., while a moderate blizzard interrupted one day.

On February 27 while working on the roof, Harrisson made an addition to our geographical knowledge. Well to the north of the mainland, and bearing a little north of east, he could trace the outline of land. Subsequently this was proved to be an island, eventually named Masson Island, thirty-two miles distant, and seventeen miles north of the mainland. It was twenty miles long and fifteen miles wide, being entirely ice-covered.

On the 28th the hut was fit for habitation, the stove was installed, and meals were cooked and eaten in moderate comfort. The interior of the house was twenty feet square, but its area was reduced by a lobby entrance, three feet by five feet, a dark-room three feet by six feet situated on one side, and my cabin six feet six inches square in one corner. The others slept in seven bunks which were ranged at intervals round the walls. Of the remaining space, a large portion was commodiously occupied by the stove and the table. The general design of the structure was the same as that of the main living hut of the Main Base Party in Adelie Land.

The next three days were occupied in completing the fittings within the hut and in sledging up coal and stores from the brink of the cliff.

Sunday, March 3, was the finest day we had up till then experienced, and, since the work was now sufficiently advanced to make us comparatively comfortable and safe, I determined to make a proper Sunday of it. All hands were called at 8.30 a.m. instead of 6 a.m. After breakfast a few necessary jobs were done and at noon a short service held. When lunch was over, the skis were unpacked, and all went for a run to the east in the direction of Masson Island.

The glacier's surface was excellent for travelling, but I soon found that it would be dangerous to walk about alone without skis, as there were a number of crevasses near the hut, some of considerable size; I opened one twenty-five feet wide. They were all well bridged and would support a man on skis quite easily.

A heavy gale, with falling snow and blinding drift, came on early the next day and continued for forty-eight hours; our worst blizzard up to that time. The temperature, below zero before the storm, rose with the wind to 30° F. Inside all were employed preparing for a sledging trip I intended to make to the mainland before the winter set in. We were

greatly handicapped by the want of a sewing machine.*
Large canvas bags made to contain two weeks' provision for
a sledging unit of three men were in the equipment, but the
smaller bags of calico for the different articles of food had to
be sewn by hand. Several hundred of these were required,
and altogether the time consumed in making them was
considerable.

Emerging on the morning of the 6th, after the blizzard
had blown itself out, we found that snow-drifts to a depth
of twelve feet had collected around the hut. For entrance
and exit, a shaft had to be dug and a ladder made. The
stores packed in heaps close by were completely covered, and
another blizzard swooping down on the 7th made things
still worse. This "blow," persisting till the morning of the
9th, was very heavy, the wind frequently attaining very high
velocities, accompanied by drift so thick that it was impossible
to go outside for anything.

When the wind abated a party set to work to dig out the
stores now buried in snow drifts. All the cases were rescued;
some were stowed alongside the hut, and the remainder
stacked up again on a new level.

On came another severe blizzard, which continued with
only a few minutes' interval until the evening of the 12th.
During the short lull, Jones, Dovers, and Hoadley took a
sledge for a load of ice from a pressure-ridge rather less than
two hundred yards from the hut. While they were absent, the
wind freshened again, and they had great difficulty in finding
their way to the entrance.

It was very disappointing to be delayed in our sledging
programme in this manner, but there was consolation in the
fact that we were better off in the hut than on the glacier,
and there was plenty of work inside. The interior was then
put in order much earlier than it would otherwise have
been.

There was no need for anxiety as to the stability of the
building, for very soon the snow piled to such a depth in our

---

* By an accident the small sewing machine belonging to Wild's Party was
landed at the Main Base.

immediate vicinity that, even with a wind of hurricane force, there was scarcely a tremor in the structure.

The morning of Wednesday, March 13, was calm and overcast. Breakfast was served at 6 o'clock. We then set to work completing the erection of the two small masts to carry the aerial for our wireless receiving instrument; by 8.50 a.m. both masts were in position. Before the job was over, a singular sight was witnessed. A large section of the glacier—many thousands of tons—calved off into the sea. The tremendous waves raised by the fall of this mass smashed into fragments all the floe left in the bay. With the sea-ice went the snow-slopes which were the natural roadway down. A perpendicular cliff, sixty to one hundred feet above the water, was all that remained, and opportunities of obtaining seals and penguins in the future were cut off until the new season's sea-ice should form again. This left us in a serious position as regards food for the dogs.

The whole of the sledging provisions and gear for our journey were brought out, weighed and packed on the sledges; the total weight being one thousand two hundred and thirty-three pounds. Dovers, Harrisson, Hoadley, Jones, Moyes and myself were to constitute the party, while Kennedy and Watson remained behind to keep the observations going at the hut. The ground was to be covered by man-hauling, for the nine dogs landed were still in very poor condition after their cramped and wet passage on the *Aurora*.

To the south of the Base, seventeen miles distant at the nearest point, the mainland was visible, entirely ice-clad, running almost due east and west. It appeared to rise rapidly to about three thousand feet, then to ascend more gradually as the great plateau of the Antarctic continent. It was my intention to travel inland beyond the lower ice-falls which extended in an irregular line of riven bluffs all along the coast, and there to lay a depot or depots for future use.

While the sledges were being loaded, ten skua gulls paid us a visit, and, as roast skua is a very pleasant change of food, Jones shot six of them.

At 1 p.m., March 13, we left the hut, marching on a general south-easterly course. The coast looked most accessible in this direction, whereas a line running south, though a shorter route, would have brought us to some unpromising ice-falls.

The surface was very good and almost free from crevasses; only one, into which Jones fell to his middle, being seen during the afternoon's march. Not wishing to do too much the first day, especially after the "soft" days we had been forced to spend in the hut during the spell of bad weather, I made two short halts in the afternoon and camped at 5 p.m., having done seven and a half miles.

For the two hours after starting next morning, the surface was tolerable and then changed for the worse; the remainder of the day's work being over a hard crust, which was just too brittle to bear the weight of a man, letting him through six to eight inches into a soft substratum. Only those who have travelled in country like this can properly realize how wearisome it is.

At 9 a.m. the course was altered to south, as there appeared to be a fairly good track up the hills. The surface of the glacier rose and fell in long undulations which became wider and more marked as the land approached. By the time we camped, they were three-quarters of a mile from crest to crest, with a drop of thirty feet from crest to trough. Despite the heavy trudging we covered more than thirteen miles.

I made the marching hours 7 a.m. to 5 p.m., so that there was time to get the evening meal before darkness set in; soon after 6 p.m.

The march commenced about seven o'clock on March 15, the thermometer registering −8° F., while a light southerly breeze made it feel much colder. The exercise soon warmed us up and, when the breeze died away, the remainder of the day was perfectly calm.

A surface of "pie-crust" cut down the mileage in the forenoon. Many crevasses were encountered from two to five feet wide, with clean-cut sides and shaky bridges. Hoadley went down to his head in one, and we all got our legs in others.

It became evident after lunch that the land was nearing rapidly, its lower slopes obscuring the higher land behind.

The crevasses also became wider, so I lengthened the harness with an alpine rope to allow more room and to prevent more than two men from being over a chasm at the same time. At 4 p.m. we were confronted with one sixty feet wide. Crevasses over thirty feet in width usually have very solid bridges and may be considered safe, but this one had badly broken edges and one hundred yards on the right the lid had collapsed. So instead of marching steadily across, we went over singly on the alpine rope and hauled the sledges along in their turn, when all had crossed in safety. Immediately after passing this obstacle the grade became steeper, and, between three and five o'clock, we rose two hundred feet.

That night the tent stood on a field of snow covering the lower slopes of the hills. On either hand were magnificent examples of ice-falls, but ahead the way seemed open.

Next morning the wind sprang up and drift began to fly. The gale raged all through the night subsiding at 11.30 a.m. the following day. On turning out we found that the tents and sledges were covered deeply in snow, and we dug continuously for more than two hours before we were able to pack up and get away. Both sledges ran easily for nearly a mile over névé, when the gradient increased to one in ten, forcing us to relay. It was found necessary to change our finnesko for spiked boots. Relaying regularly, we gradually mounted six hundred feet over névé and massive sastrugi. with a steep slope in front, a halt was made for the night. The sunset was a picture of prismatic colours reflected above the undulating ice-sheet and the tumbling cascades of the glacier.

On the evening of March 18 the altitude of our camp was one thousand four hundred and ten feet, and the slope was covered with sastrugi ridges, three or four feet high. Travelling over these on the following day we had frequent capsizes.

The outlook to the south was a series of irregular terraces, varying from half a mile to two miles in breadth and twenty to two hundred feet in height. These were furrowed by small valleys and traversed by ridges, but there was not a sign of rock anywhere.

The temperature varied from 4° to 14° F. during the day, and the minimum recorded at night was −11° F.

Another nine miles of slow ascent brought us to two thousand feet, followed by a rise of two hundred and twenty feet in seven and three-quarter miles on March 21. Hauling over high, broken sastrugi was laborious enough to make everyone glad when the day was over.

There now swept down on us a blizzard* which lasted for a whole week. Snow fell in deluges and a high wind raged threatening to demolish our tents. The wind and drift were so strong that while securing the tent I had several times to get in the lee of it to recover my breath and to clear the mask of snow from my face. To make matters worse the wind veered round from south-east to north pouring several hundredweights of snow, through the small ventilator at the peak of the tent, on the top of us as we lay toggled up in the sleeping-bags. Owing to the warmth of our bodies thawing the snow, we became very wet and the bags were like sponges.

March 28 broke with a heavy south-east wind and drift still continuing. At noon the wind eased down and the snow ceased falling, so we slipped into our burberry over-suits and climbed out to dig for the sledges.

Nothing could be seen except about two feet of the tops of the tents, which meant that there was a deposit of five feet of freshly fallen snow. The upper two feet were soft and powdery, offering no resistance; under that it was still soft, so that we sank to our thighs every step and frequently to the waist. By 4.30 p.m. both sledges were rescued, and it was ascertained that no gear had been lost. We all found that the week of idleness and confinement had weakened us, and at first were only able to take short spells at the digging.

At 5.30 a.m. next day the weather was bright and calm. As a strong wind had blown throughout the night, a harder

---

* It is an interesting fact that this blizzard occurred on the same date as that during which Captain Scott and his party lost their lives, perishing in their tent at a spot somewhat over one thousand seven hundred miles distant across the continent.

surface was expected. Outside, we were surprised to find a fresh wind and thick, low drift; owing to the tents being snowed up so high, the threshing of the drift was not audible. To my disgust the surface was as soft as ever. It appeared that the only resort was to leave the provisions for the depot on the nearest ridge and return to the Base. The temperature was −20° F., and, while digging out the tents, Dovers had his nose frost-bitten.

It took six of us well over an hour to drag the necessary food half a mile up a rise of less than one hundred feet; the load, sledge included, not being five hundred pounds. Nearly all the time we were sinking thigh-deep, and the sledge itself was going down so far that the instrument-box was pushing a mass of snow in front of it. Arriving on the ridge, Moyes found that his foot was frozen and he had to go back to camp, as there was too much wind to bring it round in the open.

Sufficient food and oil were left at this depot for three men for six weeks; also a minimum thermometer.

In a fresh breeze and flying drift we were off at 10 a.m. next day. At first we were ambitious and moved away with two sledges, sinking from two to three feet all the time. Forty yards was as much as we could do without a rest, and by lunch time nine hundred yards was the total. Now the course was downhill, and the two sledges were pulled together, creeping along with painful slowness, as walking was the hardest work imaginable. After one of the most strenuous days I have ever experienced we camped; the sledge-meter recorded one mile four hundred and fifty yards.

A spell of two days' blizzard cooped us up once more, but improved the surface slightly. Still, it was dreadfully soft, and, but for the falling gradient, we would not have made what we did—five miles six hundred and ten yards—on April 2.

Soon after leaving the hills (April 4), a direct course to the hut was made. There was no mark by which to steer, except a water-sky to the north. During the afternoon, the sun occasionally gleamed through a tract of cirro-stratus cloud and there appeared a very fine parhelion. At 4.30 p.m.

we had done seventeen and a half miles, and, as all hands were fresh and willing, I decided to have a meal and go on again, considering that the moon was full and there were only six miles to be done.

After supper the march was continued till 8.30 p.m., by which time we were due for a rest. I had begun to think that we had passed the hut.

April 5 was far from being a Good Friday for us. At 2 a.m. a fresh breeze rose and rapidly increased to a heavy gale. At 10 a.m. Hoadley and I had to go out to secure the tent; the weather-side bulged in more than half the width of the tent and was held by a solid load of drift, but the other sides were flapping so much that almost all the snow had been shaken off the skirt. Though only five yards away from it we could not see the other tent. At noon Hoadley again went out to attend to the tent and entirely lost himself within six feet of it. He immediately started to yell and I guessed what was the matter at once. Dovers and I shouted our best, and Hoadley groped his way in with a mask of snow over his face. He told us that the wind, which was then blowing a good eighty miles an hour, knocked him down immediately he was outside, and, when he struggled to his feet again, he could see nothing and had no idea in what direction lay the tent.

The space inside was now so limited by the combined pressure of wind and snow that we did not light the primus, eating lumps of frozen pemmican for the evening meal.

The blizzard continued with unabated violence until eleven o'clock next morning, when it moderated within an hour to half a gale. We turned out and had a good hot meal. Then we looked to see how the others had fared and found that their tent had collapsed. Getting at once into wind-proof clothing, we rushed out and were horrified to see Harrisson in his bag on the snow. He quickly assured us that he was all right. After carrying him, bag and all, into our tent, he emerged quite undamaged, but very hungry.

Jones and Moyes now had to be rescued; they were in a most uncomfortable position under the fallen tent. It appears that the tent had blown down on the previous morning at ten o'clock, and for thirty-six hours they had had nothing to eat. We did not take long to dig them out.

The wind dropped to a moderate breeze, and, through the falling snow, I could make out a water-sky to the west. The three unfortunates said that they felt fit to travel, so we got under way. The surface was soft and the pulling very heavy, and I soon saw that the strain was largely due to the weakness of the three who had been without food. Calling a halt, I asked Jones if it would do to go on; he assured me that they could manage to go on with an effort and the march was resumed.

Not long after, Dovers sighted the wireless mast, and a quarter of an hour later we were safely in the Hut, much to the surprise of Kennedy and Watson, who did not expect us to be travelling in such weather, and greatly to our own relief. According to the sledge-meter, the last camp had only been two miles one hundred yards from home, and if anything had been visible on the night of April 4, we could have got in easily.

I was very pleased with the way all the party had shaped. They had worked splendidly and were always cheerful, although conditions had been exceptionally trying during this journey. No one was any the worse for the hardships, except for a few blistered fingers from frost-bites. The party lost weight at the average of two and a half pounds; Harrisson was the greatest loser, being reduced six pounds. Out of the twenty-five days we were away, it was only possible to sledge on twelve days. The total distance covered, including relay work, was nearly one hundred and twenty-five miles, and the greatest elevation reached on the southern mainland was two thousand six hundred feet above sea-level.

Kennedy and Watson had been very busy during our absence. In addition to routine duties they had trained five of the dogs to pull in harness, and transported the remainder of the stores from the landing-place, arranging them in piles round the Hut. The weather at the Base had been quite as bad as that experienced by us on the land slopes.

CHAPTER XX

WINTER AND SPRING IN QUEEN MARY LAND

Frank Wild's Narrative

On Easter Sunday, April 7, a furious blizzard kept us close prisoners. It raged with such force all Sunday and Monday, that I dared not let anyone go out to feed the dogs, although we found, later, that a fast of three days did not hurt them at all.

I now thought it time to establish a winter routine. Each member had his particular duties to perform, in addition to general work, in which all hands were engaged. Harrisson took charge of the lamps and checked consumption of oil. Hoadley had the care of the provisions, making out lists showing the amount the cook might use of each article of food, besides opening cases and stowing a good assortment on convenient shelves in the veranda. Jones and Kennedy worked the acetylene plant. Jones, in addition to his ability as a surgeon, showed himself to be an excellent plumber, brazier and tinsmith, and the Hut was well lighted all the time we occupied it. Moyes's duties as meteorologist took him out at all hours. Watson looked after the dogs, while Dovers relieved other members when they were cooks. The duty of cook was taken for a week at a time by everyone except myself. A night watch was kept by each in turn.

The cook for the week was exempt from all other work. In the case of Kennedy, whose magnetic work was done principally at night, arrangements were made to assist him with the cooking.

Work commenced during the winter months at 10 a.m. and, unless anything special had to be done, finished at 1 p.m., when lunch was served. The afternoon was usually devoted to sport and recreation. Divine Service was held every Sunday, Moyes and I taking it in turn.

On going to feed the dogs during the afternoon of the 14th, Watson found that Nansen was dead; this left us with seven, as Crippen had already died. Of the remainder, only four were of any value; Sweep and the two bitches, Tiger and Tich, refusing to do anything in harness, and, as there was less than sufficient food for them, the two latter had to be shot.

A tunnel forty feet long was driven from the entrance-veranda of the hut to a situation where there was less tendency for the opening to drift up. The regular entrance from the snow-field without was a trap-door, built over the tunnel and raised well above the outside surface to prevent it being drifted over. From below it was approached by a ladder, but the end of the tunnel was left open, so that in fine weather sledges could be run in and out with loads of ice. With each blizzard the entrance was completely choked, and it gave two men a day's work to clear it out once more.

The next move was to excavate roomy caverns in the drifts to accommodate our stores and a supply of ice for the kitchen to be drawn upon during blizzards. Until the end of April almost all our time was spent in making these store-rooms and in searching for buried stores; sometimes a shaft would have to be sunk eight to twelve feet. Bamboo poles stuck in the snow marked the position of the different stores. The one marking the carbide was blown away, and it was two days before Dovers finally unearthed it. By the 30th, caves roomy enough to contain everything were completed, all being connected by the tunnel. We were now self-contained, and everything was accessible and immune from the periodic blizzards. From this time forth our winter quarters was referred to by the appropriate title of "The Grottoes."

On April 16 Kennedy had a term day. A fresh breeze was blowing and the temperature was −20° F. Some of his observations had to be taken in the open and the remainder in a tent. The series took three hours to complete and by that time he was thoroughly chilled through, his feet and fingers were frost-bitten and his language had grown more incisive than usual.

Between the 10th and the 19th we made a search for penguins and seals. Hoadley and Moyes staying behind, the rest of us with tents and equipment journeyed along the edge of the ice-shelf to the south without seeing the smallest sign of life. The margin of the ice formation was very much fissured, many of the breaches giving no sign of their presence, in consequence of which several falls were sustained.

Late in April, Kennedy, Harrisson and Jones built an igloo to be used as a magnetic observatory. On the afternoon of the 30th, the magnetician invited everyone to a tea-party in the igloo to celebrate the opening. He had the place very nicely decorated with flags, and after the reception and the formal inspection of instruments, we were served with quite a good tea. The outside temperature was −33° F. and it was not much higher inside the igloo. As a result, no one extended his visit beyond the bounds of politeness.

On May 1, Harrisson, Hoadley and Watson went away south towards the land at the head of the bay, which curved round to Junction Corner, to examine icebergs, take photographs and to search for seals. They took the four dogs with them and, as the load was a light one—three hundred and forty-two pounds—the dogs pulled easily.

I went with the others to the north, hoping that we might find a portion of the glacier low enough to give access to the sea-ice. There were several spots where the ice-cliffs were not more than forty to fifty feet high, but no convenient ramps led down from the cliffs. In any case neither penguins nor seals were to be had in the vicinity. A great, flat sheet of frozen sea stretched away to the north for quite thirty miles.

The next few days were windy once more and we had to remain indoors. Saturday was clean-up day, when the verandas, tunnel and cave were swept and tidied, the stove cleaned, the Hut and dark-room scrubbed and the windows cleaned. The last was a job which was generally detested. During the week, the windows in the roof collected a coat of ice, from an inch to three inches thick, by condensation of moisture; chipping this off was a most tedious piece of work.

One Sunday, Harrisson, Hoadley and Watson returned from their short trip; they had missed the strong winds which had been blowing at the Base, although less than twenty miles away. Some very fine old icebergs were discovered which were of interest to the two geologists and made good subjects for Harrisson's sketches. Watson had had a nasty fall while crossing a patch of rough ice, his nose being rather badly cut in the accident.

On May 7 another blizzard stopped all outside work. Moyes ventured as far as the meteorological screen at noon and got lost, but luckily only for a short time.

At this time there was much occupation for us repairing and refitting tents, poles and other sledging gear. The sleeping-bags used on the first sledging journey had been hung up near the roof. They were now taken down to be thoroughly over-hauled. As a consequence of their severe soaking, they had shrunk considerably and required enlarging. Dovers's bag, besides contracting a good deal, had lost much hair and was cut up to patch the others; a spare bag falling to his lot in place of it.

May 15 was a beautiful bright morning and I went over to Icy Cape two miles southward, with Harrisson, Hoadley, Dovers and Watson, to find a road down to the sea-ice. Here, we had good fortune at last, for, by climbing down a partly choked crevasse which opened out at sea-level into a magnificent cave, we walked straight out on to the level plain of the floe. Along the edge of the glacier there was not even a seal's blow-hole.

It was Kennedy's term night; the work keeping him in the igloo from 10 p.m. until 2.30 a.m. He had had some difficulty in finding a means of warming the observatory—an urgent necessity, since he found it impossible to manipulate delicate magnetic instruments for three or four hours with the temperature from −25° F. to −30° F. The trouble was to make a non-magnetic lamp and the problem was finally solved by using one of the aluminium cooking pots; converting it into a blubber stove. The stove smoked a great deal and the white walls were soon besmirched with a layer of soot.

During a blow on the evening of May 20, Zip and Sweep disappeared. A search on the glacier having been in vain,

Dovers and Hoadley made their way down to the floe. They found Zip well and hearty in spite of having had a drop of at least forty feet off the glacier. A further search for Sweep proved fruitless. We were forced to conclude that he was either killed by falling over the precipice or he had gone far away hunting for penguins.

A howling blizzard immured us for three days from May 22; the wind at times of terrific force, approaching one hundred miles per hour. It was impossible to secure meteorological observations at the screen, or to feed the dogs until noon on the 24th. Moyes and I went out during a slight cessation and, with the aid of a rope from the trap-door, managed to find the dogs, and gave them some biscuits. The drift was then so thick that six feet was as far as one could see.

We did not forget Empire Day and duly "spliced the main-brace." The most bigoted teetotaller could not call us an intemperate party. On each Saturday night, one drink per man was served out, the popular toast being "Sweethearts and Wives." The only other convivial meetings of our small symposium were on the birthdays of each member, Midwinter's Day and King's Birthday.

On the 25th we were able to make an inventory of a whole series of damages effected outside. The dogs' shelter had been entirely carried away, a short mast which had been erected some weeks previously as a holdfast for sledges was snapped off short and the sledges buried, and, worst of all, Kennedy's igloo had parted with its roof, the interior being filled with snow, underneath which the instruments were buried. The dogs were, however, all quite well and lively. It was fortunate for them that the temperature always rose during the blizzards. At this period when on fine days it was usual to experience $-25°$ to $-37°$ F., the temperature rose in the snow-storms to $25°$ or even $30°$ F.

May 27 was beautifully clear. The tunnel entrance was opened and some of the party brought in ice while others undid the rope lashings which had been placed over the hut. This was so completely covered in snow that the lashings were not required and I wanted to make a rope ladder to enable us to get down to the sea-ice and also to be used by Watson and Hoadley, who were about to dig a shaft in the glacier to examine the structure of the ice.

Fine weather continued until June 2. During this time we were occupied in digging a road from the glacier down to the sea-ice in the forenoons and hunting for seals or skiing in the afternoons. Kennedy and Harrisson rebuilt the magnetic igloo. A seal-hole was eventually found near the foot of the glacier and this was enlarged to enable the seals to come up.

At the end of May, daylight lasted from 9 a.m. until 3 p.m., and the sunrise and sunset were a marvel of exquisite colour.

On the days of blizzards, there was usually sufficient work to be found to keep us all employed. Thus on June 2, Watson and I were making a ladder, Jones was contriving a harpoon for seals, Hoadley was opening cases and stowing stores in the veranda, Dovers cleaning tools, Moyes repairing a thermograph and writing up the meteorological log, Harrisson cooking and Kennedy sleeping after a night-watch.

Between June 4 and 22 there was a remarkably fine spell. It was not calm all the time, as drift flew for a few days, limiting the horizon to a few hundred yards. An igloo was built as a shelter for those sinking the geological shaft, and seal-hunting was a daily recreation. On June 9, Dovers and Watson found a Weddell seal two and a half miles to the west on the sea-ice. They killed the animal but did not cut it up as there were sores on the skin. Jones went over with them afterwards and pronounced the sores to be wounds received from some other animal, so the meat was considered innocuous and fifty pounds were brought in, being very welcome after tinned foods. Jones took culture tubes with him and made smears for bacteria. The tubes were placed in an incubator and several kinds of organisms grew, very similar to those which infect wounds in ordinary climates.

The snowstorms had by this time built up huge drifts on the floe under the lee of the cliffs, some of them more than fifty feet in height and reaching almost to the top of the shelf-ice. An exhilarating sport was to ski down these ramps.

The majority of them were very steep and irregular and it was seldom that any of us escaped without a fall at one time or another. Several of the party were thrown from thirty to forty feet, and, frequently enough, over twenty feet, without being hurt. The only accident serious enough to disable anyone happened to Kennedy on June 19, when he twisted his knee and was laid up for a week.

There were many fine displays of the aurora in June, the best being observed on the evening of the 18th. Curtains and streamers were showing from four o'clock in the afternoon. Shortly after midnight, Kennedy, who was taking magnetic observations, called me to see the most remarkable exhibition I have so far seen. There was a double curtain 30° wide unfolded from the eastern horizon through the zenith, with waves shimmering along it so rapidly that they travelled the whole length of the curtain in two seconds. The colouring was brilliant and evanescent. When the waves reached the end of the curtain they spread out to the north and rolled in a voluminous billow slowly back to the east. Kennedy's instruments showed that a very great magnetic disturbance was in progress during the auroral displays, and particularly on this occasion.

Hoadley and Watson set up a line of bamboos, a quarter of a mile apart and three miles long, on the 20th, and from thence onwards took measurements for snowfall every fortnight.

On Midwinter's day the temperature ranged from −38° F. to −25° F. and daylight lasted from 10 a.m. until 4 p.m. We proclaimed a universal holiday throughout Queen Mary Land. There were speeches, toasts and a gramophone concert that evening, following a special dinner in honour of the occasion.

From this time dated our preparations for spring sledging, which I hoped would commence about August 15. Jones made some experiments with glaxo of which we had a generous supply. His aim was to make biscuits which would be suitable for sledging, and, after several failures, he succeeded in compressing with a steel die a firm biscuit of glaxo and butter mixed, three ounces of which was the equivalent in theoretical food value to four and a half ounces of plasmon biscuit; thereby also affording a pleasant variety in the usual ration.

July came in quietly, though it was dull and cloudy, and we were able to get out on the first two days for work and exercise. On the 2nd a very fine effect was caused by the sun shining through myriads of "fog crystals" which a light northerly breeze had brought from the sea. The sun, which was barely clear of the horizon, was itself a deep red, on either side and above it was a red mock-sun and a rainbow-tinted halo connected the three mock-suns.

On the 5th and 6th of July the wind blew a terrific hurricane and, had we not known that nothing short of an earthquake could move the hut, we should have been very uneasy.

At this time all were busy making food-bags, opening and breaking up pemmican and emergency ration, grinding biscuits, attending to personal gear and doing odd jobs many and various.

In addition to recreations like chess, cards and dominoes, a competition was started for each member to write a poem and short article, humorous or otherwise, connected with the Expedition. These were all read by the authors after dinner one evening and caused considerable amusement. One man even preferred to sing his poem. These literary efforts were incorporated in a small publication known as "The Glacier Tongue."

Watson and Hoadley put in a good deal of time digging their shaft in the glacier. As a roofed shelter had been built over the top, they were able to work in all but the very worst weather. They succeeded in getting down to a level of twenty-one feet below the surface of the shelf-ice.

Sandow, the leader of the dogs, disappeared on the 18th. Zip, who had been missed for two days, returned, but Sandow never came back, being killed, doubtless, by a fall of snow from the cliffs. All along the edge of the ice-shelf were snow cornices, some weighing hundreds of tons; and these often broke away, collapsing with a thunderous sound. On July 31, Harrisson and Watson had a narrow escape. After finishing their day's work they climbed down to the floe by a huge cornice and sloping ramp. A few seconds later, the cornice fell and an immense mass of hard snow crashed down, cracking the sea-ice for more than a hundred yards around.

July had been an inclement month with three really fine and eight tolerable days. In comparison with that of June (which was −14.5° F.) the mean temperature of July was high at −1.5° F. and the early half of August was little better.

On Sunday, August 11, Dovers and I went out in the wind to attend to the dogs and clear the chimney and, upon our return, found the others just recovering from rather an exciting accident. Jones had been charging the acetylene generators and by some means one of them caught fire. For a while there was the danger of a general conflagration and explosion, as the gas-tank was floating in kerosene. Throwing water over everything would have made matters worse, so blankets were used to smother the flames. As this failed to extinguish them, the whole plant was pulled down and carried into the tunnel, where the fire was at last put out. The damage amounted to two blankets singed and dirtied, Jones's face scorched and hair singed, and Kennedy had one finger jammed. It was a fortunate escape from a calamity.

A large berg frozen to the floe eleven miles north of the Hut had arrested our attention for some time. It was the more interesting, for during the past fortnight it had capsized, smashing the floe and exposing its base for observation. On the 14th, Harrisson, Dovers, Hoadley and Watson took provisions and equipment and went off to examine it.

They found that the berg was floating on its side, surrounded by some large isolated chunks, all locked fast in the floe. Embedded in what had been the bottom of the berg, Hoadley and Watson made an interesting find of stones and pebbles. Harrisson climbed the pitted and wave-worn ice to its summit, fifty feet above the level of the shelf-ice. There was no sign of open water to the north, but a few seals were observed sleeping under the cliffs.

After the departure of the party to examine the iceberg on August 14, while we were excavating some buried kerosene, Jones sighted a group of seven Emperor penguins two miles away over the western floe. Taking a sledge and camera we made after them. A mile off, they saw us and advanced with their usual stately bows. It seemed an awful shame to kill them, but we were sorely in need of fresh meat. The four we secured averaged seventy pounds in weight and were a heavy load up the steep rise to the glacier; but our reward came at dinner-time.

With several fine days to give us confidence, everything was made ready for the sledge journey on August 20. The party was to consist of six men and three dogs, the object of the journey being to lay out a food depot to the east in view of the long summer journey we were to make in that direction. Hoadley and Kennedy were to remain at the Base, the former to finish the geological shaft and the latter for magnetic work. There remained also a good deal to do preparing stores for later sledge journeys.

The weather was not propitious for a start until Thursday, August 22. We turned out at 5.30 a.m., had breakfast, packed up and left the Hut at seven o'clock.

After two good days' work under a magnificently clear sky, with the temperature often as low as -34° F., we sighted two small nunataks among a cluster of pressure-ridges, eight miles to the south. It was the first land, in the sense of rocks, seen for more than seven months. We hoped to visit these outcrops—Gillies Nunataks—on our return.

The course next day was due east and parallel to the mainland, then ten miles distant. To the north was Masson Island, while at about the same distance and ahead was a smaller island, entirely ice-covered like the former—Henderson Island.

A blizzard of three days' duration kept us in camp between the 27th and 30th. Jones, Moyes and I had a three-man sleeping-bag, and the temperature being high, 11° to 15° F., we were very warm, but thoroughly tired of lying down for so long. Harrisson, Dovers and Watson had single bags and therefore less room in the other tent.

The last day of August was beautifully bright: temperature −12° to −15° F. We passed Henderson Island in the forenoon, and, hauling up a rise to the south of it, had a good view of the surroundings. On the right, the land ran back to form a large bay, seventeen miles wide. This was later named the Bay of Winds, as a "blow" was always encountered while crossing it.

In the centre of the bay was a nunatak, which from its shape at once received the name of the Alligator. In front, apparently fifteen miles off, was another nunatak, the Hippo, and four definite outcrops—Delay Point and Avalanche Rocks—could be seen along the mainland. The sight of this bare rock was very pleasing, as we had begun to think we were going to find nothing but ice-sheathed land. Dovers took a round of angles to all the prominent points.

The Hippo was twenty-two miles away, so deceptive is distance in these latitudes; and in one and a half days, over very heavy sastrugi, we were in its vicinity. The sledges could not be brought very near the rock as it was surrounded by massive ridges of pressure-ice.

We climbed to the top of the nunatak which was four hundred and twenty feet high, four hundred yards long and two hundred yards wide. It was composed of gneissic granite and schists. Dovers took angles from an eminence, Watson collected geological specimens and Harrisson sketched until his fingers were frost-bitten. Moss and lichens were found and a dead snow-petrel—a young one—showing that the birds must breed in the vicinity.

To the south, the glacier shelf appeared to be very little broken, but to the north it was terribly torn and twisted. At each end of the nunatak there were gaping crevasses. Twenty miles to the east there appeared to be an uncovered rocky islet; the mainland turning to the southward twelve miles away. During the night the minimum thermometer registered –47° F.

An attempt to get away next morning was frustrated by a strong gale. We were two hundred yards from the shelter of the Hippo and were forced to turn back, since it was difficult to keep one's feet, while the sledges were blown sideways over the névé surface.

I resolved to leave the depot in this place and return to the Base, for our sleeping-bags were getting very wet and none of the party were having sufficient sleep. We were eighty-four miles from the Hut; I had hoped to do one hundred miles, but we could make up for that by starting the summer journey a few days earlier. One sledge was left here as well as about six weeks' allowance of food for three men. The sledge was placed on end in a hole three feet deep and a mound built around it, six feet high; a bamboo and flag being lashed to the top.

On September 4 we were homeward bound, heading first to the mainland, leaving Delay Point on our left, to examine some of the outcrops of rock. Reaching the coast about 3 p.m., camp was shortly afterwards pitched in a most beautiful spot. A wall of solid rock rose sheer for over four hundred feet and was crowned by an ice-cap half the thickness. Grand ice-falls surged down on either side.

The tents were erected in what appeared to be a sheltered hollow, a quarter of a mile from Avalanche Rocks. One tent was up and we were setting the other in position when the wind, which was blowing fresh from the west, suddenly veered right round to the east and flattened out both tents. It was almost as humorous as annoying. They were soon raised once more, facing the other way.

While preparing for bed, a tremendous avalanche came down, the noise was awful and seemed so close that we all turned to the door and started out. The fastening of the entrance was knotted, the people from the other tent were yelling to us to come out, so we dragged up the bottom of the tent and dived beneath it.

The cliff was entirely hidden by a cloud of snow, and, though the crashing had now almost ceased, we stood ready to run, Dovers thoughtfully seizing a food-bag. However, none of the blocks had come within a hundred yards of us, and as it was now blowing hard, all hands elected to remain where they were.

Several more avalanches, which had broken away near the edge of the mainland, disturbed our sleep through the night, but they were not quite so alarming as the first one. A strong breeze was blowing at daybreak; still the weather was not too bad for travelling, and so I called the party. Moyes and I lashed up our bags, passed them out and strapped them on the sledge; Jones, in the meantime starting the cooker. Suddenly a terrific squall struck the front of our tent, the poles burst through the apex, and the material split from top to bottom.

Moyes and I were both knocked down. When we found our feet again, we went to the aid of the other men, whose tent had survived the gust. The wind rushed by more madly than ever, and the only thing to do was to pull away the poles and allow the tent to collapse.

Looking round for a lee where it could be raised, we found the only available shelter to be a crevasse three hundred yards to windward, but the wind was now so strong that it was impossible to convey the gear even such a short distance. All were frequently upset and blown along the surface twenty to thirty yards, and, even with an ice-axe, one could not always hold his own. The only resort was to build a shelter.

Setting to work, we excavated a hole three feet deep, twelve feet long and six feet wide; the snow being so compact that the job occupied three hours. The sledges and tent-poles were placed across the hole, the good tent being laid on top and weighted down with snow and blocks of ice. All this sounds very easy, but it was a slow and difficult task. Many of the gusts must have exceeded one hundred miles per hour, since one of them lifted Harrisson who was standing beside me clean over my head and threw him nearly twenty feet. Everything movable was stowed in the hole, and at noon we had a meal and retired into sleeping-bags. At three o'clock a weighty avalanche descended, its fearful crash resounding above the roar of the wind. I have never found anything which gave me a more uncomfortable feeling than those avalanches.

The gale continued on September 6, and we still remained packed in the trench. If the latter had been deeper and it had been possible to sit upright, we should have been quite comfortable. To make matters worse, several more avalanches came down, and all of them sounded horribly close.

We were confined in our burrow for five days, the wind continuing to blow with merciless force. Through being closed up so much, the temperature of the hole rose above freezing point, consequently our sleeping-bags and clothes became very wet.

On Sunday, September 8, Moyes went out to feed the dogs and to bring in some biscuit. He found a strong gusty wind with falling snow, and drift so thick that he could not see five yards. We had a cold lunch with nothing to drink, so that the primus could not raise the temperature.

The long confinement was over on the 10th; the sky was blue and the sun brilliant, though the wind still pulsated with racking gusts. As soon as we were out on the ice, away from the land, two men had to hold on to the rear of each sledge, and even then capsizes often occurred. The sledge would turn and slide broadside-on to leeward, tearing the runners badly on the rough ice. Still, by 9.30 a.m. the surface changed to snow and the travelling improved. That night we camped with twenty miles one hundred yards on the meter.

There was a cold blizzard on the 11th with a temperature of −30° F. Confined in the tents, we found our sleeping-bags still sodden and uncomfortable.

With a strong beam wind and in moderate drift big marches were made for two days, during which the compass and sastrugi determined our course.

Lunch was hurried on the 14th as we were all anxious to reach the Hut that night, especially we of the three-man bag for, on account of the wetness of our gear resulting from the subterranean confinement, we had had very little sleep and plenty of shivering for the last four nights. Unfortunately during the afternoon we marched towards the Hut on a magnetic bearing from Masson Island of 149° instead of 139°; we did not discover this error, of course, until next day.

Instead of reaching home at 5 p.m. we travelled on till 8 p.m. and then camped for the night without arriving at the Hut, having done thirty-five miles one thousand yards. The last two hours were in the dark, except for a young moon, amongst a lot of crevasses and pressure ridges which none of us could recognize. At one time we found ourselves on a slope within a dozen yards of the glacier. The temperature that night was −35° F., so we had a very chilly time in our wet bags. Next day we reached home. The last camp had been four and a half miles north of the Hut. Before having a meal, we were all weighed and found the average loss to be eight pounds. In the evening, Moyes and I weighed ourselves again, he had gained seven pounds and I five and three-quarter pounds.

Comparing notes with Hoadley and Kennedy, I found that the weather at the Base had been similar to that experienced on the sledging journey.

Plans were now fixed for the summer sledging programme. There was to be a Western Coast Party under the leadership of Jones and an Eastern Coast Party directed by myself. All ideas of a march into the interior over the plateau, utilizing the depot laid in the autumn, had to be relinquished in view of the limited time at our disposal and the greater importance of the work along the coast.

In preparation for his main journey, Jones decided to lay a depot as far west as was possible during the next four weeks. His depot-laying party included Dovers, Harrisson, Hoadley and Moyes; they were to be assisted by what remained of the dog team. Their intention was to travel over the fast floe which, from experience on board the *Aurora* when first we fell in with Queen Mary Land, was known to extend for at least fifty miles to the west.

Until Jones made a start on September 26, there were ten days of almost continuous wind and drift. There was plenty of occupation indoors weighing and bagging food, repairing tents, poles, cookers and other gear damaged on the last journey and sewing and mending clothes.

At 6 a.m. on the 26th Jones reported that there was only a little low drift and that the wind was dying away. All hands were therefore called and breakfast served. Watson, Kennedy and I assisted the others down to the sea-ice by way of a long sloping snow-drift and saw them off with a good start in a south-westerly direction.

It was my intention to take Kennedy and Watson to recover the depot we had left on the highlands in March.

Watson was slightly lame at the time, as he had bruised his foot on the last trip.

After two days of blizzard Watson, Kennedy and I broke trail, but found the surface was so soft that pulling proved very severe. On the first day, September 29, we managed to travel more than nine miles, but during the next six days the snow became deeper and more impassable, and only nineteen miles were covered. Crevasses were mostly invisible, and on the slope upwards to the ice-cap more troublesome than usual. The weather kept up its invariable wind and drift. Finally, after making laborious headway to two thousand feet Kennedy severely strained the tendon at his heel and I decided to return to "The Grottoes."

At 2 p.m. on October 8, the mast was sighted and shortly afterwards we climbed down into the Hut, finding it very cold, empty and dark. The sun had shone powerfully that day and Kennedy and Watson had a touch of snow-blindness.

Two weeks went by and there was no sign of the Western Depot Party. In fact, out of sixteen days, there were thirteen of thick drift and high wind, so that our sympathies went out to the men in tents with soaking bags, waiting patiently for a rift in the driving wall of snow. On October 23 they had been away for four weeks; provisions for that time having been taken. I had no doubt that they would be on reduced rations, and, if the worst came, they could eat the dogs.

During a lull on October 24, I went to the mast-head with the field-glasses, but saw nothing of the party. On that day we weighed out provisions and made ready to go in search of them. It was my intention to go on the outward track for a week. I wrote instructions to Jones to hoist a large flag on the mast, and to burn flares each night at 10 p.m. if he should return while I was away.

There was a fresh gale with blinding drift early on the following morning; so we postponed the start. At 4 p.m. the wind subsided to a strong breeze and I again went up the mast to sweep the horizon. Westward from Icy Cape to the south a gale was still blowing and a heavy cloud of drift, fifty to sixty feet high, obscured everything.

An hour later Watson saw three Adelie penguins approaching across the floe and we went down to meet them, bringing them in for the larder. Four Antarctic petrels flew above our heads: a sign of returning summer which was very cheering.

The previous night had promised a fine day and we were not disappointed on October 26. A sledge was packed with fourteen days' provisions for eight men and we started away on a search expedition at 10 a.m.

After doing a little over nine miles we camped at 5.30 p.m. Before retiring to bag, I had a last look round and was delighted to see Jones and his party, about a mile to the south. It was now getting dark and we were within two hundred yards of them before being seen, and, as they were to windward, they could not hear our shouts. It was splendid to find them all looking well. They were anxious to get back to "The Grottoes," considering there was only one serviceable tent between them. Kennedy and I offered to change with any of them but, being too eager for warm blankets and a good bed, they trudged on, arriving at the Base at midnight.

Briefly told, their story was that they were stopped in their westerly march, when forty-five miles had been covered, by a badly broken glacier—the Helen Glacier—on the far side of which there was open sea. There was only one thing to do and that was to set out for the mainland by a course so circuitous that they were brought a long way eastward, back towards the Base. They had very rough travelling, bad weather, and were beset with many difficulties in mounting on to the land-ice, where the depot had to be placed. Their distance from the Base at this point was only twenty-eight miles and the altitude was one thousand feet above sea-level. On the ice-cap they were delayed by a blizzard and for seventeen days—an unexampled time—they were unable to move from the camp. One tent collapsed and the occupants, Jones, Dovers and Hoadley, had to dig a hole in the snow floor and to lower the partly demolished tent into it, while the gale raged overhead.

When the snow and wind at last held up, they immediately made down to the sea-ice and back towards home, and, when they met us, had done nineteen miles. All were stiff next day, and no wonder; a march of twenty-eight miles after lying low for seventeen days is a very strenuous day's work.

Final arrangements for the summer journeys were now made, Jones, Dovers and Hoadley, the Western Party, were to start about November 2. Kennedy and Watson were to accompany me to the east. I arranged that Harrisson and Moyes should remain at the Hut, the latter to carry on meteorological observations, and Harrisson biological work. Later, Harrisson begged to accompany me as far as the Hippo depot, bringing the dogs and providing a supporting party. At first I did not like the idea, as on the return, he would have to travel one hundred miles alone, but he showed me that he could erect a tent by himself and, as summer and consequently better weather was in sight, I agreed that he should come.

Each party was taking provisions for fourteen weeks, and I had an additional four weeks' supply for Harrisson and the dogs. My total load came to nine hundred and seventy pounds; the dogs pulling four hundred pounds with the assistance of one man, and three of us dragging five hundred and seventy pounds.

CHAPTER XXI

BLOCKED ON THE SHELF-ICE

Frank Wild's Narrative

WE started away on the Main Eastern Journey on October 30, a calm and cloudless day, following our former track over the shelf-ice to the Hippo Nunatak.

Rapid progress was made and at 4 p.m. on November 6 the Hippo was close at hand. Nearing the shattered ice about the depot we released the dogs and pulled both sledges ourselves.

A nasty shock was awaiting us at the depot. The sledge, which had been left on end, buried two feet deep in hard snow and with a mound six feet high built round it, had been blown completely away. The stays secured to food-bags, were both broken; one food-bag weighing sixty-eight pounds having been lifted ten feet. This was a very serious loss as the total load to be carried now amounted to one thousand one hundred and eighty pounds, which was too great a weight to be supported by one sledge.

It appeared, then, that the only thing to do was to include Harrisson in the party, so that we could have his sledge. This would facilitate our progress considerably, but against that was the fact that Moyes would be left alone at the Base under the belief that Harrisson had perished.

A gale was blowing on the 7th, but as we were partly under the lee of the Hippo, it was only felt in gusts. A visit was made to the nunatak; Harrisson to investigate the bird life, Watson for geology and photography, while I climbed to the summit with the field-glasses to look for the missing sledge. Kennedy remained at the camp to take magnetic observations.

There were hundreds of snow-petrels pairing off, but no eggs were to be seen in any of the nests or crevices.

Upon returning to camp, the search for the sledge was continued. After prospecting with a spade in possible snow-drifts and crevasse-lids, we walked out fanwise, in the direction of the prevailing wind, but with no result. I decided, therefore, to take Harrisson with me. I was extremely sorry for Moyes, but it could not be helped.

Next day the march was resumed and camp was pitched that evening on a slope close to the mainland coast.

From the Base to this spot—Delay Point—the coast ran almost due east and west and with no deep indentations except the Bay of Winds. To the west, the slope from the inland plateau was fairly gradual and therefore not badly broken, but still further west it was much steeper, coming down from two thousand feet in a very short distance, over tumbling ice-fields and frozen cascades. Several outcrops of dark rock lay to the east, one of them only two miles away.

Throughout the 9th a high gale raged confining us to the tents. The next day it moderated, the drift creeping low and thick over the ground, the land visible above it. Donning burberrys, we made an excursion to the rocks at Delay Point. Two miles and a climb of six hundred feet were rather exhausting in a strong wind. There were about eighty acres of rocks of an ancient crystalline character exposed as a prominent headland jutting out from the ice-cap. A line of moraine on the shelf-ice ran from the rocks away in an east-north-east direction.

Most of the next day was broken by a heavy gale so we passed the time in making everything ready for a start and repaired a torn tent. The rent was made by Amundsen, who dragged up the ice-axe to which he was tethered and, in running round the tent, drove the point of the axe through it, narrowly missing Kennedy's head inside.

Tuesday, November 12, was an interesting day. The greater part of the track was over rippled, level ice, thrown into many billows, through devious pressure-hummocks and between the inevitable crevasses. The coast was a kaleido-scope of sable rocks, blue cascades, and fissured ice-falls. Fifteen miles ahead stood an island twenty miles long, rising in bare peaks and dark knolls. This was eventually named David Island.

The dogs were working very well and, if only a little additional food could be procured for them, I knew they could be kept alive. Zip broke loose one night and ate one of my socks which was hanging on the sledge to dry; it probably tasted of seal blubber from the boots. Switzerland, too, was rather a bother, eating his harness whenever he had a chance.

On the 14th, a depot was formed, consisting of one week's provisions and oil; the bags being buried and a mound erected with a flag on top. Kennedy took a round of angles to determine its position.

At the end of two snowy days, after we had avoided many ugly crevasses, our course in an east-south-east line pointed to a narrow strait between David Island and the mainland. On the southern side of the former there was a heaped line of pressure-ice, caused by the flow from a narrow bay being stopped by the island. After lunch, on the 16th, there was an hour's good travelling and then we suddenly pulled into a half-mile of broken surface—the confluence of the slowly moving land-ice and of the more rapidly moving ice from a valley on our right, from which issued the Reid Glacier. It was impossible to steer the dogs through it with a load, so we lightened the weights on both sledges and then made several journeys backwards and forwards over the more broken areas, allowing the dogs to run loose. The crevasses ran tortuously in every direction and falls into them were not uncommon. One large lid fell in just as the sledge had cleared it, leaving a hole twelve feet wide, and at least a hundred feet deep. Once over this zone, the sledges were worked along the slope leading to the mainland, where we were continually worried by their slipping sideways.

Ahead was a vast sea of crushed ice, tossed and piled in every direction. On the northern horizon rose what we concluded to be a riven, flat-topped berg. Ten days later, it resolved itself into a tract of heavy pressure ridges.

Camping after nine and a half miles, we were surprised, on moving east in the morning, to sight clearly the point—Cape Gerlache—of a peninsula running inland to the south-west. A glacier from the hinterland, pushing out from its valley, had broken up the shelf-ice on which we were travelling to such an extent that nothing without wings could cross it. Our object was to map in the coast line as far as possible, and the problem, now, was whether to go north or south. From our position the former looked the best, the tumbled shelf-ice appearing to smooth out sufficiently, about ten miles away, to afford a passage east, while, to the south, we scanned the Denman Glacier, as it was named, rolling in magnificent cascades, twelve miles in breadth, from a height of more than three thousand feet. To get round the head of this ice-stream would mean travelling inland for at least thirty miles.

So north we went, getting back to our old surface over a heavy "cross sea," honeycombed with pits and chasms; many of them with no visible bottom. There was half a mile to safety, but the area had to be traversed five times, relaying the loads across. Kennedy remarked during the afternoon that he felt like a fly walking on wire netting.

The camp was pitched in a line of pressure, with wide crevasses and "hell-holes" within a few yards on every side. Altogether the day's march had been a miserable four miles. On several occasions, during the night, while in this disturbed area, sounds of movement were distinctly heard; cracks like rifle shots and others similar to distant heavy guns, accompanied by a weird, moaning noise as of the glacier moving over rocks.

November 18 was a fine, bright day; temperature 8° to 20° F. Until lunch, the course was mainly north for more than five miles. Then I went with Watson to trace out a road through a difficult area in front. At this point, there broke on us a wonderful vision of most rugged ice scenery.

The Denman Glacier moving much more rapidly than the Shackleton Shelf, tore through the latter and, in doing so, shattered both its own sides and also a considerable area of the larger ice-sheet. At the actual point of contact was what might be referred to as gigantic bergschrund*: an enormous cavern over one thousand feet wide and from three hundred to four hundred feet deep, in the bottom of which crevasses appeared to go

---

* Using the term "bergschrund" in a novel sense.

down for ever. The sides were splintered and crumpled, glittering in the sunlight with a million sparklets of light. Towering above were titanic blocks of carven ice. The whole was the wildest, maddest and yet the grandest thing imaginable.

The turmoil continued to the north, so I resolved to reconnoitre westward and see if a passage were visible from the crest of David Island.

The excursion was postponed till next day, when Kennedy, Watson and I roped up and commenced to thread a tangled belt of crevasses. The island was three and a half miles from the camp, exposing a bare ridge and a jutting bluff, nine hundred feet high—Watson Bluff. At the Bluff the rock was almost all ice-worn gneiss. The face of the summit was so steep and coarsely weathered that we took risks in climbing it. Moss and lichens grew luxuriantly and scores of snow petrels hovered around, but no eggs were seen.

Owing to an overcast sky, the view was not a great deal more enlightening than that which we had had from below. The Denman Glacier swept down for forty miles from over three thousand feet above sea-level. For twenty miles to the east torn ice-masses lay distributed in confusion, and beyond that, probably sixty miles distant, were several stretches of bare rocky islands.*

On November 20, a strong north-east wind blew, with falling snow. Nothing could be seen but a white blanket, above, below and around; so, with sudden death lurking in the bottomless crevasses on every hand, we stayed in camp.

For the next two days also a blizzard of great violence kept us confined. One consolation was that our lips, which were very sore from exposure to the sun and wind, had now a chance of healing.

Next afternoon, the gale moderated sufficiently for us to go once more to David Island, in clearer weather, to see the outlook from the Bluff. This time the sun was shining on the mainland and on the extension of the glacier past the Bluff to the north. The distant southern slopes were seamed with a pattern of crevasses up to a height of about three

---

* To which the name Hordern Islands has been given.

thousand feet. To the north, although the way was certainly impassable for twelve miles—it appeared to become smoother beyond that limit—we decided to try to cross in that direction.

We persevered on the 24th over many lines of pressure-ice and then camped near an especially rough patch. Watson had the worst fall on that day, going down ten feet vertically into a crevasse before his harness stopped him. After supper, we went to locate a trail ahead, and were greatly surprised to find sea-water in some of the cracks. It meant that in two days our descent had been considerable, since the great bergschrund farther south was well over three hundred feet in depth and no water had appeared in its depths.

A few extracts from the diary recall a situation which daily became more serious and involved:

"*Monday, November* 25. A beautiful day so far as the weather and scenery are concerned, but a very hard one. We have been amongst 'Pressure,' with a capital P, all day, hauling up and lowering the sledges with an alpine rope and twisting and turning in all directions, with waves and hills, monuments, statues, and fairy palaces all around us, from a few feet to over three hundred feet in height. It is impossible to see more than a few hundred yards ahead at any time, so we go on for a bit, then climb a peak or mound, choose a route and struggle on for another short stage. . . .

"*Tuesday, November* 26. Another very hard day's work. The first half-mile took three hours to cover; in several places we had to cut roads with ice-axes and shovels and also to build a bridge across a water-lead. I never saw or dreamt of anything so gloriously beautiful as some of the stuff we have come through this morning. After lunch the country changed entirely. In place of the confused jumble and crush we have had, we got on to névé slopes; huge billows, half a mile to a mile from crest to crest, meshed with crevasses. . . .

"We all had falls into these during the day: Harrisson dropping fifteen feet. I received rather a nasty squeeze through falling into a hole whilst going downhill, the sledge running on to me before I could get clear, and pinning me down. So far as we can see, the same kind of country continues, and one cannot help thinking about having to return through this infernal mess. The day's distance—only one thousand and fifty yards.

"*Wednesday, November* 27. When I wrote last night about coming back, I little thought it would be so soon. We turn back to-morrow for the simple reason that we cannot go on any farther.

"In the morning, for nearly a mile along a valley running south-east, the travelling was almost good; then our troubles commenced again.

"Several times we had to resort to hand-hauling with the alpine rope through acres of pitfalls. The bridges of those which were covered were generally very rotten, except the wide ones. Just before lunch we had a very stiff uphill pull and then a drop into a large basin, three-quarters of a mile in diameter.

"The afternoon was spent in vain searching for a road. . . . On every side are huge waves split in every direction by crevasses up to two hundred feet in width. The general trend of the main crevasses is north and south. . . .

"I have, therefore, decided to go back and if possible follow the road we came by, then proceed south on to the inland ice-cap and find out the source of the chaos. If we are able to get round it and proceed east, so much the better; but at any rate, we shall be doing something and getting some-where. We could push through farther east from here, but it would be by lowering the gear piecemeal into chasms fifty to one hundred feet deep, and hauling it up on the other side; each crevasse taking at least two hours to negotiate. For such slow progress I don't feel justified in risking the lives of the party."

Snow fell for four days, at times thickly, unaccompanied by wind. It was useless to stir in our precarious position. Being a little in hand in the ration of biscuits, we fed the dogs on our food, their own having run out. I was anxious to keep them alive until we were out of the pressure-ice.

From this, our turning point out on the shelf-ice, the trail lay over eighteen inches of soft snow on December 3, our former tracks, of course, having been entirely obliterated.

The bridged crevasses were now entirely hidden and many weak lids were found.

At 9 a.m. Harrisson, Watson and I roped up to mark a course over a very bad place, leaving Kennedy with the dogs. We had only gone about one hundred yards when I got a very heavy jerk on the rope and, on looking round found that Watson had disappeared. He weighs two hundred pounds in his clothes and the crevasse into which he had fallen was fifteen feet wide. He had broken through on the far side and the rope, cutting through the bridge, stopped in the middle so that he could not reach the sides to help himself in any way. Kennedy brought another rope over and threw it down to Watson and we were then able to haul him up, but it was twenty minutes before he was out. He reappeared smiling, and, except for a bruise on the shin and the loss of a glove, was no worse for the fall.

At 2.30 p.m. we were all dead-beat, camping with one mile one thousand seven hundred yards on the meter. One third of this distance was relay work and, in several places, standing pulls with the alpine rope. The course was a series of Z's, S's, and hairpin turns, the longest straight stretch one hundred and fifty yards, and the whole knee-deep in soft snow; the sledge sinking to the cross-bars.

The 4th was a repetition of the previous day—a terribly hard two and a half miles. We all had "hangman's drops" into crevasses. One snow-bridge, ten feet wide, fell in as the meter following the twelve-foot sledge was going over behind it.

The 5th was a day of wind, scurrying snow and bad light. Harrisson went out to feed the dogs in the morning and broke through the lid of a crevasse, but fortunately caught the side and climbed out.

The diary again:

"*Friday, December 6.* Still bad light and a little snowfall, but we were off at ten o'clock. I was leading and fell into at least a dozen crevasses, but had to be hauled out of one only. At 1.30 p.m. we arrived at the open lead we had crossed on the outward journey and found the same place. There had been much movement since then and we had to make a bridge, cutting away projections in some places and filling up the sea-water channels with snow and ice. Then Harrisson crossed with the aid of two bamboo poles, and hauled me over on a sledge. Harrisson and I on one side and Kennedy and Watson on the other then hauled the sledges backwards and forwards, lightly loaded one way and empty the other, until all were across. The glacier at this place is without doubt afloat, if the presence of sea-water and diato-maceous stains on the ice is of any account. We camped to-night in the same place as on the evening of November 25, so with luck we should be out of this mess to-morrow. Switzerland had to be killed as I cannot afford any more biscuit. Amundsen ate his flesh, without hesitation, but Zip refused it."

Sure enough, two days sufficed to bring us under the Bluff on David Island. As the tents were being pitched, a skua gull flew down. I snared him with a line, using dog flesh for bait and we had stewed skua for dinner. It was excellent.

While I was cooking the others climbed up the rocks and brought back eight snow-petrels and five eggs, with the news that many more birds were nesting. After supper we all went out and secured sixty eggs and fifty-eight birds. It seemed a fearful crime to kill these beautiful, pure white creatures, but it meant fourteen days' life for the dogs and longer marches for us.

Fresh breeze, light snow and a bad light on the 9th; we remained in camp. Two more skuas were snared for the evening's dinner. The snow-petrels' eggs were almost as large as hens' eggs and very good to eat when fresh. Many of them had been under the birds rather too long, but although they did not look so nice, there was little difference in the taste. I was very glad to get this fresh food, as on account of diffi-culty in obtaining seal and penguin meat we had lived on tinned meat most of the year and there was always the danger of scurvy.

The light was too changeable to make a satisfactory start until the evening of December 11, when we managed to dodge through four and a half miles of broken ice, reaching the mainland close to our position on November 16, and camping for lunch at midnight. In front was a clear mile on a peninsula and then the way led across Robinson Bay, seven miles wide, fed by the Northcliffe Glacier.

Another night march was commenced at 8 p.m. The day had been cloudless and the sun very warm, softening the surface, but at the time of starting it was hardening rapidly. Crossing the peninsula we resolved to head across Robinson Bay as the glacier's surface was still torn up. We ended with a fine march of twelve miles one thousand two hundred yards.

The fine weather continued and we managed to cross three and a half miles of heavy sastrugi, pressure-ridges and crevasses, attaining the first slopes of the mainland at 10 p.m. on December 14. The discovery of two nunataks springing out of the ice to the south lured us on.

The first rock—Possession Nunataks—loomed ahead, two hundred feet above, up a slope of half a mile. Here a depot of provisions and spare gear was made, sufficient to take us back to the Hippo. We lunched in this place and resumed our march at midnight.

The second nunatak was on the course; a sharp peak in the south, hidden by the contour of the uprising ridges. In four miles we steadily ascended eight hundred feet. While we were engaged pitching camp, a Cape pigeon flew overhead.

There were advantages in travelling at night. The surface was firmer, our eyes were relieved from the intense glare and our faces no longer blistered. On the other hand, there were disadvantages. The skirt of the tent used to get very wet through the snow thawing on it in the midday sun, and froze solid when packed up; the floor-cloths and sleeping-bags, also, never had a chance of drying and set to the same icy hardness. When we had mounted higher I intended to return to work by day.

It was not till the altitude was three thousand feet that we came in sight of the far peak to the south. We were then pulling again in daylight. The ice-falls of the Denman Glacier on the left were still seen descending from the plateau, while down on the plain we saw that the zone of disrupted ice, into which the short and intricate track of our northern attempt had been won, extended for quite thirty miles.

The surface then softened in a most amazing fashion and hauling became a slow, dogged strain with frequent spills. A little over four miles was the most we could do on the 18th, and on the 19th the loads were dragging in a deluge of dry, flour-like snow. A long halt was made at lunch to repair a badly torn tent.

The peak ahead was named Mount Barr-Smith. It was fronted by a steep rise which we determined to climb next day. On the eastern margin of the Denman Glacier were several nunataks and higher, rising ground.

Following a twenty-four hours' blizzard, the sky was overcast, with the usual dim light filtering through a mist of snow. We set off to scale the mountain, taking the dip-circle with us. The horizon was so obscured that it was useless to take a round of angels. Fifteen miles to the south was another and higher peak, to be subsequently called Mount Strathcona. The stream of ice forming the Denman Glacier, propelled by the immense forces of the hinterland, is squeezed down through a steep valley at an accelerated speed, and, meeting the slower moving Shackleton Shelf, rends it from top to bottom and presses onward. Thus chaos, icequake and ruin.

Our tramp to Mount Barr-Smith was through eighteen inches of soft snow, in many places a full two feet deep. Hard enough for walking, we knew from experience what it was like for sledging. There was only sufficient food for another week and the surface was so abominably heavy that in that time, not allowing for blizzards, it would have been impossible to travel as far as we could actually see from the summit while four miles a day was the most that could have been done. Our attempts to make east by rounding the Denman Glacier to the south had been foiled, but by turning back at that point, we stood a chance of saving our two remaining dogs, who had worked so well that they really deserved to live. On December 22 the clouds cleared away and we again visited the summit of Mount Barr-Smith to fix its position and make other observations. The altitude was found to be approximately four thousand three hundred and twenty feet. The latitude worked out at 67° 10.4′ S., and we were a little more than one hundred and twenty miles in an air-line from the Hut.

The return journey to the Hut commenced the following day. The surface snow was very sticky in places, clogging the runners badly, so that they had to be scraped every half mile.

Christmas dinner was celebrated at the depot at Possession Nunataks. After dinner the Union Jack and Australian Ensign were hoisted on the rocks and I formally took possession of the land in the name of the Expedition for the Empire.

At this lower elevation the surface was now found to be very soft during the day so henceforth night travelling was the order of the march.

At 6 a.m. on the 28th we rounded Watson Bluff on David Island and camped under its leeward face. After lunch there was a hunt for snow-petrels. Fifty-six were caught and the eggs, which all contained chicks, were given to the dogs.

It was my intention, in order to give Watson an opportunity of examining their character, to touch at all the rocks on the mainland on the way home, as time and weather permitted.

Next day the Hippo hove in sight and we found the depoted food in good condition. The course had been over high pressure-waves and in some places we had to diverge on account of crevasses and—fresh water! Many of the hollows contained water from thawed snow, and in others there was a treacherous crust which hid a slushy pool. The march of eighteen miles landed us just north of the Avalanche Rocks.

While we were erecting the tents there were several snow-slips, and Watson, Kennedy and I walked landwards after supper to try for a "snap" of one in the act of falling, but they refused to oblige us. It was found that one or more avalanches had thrown blocks of ice, weighing at least twenty tons, two hundred yards past the hole in which we spent five days on the depot journey. They had, therefore, travelled six hundred yards from the cliff.

The Alligator Nunatak was explored on January 2, 1913. It was found to be half a mile long, four hundred feet high and four hundred and fifty feet in width, and, like most of the rock we had seen, mainly gneiss.

There was half a gale blowing on the 4th and though the wind was abeam, the sail was reefed and we moved quickly. The day's run was our record up to that time—twenty-two miles. We reckoned to be at the Base in two days and wondered how poor Moyes was faring.

The march continued next day in a following gale. By 9 p.m. the gale became so strong that we struck sail and camped. Altogether the ground covered that day was thirty-five miles.

An hour's march next morning, and, through the glasses, we saw the mast and soon afterwards the Hut. Just before reaching home, we struck up a song, and in a few seconds Moyes came running out. When he saw there were four of us, he stood on his head for sheer joy.

As we expected, Moyes had never thought of Harrisson coming with me and had quite given him up as dead. When a month had elapsed—the time for which Harrisson had food—Moyes packed a sledge with provisions for Harrisson, himself and the dogs and went out for six days. Then, recognizing the futility of searching for anyone in that white waste of nothingness, he returned. He looked well, after his lonely nine weeks, but said that it was the worst time he had ever had in his life. Moyes reported that the Western party were delayed in starting by bad weather until November 7.

As we were to be in readiness to embark on the *Aurora* not later than January 30, preparations for departure were immediately commenced. Geological and biological collections were packed, stores were sorted out and cases containing personal gear were sledged to the edge of the shelf-ice.

Harrisson contrived a winch for sounding and fishing. Strong copper wire, the only material available, was wound on it and, through a crack in the sea-ice a quarter of a mile from the edge of the Shackleton Shelf, bottom was reached in two hundred and sixty fathoms. As the water was too deep for dredging with the meagre gear at his disposal, Harrisson manufactured cage traps and lowering them to the bottom, secured some fish, a squid, and other specimens.

At this time there was abundant evidence of life. Skua gulls frequently flew about the Hut, as well as Cape pigeons, Antarctic, snow, Wilson, giant and silver-grey petrels. Out on the sea-ice, there were Adelie and Emperor penguins; the latter moulting. With the aid of glasses hundreds of seals were seen on the edge of the floe, ten miles to the north.

Shortly after lunch on January 21 we caught sight of Jones's party coming in from the south and, hastening out to meet them, were soon shaking them by the hand and listening eagerly to the story of their very successful enterprise.

CHAPTER XXII

LINKING UP WITH KAISER WILHELM LAND

From Dr. S. E. Jones's Narrative

JONES, Dovers and Hoadley had set out from The Grottoes on November 7, Moyes bidding them adieu and wishing them good luck. The course lay southward over the shelf-ice towards Junction Corner where, on the following day, the rising slopes were met. Ahead, on the land-ice, half a mile from the sea cliffs, could be seen several black objects which turned out to be morainic matter—rocks, six in number.

Next day the course was continued to the west towards the depot of food laid in the spring. Marching over a polished surface with a high wind abeam it was hard work, punctuated by frequent capsizes as the sledge, driven to leeward, collided with sastrugi. Under these conditions it was not until 5.30 on the 10th that the depot was reached. From there a fine view was presented of the Helen Glacier running out of a bay which opened up ahead.

The extra sledge and the additional food recovered from the depot brought their total load up to twelve hundred pounds—including supplies for thirteen weeks. This meant relay work, for it was too much to haul as one load; accordingly, an even division was made between the two sledges.

In front, the ice of the land slopes was observed to be very broken, and so it was clear that their track would have to lie some way from the sea cliffs, at higher elevations, where the surface was less crevassed.

The march was continued, laboriously relaying the sledges over the dangerous ground. To make matters worse, gales of wind and snow storms placed additional limitations on their progress.

On the evening of November 17, after travelling for a couple of hours through thick drift, Jones's narrative continues:

"The night's camp was situated approximately at the eastern edge of the Helen Glacier. The portion of the ice-cap which contributes to the glacier below is marked off from the general icy surface on either side by a series of falls and cascades. These appeared quite impassable near sea-level, but we hoped to find a smooth passage at an altitude of about one thousand feet.

"A start was made at 7 a.m. The surface consisted of ice and névé and was badly broken by pressure mounds, ten to twenty feet high, and by numerous crevasses old and recent; many with sunken or fallen bridges. While crossing a narrow crevasse, about forty feet of the bridge collapsed lengthwise under the leading man, letting him fall to the full extent of his harness rope. Hoadley and myself had passed over the same spot, unsuspecting and unroped, a few minutes previously, while looking for a safe track. We were now nearing the approximate western edge of the Helen Glacier, and the broken condition of the ice evidently indicated considerable movement. Later in the morning a more southerly course was kept over an improving surface.

"At midday Dovers took observations of the sun and found the latitude to be 66° 47' S. Owing to the heat of the sun the fat in the pemmican had been melting in the food-bags, so after lunch the provisions were repacked and the pemmican was put in the centre of the large tanks. In the afternoon we hoisted the sail, and by evening had done four miles.

"The next day was gloriously bright, with a breeze just strong enough to make hauling pleasant. Erecting a sail, we made an attempt to haul both sledges, but found that they were too heavy. It was soon discovered that a considerable detour would have to be made to cross the broken ice on the western edge of the Helen Glacier. At 4 p.m. we arrived at what at first appeared an *impasse*.

"At this point three great crevassed ridges united to form the ice-falls on the western side of the glacier. The point of confluence was the only place that appeared to offer any hope of a passage, and, as we did not want to retrace our steps, we decided to attempt it. The whole surface was a net-work of huge crevasses, some open, the majority from fifty to one hundred feet or more in width. After many devious turns, a patch of snow between two large abysses was reached. As the ice in front seemed even more broken than that behind, camp was pitched. After tea a search was made for a way out, and it was found that by travelling along a narrow, knife-edge ridge of ice and névé, with an open crevasse on each side, a good surface could be reached within a mile of the camp. The ridge had a gradient of one in ten, and, unfortunately, also sloped down towards one of the open crevasses.

"During the next four days a heavy blizzard raged. There was a tremendous snowfall accompanied by a gale of wind, and, after the second day, the snow was piled four feet high round the tent, completely burying the sledges and by its pressure greatly reducing the space inside the tent. On the 23rd, the fourth day, we dug out the floor, lowering the level of the tent about two feet, and this made things more comfortable. While digging, a crack in the ice was disclosed running across the floor, and from this came a considerable draught. By midday the weather had improved sufficiently to allow us to move.

"The sledge and tent were excavated from beneath a great mass of soft snow; the new level of the snow's surface being four to five feet above that on which the camp had been made four days earlier. The wind having fallen, we went ahead with the sledges. While crossing the ridge of ice which led into the valley below, one man hauled the sledges while the other two prevented them from sliding sideways downhill into the open crevasse. That afternoon we noticed very fine iridescent colouring in cirro-cumulus clouds as they crossed the sun.

"The next day gave us a pleasant surprise, there being a strong breeze dead aft, while the travelling surface ahead looked distinctly favourable. Sail was hoisted and the two sledges were coupled together. The course for a short distance was downhill, and we had to run to keep up with the sledges."

The Helen Glacier was passed and below lay young floe ice, studded with numerous bergs. The march west was continued parallel to the coast at a distance therefrom of five to ten miles.

On the morning of November 25, Dovers called attention to what appeared to be an ice-covered island* on the north-north-west horizon. The lunch camp was pitched on an ice ridge from where a good view of the sea-front could be obtained. From its crest was spied a group of about a dozen rocky islets, the most distant being about five miles from the coast. All were surrounded by solid floe.

After the meal, Jones and Hoadley descended to the sea to reconnoitre a passable route down for the sledges. A descent of nine hundred feet in a distance of one and a half miles brought them to sea-level, but the surface was badly broken and not at all promising for sledges. So while Jones returned to help Dovers with his charting, Hoadley walked over the floe to the islets to ascertain the nature of the rock.

"Hoadley returned at 9 p.m. and reported that he had seen an immense rookery of Emperor penguins near the largest islet, besides Adelie penguins, silver-grey, Wilson and Antarctic petrels and skua gulls. He also said that he thought it possible to take a sledge, lightly laden, through the drifts below the brink of the glacier.

"Accordingly in the morning the eleven-foot sledge was packed with necessaries for a week's stay, although we intended to remain only a day in order to take photographs and search for specimens. Erecting a depot flag to mark the big sledge, we broke camp at midday and soon reached the sea-front. Our track then wound among the snow-drifts until it emerged from the broken ice which was observed to border the land ice-sheet for miles. The travelling became unexpectedly good for a time over highly polished, green sea-ice, and thence on to snow, amid a field of numerous

---

* This was examined in detail from the *Aurora* in January 1913, and found to be an island, which was named Drygalski Island, for it is evidently the ice-covered "high land" observed by Professor Drygalski (German Expedition, 1902) from his balloon.

small bergs. Many of these showed a marked degree of ablation, and, in places, blocks of ice perched on eminences had weathered into most grotesque forms. There were numerous streams of thaw-water running from mud-covered bergs. Perspiring in the heat, we more than once stopped to slake our thirst.

"Approaching the largest rock exposure—Haswell Island, as it was called later—we saw more distinctly the immense numbers of Emperor penguins covering several acres of floe. The birds extended in rows even on to the lower slopes of several bergs. The sound of their cries coming across the ice reminded one of the noise from a distant sports ground during a well-contested game. We camped at 5 p.m. on a snow-drift at the southern end of the island. A large rookery of Adelie penguins on a long, low rock, about a mile distant, soon made itself evident.

"Although the stay was intended to occupy only about twenty-four hours, we were compelled to remain five days on the island on account of a snowstorm which continued for practically the whole of the time. This did not prevent us from leaving the tent and wandering about; Hoadley keen on the geology and Dovers surveying whenever the light was good enough. The temperature of the rock was well above freezing-point where it was exposed, and snow melted almost as soon as it fell. Our sleeping-bags and gear soon became very wet, but we rejoiced in one compensation, and that was a change in diet. It was agreed that five Adelie penguin or ten Cape pigeon eggs made a good tasty entrée to the monotonous ration.

"Haswell Island was found to be roughly diamond shaped; three-quarters of a mile in length, the same in width, and about three hundred feet on the highest point.

"There was ample proof that it had been completely overridden by the ice sheet of former times, and many large erratics lay scattered over the surface. Two deep gorges cut through the island from south-east to north-west, in both of which were small ponds of fresh water.

"The most marked feature was the wonderful abundance of bird life, for almost all the birds frequenting the shores of the continent were found nesting there. Adelie penguins were in greatest numbers. Besides the large rookery on one of the smaller islets there were numerous others of fifty to one hundred birds each on Haswell Island. Attached to each rookery was a pair of skua gulls, who swooped down and quickly flew off with any eggs left for a moment untended.

"The Emperor penguins had their rookery on the floe, about a mile from the island. The birds covered four or five acres, but there were undoubted signs that a much larger area had been occupied. We estimated the numbers to be seven thousand five hundred, the great majority being young birds. These were well grown, most of them standing as high as the shoulders of the adults. They were all very fat, covered by a grey down. A few of the larger chicks had commenced to moult, the change of plumage being observed on the flippers.

"Daily we watched large numbers of adults departing from and returning to the rookery. The direction in which they travelled was north, towards open water, estimated to be twenty miles distant. Although more than once the return of the adults to the rookery was carefully noted, we never saw the young birds being fed, old birds as they entered the rookery quietly going to sleep.

"Hoadley on his first visit to the island had seen Antarctic petrels flying about, and a search revealed a large rookery of these on the eastern side. The nesting-place of this species of petrel had never before been discovered, and so we were all elated at the great find. About three hundred birds were found sitting in the gullies and clefts, as close together as they could crowd. They made no attempt to form nests, merely laying their eggs on the shallow dirt. Each bird had one egg about the same size as that of a domestic fowl. Incubation was far advanced, and some difficulty was experienced in blowing the specimens with a blow-pipe improvised from a quill. Neither the Antarctic nor any other petrels offered any resistance when disturbed on their nests, except by the expectoration of large quantities of a pink or green, oily fluid.

"The Cape pigeons had just commenced laying when we arrived at the island. On the first day only two eggs were found, but, on the fourth day after our arrival, forty were collected. These birds make a small shallow nest composed of chips of stone.

"The silver-grey petrels were present in large numbers, especially about the steep north-eastern side of the island. Though they were mated, laying had scarcely commenced, as we found only two eggs. They made small grottoes in the snowdrifts, and many pairs were seen billing and cooing in such shelters.

"The small Wilson petrels were found living in communities under slabs of rock.

"Skua gulls were present in considerable force, notably near the penguin rookeries. They were breeding at the time, laying their eggs on the soil near the summit of the island. The neighbourhood of a nest was always betrayed by the behaviour of these birds who, when we intruded on them, came swooping down as if to attack us.

"Although many snow-petrels were seen flying about, we found only one with an egg. The nests were located in independent rocky niches but never in rookeries.

"Vegetable life existed in the form of algæ in the pools, lichens on the rocks and mosses which grew luxuriantly, chiefly in the Adelie penguin rookeries.

"Weddell seals were plentiful about the island near the tide-cracks; two of them with calves."

On December 3 the specimens were packed and the party left for the mainland, reaching the second sledge, then buried in snow, late in the afternoon. Next morning the journey was resumed. On account of the frequency of crevasses they were driven inland high up the slopes. Below them was the fast floe dotted with bergs and beyond, some twenty miles from the coast, lay open water.

The journey for the next few days was a strenuous grind, relaying the sledges uphill through crevassed ice and hindered by frequent blizzards.

On December 12 the surface improved and aided by a fair breeze both sledges were easily hauled along coupled together. The course was almost due west, parallel to the coast.

"Open water came within a few miles of the ice cliffs, and, further north, a heavy belt of pack was observed. When the sun sank lower, the bergs on the northern horizon were refracted up to such a degree that they appeared to be hanging from the sky.

"The aid rendered by the sail under the influence of a fair breeze was well shown on the following day. In four hours, on a good surface, both sledges were transported seven miles. When we moved off, the wind was blowing at ten to fifteen miles an hour. By 10 a.m. the sky became overcast and the wind freshened. Camp was pitched for lunch at 11 a.m., as we hoped that the weather would clear again later, but the wind increased and snow began to fall heavily in the afternoon, so we did not stir. The storm continued throughout the following day and it was quite impossible to march until the 15th.

"Continuing the ascent on the 16th out of a valley we had crossed on the previous day, we halted on the top of a ridge within view of German "territory"—a small, dark object bearing due west, evidently bare rock and presumably Gaussberg. The course was altered accordingly towards this object and everything went smoothly for ten miles. Then followed an area where the ice fell steeply in waves to the sea, crossed by crevasses which averaged fifty feet in width. The snow bridges were deeply concave, and the lower side of each chasm was raised into a ridge five to ten feet high. Making fast the alpine rope on to the sledges, one of us went ahead to test the bridge, and then the sledges, one at a time, were rushed down into the trough and up on the other side. After crossing ten or more crevasses in this fashion, we were forced to camp by the approach of a rapidly moving fog driven before a strong westerly wind. While camp was being prepared, it was discovered that a tin of kerosene on the front sledge had been punctured causing the loss of a gallon of fuel. Fortunately, we were well within our allowance, so the accident was not serious. Soon after tea our attention was drawn to a pattering on the tent like rain, caused by a fall of sago snow.

"In the morning the weather was clearer, and we saw that it was impossible to reach Gaussberg by a direct route, which would have led us down on to and across the frozen sea.

The ice ahead was cleft and split in all directions, and, in places, vertical faces stood up to a height of one hundred feet. The floe, off shore, was littered with hundreds of bergs, and in several localities there were black spots which resembled small rocks, but it was impossible to approach close enough to be certain. Retracing our steps until clear of the broken surface, we steered in a south-westerly direction, just above the line of sérac and crevassed ice. The coast here trended to the south-west, forming the eastern side of Drygalski's Posadowsky Bay. The going was heavy, as the surface was covered by a layer of frost-crystals deposited during the night. A fog came up again early in the afternoon and had quite surrounded us at camping time. During the day there were fine clouds of ice crystals in the air, and at 8 p.m. a fogbow was seen in the east.

"Turning out in the morning we saw Gaussberg peeping over a ridge to the west, but were still prevented from steering direct towards it by the broken surface. When we had advanced ten miles, a heavy fog brought us to a halt at 5 p.m.

"On Friday the 20th, in spite of a sticky surface, thirteen miles were covered on a west-south-west course. The ice-cap continued to be undulating but free from crevasses. The altitude was between two thousand five hundred and three thousand feet.

"In the morning, after travelling two miles, we came in sight of Gaussberg again and steered directly towards it. The surface was good with a downward grade. At five and a quarter miles a depot was made of the small sledge and most of the food. The next day a high wind kept us tent-bound.

"Gaussberg was reached in the afternoon of the 23rd, after our track had passed through seventeen miles of dangerous country. For the first few miles the surface consisted of a series of steep, buckled ice ridges; later, it was snow-covered, but at times literally cut into a network of crevasses.

"The only approach to Gaussberg from the plateau is from the south. To the east and west there were magnificent ice-falls, the debris from which litters the floe for miles around."

Christmas Eve and Christmas Day were devoted to examining the mountain. It attains an altitude of about twelve hundred feet and is an extinct volcano, of comparatively recent geological age, fragments of sulphur still being met with on the slopes. The cone stands right on the margin of the continent, the land ice-cap abutting against it on the south side at an elevation of four hundred feet above sea level; while to the north the rocky slopes descend to the sea. These slopes are covered with loose rubble, square yards of which commence to slide at the slightest disturbance, rendering climbing difficult.

At the summit two cairns were found, the bamboo poles which had previously marked them having been blown over. Further examination revealed many other bamboos which had been used as marks, but no other record of the visit of the German expedition, ten years before, was met. Bird life was not plentiful, being limited to a few skuas, Wilson petrels and snow-petrels; the latter nesting under slabs of rock. There were large quantities of moss where thaw-water had been running.

"The ice and snow near the mountain showed evidences of marked thawing, and we had difficulty in finding a favourable spot for our camp.

"Christmas Day was gloriously fine, with just sufficient wind to counteract the heat of the sun. At midday the Christmas "hamper" was opened, and it was not long before the only sign of the plum-pudding was the tin. In the afternoon we ascended the mountain and left a record in a cairn at the top. By the route followed, Gaussberg was two hundred and fifteen miles from The Grottoes, but relay work had made the actual distance covered three hundred miles.

"We had been away from home seven weeks, and, though there was sufficient food for an outward journey of another week, there was no indication that the country would change. Furthermore, from the summit of Gaussberg one could see almost as far as could be marched in a week. Accordingly we decided to turn back at this point."

The return journey commenced on December 26. After picking up the gear at the depot a course was pursued further inland and at a somewhat higher elevation than that of the outgoing march, thereby avoiding stretches of irregular and broken ground. Though unduly hampered by bad weather a good average daily mileage was maintained.

During the morning of January 9 they were enveloped for a time in a fog and witnessed a wonderful display of mock-suns and coloured arcs and bows, the sky being literally covered with them for about ten miles. As the minute ice particles which filled the air disappeared the display faded away; illustrating very clearly how these very curious optical effects arise from refraction in the particles that fill the air at such times.

Almost daily during the first fortnight in January a Wilson petrel visited the party as they marched along, the only form of life seen on the return journey.

On the afternoon of January 19 a magnificent view of the Helen Glacier was obtained, and to the north-west Haswell Island and Drygalski Island were plainly visible.

Continuing on the same course throughout the following day, they picked up The Grottoes with the binoculars at 5 p.m. There now came a quick descent to Junction Corner.

On the lower levels there was clear evidence of thawing having occurred. The firm surface of snow which had presented itself on the outward journey was now converted into rough ice, over which they walked painfully in finnesko. Névé and ice surfaces were covered with sharp spicules and blades, and the bridges of crevasses were unmistakably thawed.

Leaving Junction Corner at 6 a.m. on January 21, they steered a course for The Grottoes running parallel to the edge of the shelf-ice. At 3 p.m. the mast was sighted, and, later, the Hut itself, concluding an achievement of which Jones, Hoadley and Dovers should feel justly proud.

Wild, continuing with his chronicle of events at the Western Base writes:

"It was very gratifying to hear their story and learn that our comrades had done so well. Our joint efforts had been successful in charting and otherwise investigating a length of about four hundred miles of coast in this very interesting region.

"Now that all were back safely at the Base it only remained for the *Aurora* to appear to dispel our final anxiety. On January 26, accompanied by several of the party I walked out over the floe towards the sea discovering that the open water now reached to within seven miles of the Hut.

"On the whole, January was a very fine month. Some of the days seemed really hot; the shade temperature on one occasion reaching 37° F., and, in several instances 33° F. It was quite a common thing for us to work outside in loose, light garments; in fact, with nothing more than a singlet on the upper part of the body. In February the weather altered for the worse, and there was not a single fine day until the 20th. A strong east-south-east wind with falling snow prevailed. As the days were shortening rapidly, all were beginning to feel anxious about the *Aurora*.

"In view of the possibility of an accident having befallen the vessel or of her not being able to penetrate the pack to our relief, large stores of seal meat for food, and blubber for fuel were accumulated to carry us through a second year if necessary. Unfortunately the nearest crack in the sea-ice where the seals were to be obtained was two miles away, so that the return journey, with a heavily laden sledge, was long and tedious. Two holes were dug in the glacier near the Hut, one for blubber, the other for meat.

"On February 20 the open water was within three miles of the Hut and the edge of the floe was rapidly breaking up. As beacons we had erected flagstaffs at two points close to the face of the shelf-ice; also a lamp screen and reflector was fitted at the mast-head and each night a hurricane lamp was placed there, which could be seen with the naked eye from a distance of eight miles.

"February 22 was the anniversary of the day the *Aurora* left us, but the weather was very different. A heavy blizzard was raging, the velocity of the wind ranging up to about eighty miles per hour. As it was Saturday, we kept the usual routine, scrubbing out and cleaning up the Hut. We could not help speculating as to whether we should have to do it for another whole year. But everyone had great faith in 'good old Davis,' and nobody was at all downhearted.

"When we 'turned out' on Sunday there was still a strong wind and drift, but this died away to a light breeze before breakfast was over, and the sun came out. I had a look round with the glasses and saw that the ice had broken away beyond a limit of one and a half miles. As there was a sledge, which Harrisson had been using for sounding within a few yards of the water's edge, Jones and I went off to bring it in. We had gone less than half a mile when we saw what at first appeared to be a penguin, standing on some pack-ice in the distance, but which we soon saw was the mast-head of the *Aurora*.

"It was evident that she could not be alongside for some time, so Jones went back to the Hut to tell the others to bring down a load of gear, and I went on to meet the ship. Before the *Aurora* had reached the fast ice, all the party were down with two sledge loads, having covered the mile and a half in record time.

"We were all anxious, of course, for news, and the first we received was the sad account of the deaths of Ninnis and Mertz; then of the wonderful march made by Dr. Mawson.

"Before closing I should like to pay a tribute to the good fellowship, unfailing industry, enthusiasm and unswerving loyalty which characterized my comrades. During the whole of the Expedition, whether carrying out monotonous routine work at the Base or under the trying conditions of sledging, all the duties were performed with never-failing good temper and perseverance.

"Should it ever be my lot to venture on a like expedition I hope to have some, if not all, of the same party with me. But whether we meet again or not, I shall always think of every man of them with the greatest affection and respect."

Wild and his seven men had certainly done well with their opportunities and were to be abundantly congratulated for the success of their efforts. They had faced great risks cheerfully and by their energy and ability had wrung its secrets from that inhospitable land.

Dovers's chart of the western section and Kennedy's chart

of the eastern extension of Queen Mary Land reflect very great credit upon both of them, and illustrate at a glance what a large field was covered.

It is only to be regretted that space does not allow us to deal more fully with the achievements of this gallant band in the rigours and dangers of a new Antarctic Polar land.

CHAPTER XXIII

THE SECOND YEAR

DURING the first busy year in Adelie Land, when the Hut was full of life and work, there were few moments for reflection. With each day came fresh diversions, and no one could foretell what the morrow had in store. So the year sped away almost too quickly.

Now there were only seven of us; the field of work which once stretched to the west, east and south had no longer the mystery of the unknown; we knew what was ahead and the weather had already given ample proof of the early approach of winter. Briefly, the prospects were decidedly duller than the previous year; yet we knew that there still remained useful work to be undertaken.

A wireless telegraph station had at last been established, and we could confidently expect communication with the outside world at an early date. Our short mile of rocks still held some geological secrets and there were biological discoveries yet to make. Even the routine of magnetic and meteorological observations was accumulating really valuable data. These were some of the obvious assurances which no one had the heart to think about at first; but, then, there was always the tonic of good companionship to carry us over dull hours.

It was to be a dreary and difficult time for the five who had remained behind facing another year in order to make a search for myself and comrades. These were men whom I had learnt to appreciate during the first year, and I now saw their sterling characters in a new light. To Jeffryes all was fresh, and we envied him the novelties of a new world, rough and inhospitable though it was. As for me, it was sufficient to feel

"...He that tossed thee down into the field
He knows about it all—He knows, He knows."

The trials of my late experience, wherein I had sounded to the lowest depths of starvation without actually perishing, had so disorganized my system that two months elapsed ere my internal arrangements were again in order. It was several weeks before normal sleep returned; during that time I did little else than potter about, eat and doze, with frequent interruptions from internal disorders. My companions were indulgent and vied with each other in making things as comfortable as possible for me.

Whilst I was recuperating, the others set to work to make the Hut, if anything, safer and snugger. This chiefly consisted in covering the roof with an old sail left by the ship, and otherwise rendering the structure more wind-proof.

Bage's time was very fully occupied, for, besides being astronomer and magnetician, he undertook the duties of storeman. The penguin-eggs, which had been stored in boxes, were stacked together on the windward side of the Hut, and a choice selection of seal and penguin steaks were at the storeman's disposal in the veranda.

Madigan, in addition to his meteorological duties, took charge of the new sledge dogs which had been landed from the ship. These fine animals had all been presented to our Expedition at Hobart by Captain Roald Amundsen on the return of the *Fram*. A number of seals had already been killed to last as food for these dogs through the winter.

Jeffryes, as operator, was occupied regularly every night listening attentively for wireless signals and calling at intervals. The continuous winds soon caused many of the stays of the wireless mast to become slack, and these he pulled taut on his daily rounds.

Bickerton, as engineer for the wireless installation, remained on duty each evening. He was also busied with many odd mechanical jobs in connection with the repairing of instruments and the like.

McLean kept the biological log and undertook the duties of ice-cutter and coal-carrier. He also dispatched ocean-letters—messages sealed in bottles—regularly, on the chance of their being picked up, thereby giving some indication of the direction of the currents.

Hodgeman continued as assistant meteorologist but also spent much time drafting, engaged upon the maps and plans of the Expedition.

On the night of February 15, Jeffryes suddenly surprised us with the exciting intelligence that he had heard Macquarie Island send a coded weather report to Hobart. The engine was immediately set going, but though repeated attempts were made, no answer could be elicited. Each night darkness was more pronounced and signals became more distinct, until, on the 20th, our call reached Sawyer at Macquarie Island, who immediately responded by saying "Good evening." The insulation of a Leyden jar broke down at the point, and nothing more could be done until it was remedied.

At last, on February 21, signals were exchanged, and by the 23rd a message had been dispatched to Lord Denman, Governor-General of the Commonwealth, acquainting him with our situation and the loss of our comrades and, through him, one to His Majesty the King requesting his royal permission to name a tract of newly discovered country to the east, King George V Land. Special messages were also sent to the relatives of Lieutenant B. E. S. Ninnis and Dr. X. Mertz.

The first news received from the outside world was the bare statement that Captain Scott and four of his companions had perished on their journey to the South Pole. It was some time before we knew the tragic details which came home, direct and poignant, to us in Adelie Land.

To Professor David a fuller account of our own calamity was sent and, following this, many kind messages of sympathy and congratulation were received from all over the world. On February 26 Lord Denman sent an acknowledgment of our message to him, expressing his sorrow at the loss of our two companions; and on March 7 His Majesty the King added his gracious sympathy, with permission to affix the name, King George V Land, to that part of the Antarctic continent lying between Adelie Land and Oates Land.

March began in earnest with much snow and monotonous days of wind. By contrast, a few hours of sunny calm was appreciated to the full. The face of the landscape was changed; the rocky crevices filling flush with the low mound of snow which trailed along and off the ridges.

On March 16 everyone was relieved to hear that the *Aurora* had arrived safely in Hobart, and that Wild and his party were all well. But the news brought disappointment too, for we had always a lingering ray of hope that there might be sufficient coal to bring the vessel back to Adelie Land. Later on we learned that on account of the shortage of funds the ship was to be laid up at Hobart until the following summer. In the meantime, Professors David and Masson were making every effort to raise the necessary money. In this they were assisted by Captain Davis, who went to London to obtain additional donations.

It was now a common thing for those of us who had gone to bed before midnight to wake up in the morning and find that quite a budget of wireless messages had been received. It took the place of a morning paper and we made the most of the intelligence, discussing it from every possible point of view. Jeffryes and Bickerton worked every night from 8 p.m. until 1 a.m., calling at short intervals and listening attentively at the receiver. In fact, notes were kept of the intensity of the signals, and of the several forms of interference which hamper the operator. Of these, the wireless man of Adelie Land is harassed by a specially troublesome disturbance arising from St. Elmo's fire in the aerial system.

Listening at the wireless receiver was very tedious work, as so many adventitious sounds had to be neglected. There was, first of all, the noise of the wind as it swept by the Hut; then there was the occasional crackling of St. Elmo's fire; the dogs in the veranda shelter were not always remarkable for their quietness; while within the Hut it was impossible to avoid slight sounds which were often sufficient to interrupt the sequence of a message. At times, when the aurora was visible, signals would often die away, apparently "damped" out, and the only alternative was to wait until they recurred, meanwhile keeping up calls at regular intervals awaiting a clearance of the ether. So Jeffryes would sometimes spend the whole evening trying to transmit a single message, or conversely, trying to receive one.

It was often possible for Jeffryes to hear Wellington, Sydney, Melbourne and Hobart, and once he managed to communicate directly with the last-named. Then there were numerous ships passing along the southern shores of Australia or in the vicinity of New Zealand whose calls were audible on "good" nights. The warships were at times particularly distinct, and occasionally the "chatter in the ether" was so confusing that Sawyer, at Macquarie Island, would signal that he was "jammed."

A coded weather report which had priority over all other messages was sent out each night, and it is surprising how often Jeffryes managed to transmit to the Commonwealth Weather Bureau, via Macquarie Island, this important intelligence.

At the beginning of April, McLean laid the foundations of *The Adelie Blizzard*, which recorded our life for the next seven months. It was a monthly publication, and contributions were invited from all on every subject but the wind. Anything from light doggerel to heavy blank verse was welcomed, and original articles, letters to the Editor, plays, reviews on books and serial stories were accepted within the limits of our supply of foolscap paper and typewriter ribbons.

It was the first Antarctic publication which could boast a real cable column of news of the day. Extracts from the April number were read after dinner one evening and excited much amusement. An "Ode to Tobacco" was very popular and seemed to voice the enthusiasm of our small community, while "The Evolution of Women" introduced us to a once-familiar subject. The Editor was later admitted by wireless to the Journalists' Association (Sydney).

Many have asked the question, "What did you do to fill in the time during the second year?"

The duties of cook and night-watchman came to each man once every week, and meteorological and magnetic observations went on daily. Then we were able to devote a good deal of time to working up the scientific work accomplished during the sledging journeys. The wireless watches kept two men well occupied, and in spare moments the chief recreation was reading. There was a fine supply of illustrated journals and periodicals which had arrived by the *Aurora* and with these we tried to make up the arrears of a year in exile. The "Encyclopædia Britannica" was a great boon, being always the last word in the settlement of a debated point. Again, whenever the weather gave the smallest opportunity, there were jobs outside, digging for cases, attending to the wireless mast and, in the spring, geological collecting and dredging. If the air was clear of drift, and the wind not over fifty miles per hour, one could spend a pleasant hour or more walking along the shore watching the birds and noting the changes which were always occurring along our short length of rocky shore.

Cooking reached its acme according to our standard, and each man became remarkable for some particular dish. Bage was the exponent of steamed puddings of every variety, and Madigan could always be relied upon for an unfailing batch of puff-pastry. Bickerton once started out with the object of cooking a ginger pudding, and in an unguarded moment used mixed-spice instead of ginger. The result, though highly spiced, was rather appetizing, so "mixed-spice pudding" was added to our list of discoveries. McLean specialized in yeast waffles, having acquired the art of tossing pancakes. Jeffryes had come on the scene with a limited experience, but his first milk scones gained him a reputation which he managed to make good. Hodgeman never failed to consult the cookery book before embarking on the task of preparing dinner; but as a result of these deliberations, at least as far as the sweet course was concerned, we might confidently and invariably expect tapioca pudding.

We had become thoroughly tired of soda bread and longed to renew our acquaintance with yeast bread. The difficulties of cultivating yeast under the cold and uncertain temperature conditions of the Hut had caused us to refrain from adopting the latter during the previous year. Now, however, we were anxious to experiment on its manufacture, but the first problem was how to obtain a culture of yeast. With this object in view, a mixture of stout (from a bottle), flour, sugar, dried fruit, etc., was left near the stove to "mature." After a few days fermentation commenced and very soon the contents of the pot became a vile-smelling mess. So rotten was it, and overgrown with moulds that the majority voted to have it cast outside. However, before this was done, a scrap of froth which showed on it was selected and added to a fresh mixture of flour, water and sugar. This, when matured, was less obnoxious and grew fewer moulds. A sub-culture was again made from and so on for several weeks, until at length an almost pure sample of yeast was produced. Bread-making was the next difficulty, but it soon came about that the first light spongy loaf was produced; then every night-watchman cultivated the art and baked for the ensuing day.

The dogs were penned in the veranda and in tolerable weather were brought outside to be fed. Carrying an axe, Madigan usually went down to the Boat Harbour, followed by the expectant pack, to where there were several seal carcases. These lay immovably frozen to the ice, and were cut about and hacked so that the meat in section reminded one of the grain of a log of red cedar, and it was certainly quite as hard. When Magidan commenced to chop, the dogs would range themselves on the lee side and "field" the flying chips.

On April 16 the last penguin was seen on a ledge over-hanging an icy cove to the east. Apparently its moulting time had not expired, but it was certainly a very miserable bird, smothered in small icicles and snow and partly exposed to a sixty-five mile wind with the temperature close to −10° F. Petrels were often seen flying along the foreshores and no wind appeared to daunt them. It was a most remarkable thing to witness a snow-petrel, small, light and fragile, making headway over the sea in the face of a seventy mile hurricane, fluttering down through the spindrift to pick up a morsel of food which it had detected. Close to the western cliffs there was a trail of brash-ice where many birds were often observed feeding on Euphausia (crustaceans) in weather when it scarcely seemed possible for any living creature to be abroad.

It was very gratifying to learn that the Macquarie Island party to a man had consented to remain at their lonely post, and from Ainsworth, their leader, I received a brief report of the work which had been accomplished by each member. We all could appreciate the sacrifice they were making. Then, too, an account was received of the success of the enterprise entrusted to Wild and his men to the west. But it was not till the end of the year that their adventurous story was related to us in full detail.

On May 23 Lassie, one of the dogs, had his abdomen ripped open in a fight and had to be shot. Quarrels amongst the dogs had to be quelled immediately, otherwise they would probably mean the death of some unfortunate animal which happened to be thrown down amongst the pack. Whenever a dog was down, it was the way of these brutes to attack him irrespective of whether they were friends or foes.

We became very fond of the dogs despite their habit of howling at night and their somewhat wolfish ferocity. They always gave one a welcome, in drift or sunshine, and though ruled by the law of force, they had a few domestic traits to make them civilized.

May was a dreaded month because it had been the period of worst wind and drift during 1912. On this occasion the wind velocities over four weeks were not so high and constant, though the snowfall was just as persistent. On the 17th and 18th, however, there was an unexpected rise to the nineties. The average over the first twenty-four hours was eighty-three, and on the 18th it attained 93.7 miles per hour. One terrific rise between 6.30 and 7.30 on the night of the 17th was shown as one hundred and three miles on the anemometer—the record up to that time.

On May 22 there were hours of gusts which came down like thunderbolts, making us apprehensive for the safety of the wireless masts; we had grown to trust the stability of the Hut. Everyone who went outside came back with a few experiences. Jeffryes was roughly handled through not wearing crampons, and several cases of kerosene, firmly stacked on the break-wind, were dislodged and thrown several yards.

Empire Day was celebrated in Adelie Land with a suitable display. At 2.30 p.m. the Union Jack was hoisted to the topmast and three cheers were given for the King. The wind blew at fifty miles an hour with light drift; temperature –3° F. Empire greetings were sent to the Colonial Secretary, London, and to Mr. Fisher, Prime Minister of Australia. These were reciprocated by return wireless.

Preceded by a day of whirlies on June 7 and random gusts on the same evening, the wind made a determined attack next morning and carried away the top and part of the middle section of the main wireless mast. It was a very unexpected event, lulled into security as we were by the fact that May, the worst month, had passed. On examination it was found that two of the topmast wire stays had chafed through, whilst another had parted. At first it seemed a hopeless task to re-erect the mast, but gradually ways and means were discussed, and we waited for the first calm day to put the theories into execution.

Midwinter's Day 1913! we had reached a turning-point in the season. Our astronomer told us that at eight o'clock on June 22 the sun would commence to return, and everyone took note of the fact. The sky was overcast, the air surcharged with drifting snow, and the wind was forty miles an hour—a representative day as far as the climate was concerned. The cook made a special effort and the menu bore the following foreword:

> "Now is the winter of our discontent
> Made glorious summer. . . ."

Almost a fortnight now elapsed, during which the weather was "impossible." In fact, the wind was frightful throughout the whole month of July, surpassing all its previous records and wearing out our much-tried patience. All that one could do was to work on and try grimly to ignore it.

On July 2nd it was as thick as a wall outside and an eighty-five mile wind blowing; though almost entirely buried, the whole Hut trembled and the stove-pipe vibrated so that the two large melting pots on the stove rattled continuously. And so it commenced and continued for a day, subsiding slowly through the seventies to the fifties and then suddenly redoubling in strength, rose to a climax about midnight on the 5th *one hundred and sixteen miles in an hour!*

For eight hours it maintained an average of one hundred and seven miles an hour, and the timbers of the Hut seemed to be jarred and wrenched as the wind throbbed in its mightier gusts. These were the highest wind-velocities recorded during our two years' residence in Adelie land and are probably the highest sustained velocities ever reported from a meteorological station.

On the 11th there was an exceptionally low barometer at 27.794 inches. At the same time the wind ran riot once more—two hundred and ninety-eight miles in three hours. The highest barometric reading was recorded on September 3, 30.4 inches, and the comparison indicates a wide range for a station at sea-level.

From July 26 onwards the sky was cloudless for a week, and each day the northern sun would rise a fraction of a degree higher. The wind was very constant and of high velocity.

It was a grand sight to witness the sea in a hurricane on a driftless, clear day. Crouched under a rock on Azimuth Hill, and looking across to the west along the curving brink of the cliffs, one could watch the water close inshore blacken under the lash of the wind, whiten into foam farther off, and then disappear into the hurrying clouds of spray and sea-smoke. Over the Mackellar Islets columns of spray would shoot up like geysers, and fly away in the mad race to the north.

Early in July Jeffryes became very ill, for some weeks his symptoms were such as to give everyone much anxiety. His work on the wireless had been assiduous at all times, and there is no doubt that the continual and acute strain of sending and receiving messages under unprecedented conditions was such that he eventually had a mental breakdown. Unfortunately the weather was so atrocious, and the conditions under which we were placed so peculiarly difficult, that little could be done to brighten his prospects. McLean considered that as the spring returned and it became possible to take more exercise outside, the mental exhaustion would pass off. In the meantime Jeffryes took a complete rest, and slowly improved as the months went by and our hopes of relief came nearer. It was a great misfortune for our comrade, especially as it was his first experience of such a climate, and he had applied himself to work with enthusiasm and perhaps in an over-conscientious spirit.

July concluded its stormy career with the astonishing wind-average of 63.6 miles an hour. We were all relieved to see Friday, August 1, appear on the modest calendar, which it was the particular pleasure of each night-watchman to change.

After an immense deluge of snow on August 4, followed a day of calm. The Hut was almost completely buried and everywhere the landscape was smothered to an unusual depth in very light, flaky, dry snow. The dogs delighted to race about following in each other's tracks; the leader in order to make any headway at all, proceeding by a series of plunges. At each bound they sank to nearly double their depth in the snow, so it was quite remarkable that they had sense enough to steeplechase along as they did. The exercise must have been exhausting, for some of them soon tried pushing their way along under the snow; and in response to a call one would observe, gradually approaching, a commotion on the surface indicating the existence of the dog beneath.

We did not linger over the scenery, but set to work to complete the reconstruction of the wireless aerial. With the object of replacing the broken mast, advantage had been taken of every available opportunity that had presented itself since the mishap on June 7. Fortunately these operations had proceeded with great success, thanks to Bickerton, who was the leading spirit in the work. By evening that day all was complete and it only remained to test whether the somewhat diminished height of mast would answer satisfactorily.

At eight o'clock that night, Jeffryes, who felt so benefited by his rest that he was eager to commence operating once more, had soon tuned his instrument to Macquarie Island, and in a few minutes communication was re-established and continued unbroken until November 20, when the interference of continuous daylight caused us to close down.

During August we were able to do more work outside, thus enlarging our sphere of interest. A shaft was sunk in the bay-ice and another, up on the glacier, excavated to a depth of twenty-four feet just above and into the zone where the ice was loaded with stones and debris—the ground-moraine. I was able to make measurements of ablation on the glacier; to take observations of the temperature and salinity of the sea-water; and to estimate the forward movement of the seaward cliffs of the ice-cap. Geological collecting now became quite a popular diversion, so I had plenty of assistance in that department. The specimens were cached in heaps, to be later brought home by the dogs, some of which were receiving their first lessons in sledge-pulling.

Bage, who had been continually disappointed in his astronomical work, owing to the persistence of wind and drift which rendered futile his heroic endeavours, was at length rewarded with suitable conditions. Employing wireless time signals, sent by Dr. Baldwin from the Melbourne Observatory, in conjunction with star observations made with the aid of a transit in his observatory he was able to determine with great accuracy a meridian of longitude—the first on the Antarctic Continent to be determined with such precision.

We heard by wireless that the Macquarie Islanders, on account of a mishap to a supply ship, had for some time been out of all food except sea-elephant or other meat that they could kill. On August 20 they had their reward in the arrival of the *Tutanekai* from New Zealand with supplies, and, piecing together a few fragments of evidence "dropped in the ether," we judged that they were having a night of revelry. The following day the *Tutanekai* returned and with her went Sawyer, whose health needed medical attention.

The wind was in a fierce humour on the morning of August 16, mounting to one hundred and five miles per hour between 9 and 10 a.m., and carrying with it a very dense drift.

Of one thing we were certain, and that was that Adelie Land was the windiest place in the world. To state the fact more accurately: such wind-velocities as prevailed at sea-level in Adelie Land are known in other parts of the world only at great elevations in the atmosphere. The average wind-velocity for our first year proved to be approximately fifty miles per hour. The bare figures convey more when they are compared with the following average annual wind-velocities quoted from a book of reference: Europe, 10.3 miles per hour; United States, 9.5 miles per hour; Southern Asia, 6.5 miles per hour; West Indies, 6.2 miles per hour.

Reference has already been made to the fact that often the high winds ceased abruptly for a short interval. Many times during 1913 we had opportunities of judging this phenomenon, and as an example, may be quoted September 6.

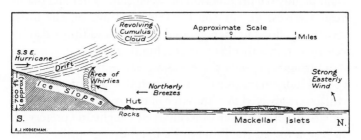

Sketch illustrating the Meteorological Conditions at Cape Denison, Noon, September 6, 1913.

As far as the Mackellar Islets the waters remained calm, while beyond them to the north the sea could be observed to be strongly agitated by an easterly wind: while about the Hut itself there were light northerly airs. Later in the day the zone of southerly wind and drift crept down and once more overwhelmed us. Evidently the "eye" of a cyclonic storm had passed over.

Early in September, Jeffryes had to be relieved of his work and Bickerton took over the wireless operating. Though at first signals could only be received slowly, Bickerton gradually improved with practice, and was altogether eminently successful during his term of office.

On September 11, although there was a wind of seventy miles per hour, the sea-ice which had become very solid during a few days of low temperature was not dispersed. The next day Madigan and McLean visited the Mackellar Islets; the first occasion that it had been possible to reach them in safety over the frozen sea.

On September 24, McLean reported a unique experience. He was quarrying ice in a fifty-mile wind with moderate drift close to the Hut, and, on finishing his work, walked down to the harbour to see if there were any birds about. He was surprised suddenly to leave the wind and drift behind and to walk out into an area of calm. The water lapped alongside the ice-foot, blue in the brilliant sun-light. Away to the west a few miles distant a fierce wind was blowing a torrent of snow over the brink of the cliffs. Towards the north-west one could plainly see the junction between calm water and foam-crested waves. To the south the drift drove off the hills, passed the Hut, and then gyrated upwards and thinned away seawards at an altitude of several hundred feet.

During September there was a great revival in biological work. Hodgeman constructed several kinds of bag-traps which were lowered over the edge of the bay-ice, and a variety of marine worms and crustaceans were caught and preserved. Bickerton forged the frame for a hand-dredge which, when completed, came in for much use, dredging in five fathoms across the entrance of the Boat Harbour. McLean and I spent many interesting days sorting over the dredgings and secured notable additions to Hunter's collection of the previous year.

The wind rose to the "seventies" on September 17, and the bay-ice was scattered to the north. On the 19th—a fine day—a large sea-leopard was observed sunning itself on a massive piece of detached floe floating adjacent to the shore in an ice-girt cove to the west. We determined if possible to secure it. It fell to Madigan to dispatch the animal, which was unusually alert, before it could escape into the water. It proved to be a large female and the skin was a valuable addition to our collection, for only three of these sea-leopards were seen at Cape Denison during our two years' occupation. On the pack-ice a few miles to the north, of course, they were very abundant.

Large purple and brown jelly-fish came floating to the ice-foot, and many were caught in a hand-net and preserved.

Within a couple of hours on one calm afternoon in October two men caught fifty-two fish, using a hand-line, in a few feet of water off the ice-foot in the Boat Harbour.

A moment after they were landed they froze stiff and remained so in our store to be drawn upon as required to introduce variation in the menu.

By October 13, everyone was on the *qui vive* for the coming of the penguins, for in 1912 they had arrived on October 12. As there was much floating ice on the northern horizon, we wondered if their migration to land had been impeded.

The winds were very high for the ensuing two days, and on the 17th the horizon was clearer and more water-sky was visible. Before lunch on that day there was not a living thing along the steep, overhanging ice-foot, but by the late afternoon thirteen birds had effected a landing, and those who were not resting after their long swim were hopping about making a survey of the nearest rookeries. One always has a "soft spot" for these game little creatures—there is something irresistibly human about them—and, situated as we were, the wind seemed of little account now that the foreshores were to be populated by the penguins—our harbingers of summer and the good times to be. Three days later, at the call of the season, a skua gull came flapping over the Hut.

It was rather a singular circumstance that on the evening of the 17th, coincident with the disappearance of the ice on the horizon, wireless signals suddenly came through very strongly in the twilight at 9.30 p.m., and for many succeeding nights continued at the same intensity. On the other hand, during September, when the sea was either firmly frozen or strewn thickly with floe-ice, communication was very fitful and uncertain. The fact is therefore suggested that wireless waves are for some reason more readily transmitted across a surface of water than across ice.

The penguins had a tempestuous time building their nests and resuming once more the quaint routine of their rookery life. In the hurricanes they usually ceased work and crouched behind the rocks until the worst was over. A great number of birds were observed to have small wounds on the body which had bled and discoloured their feathers. In one case a penguin had escaped presumably from a sea-leopard, with several wounds, and had staggered up to a rookery, dying there from loss of blood. Almost immediately the frozen carcase was mutilated and torn by skua gulls.

At odd times during the winter, Bickerton assisted by Hodgeman had been busy constructing a massive memorial cross for our two lost comrades, Ninnis and Mertz. Strength was essential in order to brave the hurricanes; so they selected lengths from the broken wireless masts—Oregon timbers eight inches square in cross-section. A substantial tablet, suitably inscribed, was prepared to go at the foot where it would be less of a target for the wind. The several parts were bolted together and bound with heavy strips of brass. When completed it appeared solid enough to last for a hundred years even in that strenuous climate. With the advent of suitable weather the opportunity was taken to raise this cross, building it solidly into the rock on the highest point of Azimuth Hill.

In his biological excursions McLean happened on a small rocky ravine to the east where, hovering amongst nests of snow-petrels and Wilson petrels, a small bluish-grey bird, apparently a new species but not unlike *Prion Banksii*, was discovered. Four specimens were shot, and, later, several old nests were found containing the unhatched eggs of previous years.

On October 31 the good news was received that the *Aurora* would leave Australia about November 15. There were a great number of things to be packed, including the lathe, the motor and dynamos, the air-tractor engine, the wireless, magnetic and other instruments. Outside the Hut, many cases of oil and provisions, which might be required for the ship, had been buried to a depth of twelve feet in places during the south-east hurricane in September. So we set to work in great spirits to prepare for the future.

A calm evening in November! At ten o'clock a natural picture in shining colours is painted on the canvas of sea and sky. The northern dome is a blush of rose deepening to a warm terra-cotta along the horizon, and the water reflects it upward to the gaze.

Tiny Wilson petrels flit like swallows; from their nests in the crannies of the grey rock hills come the love carols of the snow petrels; seals raise their dark forms above the placid surface; the shore is lined with penguins squatting in grotesque repose. The south is pallid with light—the circling sun. Adelie Land is at peace!

For some time Madigan, Hodgeman and I had been prepared to set out on a short sledge journey to visit Mount Murchison and to recover if possible the instruments cached by Madigan's and Bage's parties of the previous year. It was not until November 23 that the weather broke definitely, and we started up the old glacier wall assisted by a good team of dogs.

Aladdin's Cave was much the same as I had left it in the previous February, except that a fine crop of delicate ice crystals had formed on the walls. A course was made via Madigan Nunatak and camp pitched at the summit of Mount Murchison on the evening of November 28. The search for the cache in the valley below was unsuccessful as an enormous amount of snow had fallen, deeply burying the old surface. Indeed, on the very crown of Mount Murchison, where a ten-foot flag-pole had been left, snow had accumulated so that less than a foot of the pole was showing. Nine feet of névé compressed so hard as to be scarcely marked by one's footsteps—the contribution of one year! To such a high isolated spot, drift-snow would not reach, so that the annual snowfall must considerably exceed the residuum found by us, for the effect of the prevailing winds would be to reduce it greatly.

On the third day after leaving Mount Murchison for Bage's depot, sixty-seven miles south of winter quarters, driving snow commenced. In such thick weather it was impossible to locate anything, so we remained in camp waiting for improvement. Seven days later the drift moderated but still the limit of vision was very circumscribed; as the ship was already due we were forced to abandon the search and make direct for the Hut.

Descending the long blue slopes of the glacier just before midnight on December 12, from an outlook of a thousand feet above the Hut, I sighted a faint black bar on the seaward horizon; with the aid of glasses a black speck was discernible at the windward extremity of the bar—and it could be nothing but the smoke of the *Aurora*! The moment of which we had dreamt for months had assuredly come. The ship was in sight!

There were wild cheers down at the Hut when they heard the news. They could not believe us and immediately rushed up with glasses to the nearest ridge to get the evidence of their own senses. The masts, the funnel and the staunch hull rose out of the ocean as we watched on the hills through the early hours of a superb morning. The sun was streaming warmly over the plateau at 4 a.m., as the *Aurora* rounded the Mackellar Islets and steamed up to her old anchorage. We picked out familiar figures on the bridge and poop, and made a bonfire in a rocky crevice in their honour. As there was no indication of a boat coming off, we judged that they intended to wait developments of the weather, for a cool land breeze had sprung up. So we returned to the Hut to take a short rest after the night's vigil. Just as most of us were dozing off an unusual sound floated in from without and the next moment in rushed Captain Davis, breezy, buoyant, brave and true. He had come ashore in the whale-boat, manned by Hurley, Hunter and two of the Macquarie Islanders (Hamilton and Blake). His cheery familiar voice rang through the Hut as he pushed a way into the gloom of the living room. It was an indescribable moment, this meeting after two years.

On the ship we greeted Gillies, Gray, de la Motte Ainsworth, Sandell and Correll. It was splendid to know that the world contained so many people, and to see these men who had stuck to the Expedition through thick and thin. Then came the fusillade of letters, magazines and parcels.

We were anxious to hear the story of the Macquarie Island Party and rallied round those sub-Antarctic beach-combers. Ainsworth narrated the adventures and achievements of their two years' existence on the island. Accounts of the varied life that teems in that southern metropolis made us quite envious of their experiences. They all received our hearty congratulations for the success of their operations and the able way that they had maintained the prestige of the Expedition.

At dinner we sat down reunited in the freshly painted ward-room, striving to collect our bewildered thoughts at the sight of a white table-cloth, fresh mutton and vegetables, fruit and many delicacies.

The two long years were over—for the moment they were to be effaced in the glorious present. We were to live in a land where drift and wind were unknown, where rain fell in mild refreshing showers, where the sky was blue for long weeks, and where the memories of the past were to fade into a dream—a nightmare?

> "Seven men from all the world, back to the town again,
> Seven men from out of hell...."—KIPLING.

CHAPTER XXIV

LIFE ON MACQUARIE ISLAND

George F. Ainsworth's Narrative

LEFT on an island in mid-ocean!

It suggests the romances of youthful days—Crusoe, Sindbad and all their glorious company. Still, when this narrative is completed, imagination will be seen to have played a small part. In fact, it is a plain tale of our experiences, descriptive of a place where we spent nearly two years and of the work accomplished during our stay.

The island was discovered in 1810 by Captain Hasselborough of the ship *Perseverance*, which had been dispatched by Campbell and Sons, of Sydney, under his command to look for islands inhabited by fur-seals. Macquarie Islands, named by Hasselborough after the then Governor of New South Wales, were found to be swarming with these valuable animals, and for two years after their discovery was made known, many vessels visited the place, landing gangs of men to procure skins and returning at frequent intervals to carry the proceeds of their labours to the markets of the world.

The slaughter of the seals was so great that the animals were almost extinguished within a few years. One ship is known to have left Macquarie Island with a cargo of 35,000 skins during the first year of operations.

The sealers killed without discrimination; both male and female, old and young were ruthlessly slaughtered, with the obvious result—the extermination of the species. If supervision had been exercised and restrictions imposed, there is no doubt that the island would still be used by the fur-seal as a breeding-ground. During our stay none were seen, but Mr. Bauer, at that time head man of the sealing gang, who had visited the island each summer for eleven years, stated that he had seen odd ones at infrequent intervals.

Associated as the island has been since the year 1812 with sealing ventures, it follows that a history has been gradually developed; somewhat traditional, though many occurrences to which we shall refer are well authenticated.

It might be supposed from the foregoing that a good deal is known about the place, but such is not the case. Several scientific men from New Zealand, recognizing the importance of the island as a link between Australasia and Antarctica, visited it at different times within the past twenty years, only remaining long enough to make a cursory examination of the eastern side. They had to depend on the courtesy of captains of sealing ships for a passage, and the stormy conditions which are ever prevalent made their stay too brief for any exhaustive work.

A Russian Antarctic expedition, under the command of Admiral Bellingshausen, called there in 1821 and stayed there for two days, collecting a few bird and animal specimens. They referred to the island as being "half-cooled down," in a short but interesting account of their visit, and remarked upon the larvge number of sea-elephants lying on the shores.

In 1840 the ship *Peacock*, one of the exploring vessels of the American Expedition under Wilkes, landed several men after much difficulty on the north-west end of the island, but they remained only a few hours, returning to their ship after securing some specimens of birds.

The next call of an Antarctic expedition was made by Captain Scott in the *Discovery* in November 1901. He, with several naturalists, landed on the eastern side to collect specimens, but remained only a few hours. He refers to the penguins, kelp-weed and tussock-grass; certainly three characteristic features.

Captain Davis, during his search for charted sub-Antarctic islands at the close of Sir Ernest Shackleton's expedition, called there in the *Nimrod* in 1909. He landed a party of men who secured several sea-elephants and some penguins.

It will thus be seen that very little had been done which was scientifically important or generally interesting.

So it came that we five men of Dr. Mawson's Expedition were landed on December 22, 1911, with a programme of work outlined by our leader. H. Hamilton was biologist, L. R. Blake surveyor and geologist, C. A. Sandell and A J. Sawyer were wireless operators, the former being also a mechanic, and I was appointed meteorologist and leader of the party.

We stood on the beach in the dusk, watching the boat's party struggle back to the *Aurora*, which lay at anchor one and a half miles from the shore. Having received a soaking in the surf as we helped the boat out and being tired out with the exertions of the day, we started back to our temporary shelter. We had not gone very far when a mysterious sound, followed by a tremor of the earth, made us glance at each other and exclaim, "An earthquake!" The occurrence gave rise to a discussion which carried us to bed.

Seeing that we were to spend a long time on the island, the question of building a hut was the first consideration. Through the kindness of Mr. Bauer, who had just left the island in the S.S. *Toroa*, we were able to live for the time being in the sealers' hut.

It was urgent to get the wireless station into working order as soon as possible. The masts and operating hut had been erected during the stay of the *Aurora*, but there yet remained the building of the engine hut and the installation of the machinery and instruments, as well as the construction and erection of the aerial. Accordingly we proceeded with the living-hut on the spot near the shore and the job on Wireless Hill at the same time, working on the hill most of the day and at the hut in the evening.

Wireless Hill rose to three hundred and fifty feet in height, and formed part of a peninsula running in a north-easterly direction from the main island. It had been chosen by Hannam of the Adelie Land party because of its open northerly aspect, and because "wireless" waves would probably have a good "set-off," south-ward to the main station to be erected in Antarctica.

Just a few yards from the base of the hill on its south-western side was a huge rock in the lee of which, upon the easterly side, we decided to build our dwelling. The timbers for the hut had been cut and fitted in Hobart, so all that remained for us was to put them together.

After working at high pressure until December 30, we were able to establish ourselves in a home. The doorway faced to the east, and the rock protected the small structure from the strong westerly weather which is invariable in these

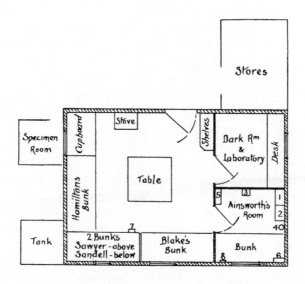

Plan of Hut - Macquarie Island

Scale of Feet

Plan of the Macquarie Island Hut.

latitudes. The dimensions were twenty feet by thirteen feet, the front wall being nine feet six inches high, sloping to seven feet six inches at the back. All the timbers were of oregon and deal, and particular attention was paid to bracing and strengthening the building, which rested on piles just clear of the sandy surface. The inside was lined and ceiled, and the roof of galvanized iron was set flush with the front wall, fascia boards along the front and sides being designed to keep the fine snow from blowing under the corrugation and lodging on the ceiling. This villa, our home for two years to come, was never referred to as anything else but the Shack.

We amplified our Christmas dinner with fresh mutton—a joint from one of the twelve live sheep landed for our use by the *Aurora*. These sheep had been put to grass on Wireless Hill, where they were restricted from straying far afield.

From the wreck of the *Clyde*, on the beach nearly half a mile away, a two hundred gallon tank had been saved, and we managed on Christmas morning, after two hours of carrying and trundling, to place it at the end of the Shack. This was a valuable find, ensuring in the future a constant, convenient supply of rain water. Further, we made use of the timber of the wreck for building, and the broken pieces strewn about were stored up as firewood.

On the 26th we all went to the wireless station, and, as Sandell had the aerial made, we pulled it into position. In the afternoon I unpacked all my instruments and started them off so as to make sure that all were working correctly. I did not intend to record any observations till January 1, 1912, and therefore did not erect the meteorological screen until the 28th.

On moving into our abode domestic arrangements were made. With regard to cooking, each man took duty for a week, during which he was able to write up his work and to wash and mend clothes. To Hamilton and Sandell, who had had previous experience, frequent appeals were made as to methods of cooking various dishes, but by degrees each one asserted his independence. There were several cookery books for reference and each week saw the appearance of some new pudding, in each instance prefaced by the boast: "This is going to be the best pudding ever turned out on the island!" The promise was not always made good.

We had a good deal of difficulty at first in making bread, and several batches were very "heavy" failures. This difficulty, however, was soon overcome and, after the first few months, the cooking standard was high and well maintained. Our stove was very small and only two loaves of bread could be cooked at once. It frequently happened, therefore, that the others, which would go on rising in the tins, overflowed; a matter which could only be set right by experience.

On New Year's Day, 1912, we carried timber in relays from the wreck to the top of Wireless Hill, so that the building of the engine-hut could be started. The next few days were occupied in getting food-stuffs, medicines, stationery, clothing and other necessaries over to the Shack from the landing-place on the beach. Blake and Hamilton unpacked their instruments and appliances, fitting up a small laboratory and photographic dark-room in one corner of the hut.

Some kind Hobart friend had sent four fowls to me on the day of sailing, requesting me to take them to Macquarie Island. They were housed in one of the meteorological screens, but on the third day from Hobart a heavy sea broke on board, upset the temporary fowl-house and crushed the rooster's head. The three hens were landed safely and appeared to be thoroughly reconciled to their strange surroundings, though the presence of so many large birds soaring about overhead had a terrifying effect on them for several days. They did not appear to pick up much food amongst the grass, but scratched away industriously all the same. I must say that they were very friendly and gave the place quite a homely aspect. One of them was christened "Ma" on account of her maternal and somewhat fussy disposition.

On the first Sunday in the new year all except myself went along the coast towards West Point. The party reported immense numbers of sea-elephants, especially young ones. They also saw many wekas and three ducks, shooting nine of the former for the kitchen.

The wekas or Maori hens are small, flightless birds, averaging when full grown about two and three-quarter pounds. They were introduced from New Zealand twenty-five years ago by a sealer, and multiplied so fast that they are now very numerous. They live among the tussocks, and subsist for the most part upon the lame of the kelp-fly, small fish and other marine life which they catch under the stones along the rocky shores at low tide. They are exceedingly inquisitive and pugnacious and may easily be caught by hand.

Usually, when disturbed, they will pop under a rock, and on being seized immediately commence to squeak. This is sufficient to bring every weka within a quarter of a mile hurrying to the spot, and, in a few minutes, heads may be seen poking out of the grass in every direction. The man holding the captured bird then crouches down, preferably just on the border of the tussock, holding the protesting bird in one hand. Soon there will be a rustle, then a rush, and another furious weka will attack the decoy. The newcomer is grabbed and, if the birds are plentiful, five or six of them may be taken in one spot.

Their call is peculiarly plaintive and wild and may be heard night and day. Though we saw and caught innumerable young ones of all sizes, we were never able to find the nests of these Maori hens.

A depot of stores had been laid by the *Aurora* at Caroline Cove, twenty miles from the Shack at the south end of the island, and it was deemed advisable to lay several more intermediate food-depots along the east coast.

The sealers had a motor-launch which they kindly placed at our disposal, and a supply of stores was put on board for transport. At 8 a.m., January 9, Sandell, Blake, Sawyer and Hamilton started out accompanied by two sealers who offered to point out the positions of several old huts along the coast. These huts had been built by sealing gangs many years ago and were in a sad state of disrepair.

The first call was made at Sandy Bay, about five miles from the Shack. Stores were landed and placed in the hut, and the party proceeded to Lusitania Bay, eleven miles farther on, where they stayed for the night. At this place there were two huts, one being a work-hut and the other a living-hut. They had not been used for sixteen years and, as a result, were found to be much dilapidated. In the locality is a large King penguin rookery, the only one on the island, and two dozen eggs were obtained on this visit, some fresh and some otherwise.

As the next morning was squally, it was decided that the stores should be deposited in the hut at the south end; a distance of five miles across country. Through bog and tussock it took the party four hours to accomplish this journey. The hut was found in the same condition as the others and a rather miserable night was spent. A short distance from this spot is situated the largest penguin rookery on the island. On returning to the launch, the six men had a quick run of three hours back to the north end.

Sandell and Sawyer were still making tests with and improving the wireless apparatus, but before the end of January it was in such condition that they daily expected communication with Australia.

On the 17th Blake commenced his charting of the island. Hamilton was kept busy with marine collecting and securing specimens of the varied bird life.

Hamilton's biological work had a special interest, for it was to have a very important bearing upon a theory widely supported, namely, that the continental land masses of the Southern Hemisphere were, at one period or another, all joined together. This theory had been advanced to explain the anomalies in the distribution of plant and animal life. Our own immediate interest in the problem lay in the suggested connection of Australia with South America through Antarctica. Perhaps a study of the fauna and flora would reveal that Macquarie Island was an unsubmerged relic of a former land bridge connecting these places. So it was evident that our scientific opportunities were unique.

On January 28, Sandell, Sawyer and I decided to climb on to the main ridge or plateau of the island. We had already discovered that the easiest way to get on to the hills was to follow up one of the many ravines or gullies which run down to the sea. This necessitates walking in water most of the way, but one soon gets accustomed to wet feet on Macquarie Island.

The slopes rise in a series of terraces which are generally soggy and covered with tussock (pleurophyllum) and with scattered cushions of *Azorella*. The summit of the ridge is a barren waste, over which loose rocks are scattered in every direction, while a wavy effect due to the action of wind is

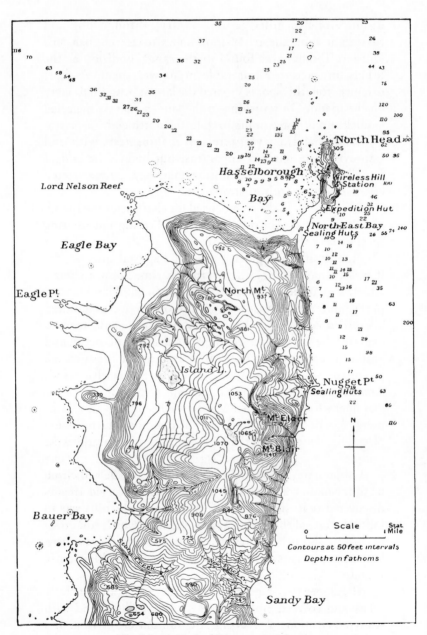

The North End of Macquarie Island.

plainly visible over the surface of the ground. The steep, descending sides are very soft and sodden, supporting a scanty growth of vegetation, including the small burr known as the "biddy-bid."

Hundreds of tarns and lakes are visible along the plateau-like ridge, which extends throughout the length of the island. Several of the lakes are half a mile long and very deep. The tarns are, for the most part, shallow with hard stony bottoms. The water is beautifully fresh and apparently contains no visible life.

Skua gulls were plentiful and washed themselves, with a great flapping of wings, in the shallow waters at the edge of the lakes. They paid particular attention to our dog "Mac," swooping down and attempting to strike her with their wings. A yelp at intervals came from Mac if they were successful, though if quick enough, she would spring at the bird and retaliate by getting a mouthful of feathers.

We eventually came out on to a point about seven hundred feet high, overlooking the west coast, and it could be seen that the space between the base of the hills and the ocean was occupied by a plain which sloped very gradually to the beach. Here and there across its surface were huge mounds of earth and rock and, occasionally, a small lakelet fringed with a dense growth of tussock and Maori cabbage.

A descent was made to explore the place. A fairly large volume of water flowed rapidly downward by several deep gullies and, coming to the terrace, cut narrow, sinuous channels which were soon lost to view in the tussocks. Examination of the watercourses revealed that this tract was simply a raised beach covered with sodden peat and carrying a rather coarse vegetation. The ground was decidedly springy and shook to our tread; moreover, one sank down over the ankles at each step. Occasionally a more insecure area was encountered, where one of us would go down to the thighs in the boggy ground.

As the shore approached we came to thick tussock and Maori cabbage, and the travelling became much rougher. A group of earthy mounds and rock was sighted some distance away and we decided to reach them and have our lunch. A nearer view showed us a large opening in one of these prominences and we scrambled up to examine it.

Inside there was a small cave, high in front but sloping sharply towards the back for a distance of thirty-five feet. The roof and walls were blackened by smoke, and spikes and nails driven into crevices were evidences that the place had once been occupied. Eagle Cave it is called, and its story was afterwards related to us.

Between thirty and forty years ago the schooner *Eagle*, in attempting to make the island, had been caught in a gale and wrecked on the rock-bound western coast. As far as can be learned, there were nine men and a woman on board, all of whom were saved. They lived in this cave for almost two years, subsisting on what they could catch. Decayed tussock grass, a foot in depth, now covers the floor, showing that some attempt had been made to improve the comfort of the place, while bones lying strewn about in all directions indicate that gulls, penguins and cormorants must have supplied a good deal of their food. It is presumed that some of them made a journey to North Head periodically to look out for relief, as a well-defined track to that point is still visible in places.

The tale, however, has its tragic side, for the woman died on the very day when the rescuing ship called at the island. She was buried on the isthmus, not far from our Shack. One would think that death was rather a relief from such an existence as this unfortunate woman must have endured, but, at the same time, it seems hard that she did not live to participate in the joy of deliverance.

We ate our lunch and had a smoke, after which we decided to walk homewards along "Feather Bed" terrace. A few minutes after leaving the cave, Sawyer and Sandell caught three young ducks, which they carried back, intending to rear them, but they died several days later. A weary tramp brought us, thoroughly tired, to the Shack, where Hamilton had an excellent meal awaiting us.

The weather during January was rather trying. Precipitation in the form of either rain, hail, sleet or snow occurred on twenty-six days, sometimes all forms being experienced on the same day. As a result, the supply of water was well maintained; in fact, the amount caught exceeded the consumption, and we finished the month with the tank almost full. Gales were experienced on eight days, the maximum wind force being forty-two miles an hour. The sky was mostly heavily clouded or absolutely overcast and on many days the sun was not seen. Fog hung about the hills almost continuously, and driving mist accompanied the northerly winds.

January 24 was a glorious day, calm and sunny, with a maximum temperature of 51.3° F. The habit of former days induced Sandell and myself to have a dip in the surf, but as the temperature of the water was about 42° F., we stayed in as many seconds.

My first view of the island when the *Aurora* arrived in December 1911 left rather an agreeable impression. The day of our approach was marked by fine calm weather and the dark green tussock-clad hillsides were rather attractive. On the other hand, one was immediately struck with the entire absence of trees, the steep precipices, cliffs and the exceedingly rugged nature of the coast-line.

Closer scrutiny shows that the tussock grass radiates closely from a semi-decayed mass of leaf sheaths, with the blades of grass shooting upwards and outwards as high as three or four feet. Scattered through it are patches of *Stilbocarpa polaris*, locally known as Maori cabbage. It is of a more vivid green than the tussock and is edible, though somewhat stringy and insipid. Our sheep ate it readily, even nibbling the roots after the plant had been cropped down.

There were several Victoria penguin colonies round about the rocky faces of the hills in the vicinity of the Shack, and their hubbub and cackling uproar were something to remember. The rearing of the young appeared to be rather a busy process. The young ones look like bundles of down and seem to grow at a remarkable rate, while the attempt of the parent to shelter the usual two chicks is a very ludicrous thing to watch.

The material for the nest made by these birds seems to depend almost entirely on its immediate surroundings. The rookery is established on a broken rocky face close to the water's edge and the nests are made under rocks, in niches and passages, as well as amongst the tussock growing on the rocks. Those under the rocks are constructed of small stones and a few blades of grass, while those in the passages and fissures are usually depressions in soft mud. Amongst the tussock a hole is first made in the soft earth and then neatly lined with blades of grass.

The birds lay two or three eggs of a white or greenish-white colour, but I have never seen three chicks hatched. The eggs are edible, and we used many dozens of them during our stay.

The period of incubation is about five weeks, and male and female take turns at sitting. A young one is fed by placing the beak within that of the parent bird where the food—mainly crustaceans—is taken as it regurgitates from the old bird.

Although the smallest species on the island, the Victoria penguins are the most spiteful, and a scramble through the rookery invites many pecks and much disturbance. They have a black head and back, white breast and yellow crest, the feathers of which spread out laterally. During the moulting season they sit in the rookery or perched on the surrounding rocks, living apparently on their fat, which is found to have disappeared when at last they take to the sea. They come and go with remarkable regularity, being first seen about the middle of October, and leaving during the first week of May. The same rookeries are occupied year after year, and the departure of the birds adds to the general desolation during the winter months.

Their destination on leaving the land is still a mystery. Although they are never seen, it is conjectured that they spend the winter at sea. Their natural enemy in the waters round Macquarie Island is the sea-leopard, and the stomachs of all specimens of this animal taken by us during the penguin season contained feathers.

On the night of February 2, Sawyer reported that he had heard the Wellington wireless operator calling Suva station, but, as no further signals were heard from anywhere, he was inclined to the idea that it was the experience of a "freak night." In explanation of this term, I may say that it is used in reference to nights on which the atmospheric conditions are abnormally favourable for wireless work.

The news was particularly encouraging, and for the next few days we were on the tip-toe of expectation.

In the early morning of the 5th a howling gale sprang up and, increasing in force as the day wore on, rendered work impossible. A tremendous sea worked up, and the ocean for a distance of a mile from shore was simply a seething boil of foam. Huge waves dashed on shore, running yards beyond the usual marks, and threatening to sweep across the isthmus. Masses of tangled kelp, torn from the outlying rocks, were washed backwards and forwards in the surf or carried high up among the tussocks. The configuration of the shingly beach changed while one looked at it. The tops of the waves could be seen flying over Anchor Rock, seventy feet high, and spray was blowing right across the isthmus.

On the advice of the sealers we had shifted our stores farther back from the beach and it was just as well we did so, as the waves reached to within a few feet of the nearest box. Meanwhile I began to wonder how our benzine and lubricating oil were faring. Both had been stacked in cases among the tussock and rocks, well back from the waters of Aerial Cove on the western side of Wireless Hill.

Accordingly, Hamilton, Sandell and I went round in that direction the following morning, while Sawyer made his way up to the wireless station to see if there were any damages there. We worked along round the cliff front through a cave rejoicing in the name of "Catch Me," from the fact that the waves rushed into it, frequently catching and thoroughly wetting any unfortunate taken off his guard. A massive rock, evidently broken from the roof, lay right across its centre, while on either side of the obstruction were masses of greasy decaying kelp. We were "caught" and floundered about in the kelp while the water surged around us. Arriving at the Cove, we found that several cases were missing. One was discovered buried in kelp, and a little later we came upon a tin battered almost out of recognition. The loss was not serious, but the precaution was taken to shift the oil still farther back.

While we were engaged on this task, Sawyer appeared on the front of the hill above and signalled to us that the aerial had been blown down. The three-inch rope keeping the aerial taut had broken off close to the bridle and torn the halyard with it. It meant that someone would have to climb the mast to pass a rope through the block, and the wind was at this time too strong for anything to be done.

On February 7, Blake and Hamilton, who had been making preparations for several days past, set out for Sandy Bay, intending to do some work in that locality. Their blankets, sleeping-bag, instruments and other gear made rather heavy swags, but they shouldered them in true bush style and tramped away.

Sandell, Sawyer and I went up Wireless Hill to fix the aerial. Sandell, the lightest of the three, was being hoisted up the first section of the mast with some one-and-a-half-inch rope when the hauling line gave way. Fortunately, he had a strap securing him to the mast, otherwise his fall would have been from twenty feet. This was the only rope we had, so we had to think of some other means of reaching the top. After a short discussion, I suggested that decking-spikes should be secured from the wreck of the *Clyde* and driven into the mast at intervals. The idea was followed with great success, and Sandell was able to run the halyard through the block at the top (ninety feet). The aerial was then hauled into position, the stay-wires were tightened, an extra "dead-man" was put in and the station was once more ready for work.

Hamilton returned from Sandy Bay on the 11th laden with botanical trophies and four specimens of a small land bird, apparently an endemic finch, which we had never before seen. He and Blake who remained behind had fixed up the hut there so that it afforded decent shelter.

On the night of the 13th what we had long expected happened. Wireless communication was established for the first time with a ship—S.S. *Ulimaroa*. Sandell and Sawyer were complimented on their success.

On the following night communication was held with Sydney, S.S. *Westralia*, S.S. *Ulimaroa* and H.M.S. *Drake*; the latter very courteously sending us time signals. We heard that a wireless station had just been established in Melbourne, and that the Hobart station would be working in about one month. It was with the latter station that we expected to do most of our business. There was great joy in the camp now that this stage of practical efficiency was reached and because we were no longer isolated from the world.

Blake came back from Sandy Bay on February 16 with news that he had almost finished the survey of that section. Foggy or misty weather gave him a good deal of trouble in getting sights with the theodolite, and it became part of his future programme to devote the "impossible" days to plotting data, writing up field-notes, and making geological collections.

The afternoon of the 17th was fine, and I went along the beach towards West Point and found it very rough travelling.

Large numbers of skua gulls, creating a dreadful din, drew my attention to a spot amongst the rocks, and, on nearing it, I found them squabbling around the carcase of a xiphoid whale, about sixteen feet long, which had been cast up apparently only a few hours before.

The skuas of Macquarie Island are large brown birds very similar to the somewhat different species which inhabits the ice regions of the Antarctic further south. They resort to the island in great numbers for the purpose of breeding and stay longer than any other migrant, being absent only three months during the depth of winter. Returning early in August, they do not start nesting until the beginning of October. The nests, nicely made of grass and plant leaves, are generally built on the terraces and slopes amongst the hills. The ideal site, however, is a pleurophyllum flat adjoining a penguin rookery. Two or three eggs of a brown or greenish-brown colour with darker spots or blotches are laid about the end of October, and, from this time till the chicks are reared, the parent exhibits much annoyance at the presence of any person in the vicinity. They utter shrill cries and swoop down continuously in an attempt to strike the invader with their wings. Several of our party received black eyes as a result of attacks by skuas.

The young grow rather quickly, and not much time elapses before they leave the nest to stagger round and hide amongst the vegetation. The parents fly down and disgorge food, which is immediately devoured by the young ones. The skuas are bare-faced robbers and most rapacious, harassing the penguins in particular. They steal the eggs and young of the latter and devour a great number of prions—small birds which live in holes in the ground. The skuas are web-footed, but are very rarely seen in the water.

By this time many improvements had been effected in the interior of the Shack. Shelves lined the walls wherever it was convenient to have them, and many perishable foodstuffs had been brought inside. Comfort, after all, is but a relative matter, and, as far as we were concerned, it was sufficient.

Our clothing answered the requirements of the climate admirably with the exception of the boots. The latter were not heavy enough, and soon showed the effect of travelling from a water-logged surface to one of rock and vice versa. In fact, our boots were very rarely dry on Macquarie Island.

An event of some moment occurred on the 28th. The fowls, in order to justify our confidence in them and as a return for their constant care, commenced to lay and, strange to say, all began to lay at the same time. Ma, who was greatly concerned during the turn of affairs, suffered from prolonged attacks of cackling.

During the opening days of March, Blake and Hamilton were engaged in field work down the island. They went as far as The Brothers, a rocky promontory about two miles south of Sandy Bay. Wekas were so plentiful that they lived almost entirely on them. Blake, on returning to the Shack, had a badly blistered heel which kept him indoors for a few days. Hamilton, who had secured a goodly number of specimens, had to attend immediately to their preservation.

There were many rats on the island and we frequently heard them scuttling about on the ceiling of the Shack and slithering down between the lining and the wall. Hitherto they had contented themselves by doing this, but on the night of the 7th several of them flopped one after another into the hut, awakening the inmates. On getting out to investigate I found a hole through the lining, about seven feet from the floor, and two or three were rushing about on the shelves. After much shifting of boxes and searching behind tins, the intruders were killed.

On March 10 our station had communicated with Suva at a distance of two thousand four hundred miles; a remarkable performance for a one-and-a-half-kilowatt wireless set.

Hamilton and I set out for West Point and Eagle Cave on the 11th with the object of examining the flora of the locality, and incidentally, to shoot ducks which frequent the pools on the "Feather Bed" terrace. The weather was dull and misty and the walk very uncomfortable. We made our way across this treacherous tract, often sinking knee-deep. As we neared the first pool a duck rose and immediately paid the penalty. Although we saw at least two hundred, only one was shot, owing to the fact that there is no cover about and the ducks are too easily scared.

Close to Eagle Cave Hamilton gathered some plant specimens and, after lunching, we set off home. Light, steady rain set in about 3 p.m. and wet us thoroughly. We travelled back along the coast, finding it fearfully rough but not so tiring as walking on the terrace.

Cooking was still on the up grade. Everybody, as his turn arrived, embarked on something new. Blake turned out a magnificent meat pudding during his week, and Sawyer manufactured a salmon kedgeree. Sandell's treacle pudding and Hamilton's soda rolls and date pudding were equally good, while I fairly surpassed myself with a roly-poly and some pan-cakes.

Hitherto, Sawyer and Sandell had been coming down to the Shack each night after finishing the wireless work, but on account of the bad weather they determined to sleep up there and, with that end in view, each built a bunk for himself; Sawyer, in the operating-hut, had ample room for the improvement, but Sandell had more difficulty in the engine-hut, finding it necessary to add a small structure to the original one.

Good wireless work was now being done, and almost every ship trading to eastern Australian ports gave us a "call up." Much difficulty was experienced with the stays securing the masts which frequently required tightening on account of the "dead-men" working loose in the yielding peaty soil. There were seven stays required for each mast, and Sandell spent much time in attending to them.

Hamilton had found, some weeks previously, several nests of the sooty albatross along the cliff-front on the eastern side of Wireless Hill, and on the 21st he visited them for the purpose of photographing the young in the nest. They were still in the downy stage, and vomited vigorously on being approached.

These birds build their nests on ledges along the face of a steep cliff and always betray the whereabouts of their nesting-place by wheeling and soaring around the vicinity. When sitting, the bird utters piercing calls for its mate, and is thereby easily located. They make a nest of grass, generally at the root of a tussock growing on the cliff-front, and when the building is in progress the two birds sit side by side entwining their necks, rubbing beaks and at intervals uttering their harsh cries. One can approach and catch them quite easily, either at this time or when sitting. The female lays one large white egg, which has a peculiar and rather disagreeable odour. They have beautiful slaty or bluish-grey plumage with a dark soot black head, while encircling the eye is a white ring which stands out conspicuously from the dark feathers surrounding it. Like most other sea-birds they have the rather revolting habit of vomiting quantities of partly digested food and fluid when an attempt is made to get close to them. In this respect old and young are alike. Their food is procured at sea, and consists of the small forms of marine life.

Sandell and Hamilton went round to Aerial Cove on the 25th to collect shells and to search for the missing lubri-cating oil. When coming home, after a successful day, they discovered a cave quite close to Catch Me. A lantern was secured from the Shack and they went back to examine it. It penetrated for a considerable distance and opened out on the hill side about eight feet above sea-level. Many rocks

Great cone of névé dumped in the lee of the coastal cliffs (*Hurley*)

Penguin visitor to motor launch at the ice front,
boat harbour, Cape Denison (*Hurley*)

The S.Y. *Aurora* lying at the anchorage in Commonwealth Bay—
a view from Cape Denison. The ice slopes of the mainland are
seen encircling the bay and, where visible on the sky-line,
have reached an elevation of 3500 feet (*Hurley*)

Frozen spray built up by the blizzards along the shore (*Hurley*)

The members of the Macquarie Island base

In an ice bower: a silver-grey petrel on the nest (*Hurley*)

The cliffs at Land's End, Cape Denison. On the brow
of the cliff in front of the figure (Mertz) is a
good example of snow cornice (*Hurley*)

First stage in the development of ice flowers on young ice
on the Boat Harbour, Cape Denison (*Hurley*)

Thermiting a broken vice in the workshop (*Hurley*)

In the blizzard—a photograph portraying the efforts of
Whetter and Close to get ice for domestic purposes
from the glacier adjacent to the hut (*Hurley*)

Mertz in the snow tunnels on his way to the hut with
a box of ice for the melters (*Hurley*)

Mertz in an ice ravine (*Hurley*)

The corner of the bay at Land's End in winter (*Hurley*)

A social evening in the hut, Cape Denison (*Hurley*)

The margin of the ice-capped land (*Hurley*)

Washing up after dinner at Winter Quarters, Cape Denison—
Left to right: Hunter, Hodgeman, Bage

The S.Y. *Aurora* anchored to floe ice in Lat. 65.5 Long. 1.6
(Figure is Blake) (*Hurley*)

Three men with partial ice masks (*Hurley*)

Erected to commemorate the supreme sacrifice made by
Lieut. B.E.S. Ninnis, R.F. and Dr X. Mertz in the cause of science -
A.A.E. 1913

An illustration of the life on the Mackellar Islets (*Hurley*)

Ninnis driving a team of dogs (*Mertz*)

The S.Y. *Aurora* at anchor, from near Aerial Cove,
Macquarie Island (*Hurley*)

Midwinter dinner, Adelie Land (*Hurley*)

hung down from overhead, and altogether it appeared a very unsafe place.

We built a kind of annex to the Shack out of the cases of provisions; each case being numbered and a list being drawn out setting forth the contents of each case. This list was nailed on to the wall inside, and besides being convenient for procuring the provisions, gave the cook at a glance exact information and afforded him a glorious scope.

To eke out the coal supply the weekly cook limited himself to three briquettes, and these he supplemented with sea-elephant blubber and wood, which he gathered and cut up for use.

Each man commenced his cooking week on Saturday morning, and continued until the following Friday night, when, after having cleared up, washed the towels and cleaned the stove, he retired. The incoming cook, who for half an hour had been prowling about keenly observant of "over-looked" dirty "things" and betraying every sign of impatience to make a start, proceeded at once to set a batch of bread sufficient for one week, which was baked early on Saturday morning. Five loaves had to be baked, and as only two could be dealt with at a time, the chance of producing at least one doughy loaf was reasonably high until everyone became a master baker.

For a time we had been rather hard put to it in the matter of having baths, but the disability had been overcome by means of sawing a cask in two; an expedient which answered very well. The bath was able to be used as a wash-tub, each man taking charge as his cooking week came round. The clothes were dried inside the Shack along a number of strings at the back of the stove. Darning and mending took a little time, and our experiences in this direction were such as to demonstrate the wisdom of putting in "a stitch in time."

In going over to the meteorological screen one morning I saw a giant petrel flapping about in the tussock, gorged to such an extent that it could not rise. I killed the loathsome bird with the rib-bone of a sea-elephant, and Hamilton made a fine specimen of it later on.

These birds, properly called giant petrels, are usually known as "nellies" or "stinkers"; the latter title being thoroughly justified on account of the disagreeable smell which comes from them. As may be inferred from the name, they are the largest of all the petrels, and measure about seven feet from tip to tip on the wing. The colour ranges through various shades from almost pure white to a dark greyish-brown; some even appearing almost black. Very large and ungainly when on the ground, they become most graceful when in the air, and soar about without the slightest effort even on the stormiest days. I have seen them flying into a forty-mile wind with absolute ease, never moving a wing, but occasionally adjusting their balance. They are gross scavengers, and eat apparently for the sake of eating. A carcase on the rocks or beach attracts them in large numbers, and very soon they can be seen pulling and tearing at it until thoroughly gorged, when they waddle away into the water and sit there wholly unable to rise till digestion takes place. If disturbed, they immediately disgorge and fly off. They nest on the ground and lay one large white egg. When sitting, they are reluctant to leave the nest and will squat there, vomiting evil-smelling, partly digested food and fluid at any intruder. The young, even in the downy stage, have the same habit.

When mating they go on with a queer kind of performance, which consists of running around each other on the shore with wings outspread as if displaying their charms, finally flying off or waddling into the water.

Exceptionally low tides at the end of the month gave Hamilton a fine opportunity of collecting marine specimens, and he secured amongst many other things some striking anemones.

Blake had very little opportunity of doing much survey work during the month, as he was hampered by a sore foot and the weather was wretched. He therefore spent most of his time plotting data, making geological investigations and collecting and naming specimens.

He and Hamilton had so far confined their attention to the northern half of the island, and had resolved to complete the study of this area before tackling the southern half.

The weather throughout March was rather severe, and only two days were really good. Precipitation occurred on twenty-five days, but the worst feature was the continuity of strong winds. Temperatures, as might have been expected, were beginning to go down, and we experienced several very cold days. The average temperature for March was 41.8°.

On the evening of April 1 the rope supporting the aerial again parted. As before, the halyard soon carried away and Sandell henceforth resolved to shackle one end of the aerial to the mast, using a short length of chain instead of rope. The wreck of the *Clyde* was once more our stand-by, providing a suitable length of chain and four shackles. After completing this job, they had very little subsequent trouble with the aerial.

Hamilton and Sawyer caught several three-pound fish on April 2, and Sandell served them in good style. They were good eating, but, unfortunately, were very much worm-infested. These parasitical worms are about an inch and a half long and taper to a point at each end. They penetrate right through the flesh and are plainly noticeable after the fish is cooked. One has to dodge the worms as the meal proceeds: either that or persuade oneself that they do not matter.

The contours of the land in the vicinity of The Nuggets suggested glacial action to Blake, and on the 4th, while making geological investigations in that locality, he lit upon a well-defined basal moraine. He brought home a number of polished, striated boulders as convincing evidence of his discovery. This was very interesting indeed for, at the present day, there is no permanent ice lodged on the island.

It was rather disappointing to find that the potatoes and onions we had planted in some sandy soil near the Shack were making little progress. They would shoot up at first very strongly, like the "seed that fell on stony ground," but, as soon as a gale arose, the tops turned black and shortly afterwards withered away. It was apparently an effect of the salt spray which, in rough weather, used to blow across the isthmus. Hamilton planted some willows and other cuttings, which shared the same fate.

The winter had now arrived in real earnest, and the months which followed were punctuated by a succession of gales, while we came to recognize that it was an exceptional day when the hills were not shrouded in mist.

CHAPTER XXV

A LAND OF STORM AND MIST

By George F. Ainsworth

A HEAVY north-west gale was experienced on April 12, the wind attaining a force of over fifty miles an hour. As usual, a tremendous sea worked up very quickly, and sheets of spray shredded across the isthmus. During the night the wind moderated, heavy snow fell and, when morning dawned, all the pools were frozen over and the island was draped in white. It was the heaviest fall we had so far experienced.

On the 15th Hamilton and I shot several gulls for specimens.

These Dominican or black-headed gulls are very numerous and remain on the island all the year round. They are rather pretty, being snow-white, except on the upper part of the wings and back. Ordinarily their food is obtained from the water, but at Macquarie Island they live almost entirely upon the carcases left by the sealers, and are usually seen defending their rights against skuas and giant petrels. They build nests of tussock on rocks close to the water or maybe on the ground. Three eggs, much like those of the skua in colour, but with a greener tint and smaller, are laid, but generally only two are hatched. The young leave the nest early and hide amongst the rocks, whither the old ones come to feed them.

We now considered it advisable to prepare for the winter, and with that end in view papered the inside of the Shack in various places. As the cold winds were particularly searching, all faulty joints in the lining were pasted over with any kind of paper we could find. A leak down the outside of the stove-pipe was remedied, after a good deal of trouble, by soldering a collar round the pipe where it passed through the roof. Firing was an important consideration, so each man now brought home several loads of driftwood every day, until we had enough to keep us going for some months. There was a complete boot-mending outfit which was put to a good deal of use, for the weathered rocks cut the soles of our boots and knocked out the hobnails. Our supply of the latter article did not last long, and several of the party used strips of hoop-iron in their stead.

Although they had intended to leave the work on the southern half of the island until the spring, Hamilton and Blake set out for Lusitania Bay on April 23 to make a short reconnoitring trip. It was thought advisable to spend a few days down there, to improve the hut and generally speaking to have a look round. At 8 a.m. they started off, carrying their blankets, sleeping-bags and a few other articles. Their proposal was to go along the coast as far as Sandy Bay and from thence along the hill-tops for the remaining ten miles.

Hail and snow storms succeeded each other at frequent intervals, and by the time they reached Sandy Bay all hope of proceeding along the hill-tops was dissipated. They therefore kept near the coast. The going was frightfully rough and the weather was very bad, so on making Green Valley they camped in a small cave for the night. The floor was covered with tussock, and, by searching amongst the rocks, enough pieces of wreckage were found to keep the fire going. On the whole they passed a fairly comfortable night. Mac proved a bit troublesome by persisting in her attempts to curl up on or between the sleeping-bags, and by finally eating the jam which had been saved for breakfast. The weather was quite as bad next morning, but, after a meal of dry biscuit and cocoa, they pushed on, taking four and a half hours to do the six miles. The next day was spent making the hut weather-proof and fixing up a couple of bunks. The provisions which had been cached were in good order and abundance of firewood lay around, in the shape of barrel-staves. Just close to the living-hut was a works-hut containing boilers and digestors which years ago had been used for procuring penguin oil, while there was a rookery a few yards away from which the victims had come.

This rookery was the resort of King penguins, the largest of the four species which are to be found on the island. They are magnificently coloured birds, being bluish-grey on the back while the head is greenish-black and on each side of the neck there is a brilliant yellow band, shading to a greenish-yellow on the upper part of the breast, and gradually merging into the glossy white of the lower part of the body. They attain to a height of about three feet and weigh thirty pounds approximately. The side of their rookery is a stony flat about a hundred yards from the water, and here are collected between five and six thousand—all that remain on the island.

The King penguin is nearly related to the Emperor penguin of the ice-zone, and their methods of hatching the egg closely correspond. They make no nest, the single egg laid being supported on the feet, and kept in position and incubated in a kind of skin pouch which conceals it from view. One would never guess the egg was there, for, on being disturbed, the bird shuffled along, carrying it in the manner described. The egg is large, tapering very much at one end and resembling a pear in shape. They lay during December and January, and the young are hatched in about six weeks. A peculiar feature about the young birds is that the parents feed them for two seasons. They are covered with a coarse, greyish-brown furry growth, and a year-old chick looks bigger than the old bird. This furry growth is lost during the second year, and the adult plumage replaces it. The young utter a peculiar sound, something between a squeak and a whistle. It is probable that the King penguins were never so numerous as the Royal or Victoria penguins, but the fact remains that they have not yet recovered from the wholesale slaughter to which they must have been subjected over sixteen years ago.

Down on a strip of shingly beach the birds parade, when not in the rookery or at sea getting food. Their proceedings strike one as being extraordinarily human, while the dignity and gravity of the participants are beyond description. On one occasion, a large number marching along the beach were seen to halt suddenly and talk excitedly. Three birds then left the main body, consulted together for a short time, and then separated. The other birds immediately separated into three companies, and each company stood behind one of the three already mentioned, who were now some distance apart. The individuals of each party then talked among themselves for several minutes, after which two parties joined forces and marched off, leaving the third party staring after them.

I have lost myself for the time being amongst the penguins and shall now return to Blake and Hamilton, who climbed on to the hill-tops the following morning to spy out the land. There the island is, generally speaking, higher for all the more elevated peaks are on the southern half.

They saw numerous rabbits, of which many were coloured black and Mac had the day of her life amongst them. These animals were introduced to the island about twenty-five years ago, and have gradually withdrawn to the lonelier southern part, though occasionally odd ones are seen about the northern end. They are very tame and live in holes amongst the rocks or make burrows in the gully banks and broken hill sides.

Many lakes, frozen over, were seen, several of which were fairly large. Altogether, the topography is similar to that of the northern end.

In an endeavour to improve the evening fare, a sweet broth consisting of biscuit, milk, jam and sugar was tried but it was not a success; Hamilton remarking that "even Blake had only one helping." On the following morning they started for the Shack and chose the route on the hill-tops, as the ground was frozen hard; and, though there were frequent snow-drifts into which they floundered occasionally, the surface for travelling was much better than along the coast.

An earthquake shock was felt at 9.15 p.m. on April 27. I was sitting in the Shack writing up records at the time, and it seemed as if somebody had struck the south-west end of the place a severe blow with a bag of sand. Immediately afterwards a crashing sound, apparently some distance away on the eastern side, indicated that some rocks on the cliff-front had been dislodged.

Much rough weather was experienced during the month, and it rained, hailed and snowed on twenty-five days. The wind attained moderate to fresh gale-force on six days, and fog and mist were almost invariable.

We found it necessary to use sea-elephant blubber in the stove in order to warm the Shack, and a very small piece put on the fire at intervals always ensured a good heat. Sea-elephants had become scarce, so, in order to lay in a supply of fuel for the next few weeks, we went round to Aerial Cove on May 3 and killed the largest animal we could find, afterwards carrying the blubber round to the Shack. We came through Catch Me and had the same old experience. Hamilton examined the contents of the stomach of the sea-elephant and found gravel, stones, cuttlefishes' beaks and parasitic worms in abundance.

There was a violent north-westerly gale throughout the early morning hours of the 4th, reaching a maximum velocity of fifty-two miles per hour, but as the day progressed the wind veered more to the south and weakened rapidly.

In the afternoon Blake and I had a trip down to the moraine which he had found a few days previously. After a heavy one-and-a-half-hours' walk, the last half-mile of which was along a creek bed, with water ankle-deep all the way, we reached the spot: the site of one of the large penguin rook-eries up on the hills at the back of The Nuggets. The sun showed between squalls, and Blake took some interesting photographs showing striated rock faces the result of past glacial action. We battled with one enormous boulder for some time before getting it into a suitable position for the camera, and afterwards walked right through the glacial area.

Hobart wireless station was by this time in working order, a fact which greatly facilitated wireless business. We received a message on the 7th, saying that the *Aurora* was leaving Hobart on about the 13th for a sub-Antarctic cruise and would call at the island. At the same time I was requested to send a list of articles required.

A persistent area of high pressure affected the weather conditions of the island to the extent of shrouding us in fog from the 6th to the 10th inclusive, and we did not catch a glimpse of the sun during that period. The average daily temperature-range during this time was only 2.3°. Such conditions have a rather depressing effect on the spirits, but the cheering news we received on the 7th made some amends for the lack of sunshine.

The sun appeared at last on the 11th and shone strongly, so Blake went up on Wireless Hill to work with his theodolite. After assisting for a while I was joined by Sandell and we went off to round up the sheep.

From the hill-top we could see Hamilton engaged in skinning a large sea-leopard on the coast, so we climbed down to render any necessary assistance. It was a beautifully marked animal, about eleven feet long, and made a fine specimen.

Sea-leopards frequent Macquarie Island in great numbers from the late winter to the early summer, and may be seen lying about, sleeping close to the water and apparently always very tired. They do not give birth to the young on the island, and our observations indicated that they were born at sea. Until the young one is weaned, its habitat is evidently in the water as we never saw an adult suckling its offspring.

Sea-leopards—long, lithe creatures with a reptilian cast of head—are remarkably quick in the water. If one is disturbed on shore it opens its mouth very wide, revealing a wicked-looking row of teeth in each jaw; the canine teeth or tusks being very long and slightly curved.

Unlike sea-elephants and seals they are solitary animals, and should several of them be found on a small gravelly patch of beach they are seen to be as far as possible from one another. We have never seen them attempt to fight on the shore, but the gaping wounds and scars with which they are frequently covered appear to indicate that they treat each other very severely in the water. They live on penguins, gulls, shags and fish.

I saw several shags on one occasion very busy fishing, and between diving intervals they would sit on the water. Suddenly one disappeared under the water and the rest flew off: but in a few seconds the one which had disappeared was thrown into the air and caught by a sea-leopard, who played in this fashion with the maimed bird for several minutes before devouring it.

From May 12 onwards a daily weather report was sent nightly to Dr. S. C. Bates, the New Zealand Meteorologist, at Wellington, a distance of eleven hundred miles.

The two species of penguins which leave the island during the winter months had disappeared, and silence now reigned where formerly were busy, noisy colonies. The departure of the migrants made the place seem lonelier, and, during the depths of winter when snow covers the ground and the birds and animals are few in number, a more dreary spot would be difficult to find.

The weather conditions were now rather severe, and as Sawyer and Sandell worked from 8 p.m. till 2 or 3 a.m. every night and slept at the wireless station, they were exempted from the necessity of coming down to breakfast during their cooking weeks. They now rested till about noon, and arrived at the Shack every day in time for lunch. Hamilton, Blake and I, each outside his own cooking week, took it in turns to prepare breakfast.

Blake's field-work at the north end, more particularly in the vicinity of West Point and North Head, was just about finished. West Point proved to be an area of gabbro, a coarse-grained eruptive rock of a basic character, while North Head was composed of agglomerate, and volcanic bombs were numerous.

Hamilton had got together a good collection of bird specimens, and was now in quest of skeletons.

On the night of May 13 we witnessed a rather pretty auroral manifestation. It was in the form of parallel bands stretching across the whole sky. As seen in perspective the bands appeared to converge to two opposite points on the horizon. The light was a pale yellow, no other tint being visible. In addition, a nebulous glow appeared at intervals in the south.

We heard on the 16th that the *Aurora* had sailed on that day from Hobart for a sub-Antarctic cruise and would call at Macquarie Island in about three weeks' time. This was indeed cheerful news, and we began to look forward to her arrival.

A fresh west-south-west gale during the early morning hours of the 17th was accompanied by soft hail and snow-squalls. Snow never lay long on the lower ground, for as soon as the wind shifted to the north of west it melted and rapidly disappeared.

Through the courtesy of the naval officials, H.M.S. *Drake* sent us time signals twice a week, and though we had so far no sound from Adelie Land, there was a possibility that they could receive messages from us. Sawyer therefore sent out time-signals as a matter of routine.

Hamilton made a trip to the west coast on the 28th and returned with thirteen wekas. Sawyer did not care for these birds, but each of the others could account for one at a meal. They seem to be better eating if plucked like a fowl and roasted, but the plucking takes too long and we generally skinned and boiled them. It is advisable to hang them for several days before cooking as it certainly makes them tender.

Rough, stormy weather prevailed during the greater part of the month and the wind reached the force of a gale on nine days. Much snow, soft hail and sleet fell and some very cold days were experienced. The average temperature was 40°, the maximum being 44.7° and the minimum 27.8° F.

In anticipation of the *Aurora's* arrival, Blake and Hamilton collected some stores together in the hope that Captain Davis would transport them down to Lusitania Bay, thus obviating the necessity of carrying them down on foot. As Blake reckoned that he would remain there fully three months and Hamilton about two months, it was thought that such another opportunity might not present itself.

A heavy snowfall occurred during the early morning hours of June 3, and the temperature was below freezing-point all day. In the afternoon we had rather an enjoyable time tobogganing down a steep talus-slope on the east coast.

A considerable struggle was necessary in order to get the sledge to the top, but the lightning slide to the bottom more than compensated for the labour.

Hamilton killed a very fine sea-leopard on the 5th and the skin, apart from being unscarred, was handsomely marked. It should make a splendid specimen. The stomach contained more than the usual number of the common worms, and one tape-worm.

Everything was going along in the usual placid manner on the 7th, when, as we were just taking our seats for lunch, someone rushed in with the information that the *Aurora* was in sight. There was a scramble to various points of vantage and she was soon observed coming up the east coast very slowly. At 2.30 p.m. she dropped anchor in North-East Bay, but, as it was blowing strongly and a nasty sea was running, no boat was launched, though one may imagine how anxiously we watched for some movement in that direction. As soon as it became dark a message was sent to us by signalling-lantern to the effect that a boat would bring mails and goods ashore in the morning if the weather moderated, and with that we had to be content. Needless to say, business ashore was for the time being paralysed, but a message was sent to Hobart advising her arrival.

True to his intimation of the previous night, Captain Davis brought a boat ashore at 9.30 a.m. and with him came several visitors who were to be our guests for some days. They were Mr. E. R. Waite, naturalist, and his taxidermist, and Mr. Primmer, cinematographer. Conspicuous in the boat was a well-laden mail bag and no time was lost in distributing the contents. Letters, papers, and magazines were received by every member of the party, and all the news was "good." Some stores were brought along and, after getting these ashore, we took the visitors across to the Shack and invited them to make themselves at home.

Blake went off to the ship again, taking the stores which had been got ready for transport to Lusitania Bay, as the Captain had agreed to land them when he visited there in a few days' time.

Captain Davis sent a boat ashore on the morning of the 12th with an invitation to come on board and lunch.

I accordingly went out to the vessel and, after lunching, had a thorough look over her, mentally contrasting her spick-and-span appearance at the time with what it had been when I left her laden with deck-cargoes in December. I went ashore again in the afternoon and assisted the visitors to get their loads down to the boat, as they were returning to the ship, which was leaving next morning on a sounding trip down the island.

Several days were occupied in carrying our stores half a mile along the beach to the Shack and stowing them. Also several new instruments were put into commission; the chief of which, the tide-gauge, occupied Sandell and myself for several days.

The *Aurora* returned from the south of the island on the 19th and reported having had a rough experience in the north-east to south gale which blew on the two previous days. The wind came out of the north-east very suddenly on the 17th, and some very strong squalls were experienced. A calm prevailed for several hours in the evening, but a south-east gale then sprang up and blew all day on the 18th, gradually working into the south and dying away during the night.

Early on the 20th the *Aurora* steamed out of the bay, bound north as we thought, but she returned again in the evening, and we signalled to know if anything were wrong. They replied, "All well, but weather very bad outside." She lay at anchor in the bay all next day, as it was snowing and blowing very hard from the south-west, but early on the 22nd she disappeared in the north and we did not see her again for some months. A few hours after her departure the wind increased in force, and a gale accompanied by hail and snow-squalls raged until the end of the month.

A tremendous sea was running on the 25th. Spray was scudding across the isthmus, and the sea for a mile from the shore was just a seething cauldron.

Something in the nature of a tidal wave occurred during the night of the 28th, for, on rising the following morning, I was considerably astonished to see that the sea-water had been almost across the isthmus. To effect this, a rise of twenty to twenty-five feet above mean sea-level must have taken place and such a rise appeared abnormally high. Our coal heap, which we had hitherto regarded as perfectly safe from the sea, was submerged, as shown by the kelp and sand lying on top of it, and the fact that seven or eight briquettes were found fifteen feet away from the heap.

Nothing at the wireless station was damaged and work went on as usual. The wind used to make a terrific noise in the aerial wires, but this did not affect the transmission of messages. The howling of the wind round the operating-hut interfered with the receiving, at times making it extremely difficult to hear signals.

Hamilton was at this time concentrating his attention on the cormorants, or shags as they are frequently called. This species of cormorant is peculiar to the island, being found nowhere else. They are blue-black, with a white breast, and on the head they have a small black crest. At the top of the beak are golden lobes, while the skin immediately round the eye is pale-blue. They remain on the shores of the island all the year and nest on the rocks in or very close to the water. They form rookeries and build nests of grass, laying three eggs about the end of November. Neither the birds nor the eggs are palatable. They are very stupid, staring stupidly till one gets almost within reach of them, when they flap heavily into the water. They are easily caught when sitting on the nest, but a shag rookery, like most other rookeries, is by no means a pleasant place in which to linger.

Hamilton had a lobster pot set some distance from the shore and anchored to a float, but unfortunately the pot was lost in the rough seas at the end of June. He had a couple of fish-traps also, but, in view of this disaster, he decided to set these in Aerial Cove, where the water was quieter. Here he was successful in trapping several varieties of fish, but a month later the traps were found to have disappeared, the wire having broken apparently through continual friction against the rock.

Taking advantage of a bright sun on the following day, Blake and Hamilton went to The Nuggets to obtain photographs of geological and biological interest. They had occasion to enter one of the unoccupied huts down there and found a wild cat a little more than half-grown, which they caught and carried home with them. He was the usual tabby colour and by no means fierce, quickly yielding to the coaxing treatment of his captors. He made himself quite at home in the Shack, and we looked forward to a display of his prowess as a rat-catcher. These wild cats are the descendants of the domestic variety brought to the Island by sealers.

A bright display of the aurora occurred on the night of July 4, the ribbons and streamers of light being well defined and occasionally slightly coloured. We could establish no connection between this extraordinary outburst and the fact that it occurred on American Independence night, but it was certainly the most energetic manifestation of the phenomenon we had so far witnessed.

The operator was requested by the Pennant Hills high-power wireless station at Sydney to listen for signals tapped out during the daytime, and Sawyer spent a couple of hours on certain mornings assisting in these tests, which were attended with some success. We occasionally received Press news from land stations or from ships passing across the Tasman Sea, but it was only a brief summary of the cable news: enough to whet one's curiosity, rarely ever satisfying it.

Our tank water gave out for the first time on the 12th. The precipitation for a fortnight had been in the form of dry powdery snow and soft hail; the wind blowing it off the roof before it had a chance to thaw, thus robbing us of our usual water supply. For a while we had to use swamp water, which contained a good many insects of various kinds and had a distinctly peaty flavour. Finding good water running from the hill-tops down a deep gully on the east coast, three-quarters of a mile away, we carried drinking water from there, using the less palatable quality for other purposes.

During the third week in July a very low tide exposed rocks, ordinarily submerged, and Hamilton was occupied all the week in collecting marine organisms, worms and plants, and then preserving, bottling and labelling them.

A most peculiar sight was witnessed on the 17th. Aerial Cove is a favourite nesting-place for shags, and they may be seen in twos and threes flying round in that direction almost any time during the day; but on this particular day a kind of wholesale exodus from the cove took place, and large flocks of them followed each other for a couple of hours. They congregated on the rocks along the east coast, or settled on the water in scores; the latter fact suggesting that the probable reason for this extraordinary behaviour was the presence of unusual shoals of fish.

We used to relax and have a game of cards occasionally, while our small organ became a medium of much enjoyment. Four of us played well enough to amuse ourselves; there was a distinct predilection in favour of ragtime.

The pursuit and killing of a sheep had now become something in the nature of an experience, and when Sandell and I were hunting for one on the 20th, we realized it before we reached home. The flock was very timid, and when disturbed on North Head invariably came past the wireless station close to the engine hut. Sandell concealed himself there with a rifle while I went out to startle the animals. They did not fail to do their part, but Sandell missed and the shot frightened them. He then rushed out and fired another shot as they were running, managing to hit one, which immediately dropped behind and ran to the edge of the cliff. We did not want to shoot the sheep at this moment, as it would have fallen about two hundred feet, so we cautiously approached to drive it away. The poor creature simply took a leap out into space and landed on the talus below, down which it rolled to the water's edge. We scrambled down and skinned it, having to carry the carcase along the rocks at the base of the cliffs, and getting many duckings on the way.

During the last week of the month we all had our hair cut. On arrival at the island, several of us had it shorn very closely with the clippers and had not trimmed it since then, growth being very slow. We had a proper hair-cutting outfit and Blake, Hamilton and Sandell acted as barbers.

Blake was an expert with the needle and did some really neat mending, while with the aid of some woollen thread and a mug he darned holes in his socks most artistically. He was the authority on how, when and where to place a patch or on the only method of washing clothes. The appearance of his articles when washed, compared with mine, made me wonder.

Hamilton was busy, about this time, dredging in swamp pools and securing specimens of the rockhopper or gentoo penguin.

The small gentoo penguins, like the King penguins, do not migrate and are few in numbers. They form diminutive colonies, which are always established on mounds, amongst the tussock, or on the hill-sides not far from the water. Their eggs are about the best of the penguin eggs for eating, and if their nests are robbed the birds will generally lay again. They build their nests of grass and plant leaves. They are more timid than any other specimen of penguin, and leave the nests in a body when one ventures into the rookery. The skuas take advantage of this peculiarity to the length of waiting about till a chance presents itself, when they swoop down, pick up an egg with their beak and fly off. The penguin makes a great fuss on returning to find that the eggs are gone, but generally finishes up by sitting on the empty nest. We have frequently put ten or a dozen eggs into one nest and watched the proprietress on her return look about very doubtfully and then squat down and try to tuck the whole lot under herself with her beak.

July passed away with a mean temperature of 37.7° F., with extremes of 43.3° and 26° F. It had proved a bleak, windy month with only occasional quiet days.

Now that our life was one of smooth routine I devoted a good deal of time to reducing the meteorological observations. This inactive operation meant enduring the inevitable cold feet, for the floor of the Shack was never warm.

Mac developed a great animosity against the rats and thoroughly enjoyed rooting them out on all occasions. The only explanation of their presence on the island is that they had arrived in the ships which were wrecked along the coasts.

They got into the Shack several times, and we simply brought in Mac and shifted things about till she caught them.

Rough weather occurred during the first week of August, the wind reaching fifty miles an hour at different times.

Blake found a cave running through North Head and went round, on August 5, to examine it. He proved it to be about sixty yards from opening to opening, and to widen out inside; the roof being about fifteen feet above the floor.

Hamilton and Sandell went along the coast on the 6th and brought home a dozen Maori hens for the pot. Hamilton secured some spiders, parasites on birds and many beetles under the moss and stones on the site of a penguin rookery, besides shooting a few terns.

The tern frequenting Macquarie Island is a very pretty bird with light grey plumage, a black head and red beak and feet. We found no nests on the island, though the fact that the birds remain throughout the year implies that they breed there. They fly very fast while not appearing to do so, but their movements are by no means graceful. They flit about over the water close to the shore, every now and then dipping down, picking up morsels and keeping up a constant, shrill squeaking.

A very heavy fall of snow, with flakes the size of half-a-crown, occurred on the afternoon of the 7th, and within an hour the island was quite white.

Bright sunny intervals alternated with light snow-squalls on the 10th, and the temperature was below freezing-point all day. It was pleasant to be out of doors, and I walked along to the west coast to see if there were any signs of activity amongst the sea-elephants.

An unmistakable sign of the near approach of the breeding season was the presence of an enormous old bull, almost too fat to move, lying on the beach. Very few small ones were seen, as, on the arrival of the adult males and females for the breeding season, the younger ones leave for a while, presumably to get fat for the moulting period, or because they are afraid of the bulls, who are particularly savage at this time. The full-grown bulls attain to a length of quite twenty feet, and have a fleshy proboscis about eight or ten inches in length hanging over the mouth, suggesting the trunk of an elephant. They are elephantine in size for these big fellows weigh several tons each.

There is a considerable disparity of size between the adult male and female, the latter very rarely exceeding eleven feet, though we have seen a few twelve and thirteen feet long. The females are devoid of the trunk-like development characteristic of the males. The adults are called bulls and cows in common with all members of the class Phocidæ. The local sealers at Macquarie Island, however, referred to the young ones as pups instead of calves, confusing the term applicable to the young of the class Otaridae. The places where large numbers of these sea-elephants gather together during the breeding season are, curiously enough, known as rookeries.

The calves, born during September or early October, are covered with a long, black, wavy fur, which they lose when about two months old, and in its place comes a growth of silver-grey hair, which changes later into the ordinary brown colour of the full-grown animal.

The old males and females leave the island about the end of January, and are not seen again (except a few stray ones) till August in the case of the males, and until September in the case of the females.

The rookeries vary in size, containing from half a dozen to four or five hundred cows; in the last case, of course, being an aggregation of smaller rookeries, each with its proprietor, in the shape of an old bull, lying in or somewhere near the centre. The normal rookery, as far as I could judge, seemed to be one that contained about fifty cows, but once the nucleus was formed, it was hard to say how many cows would be there before the season ended, as females keep arriving for a period of about three weeks.

The young, varying in length from three and a half to four and a half feet, are born within a few days of arrival and suckled for about a month, becoming enormously fat. The cow, who has not eaten during the whole of this time and has become very thin, then leaves the calf, but remains in the rookery for about two days, after which she escapes to sea, remaining there till the beginning of January, when she returns to the island to moult. The calves when weaned get such rough usage in the rookery that they soon make off into the tussock and sleep for about a month, living on their fat and acquiring a new coat. The noise in one of the large rookeries is something to remember—the lowing of the mothers, the whimpering and yelping of the calves and the roaring of the bulls.

Another feature in connection with the rookery is the presence of what may be called unattached bulls, which lie around at a little distance from the cows, and well apart, forming a regular ring through which any cow wishing to desert her calf or leave the rookery before the proper time has very little chance of passing, as one of these grips her firmly with his powerful flipper and stays her progress. The lord of the harem, in the meantime, hastens to the scene of the disturbance, whereupon the other bull decamps.

The sea immediately in the vicinity of a large rookery is generally swarming with unattached bulls, who may be seen with their heads out of the water eyeing each other and keeping a bright look out for escaping cows. Now and again one may see a bull in the water gripping a cow with his flipper, despite her struggles, and roaring at a couple of others who show up menacingly quite close to him.

It may be remarked that towards the end of the season changes in the proprietorship of a rookery are rather rapid, as continuous raids are made by individuals from the outside. The need of continuous vigilance and the results of many encounters eventually lead to the defeat and discomforture of the once proud proprietor.

I have never seen two bulls fight without first indulging in the usual preliminaries, that is, roaring and advancing a few yards and repeating the performance till within striking distance. Then both animals rear high up, supporting themselves on the lower part of the body, and lunge savagely with their whole weight each at his opponent's head or neck, tearing the thick skin with their teeth and causing the blood to flow copiously. Several lunges of this kind generally finish the battle, whereupon the beaten one drops to his flippers and makes all haste towards the water, glancing fearfully behind him on the way. We have seen bulls with their snouts partly torn off and otherwise injured, but worse injuries must occur in the rare, desperate battles which sometimes take place between two very much enraged animals.

When a bull in the centre of the rookery has occasion to rush at an interloper, he does so without regard to anything in his way, going over cows and calves alike and very often crushing some of the latter to death. Again, it seems as if all the outlying bulls recognize the noise of the rookery bull, because each time he roars they all lift up their heads and take notice, whereas others who have just been roaring have not the slightest regard paid to them, except perhaps by one immediately concerned.

The bull, during the breeding season, will on provocation attack a man, and it is surprising how quickly the former covers the ground. But on the whole he is an inoffensive animal. It is, of course, impossible to venture into a rookery, as the cows are very savage when they have the calves with them, but one can approach within a few yards of its outskirts without danger. Their food consists of cuttlefish, crabs and fish.

The skuas were now returning to the island and their numbers and corresponding clamour were daily increasing. They were the noisiest and most quarrelsome birds we had, but their advent, we hoped, marked the return of less rigorous weather.

Blake left for Lusitania Bay on August 17, intending to spend several months there in order to survey and geologically examine the southern end, so we gave him a send-off dinner. He had a very rough trip to the place, having to spend two nights in a cave about six miles from his destination, as a result of getting lost in a dense fog.

We heard that the *Rachel Cohen*, a sealing vessel, had sailed for Macquarie Island and was bringing a few articles for us, so there was something to which we could look forward in the immediate future.

At length August came to an end, a month of gales and rain. Either snow or rain had fallen on twenty-seven out of the thirty-one days, and it had been overcast with cloud almost all the time.

Bull elephants were now arriving in great numbers, and these monsters could be seen lying everywhere on the isthmus, both up in the tussock, on the beaches, and among the heaps of kelp. Now and again one would lazily lift a flipper to scratch itself or heave its great bulk into a more comfortable position.

The island is the habitat of two kinds of night-birds, one kind—a species of petrel (Lesson's)—being much larger than the other, both living in holes in the ground. They fly about in the darkness, their cries resembling those made by a beaten puppy. The smaller bird was occasionally seen flying over the water during the day, but the larger ones come out almost exclusively at night. A light attracts them and Hamilton, with the aid of a lantern and butterfly-net, tried to catch some. Others swooped about, well out of range, shrieking the while in an uncanny way. Numbers of them were secured afterwards by being dug out of their holes, Mac being just as keen to locate them as Hamilton was to secure their skins. They cannot see well during the day, and seem to have almost lost the use of their feet. They lay two small, white, thin-shelled eggs at the end of their burrow; and in certain parts of the island, where the burrows are numerous, the sound made by hundreds of them at once, during the nesting season, somewhat resembles that made by a high-power Marconi wireless set at close range.

Before Blake left Lusitania Bay, I promised to see that the hut on Sandy Bay was re-stocked with provisions by the middle of the month, so, on the 8th, Hamilton, Sandell and I carried a supply of stores down there, leaving a note which informed him that we expected the *Rachel Cohen* to arrive any day, and asking him to return to the Shack. On the way down we came upon a vast quantity of wreckage piled up on the beach, midway between The Nuggets and Sandy Bay. This was all that remained of the sealing schooner, *Jessie Nichol*, which had been wrecked in December 1910. Three men were drowned, their bodies being interred among the tussock, each marked by a life-belt and a small board on which the name was roughly carved.

On our homeward trip we caught some wekas for the pot and duly arrived at the Shack, tired, wet and hungry.

Next day, while sitting in the Shack reducing records, I heard a yell from Hamilton to the effect that the *Rachel Cohen* was in sight, and about an hour later she dropped anchor in North-East Bay.

The sea was fairly smooth and no time was lost in bringing a boat ashore with the mails, of which each man received a share. A gang of sealers was landed with a view to obtaining sea-elephant and penguin oil. I had wirelessed asking for a dinghy to be sent down, which would enable Hamilton to do more marine work; and it now came to hand. Further, we received an additional supply of photographic material and some rubber tubing for the anemometer, but the much-needed boots did not arrive.

On the 18th a strong southerly gale sprang up and compelled the *Rachel Cohen* to seek safety in flight; so she slipped her cable and put to sea. She had not yet landed all the sealers' stores and was forced to hang about the island till the weather moderated sufficiently for her to return to an anchorage.

The gentoo penguins, which had been observed at the beginning of the month, building their nests, commenced to lay, and the first ten eggs were collected by us on September 18. Many sea-elephant rookeries were now well-formed as the cows began to arrive about the 11th and were soon landing in large numbers. The first calves were heard on the 20th, and Bauer and I walked along to the rookery from which the noise came and had a look at the new-comers. There were only four, none of which was more than a few hours old, but they yapped their displeasure, and the mothers made frantic lunges at us when we approached to get a close view of them.

The sealers always gave the animals time to form their rookeries and then killed the bulls for oil. The cows being small never have a very thick coating of blubber, but I have seen bulls with blubber to a depth of eight inches, and some of them yield nearly two thousand pounds, though I should estimate the average yield at about one thousand pounds. The sealers in the early days used to obtain the oil by cutting the blubber up into very small pieces and melting it down in "trying" pots. These pots, many of which may be still seen about the island, were made of thick cast-iron and the fuel used was the refuse taken from the pot itself. In the present method steam digestors are used, and the oil from the melted blubber is drawn off, after steam has been passing for twelve hours. Coal is brought down by the sealing-vessel to be used as fuel. The "elephant season" lasts only about three months, and within about four weeks of its conclusion, the "penguin season" begins; the same gang of men being employed as a rule.

We heard sounds from Adelie Land wireless station for the first time on September 25, 1912, but the signals were very faint and all that we could receive was: "Please inform Pennant Hills." Sawyer called them repeatedly for several hours, but heard no acknowledgment. Every effort was made to get in touch with them from this time forward, Sawyer remaining at the instrument until daylight every morning.

The Royal penguins returned to the island on September 27, and immediately commenced to make their way to the rookeries. They had been absent since April and were very fat after their long migration.

On the 28th Blake and Hamilton started out in the dinghy for Lusitania Bay. With the aid of a make-shift sail the frail craft ran before a light breeze. Having a fair wind they made good headway along the coast, dropping in at a gentoo penguin rookery *en route*, and collecting about two hundred and twenty eggs. Mac was a passenger and was a very sick dog all the trip.

Shortly after their departure, the *Rachel Cohen*, which had been blown away on the 18th, reappeared and again anchored. The captain reported having seen numerous icebergs, several of which were very large, some about thirty miles to the eastward of the island. The sealers immediately commenced to get away the rest of their stores and coal and also to put some oil aboard the vessel, but on the following day the wind increased to such an extent that, in attempting to reach the ship with a raft of oil, they were blown down the coast and had to beach the boat several miles away.

On the night of the 29th Adelie Land wireless station was again heard tapping out a message apparently with the hope that some station would receive it. All we got was: "Having a hell of a time waiting for calm weather to put up our masts." Sawyer again repeatedly called, but they evidently could not hear him as no reply was received, and the above message was repeated time after time. On several occasions later on, messages were picked up but it was not until the following February that communication was properly established.

The weather during September was not quite so rough as that of the previous two or three months, but misty days were very frequent.

October was ushered in by a strong gale and rather heavy rain-squalls. The *Rachel Cohen* had a severe buffeting, though she was lying on the lee side of the island.

Just about three-quarters of a mile to the west of the Shack were two large sea-elephant rookeries, very close to each other, and on the 3rd Sandell and I went along to see what was happening there. We found about two hundred and fifty cows in the nearer one, and, as closely as we could count, about five hundred in the adjacent colony. The babel of sounds made one feel thankful that these noisy creatures were some distance from the Shack. Nearly all the cows had calves, some of which had reached a fair size, while others were only a few hours old. We saw several dead ones, crushed out almost flat, and some skuas were busily engaged gorging themselves on the carcases. These birds are indeed professional plunderers, and will venture almost anywhere in pursuit of food.

Hamilton and Blake were busy at Lusitania Bay during the first two weeks of October securing sea-elephant specimens and collecting eggs. They visited Caroline Cove where is established a giant petrel rookery containing about four hundred birds, and gathered a large number of eggs—purely specimens—as they are no use otherwise.

The *Rachel Cohen* finally left us on the 8th, expecting to pay another visit in December for the purpose of taking off the sea-elephant oil procured by the sealers. Sandell and I visited the gentoo penguin colony in Aerial Cove during the afternoon, for the purpose of getting a few eggs. We found plenty there and collected as many as we required. On returning to the empty nests, the birds would first of all peer round to assure themselves that the eggs were really missing, and then throw their heads back, swaying them from side to side to the accompaniment of loud, discordant cries.

About the middle of the month the Royal penguins commenced to lay, and on the 17th Sandell and I went to their rookeries at The Nuggets and collected about fifteen dozen eggs, which we buried in a hole in the bank of the creek for preservation. This species of penguin is the one which is killed for oil, not because it is any fatter than the others, but because it lives in such large colonies. There is one rookery of these birds on the south end of the island which covers an area of sixteen and a half acres, whilst at The Nuggets there are numbers of them scattered along the banks of a creek which reaches the sea, aggregating ten acres. At the latter place are situated the oil works belonging to the sealers.

This species resembles the others in habits, and I shall not describe them at any length. They are of the same colour as the Victoria penguins, but have a more orderly crest. Their rookeries are always on or very close to a running stream, which forms the highway along which they travel to and fro. There is no policeman on duty, but a well-ordered procession is somehow arranged whereby those going up keep to one side and those coming down keep to the other. Once they are in the rookery, however, different conditions obtain. Here are fights, squabbles and riots, arising from various causes, the chief of which appears to be a disposition on the part of some birds to loiter about. During the nesting time much disorder prevails, and fights, in which beaks and flippers are energetically used, may be seen in progress at various places throughout the rookery. The nests are made of small stones, and occasionally a bone or two from the skeleton of some long-dead relative forms part of the bulwarks. The attempt on the part of some birds to steal stones from surrounding nests is about the most fruitful cause of a riot, and the thief generally gets soundly thrashed, besides which all have a peck at him as he makes his way with as much haste as possible from the danger-zone. As the season advances, these rookeries become covered with filthy slush, but it seems to make no difference to the eggs, as the chicks appear in due course. When the moulting process is in full swing the rookeries are very crowded, and feathers and slush then become mixed together, making the place anything but fragrant.

Hamilton returned from Lusitania Bay in the dinghy on the 21st, but Blake stopped there as he had not yet finished his work in that locality. The dinghy was well laden with specimens of various kinds and, on the way up, some wood and pickets were left at Green Valley for future requirements.

During the last week of the month several of us made journeys to the west coast in search of plants and birds' eggs, adding considerably to the collection.

On October 28 two earthquake shocks were felt, but did no damage other than bring down some loose rock.

During the evening of October 30, I received a message from Captain Davis stating that the *Aurora* would visit us in about three weeks' time and inquiring if we needed any supplies. This was entirely unexpected, as we thought that no more would be seen of the ship until she came to take us home at the end of March 1913.

Hamilton and I when on a photographic expedition on November 3 heard the discordant but mournful cry of a sooty albatross coming from the cliff-front, so Hamilton climbed up and, after scrambling about for a while, succeeded in finding a nest, which contained one egg. This led him to look along the cliff's fronting the east coast, and on the following morning he found several nests and caught two birds, both of which were taken by hand while on the nest. They had beautiful plumage and made very fine specimens.

Blake returned from Lusitania Bay during the afternoon of the 4th and reported that he required only four or five days to complete the survey. The configuration of the island at the southern end is vastly different from that shown in the rough outline composing the only existing map then published, and this became more apparent as Blake's figures were plotted.

The news that Piastre had won the Melbourne Cup was flashed about all over the Southern Ocean during the evening and we picked it up; but as this was the first we had heard of the animal, nobody seemed much interested. It certainly gave a turn to the conversation, and quite a sporting tone permeated the discussion of the ensuing two or three days.

Blake and Hamilton went to Sandy Bay in the dinghy on the 6th in order to complete some work. They improved the hut there, to the extent of making a fireplace and laying barrel-staves on the floor, afterwards bringing a boat-load of timber from the *Jessie Nichol* wreck and rigging up a board bunk sufficiently large to accommodate both of them.

While walking down to the *Clyde* wreck for some wood on the 7th I saw a strange bird on the beach, and, returning to the Shack for the gun, I got him at the second shot. He was a land bird and had evidently been blown out of his course, as none of his kind had been seen before on the island.

On getting up on the following morning I found poor old Ma lying dead, and the feathers which lay about indicated that she had been the victim of a savage assault, but whether at the teeth of a dog or the beak of a skua I was unable to determine. This was most unfortunate, as the hens had all started to lay again two days previously; but apart from this she was a funny old creature and one could almost hold a conversation with her, so we regretted her loss. However, to make amends for this disaster the Victoria penguins started to lay on the same day, and as several of their rookeries were only a few minutes' walk from the Shack, the position was much the same as if we owned a poultry farm.

At 6.30 p.m. on November 22 the *Aurora* steamed into North-East Bay and dropped anchor. Hamilton, Blake and Sawyer launched the dinghy and pulled out to receive the mails, which they brought ashore for distribution. All on board were well and Captain Davis sent word to say he would land in the morning, bringing our goods and some visitors—Professor Flynn of Hobart and his assistant Mr. Denny.

The *Aurora* next day steamed round North Head and took a series of soundings between the main island and the Judge and Clerk. These latter islets lie about eight miles to the north of North Head, and are merely rocks about eighty feet high upon which thousands of shags and other birds have established rookeries. On the following morning we said good-bye to the ship, which weighed anchor and steamed away, leaving us once more to our own devices.

All the flowering plants were now showing their extremely modest blooms, and the tussock looked like a field of wheat, each stem having a decided ear. The gentoo penguins, as well as the giant petrels, had hatched their eggs, and the parent birds were shouldering full responsibilities.

A distinct rise in temperature was noticeable during November, but there was a frequency of foggy and misty days.

On December 2, Blake and I packed our sleeping-bags and blankets and started for Sandy Bay. The swags weighed only thirty-five pounds each and we made a rather quick trip.

After repairing the dilapidated hut there we sallied out for the purpose of catching our evening meal, and with the aid of Mac soon succeeded in getting eight wekas. A sea-elephant was then killed, and the blubber, heart and tongue taken; the first named for use as fuel and the others for food. We cleaned the wekas and put them in the pot, cooking the whole lot together, a proceeding which enabled us to forgo cooking a breakfast in the morning. The beach was swarming with young sea-elephants and many could be seen playing about in a small, shallow lagoon.

Feeling a little weary, I sought the hut about 9 p.m. and turned into the sleeping-bag, which was placed on a board bottom covered with tussock, which was by no means uncomfortable. The old place smoked so much that we decided to let the fire die down, and as soon as the smoke had cleared away the imperfections of the hut became apparent; rays of moonlight streaming through countless openings in the walls and roof.

After breakfast next day we set out for Green Valley, but had not gone very far when it began to blow very hard from the south, straight in our faces, and we scrambled on towards our destination amidst squalls of snow, hail and sleet. Eventually we reached the valley and had a somewhat meagre lunch in a small cave.

On the whole, the length of the coast we had traversed was found to be as rough as any on the island. There is not a stretch of one hundred yards anywhere that can be termed "good going." In many places we found that the steep cliffs approached very close to the water, and the mournful cry of the sooty albatross could be heard coming from points high on the face of the cliffs, while the wekas were so tame that one could almost walk up and catch them.

We arose early next day and breakfasted on porridge, weka, fried heart, hard-tack and cocoa. Leaving the hut shortly afterwards we climbed on to the hills and travelled south for several miles in order to fix the position of some lakes and creeks. There was one lake in the vicinity about half a mile long and to all appearances very deep. It lay between two steep hills, and the grassy bank at one end and the small sloping approach at the other gave it an artificial appearance, while the water was beautifully clear and perfectly fresh. At the sloping end, dozens of skuas were busily engaged washing themselves, and the flapping of their wings in the water made a remarkable noise, audible at a considerable distance on the hill-tops. On returning to the hut at Sandy Bay several rabbits secured by Mac were cleaned and put on to boil.

Next morning a dense mist shrouded the island till about 11 a.m., but then the weather becoming fine and bright, we started for the west coast about noon. During our progress along the bed of a creek, Blake discovered what was believed to be a glacial deposit, containing fossil bones, and considerable time was spent in examining this and attempting to extract whole specimens, thereby making it too late to proceed to the west. On returning to the hut we decided to pack the swags. We reached home just in time for tea, finding that nothing unusual had occurred during our four days' absence.

Hamilton and Blake went out fishing in the dinghy on the 9th and made a remarkable haul of fish, sixty in number, ranging in size from a few ounces to twelve and a half pounds. They were all of the same species, somewhat resembling rock cod.

On December 11 we had a gale all day, the anemometer recording "bursts" of over fifty miles an hour frequently, while the average exceeded forty miles an hour throughout. Twelve months ago on that day we had made our first landing on the island from the *Aurora*, but vastly different weather conditions prevailed at that time.

Christmas Day was now very close at hand, and as Blake and Hamilton were going to celebrate at the other end of the island, whence they had gone on the 10th, Sawyer, Sandell and I arranged a little "spread" for ourselves. Sawyer produced a cake which he had received in the recent mail, and some friend had forwarded a plum pudding to Sandell, so on Christmas Day these, with a boiled ham, some walnuts, mince rolls and a bottle of stout were spread on the table, which had been decorated with tussock stuck in sea-elephants' tusks. The highest temperature registered on the island during our stay −51.8° F.—was recorded on Christmas Day, and the sun seemed so warm that Sandell and I ventured into the sea for a dip, but the temperature of the water was not high enough to make it an agreeable experience.

The King penguins and night-birds had laid by this time, and Hamilton added more eggs to his collection. He found for the first time a colony of mutton birds near the south end. He also came upon a mollymawk rookery on the south-western point of the island, and managed to take one of the birds by hand.

Blake and he had an accident in the dinghy on the 29th, fortunately attended by no serious results. They had gone from Lusitania Bay to the south end, and while attempting to land through the surf, the boat struck a rock and capsized, throwing them into the water. They had many things in the boat but lost only two billies, two pannikins, a sounding line and Hamilton's hat, knife and pipe. Their blankets floated ashore in a few minutes, and the oars came floating in later in the day. After the capsize Hamilton managed to reach the boat and turn her over, and Blake made for a kelp-hung rock, but, after pulling himself up on to it, was immediately washed off and had to swim ashore. The boat was afterwards found to be stove-in in two places, though the breaks were easily patched up subsequently.

New Year's Eve came and with keen anticipations we welcomed the advent of 1913.

CHAPTER XXVI

SHORT COMMONS

George F. Ainsworth's Narrative

WE had now thrown a year behind and the work we set out to accomplish was almost finished; so it was with pleasurable feelings that we took up the burden of completion, looking forward to the arrival of April 1913 which should bring us final relief and the prospects of civilization. After the return of Blake and Hamilton from Lusitania Bay on January 8, our life was one of routine; much time being devoted to packing and labelling specimens in anticipation of departure.

The first business of the year was to overhaul the wireless station, and on the 6th, Sawyer, Sandell and I spent the day laying in a supply of benzine from Aerial Cove, changing worn ropes, tightening wire stays, straightening the southern mast and finally hauling the aerial taut.

Blake and Hamilton returned on January 8 and reported that their work was finished at the southern end. Thenceforth they intended to devote their time to finishing what remained to be done at the northern end and in adding to their collections.

Hamilton made the discovery that a number of bird specimens he had packed away were mildewed, and as a result he was compelled to overhaul the whole lot and attend to them. He found another colony of mutton birds on North Head, the existence of which was quite unexpected till he dug one out of a burrow thought to contain night-birds.

The *Rachel Cohen* again visited the island on January 26, but this time she anchored off The Nuggets, whither the sealers had gone to live during the penguin season.

The end of the first month found Blake and Hamilton both very busy in making suitable boxes for specimens.

Many of the larger birds could not be packed in ordinary cases, so Hamilton had to make specially large ones to accommodate them, and Blake's rock specimens being very heavy, extra-strong boxes had to be made, always keeping in view the fact that each was to weigh not more than eighty pounds, so as to ensure convenient handling.

After a silence of about four months, we again heard Adelie Land on February 3, but the same old trouble existed, that is, they could not hear us.

The next evening Adelie Land sent out a message saying that Dr. Mawson had not yet returned to the Base from his sledging trip and Sawyer received it without difficulty, but though he "pounded away" in return for a considerable time, he was not heard, so no reply or acknowledgment was made.

The *Rachel Cohen* remained till the 5th, when a northerly gale arose and drove her away. As she had a good cargo of oil on board no one expected her to return. We had sent our mail on board several days previously as experience had shown us that the sailing date of ships visiting the island was very uncertain.

Sandell met with a slight though painful accident on the 7th. He was starting the engine, when it back-fired and the handle flying off with great force struck him on the face, inflicting a couple of nasty cuts, loosening several teeth, and lacerating the inside of his cheek. A black eye appeared in a day or two and his face swelled considerably, but nothing serious supervened. In a few days the swelling had subsided and any anxiety we felt was at an end.

We now had only two sheep left, and on the 8th Blake and I went to kill one. Mac accompanied us. Seeing the sheep running away, she immediately set off after them, notwithstanding our threats, yells and curses. They disappeared over a spur, but shortly afterwards Mac returned, and, being severely thrashed, immediately left for home. We looked for the sheep during the rest of the day but could find no trace of them, and though we searched for many days it was not till five weeks had elapsed that we discovered them on a small ledge about half-way down the face of the cliff. They had apparently rushed over the edge and, rolling down, had finally come to a stop on the landing where they were found later, alive and well.

On the 8th Adelie Land was heard by us calling the *Aurora* to return at once and pick up the rest of the party, stating also that Lieutenant Ninnis and Dr. Mertz were dead. All of us were shocked at the grievous intelligence and every effort was made by Sawyer to call up Adelie Land, but without success.

On the following day we received news from Australia of the disaster to Captain Scott's party.

Blake, who was now filling in geological detail on his map which so far as illustrating the geography of Macquarie Island was now completed, discovered several lignite seams in the hills on the west coast.

The land meets the sea in steep cliffs and bold headlands. Numerous tarns and lakes are scattered amongst the hills, the tops of which are barren, wind-swept and weather-worn. The hill sides are deeply scored by ravines, down which tumble small streams, forming cascades at intervals on their hurried journey towards the ocean. Some of these streams do not reach the sea immediately, but disappear in the loose shingly beaches and peaty swamps. The west coast is particularly rugged, and throughout its length is strewn wreckage of various kinds, some of which is not one hundred yards from the water's edge. Very few stretches of what may be called "beach" occur on the island; the fore-shores consisting for the most part of huge water-worn boulders or loose gravel and shingle, across which progress is slow and difficult.

A very severe storm about the middle of the month worked up a tremendous sea, which was responsible for piling hundreds of tons of kelp on the shore, and for several days tangled masses could be seen drifting about like small floating islands.

On the 20th an event occurred to which we had long looked forward, and which was now eagerly welcomed. Communication by wireless was established with the Main

Base in Adelie Land! A message was received from Dr. Mawson confirming the deaths of Ninnis and Mertz, and stating that the *Aurora* had not picked up the whole party. Sawyer had a short talk with Jeffryes, the Adelie Land operator, and among other scraps of news told him we were all well.

Finding that provisions were running rather short on the last day of February, we reduced ourselves to an allowance of one pound of sugar per week each, which was weighed out every Thursday. Altogether there were only forty-five pounds remaining. Thenceforth it was the custom for each to bring his sugar-tin to the table every meal. The arrangement had its drawbacks, inasmuch as no sugar was available for cooking unless a levy was made. Thus puddings became rareties, because most of us preferred to use the sugar in tea or coffee.

March came blustering in, accompanied by a sixty-four mile gale which did damage to the extent of blowing down our annex, tearing the tarpaulin off the stores at the back and ripping the spouting off the Shack. A high sea arose and the conformation of the beach on the north-western side of the isthmus was completely changed. Numbers of sea-elephants' tusks and bones were revealed, which had remained buried in the shingle probably for many years, and heaps of kelp were piled up where before there had been clean, stony beach. The Macquarie Island kelp is a very tough seaweed, but after being washed up and exposed to the air for a few days, begins to decay, giving forth a most disagreeable smell.

At this time we caught numerous small fish amongst the rocks at the water's edge with a hand line about four feet long. It was simply a matter of dropping in the line, watching the victim trifle with destiny and hauling him in at the precise moment.

Wireless business was now being done nightly with Adelie Land, and on the 7th I received a message from Dr. Mawson saying that the party would in all probability be down there for another season, and stating the necessity for keeping Macquarie Island station going till the end of the year. This message I read out to the men, and gave them a week in which to view the matter. The alternatives were to return in April or to remain till the end of the year.

I went through the whole of the stores on the 10th, and found that the only commodities upon which we would have to draw sparingly were milk, sugar, kerosene, meats and coal. The flour would last till May, but the butter allowance would have to be reduced to three pounds per week.

It was on the 12th that we found the lost sheep, but as we had some wekas, sufficient to last us for several days, I did not kill one till the 15th. On that day four of us went down towards the ledge where they were standing, and shot one, which immediately toppled off and rolled down some distance into the tussock, the other one leaping after it without hesitation. While Blake and Hamilton skinned the dead sheep, Sandell and I caught the other and tethered it at the bottom of the hill amongst a patch of Maori cabbage, as we thought it would probably get lost if left to roam loose. However, on going to the spot next day, the sheep was nearly dead, having got tangled up in the rope. So we let it go free, only to lose the animal a day or two later, for it fell into a bog and perished.

A message came on the 27th saying that the *Rachel Cohen* was sailing for Macquarie Island on May 2, and would bring supplies as well as take back the men who wished to be relieved, and this was forwarded in turn to Dr. Mawson.

He replied, saying that the *Aurora* would pick us up about the middle of November and convey us to Antarctica, thence returning to Australia; but if any member wished to return by the *Rachel Cohen* he could do so, though notification would have to be given, in order to allow of substitutes being appointed. All the members of the party elected to stay.

The loyalty of my fellows was undoubted, and though any of them could have returned if he had felt so inclined, I am proud to say that they all decided to see it through. When one has looked forward hopefully to better social conditions, more comfortable surroundings and reunion with friends, it gives him a slight shock to find that the door has been slammed, so to speak, for another twelve months. Nevertheless, we all found that a strain of philosophy smoothed out the rough realities, and in a short time were facing the situation with composure, if not actual contentment.

We decided now to effect a few improvements round about our abode, and all set to work carrying gravel from the beach to put down in front of the Shack, installing a sink-system to carry any waste water, fixing the leaking roof and finally closing up the space between the lining and the wall to keep out the rats.

We expected the *Rachel Cohen* to leave Hobart with our stores on May 2, and reckoned that the voyage would occupy two weeks. Thus, it would be six weeks before she arrived. I was therefore compelled on April 10 to reduce the sugar allowance to half a pound per week. We were now taking it in turns to go once a week and get some wekas, and it was always possible to secure about a dozen, which provided sufficient meat for three dinners. Breakfast consisted generally of fish, which we caught, or sea-elephant in some form, whilst we had tinned fish for lunch.

Sandell installed a telephone service between the Shack and the wireless station about the middle of April, the parts all being made by himself; and it was certainly an ingenious and useful contrivance. I, in particular, learned to appreciate the convenience of it as time went on. The buzzer was fixed on the wall close to the head of my bunk and I could be called any time during the night from the wireless station, thus rendering it possible to reply to communications without loss of time. Further, during the winter nights, when auroral observations had to be made, I could retire if nothing showed during the early part of the night, leaving it to Sandell, who worked till 2 or 3 a.m. to call me if any manifestation occurred.

We had heavy gales from the 12th to the 17th inclusive, the force of the wind during the period frequently exceeding fifty miles per hour, and, on the first-mentioned date, the barometer fell to 27.8 inches. The usual terrific seas accompanied the outburst.

Finding that there were only eight blocks of coal left, I reduced the weekly allowance to one. We had a good supply of tapioca, but neither rice nor sago, and as the sealers had some of the latter two, but none of the former, we made an exchange to the extent of twelve pounds of tapioca for eight pounds of rice and some sago. Only fifteen pounds of butter remained on the 20th, and I divided this equally, as it was now one of the luxuries, and each man could use his own discretion in eating it. As it was nearing the end of April, and no further word concerning the movements of the *Rachel Cohen* had been received, I wirelessed, asking to be immediately advised of the exact date of the vessel's departure. A reply came that the ship would definitely reach us within two months, I answered, saying we could wait two months, but certainly no longer.

With a view to varying the menu a little, Blake and I took Mac up on the hills on April 26 to get some rabbits and, after tramping for about six hours, we returned with seven. In our wanderings we visited the penguin rookeries at The Nuggets, and one solitary bird sat in the centre of the vast area which had so lately been a scene of much noise and contention.

On May 1 I took an inventory of the stores and found that they would last for two months if economically used. Of course, I placed confidence in the statement that the *Rachel Cohen* would reach the island within that time.

With the coming of May wintry conditions set in, and at the end of the first week the migrants had deserted our uninviting island. Life with us went on much the same as usual, but the weather was rather more severe than that during the previous year, and we were confined to the Shack a good deal.

The sealers who were still on the island had shifted back to the hut at the north end so that they were very close to us and frequently came over with their dog in the evenings to have a yarn. The majority of them were men who had "knocked about" the world and had known many rough, adventurous years. One of them in particular was rather fluent, and we were often entertained from his endless repertoire of stories.

On the 23rd, finding that there were seventy-seven and a half pounds of flour remaining, and ascertaining that the sealers could let us have twenty-five pounds, if we ran short, I increased the allowance for bread to twelve and a half pounds per week, and this, when made up, gave each man two and three-quarter pounds of bread. Our supply of oatmeal was very low, but in order to make it last we now started using a mixture of oatmeal and sago for breakfast; of course, without any milk or sugar.

Just about this time Mac gave birth to six pups and could not help us in obtaining food. She had done valuable service in this connection, and the loss in the foraging strength of the party was severely felt for several weeks. She was particularly deadly in hunting rabbits and wekas, and though the first-named were very scarce within a few miles of the Shack, she always managed to unearth one or two somewhere. Slippers were made out of the rabbit skins and they were found to be a great boon, one being able to sit down in the hut for a while without his feet freezing.

June arrived and with it much rough cold weather. The *Rachel Cohen* was expected to come to our relief, at the very latest, by the 30th. We had a very chilly period during the middle of the month, and it was only by hand-feeding the water-jacket of the engine that any work could be done at the wireless station, as the tank outside was almost frozen solid.

We had ascertained that the *Rachel Cohen* was still in Hobart, so on the 23rd I wirelessed asking when she was to sail. The reply came that the date was now fixed for June 26.

Our supply of kerosene was exhausted by the end of the month, despite the fact that the rule of "lights out at 10 p.m." had been observed for some time. Thus we were obliged to use sea-elephant oil in slush lamps. At first we simply filled a tin with the oil and passed a rag through a cork floating on the top, but a little ingenuity soon resulted in the production of a lamp with three burners and a handle. This was made by Sandell out of an old tea-pot and one, two or three burners could be lit as occasion demanded. During the meal times the whole three burners were used, but, as the oil smoked and smelt somewhat, we generally blew out two as soon as the meal was finished. This was the general lamp, but each man had, as well, one of his own invention. Mine was scornfully referred to as the "house-boat," since it consisted of a jam-tin, which held the oil, standing in a herring-tin which caught the overflow.

The end of the month arrived and, on making inquiries, we found that there was no news of the *Rachel Cohen* having left Hobart. We had enough flour to last a fortnight, and could not get any from the sealers as they possessed only three weeks' supply themselves. However, on July 8, Bauer came across and offered to let us have some wheatmeal biscuits as they had a couple of hundredweights, so I readily accepted twenty pounds of them. We now had soup twice a day, and managed to make it fairly thick by adding sago and a few lentils. Cornflour and hot water flavoured with cocoa made a makeshift blancmange, and this, with sago and tapioca, constituted our efforts towards dessert.

On the 12th I received a message stating that the *Rachel Cohen* had sailed on July 7; news which was joyfully received. We expected her to appear in ten or twelve days.

On the 18th we used the last ounce of flour in a small batch of bread, having fully expected the ship to arrive before we had finished it. Next day Bauer sent us ten pounds of oatmeal and showed us how to make oatmeal cakes. We tried some and they were a complete success, though they consisted largely of tapioca, and according to the respective amounts used, should have been called tapioca cakes.

When the 22nd arrived and no ship showed up, I went across to see what the sealers thought of the matter, and found that they were all of opinion that she had been blown away to the eastward of the island, and might take a considerable time to make back.

On this date we came to the end of our meats, which I had been dealing out in a very sparing manner, just to provide a change from sea-elephant and weka. We had now to subsist upon what we managed to catch. There were still thirty-five tins of soup, of which only two tins a day were used, so that there was sufficient for a few weeks. But we found ourselves running short of some commodity each day, and after July 23 reckoned to be without bread and biscuit.

At this time strong winds prevailed, and on the 24th a fifty-mile gale accompanied by a tremendous sea beat down on us—a bad look-out for the *Rachel Cohen*. On that day we divided evenly amongst us the ten remaining biscuits; also our last tin of fruit was eaten, twelve tins having lasted us since March 31. We were short of bread, flour, biscuits, meats, fish, jam, sugar and milk, but had twenty tins of French beans, thirty tins of cornflour, some tapioca, and thirty tins of soup, as well as tea, coffee and cocoa in abundance. We had not been able to catch any fish for some days as the weather had been too rough, and, further, they appeared to leave the coast during the very cold weather.

Sea-elephants were very scarce, and we invariably had to walk some distance in order to get one; each man taking it in turn to go out with a companion and carry home enough meat for our requirements. We were now eating sea-elephant three times a day (all the penguins having migrated) and our appetites were very keen. The routine work was carried on, though a great deal of time was occupied in getting food.

The sealer Bauer very generously offered to share his biscuits with us, but while appreciating the spirit which prompted the offer, we unanimously declined to accept them. We now concluded that something had happened to the ship, as at the end of July she had been twenty-four days out.

On August 3 a strong gale raged, the wind reaching a velocity of sixty-three miles per hour. Needless to say there was a mountainous sea running, and the *Rachel Cohen*, if she had been anywhere in the vicinity, would have had a perilous time.

Three days later a message was received stating that the *Rachel Cohen* had blown into New Zealand badly damaged, and that negotiations were in progress to secure relief for us.

Splendid news came along on the 9th to the effect that the New Zealand Government's steamer *Tutanekai* would tranship our stores from the *Rachel Cohen* and sail direct for the island.

Sawyer now became ill and desired me to make arrangements for his return. So it came about that Sandell took over the operating and I assisted by running the engine.

Everybody now looked forward eagerly to the arrival of the *Tutanekai*, but things went on as before. We found ourselves with nothing but sea-elephant meat and sago, with a pound tin of French beans once a week and two ounces of oatmeal every morning.

The *Tutanekai* was equipped with wireless, which enabled us on the 18th to get in touch with her; the operator on board stating that they would reach us early on the morning of the 20th.

On the evening of the 19th we gave Sawyer a send-off dinner; surely the poorest thing of its kind, as far as eatables were concerned, that has ever been tendered to anyone. The fare consisted of sea-elephant's tongue "straight," after which a bottle of claret was cracked and we drank heartily to his future prosperity.

At 7.30 a.m. on the 20th the *Tutanekai* was observed coming up the east coast, and as we had "elephanted" at 6 a.m. we were ready to face the day. I went across to the sealers' hut and accompanied Bauer in the launch to the ship, which lay at anchor about a mile from the shore. We scrambled on board, where I met Captain Bollons. He received me most courteously, and, after discussing several matters, suggested landing the stores straight away. I got into the launch to return to the shore, but the wind had freshened and was soon blowing a fresh gale. Still, Bauer thought we should have no difficulty and we pushed off from the ship. The engine of the launch failed after we had gone a few yards, the boat was blown rapidly down the coast, and we were eventually thrown out into the surf at The Nuggets. The captain, who witnessed our plight, sent his launch in pursuit of us, but its engines also failed. It now became necessary for the crew of the whale-boat to go to the assistance of the launch. However, they could do nothing against the wind, and, in the end, the ship herself got up anchor, gave the two boats a line and towed them back to the former anchorage. The work of unloading now commenced, though a fairly heavy surf was running. But the whale-boat of the *Tutanekai* was so dexterously handled by the boatswain that most of our stores were landed during the day.

On the following morning, some sheep, coal and flour were landed, and, with a whistled good-bye, the *Tutanekai* started north and with her went our comrade Sawyer.

Our short period of stress was over and we all felt glad. From that time onward we ate no more elephant meat "straight." A sheep was killed just as the *Tutanekai* left, and we had roast mutton, scones, butter, jam, fruit and rice for tea. It was a rare treat.

The beginning of September found me very busy, for in addition to my usual work I had to spend the evenings assisting at the wireless station.

The sea-elephant season was now in progress, and many rookeries were well formed by the middle of the month. The skuas had returned, and on the 19th the advance-guard of the Royal penguins arrived. The gentoos had established themselves in their old "claims," and since the 12th we had been using their eggs for cooking.

During September and October several trips to Sandy Bay and other stations down the island were made by Blake and Hamilton. Again on October 30 Blake made a special trip to Sandy Bay to bring back some geological specimens and other things he had left there, but on reaching the spot found that the old hut had been burned to the ground, apparently only a few hours before, since it was still smouldering. Many articles were destroyed, among others were two sleeping-bags, a sextant, gun, blankets, photographic plates, bird specimens and articles of clothing. It was presumed that rats had originated the fire from wax-matches which had been left lying on a small shelf.

On November 9 we heard that the *Aurora* would leave Hobart on the 19th for Antarctica, picking us up on the way and landing three men on the island to continue the wireless and meteorological work.

On November 18 the *Rachel Cohen* arrived bringing the remainder of our coal and some salt for Hamilton for the preservation of specimens; the latter too late to be of much use.

Everybody now became busy making preparations for departure. Time passed very quickly, and November 28 dawned fine and bright. The *Rachel Cohen*, which had been lying in the Bay loading oil, had her full complement on board by 10 a.m., and shortly afterwards we trooped across to say good-bye to Bauer and the other sealers, who were all returning to Hobart. It was something of a coincidence that they took their departure on the very day our ship was to arrive. Their many acts of kindness towards us will ever be recalled by the members of the party, and we look upon our harmonious neighbourly association together with feelings of great pleasure.

A keen look-out was then kept for signs of our own ship, but it was not until 8 p.m. that Blake, who was up on the hill-side, called out, "Here she comes," and we climbed up to take in the goodly sight. Just visible away in the north-west there was a line of thin smoke, and in about half an hour the *Aurora* dropped anchor in Hasselborough Bay.

CHAPTER XXVII

THE HOMEWARD CRUISE

We bring no store of ingots,
Of spice or precious stones:
But what we have we gathered
With sweat and aching bones.—KIPLING.

As we sat in the wardroom of the *Aurora* exchanging the news of months long gone by, we heard from Captain Davis the story of his fair-weather trip from Hobart. The ship had left Australian waters on November 19, and from the outset the weather was quite ideal. Nothing of note occurred on the run to Macquarie Island, where a party of three men were landed and Ainsworth and his loyal comrades picked up. The former party, sent by the Commonwealth Weather Bureau, were to maintain wireless communication with Hobart and to continue dispatching meteorological reports. A week was spent at the island and all the collections were embarked, while Correll was enabled to secure some good colour photographs and Hurley to make valuable additions to his cinematograph film.

The *Aurora* had passed through the "fifties" without meeting the usual gales, sighting the first ice in latitude 63° 33′ S., longitude 150° 29′ E. Davis stopped to take a sounding every twenty-four hours, adding to the large number already accumulated during the several cruises. The pack was so loosely disposed, that the ship had made a straight course for Commonwealth Bay.

There was a twenty-five-mile wind and a small sea when we pulled off in the whale-boat to the ship, but, as if conspiring to give us for once a gala day, the wind fell off, the bay became blue and placid and the sun beat down in full thawing strength on the boundless ice and snow. The Adelians, if that may be used as a distinctive title, sat on the warm deck and read letters and papers in voracious haste, with snatches of the latest intelligence from the Macquarie Islanders and the ship's officers. No one of us could ever erase that day from the tablets of his memory.

Late in the afternoon the motor-launch went ashore, and the first of the cargo was sent off. The weather remained serenely calm, and for the next six days, with the exception of a "sixty-miler" for a few hours and a land breeze overnight, there was nothing to disturb the embarkation of our bulky impedimenta which almost filled the outer hut. Other work went on apace.

During 1912 Laseron had preserved a fine lot of skins, of all kinds and additions had been made during our second year. Now the skua gulls and the Wilson petrels were laying their eggs, and Hamilton, who was an adept skinner, went ashore to secure specimens and to add to our already considerable collection. Hunter was very busy securing and preserving marine life. Ainsworth, Blake and Sandell, making their first acquaintance with Adelie Land, were most often to be seen quarrying ice on the glacier to replenish the ship's water supply, or pulling loaded sledges down to the harbour.

On the 18th I arranged for a visit to the Mackellar Islets in company with Hunter, Hurley and Hodgeman, to spend two days surveying and making other observations.

These islets, over thirty in number, are clustered mainly in a group about two miles off shore. Under a brilliant sun, across the pale blue water, heaving in a slow northerly swell, the motor-launch threaded her way between knobs of gneissic granite, capped with accumulations of solid spray. The waves had undermined the white canopies so that they stood several feet above the waters, perched on the dark, kelp-fringed rocks; some of them like fairy mushrooms of gargantuan proportions. Entering a natural harbour, bordered by a low ice-foot on which scores of Weddell seals lay in listless slumber, we landed on the largest islet—a succession of salt-encrusted ridges covered by scattered penguin rookeries. The place just teemed with life.

It was calculated that the penguin population exceeded one hundred and fifty thousand in number. Snow-petrels, skua gulls and Wilson petrels soon betrayed their nests to the biologists. The ingenious and industrious Hurley was at last able to photograph a Wilson petrel on its nest; an awkward proposition that had defied all previous attempts, for these little birds lay their eggs in narrow and dark recesses far under the rocks.

Several days later we turned our attention to a rocky outcrop protruding beneath the ice-cap eight miles away to the west of Cape Denison. For two years we had looked curiously at that patch of rocks, but as it had been difficult of access to sledging parties, Cape Hunter, as it was ultimately called, was reserved for the coming of the ship.

In perfect weather, the anchor was raised on the forenoon of December 22, and the *Aurora* steamed out at half-speed, stopping within three miles of the cape; there a sounding showed the depth to be four hundred and twenty-four fathoms. The launch was dropped and a small party of us set off for the rocks. Through field-glasses much had already been seen; enough to arouse an intense interest.

Penguins soon began to splash around; Wilson petrels came glancing overhead and we could descry great flocks of Antarctic petrels wheeling over cliff and sea. Reefs buried in frothing surge showed their glistening mantles, and the boat swerved to avoid floating streams of brash-ice.

The rocky cliffs, about eighty feet in height at the highest point, were formed of vertically-lying slate rocks. At their base lay great clinging blocks of ice deeply excavated by the restless swell. Round to the west of the point and indenting the ice cliffs was a curving bay into which we steered, finding at its head a beautiful cove fringed with a heavy, undermined ice-foot canopying a margin of brown rocks on to which swarms of penguins leapt through the splashing surf. Overhanging the water, hollowed out of a bridge of ice thrown from the glacier to the rocks, was a cavern embellished with pendant icicles along its cornice.

The swell was so great that an anchor had to be run out astern. As soon as the rest of us had jumped in safety to a rocky ledge, the launch was hauled off astern and rode to the anchor, two men remaining on board in charge.

Over the first ridge of rocks we walked, suddenly coming upon an area of several acres occupied by Antarctic petrels. There had always been much speculation as to where these birds nested. Jones's party of our Western Base had, the previous summer, at Haswell Island happened upon the first nests of Antarctic petrels ever discovered. But here was a spot in the great wilderness peopled by their thousands. Every available nook and crevice was occupied along a wide slope which shelved away until it met the vertical cliffs falling to the ocean. One could sit down among the soft, gentle birds, who were fearless at the approach of man. Some sat in pairs at their nests, others rested close by on snow banks. The eggs were laid on bare rock or amongst fragments of slate loosely arranged to resemble a nest. Many eggs were collected and the birds, losing confidence in us, rose in the air in flocks, gaining in feathered volume as they circled in excitement above this domain of rock and snow which had been theirs for generations.

In adjoining rookeries the Adelie penguins, with their fat, downy chicks, were very plentiful and more precocious than usual. Skuas, snow-petrels and Wilson petrels were all represented. Down on the low ice-foot at the mouth of a rocky ravine, a few seals had effected a landing. Algæ, mosses and lichen made quite a display in moist localities.

The afternoon was so peaceful and the calm hot weather such a novelty to us that it was with reluctance that we pushed off to the *Aurora* after an eventful day.

Those on board had had a busy time dredging, and their results were just as successful as ours. In two hundred and fifty fathoms a big haul was made of sponges, starfish, sea-eggs, lace-corals, fish and other forms of life in such quantity that Hunter and Hamilton were occupied in sorting the specimens until five o'clock next morning. Meanwhile the *Aurora* had returned to her old anchorage close to Cape Denison.

The sky banked up from the south with nimbus clouds, and early on the 23rd a strong breeze ruffled the water. In view of the ominous outlook in the weather, I issued orders for the abandonment of the hut, where Ainsworth, Sandell and Correll were still residing in charge of the dogs.

An hour later the motor launch, with Madigan and Bickerton, sped away for the last load through falling snow and a rising sea. Hodgeman had battened down the windows of the hut, the chimney was stuffed with bagging, the veranda entrance closed with boards and, inside, an invitation was left for future visitors to occupy and make themselves at home. After the remainder of the dogs and some miscellaneous gear had been shipped, the launch put off and came alongside in a squally wind, through thick showers of snow. Unfortunately, the launch was too long to be swung inboard on any of the davits, for the latter were designed merely for whale-boats. As it was a lengthy business rigging the tackle necessary to swing the launch from the water on to the deck, temporary measures had to be adopted. So the moment that willing hands had unloaded it, the launch was hauled up out of the water and left swinging over the side in the davits, there to await more propitious weather before bringing it right inboard with the derrick. Everyone was at last safe on board, and in future all operations were to be conducted from the ship.

During the night the wind rose and the barometer fell, while the air was filled with drifting snow. On the 24th—Christmas Eve—the velocity of the wind gradually increased to the seventies until at noon it blew with the strength of a hurricane. Chief Officer Blair, stationed with a few men under the fo'c'sle head, kept an anxious eye on the anchor chain and windlass.

After lunch the anchor was found to be dragging* and we commenced to drift before the hurricane. All view of the land and lurking dangers in the form of reefs and islets were cut off by drifting snow. It was a moment of intense anxiety for, with an unresponsive compass, Captain Davis had little to give him direction except the wind itself which, there was reason to believe, was veering considerably.

---

* Actually, as was discovered later, one of the flukes of that heavy anchor had broken clean off.

The wind twanged the rigging to a burring groan that rose to a shriek in the shuddering gusts. The crests of the waves were cut off and swept away in fine spindrift. Under full steam Davis kept the ship head to wind in order to reduce the drifting of the vessel to a minimum; at the same time every effort was exerted to ensure that such residual drift would be towards where he vaguely felt that the open sea must lie. Meanwhile the chain cable and damaged anchor were being slowly hauled in under most difficult circumstances. The ship's chances looked very small indeed, but, owing to Captain Davis's skill and a certain amount of luck, disaster was averted. Soon the vessel was in a short, steep sea that buried the bows every few seconds.

Each time the ship lifted on a huge roller the motor launch, lashed in the davits, would rise and then descend with a crash on the water, and, as the lashings loosened, be violently bumped against the bulwarks. Everything possible was done to save the launch, but our efforts proved fruitless. As it was being converted into a battering ram against the ship itself it had to be cut away, and was soon swept astern and lost to sight.

Most unexpectedly there came a lull in the wind, so that it was almost calm, though the ship still laboured in the seas. A momentary clearance in the atmosphere was also noticeable, for Cape Hunter became dimly discernible to the west towards which we found ourselves rapidly drifting. The sight of this landmark was a great satisfaction to us, for we then knew our approximate position and the direction of the wind.

The lull lasted scarcely five minutes, when the wind came back from a somewhat different quarter, north of east, as violent as ever. The eye of the storm had passed over us, and the gale continued steadily for several days, blowing from the south-east. Davis stood the ship well out from the land and through an atmosphere dense with snow felt his way east for the shelter of the Mertz Glacier Tongue. That night and the two following days the struggle with the elements was kept up by the officers and the crew, assisted by members of the shore party, who took the lee wheel or stood by in case of emergency.

It was a miserable Christmas Day and but little better on the 26th. That afternoon, however, it cleared sufficiently to reveal a hazy view of the coast. By 10 p.m. the ice wall of the Mertz Glacier Tongue was visible on the port bow, and to starboard there was an enormous tilted berg which, in the dim light, appeared to be magnified to giant proportions.

Allowing a day for the weather to become clearer and more settled, we got out the trawl on the 28th and made a successful dredging in three hundred fathoms close to the Glacier Tongue. In addition to the usual items, several fragments of fossilized wood and coaly matter were discovered embedded in the oozy mud which came up in quantities with the catch. Bage assisted Davis taking temperatures and collecting water samples at regular intervals from the surface to the bottom.

On the 29th a cold south-easter blew off the ice cliffs and the sun was trying to pierce a pall of gauzy altostratus clouds. The *Aurora* steamed north-east, it being our intention to round the northern limit of the Mertz Glacier Tongue. Soon, however, a field of heavy pack-ice was encountered, barring further progress east, so the ship was put about.

On December 30 the *Aurora* lay within a cordon of bergs, about one mile distant from a small, steep islet of the Way Archipelago. Immediately after breakfast I took a party of seven men in the whale-boat to investigate Stillwell Island, as we called it. The weather was gloriously sunny and everyone was eager at the prospect of fresh discoveries. Cape Hunter had proved a stronghold of the Antarctic petrel, and on this occasion we were singularly fortunate in finding a resort of the Southern Fulmar or silver-grey petrel. During the previous summer, two of the eastern sledging parties had discovered nests of these birds among isolated rocks outcropping on the coast. But here there was a stronghold of many hundreds of these petrels, sitting on their eggs in niches among the boulders or ensconced in bowers partially or wholly covered with snow which had drifted over some parts of the island. The scientific treasures were exhausted by midday, and the whale-boat was well laden when we rowed back to the ship.

Throughout a warm summer afternoon, the *Aurora* threaded her way west between stately bergs and ice-capped islets. At midnight, with the aid of glasses, we could see serpentine trails of drift floating down the slopes around Commonwealth Bay. Doubtless it was blowing at the Hut! and the thought was enough to make us thankful that we were on our good ship leaving Adelie Land for ever.

On the morning of December 31 Point Alden was abeam, and a strong wind swept down from the highlands. Bordering the coast there was a linear group of islets, the Curzon Group, and outcropping rocks on the coast itself at which we had hoped to touch. After beating up and down for some hours in the hope of a lull, the wind still continued to blow so hard that the idea of landing was abandoned, and our course was directed towards the north-west to clear a submerged reef which had been discovered in January 1912.

The wind and sea arose during the night, causing the ship to roll in a reckless fashion and carrying us a good way to the north and west. Yet the celebration of New Year's Eve was not marred, and lusty choruses came up from the ward-room till long after midnight.

On January 2, 1914, the wind having fallen off, the ship was brought to the south again. The mainland was sighted near Cape Pepin and a stretch of high coast could be traced extending far away to the west—a greater length of coast than the Ship's Party had seen in January 1912, and carrying the coast beyond the limits shown in D'Urville's chart. At that point, however, we were prevented from either a nearer approach to the coast or from proceeding to the west by pack-ice held together by innumerable grounded bergs. So the ship was put about, steering to the north and west, hugging the heavy ice and searching for an opening to penetrate to the land.

Alas! We were to be much disappointed, for the impenetrable pack-ice proved to extend further north than in either of the preceding years, thus effectively blocking the way to the south. So the days went by as we steamed steadily towards the west, repeatedly changing course to double great sheets of pack which streamed away to the north; pushing through them in other places where the welcome water-sky showed strongly ahead; making south for days following the trend of the ice, then grappling with it in the hope of winning through to the land, and at last returning to the western track along the margin of the brash which breaks the first swell of the Southern Ocean.

For the next fortnight the weather was mostly overcast, with random showers of light snow and mild variable winds on all but two days, when there was a moderate blow and a considerable sea in which the ship seemed more active than usual. During this time, though we were unable to penetrate to land as we had hoped, valuable observations were made and important additions to the zoological collections effected.

Little has yet been said of the big Monagasque trawl which, from time to time, brought up rich hauls of life from the floor of the deep sea. This trawl consisted of strong wrought-iron jaws about six feet across, to which was attached an eighteen-foot net bag of hemp rope. It was lowered and raised by a winch actuating a powerful steel wire cable some three thousand fathoms in length.

When trawling the ship continued to steam ahead at quarter speed after the trawl had reached the bottom, then, within half an hour or hour, the hauling up was commenced. This sounds very easy, but when working in deep water much time is absorbed and for good results considerable skill and experience are required. It took us from ten to twelve hours to dredge in depths of about eighteen hundred fathoms. After the experience of the previous cruises Davis proved to be a thorough master of the trawling gear and almost every haul of the voyage was attended with splendid results.

Dredging was a source of never failing interest, for the wonders of the sea floor at various depths were day by day revealed, from the rich and diverse life of the shallow coastal waters to the grotesque and sparse representatives in the cold and silent depths of the deep sea.

Unfortunately for biological considerations, our catches often partook too much of a geological character; stones great and small, several of which hauled on board actually weighed half a ton each, were most unwelcome items, for they tore the net and crushed the contents. It was thus ascertained that the oozy floor of the sea in those waters is abundantly sprinkled with rocks which arrived at their present resting-place upon release from icebergs, embedded in which they had floated out from the land. Each stone showed just how far it had been sunk in the mud, for the upper protruding part was blackened with a curious deposit of manganese oxide.

The strength of the dredging cable was illustrated on two occasions when the trawl caught on some immovable object and the ship, though with engines still turning at a slow speed, was held stock still—anchored on the high seas, on each occasion in water over ten thousand feet in depth.

There was no dearth of life in the surface waters and at intermediate depths, so tow-nets, both large and small, were employed with their capture. The simple tow-net is a long tapering bag of fine-mesh silk trailed from the ship to capture microscopic life at the surface. But through the generosity of H.S.H. the Prince of Monaco who supplied us with much apparatus from his laboratory, we were also equipped with larger and more elaborate nets of the kind which could be automatically opened and closed at any desired depths, so securing samples of the free-swimming life in depths far below the surface. Many of the organisms in the deeper zones were observed to be strongly phosphorescent.

So there were many occupations to keep all hands busy and absorbed during those days as the *Aurora* progressed west.

Gillies, with his mechanical knowledge, was a great assistance in connection with the repairing and improving of the sounding and dredging gear. The other ship's officers, Blair, Grey and de la Motte, were all kept busy at high pressure by reason of our varied activities.

Late one evening an immense iceberg, rising to two hundred and ten feet above the sea, the highest of which we had any record, passed close by, ghostly in the waning light.

Its peaked summit was tinged with the palest lilac; the mighty pallid walls were streaked with deep azure; the green swell sucked and thundered in the wave-worn caverns. A turreted castle—a keep of the icy solitudes!

The morning of January 16 found us in the neighbourhood of Queen Mary Land skirting heavy pack-ice more formidable than any met with in that locality on preceding voyages, boding ill for our chances of reaching the open waters of the Davis Sea where we hoped to conduct investigations. Many petrels flew around and resting on the pack at its margin were dark swarms of terns which, from time to time, startled by the approach of the ship, rose in great flocks.

Schools of killer whales patrolled the waters at the edge of the pack in search of seals and penguins. Every few seconds there would be a momentary glimpse of a dark back blotched with yellow, and then all would disappear.

Presently, through the perfectly still air, the unmistakable blast of finner whales could be heard. There, several miles ahead, jets of spray blown high into the air were descried. Soon we were amongst them as they played about wallowing at the surface and plunging in swirls of foam. The finners, or rorquals as they are sometimes called, are the largest of the whale class. These were fine specimens of their kind.

One day about that time we met a rorqual which showed an unusual interest in the ship, following us for more than an hour, for a time close alongside, so that the spray from his blasts moistened our faces. Every few minutes he increased his distance from the ship and turning at right angles headed straight for us; as we stood at the rail the full length of his great blue body was clearly visible as it passed under the keel to emerge on the other side. The monster continued amusing himself in this way for some time; meanwhile there was growing anxiety lest this energetic torpedo, which was more than half the length of the vessel, should turn its attention to our really vulnerable part—the rudder and propeller—in which case the consequences would have been serious for us.

After lunch, with the intention of "watering ship," we ran for a mile or so into dense pack where the ocean swell was beaten down. The sky had cleared and the sun was warm and brilliant by the time a party had landed with baskets, picks and shovels on the snow-covered fragment of floe. When the baskets had been filled, they were hoisted by hand-power on to a derrick which had been fixed to the mizen-mast, swung inboard and then shovelled into a melting tank alongside the engine-room. The melter was a small tank through which ran a coil of steam pipes. The ice came up in such quantities that it was not melted in time to keep up with the demand, so a large heap was made on the deck. Late in the afternoon it was found that holes chipped in the sea-ice to a depth of six or eight inches filled quickly with fresh-water, and soon a gang of men had started a service with buckets and dippers between these pools and the ship. At 9 p.m. work was stopped and we once more resumed our western cruise.

On the 17th and for two days following, rapid progress was made to the south on a south-westerly course through slack ice and across occasional bars of heavier pack. At 10 p.m. on the 19th there was dense pack ahead, but beyond it, on the horizon, a dark line of open water was visible. From the crow's-nest it was seen to the south stretching east and west within the belt of pack-ice—the Davis Sea. We had broken through the pack less than twenty-five miles north of where the *Gauss* had wintered.

On reaching open water a course was set for Drygalski Island, which was reached on January 21. In appearance this island resembles an immense iceberg, and it was not until we had measured its height and sounded around it finding only sixty or seventy fathoms of water deepening towards the mainland, which was just visible on the southern horizon, that we could be certain that it was an island. In shape it is like a flattened dome, about nine miles in diameter and twelve hundred feet in height at its centre, bounded by perpendicular cliffs of ice, with no visible evidence of outcropping rocks.

Later in the day we steamed south towards the mainland. During the evening the crevassed slopes rose clear to the south reminding us of sections of the Adelie Land coast. The bows were turned towards Haswell Island, and after reaching to within eight miles we were cut off by solid floe which was seen to continue right along the coast in that neighbourhood. It was 1 a.m. by the time the floe was reached, so Davis had the ice-anchors run out and we tied up for the night. The biologists were elated in making an unexpected find of six Ross seals all sleeping on the floe within a mile of the ship. Up to that time the museums of the world contained less than double that number of Ross Seal skins, so we were all very pleased with our good fortune. Before leaving next day, many Emperor penguins were secured and the ship was never so busy with skinning as at that time.

On the night of the 22nd, the *Aurora* was headed north-east for the Shackleton Ice-Shelf. In the early hours of the 23rd a strong east-south-east gale sprang up and rapidly increased in violence, reaching a velocity of quite seventy miles an hour. A pall of nimbus overspread the sky, and blinding snow commenced to fall.

We were caught with Drygalski Island and the pack-ice on our lee, which was no comforting thought as we fought with the wind during the many hours that followed. Davis decided that the best thing to do was to try to make the lee of the thirty-mile long grounded berg which, on the two previous voyages, had been met twenty-five miles west of the Shackleton Shelf.

Then began a beat of forty miles to windward in dense driving snow, through a raging sea littered with bergs and fragments of ice. During the midnight hours of semi-darkness we had to count on our luck as much as on the splendid energy and resource of Davis and his officers and crew.

The night of the 23rd had a touch of terror. The wind was so powerful that, with a full head of steam and steering a few points off the eye of the wind, the ship could just hold her own. But when heavy gusts swooped down and the propeller raced on the crest of a mountainous wave, it was impossible to keep steerage way.

Drift and spray lash the faces of officer and helmsman, and through the grey gloom misty bergs glide by on either hand. A long slow struggle brings us to a passage between two huge masses of ice. There is a shock as the vessel bumps and grinds along a great wall. The engine stops, starts again, and stops once more. The yards on the foremast are swung into the wind, the giant seas are broken by the solid barriers of ice, the engine commences to throb with its old rhythm, and the ship slowly creeps out to meet the next peril.

Early on the morning of the 24th the martingale carried away as the ship plunged into a deep trough striking a "bergy-bit." The chain-stay parted and the foremast sprang back loose in danger of being worked out of the ship by the labouring of the vessel. This required most urgent attention, so all hands assembled forward and Davis swung the ship around away from the wind so as to give the men a chance of working under the bowsprit. There was some heroic work done by the boatswain and a couple of the sailors. Eventually a jury stay was fixed up which served admirably. The fo'c'sle, plunging and swaying in the great waves, was encased in frozen spray, and along all the ropes and stays were continuous cylinders of ice. The *Aurora* then resumed her easterly course against the blizzard.

At 11.30 p.m. that day the waves perceptibly decreased and it was surmised that we were approaching the lee of the berg. A few hours afterwards all anxiety had passed, for we were under the face of the ice wall, steaming up and down, waiting for the wind to subside, which it did late on the 26th.

Several days were spent dredging and sounding along the face of the Shackleton Shelf, working northward and accurately charting its outline. On the evening of January 29 the ship was anchored for the night to thick floe ice occupying an irregular embayment in a shattered section of the shelf-ice. There we found Emperor penguins unusually plentiful on the sea-front.

Advantage was taken of a clearing in the weather to walk over the floe to a berg embedded in it two and a half miles away, from the summit of which it was hoped some sign of land might be apparent. Away in the distance, perhaps five miles further on, could be seen an immense congregation of Emperor penguins—evidently another rookery.

From the rail of the ship, as we lay against the ice that night, a sea-leopard was observed strenuously endeavouring to seize a crab-eater seal. They appeared and disappeared time and again, but always the crab-eater by greater agility evaded his foe and returned safely to a nook in the shallow water on the ice-foot. Presently a second crab-eater appeared, and when we last saw them, the sea-leopard, with his attention thus divided, seemed less likely than ever to be successful.

The cruise was now continued to the north, for we intended if possible to proceed round the northern extremity of the shelf-ice and outline its eastern limits. Wild's Party had proved that it extended at least two hundred miles in an east and west direction. Observations from the ship showed that it was approximately six hundred feet thick and projected over one hundred and eighty miles from the continent—a mighty slab of land-ice extending like a giant pontoon from the coast far out into the ocean.

This vast block of ice originates fundamentally from the glacial flow over the southern hinterland. Every year an additional layer of consolidated snow is added to its surface by the frequent blizzards. These annual additions are clearly marked in the section exposed on the dazzling white face, near the brink of the ice cliff. There is a limit, however, to the increasing thickness, for the whole mass is ever moving slowly to the north, driven by the irresistible pressure of the land-ice behind it. Thus the northern face crumbles down into brash or floats away as bergs severed from the main body of the shelf-ice.

On the morning of January 30 we had the unique experience of witnessing this crumbling action in progress—a cataclysm of snow, ice and water. The ship was steaming along within three hundred yards of the cliff, when some loose drifts slid off from its edge, followed by a slice of the face extending for many hundreds of feet and weighing perhaps one million tons. It plunged into the sea with a deep booming roar and then rose majestically, shedding great white masses of itself which pushed towards the ship in an ever-widening field of ice. The main body of the berg alternately rose high out of the water and sank down out of sight; this was enacted repeatedly and all the while the crumbling continued, leaving the residual berg smaller and smaller, and bluer and bluer. When the commotion subsided there was a beautiful blue berg amidst acres and acres of white fragments—the heart of a flower amongst its fallen petals. It was a grand scene staged in the subdued limelight of an overcast day.

During the afternoon the *Aurora* threaded her way through a wonderful sea of grounded bergs, passing along narrow lanes between towering walls where architectural wonders were revealed. On reaching the extremity of the shelf-ice the pack was found to be dense and in massive array. Davis drove the ship through some of it and entered an open lead which ran like a dark streak away to the east among ice which grew heavier and more marked by the stress of pressure.

Our time was now limited, and it seemed to me that there was little chance of reaching open water by forcing a passage either to the east or north. We therefore turned on our tracks and broke south-west into the Davis Sea, intending to steam back to the spot where we had gained an entrance, two weeks previously.

On February 4 the pack to the north was beginning to slacken. Several short cuts were taken across projecting tongues and then on February 5, finding the ice much tighter than when we entered, Davis anxiously drove the vessel into a promising part and we commenced to push through for dear life, for there was quite a fair prospect of our being frozen in for another year. No one slept well during that night as the ship bumped and ground into the ice which crashed and grated along her stout sides. Davis was on watch for long hours, directing in the crow's-nest or down on the bridge, and throughout the next day we pushed on northwards towards the goal which now meant so much to us—Home!

At four o'clock the sun was glittering on the great ocean outside the pack-ice. Many of us climbed up in the rigging to see the fair sight—a prevision of blue skies and the calm delights of a land of eternal summer. Our work was finished, and the good ship was rising at last to the long swell of the southern seas.

On February 12, in latitude 55° S., a strong south-wester drove behind, and under half steam and with all sails set, the *Aurora* made eight knots an hour. The last iceberg was seen far away on the eastern horizon. Albatrosses followed in our wake, accompanied by their smaller satellites—Cape hens, prions and Lesson's petrels.

Before leaving the ice, Sandell and Bickerton had fixed an aerial between the fore- and mizen-masts, while the former installed a wireless receiving apparatus within the narrow limits of his cabin. There was no space on the ship to set up the motor engine, dynamos and other instruments necessary for transmitting messages over a long distance.

As the nights began to darken, Sandell listened eagerly for distant signals, until on February 16, in latitude 47° S., the "calls" of three ships in the vicinity of the Great Australian Bight were recognized. After this date news was picked up every night, and all the items were posted on a morning bulletin pinned up in the ward-room.

The first real touch of civilization came unexpectedly early on the morning of February 21. A full-rigged ship on the southern horizon! It might have been an iceberg, the sails flashed so white in the morning sun. But onward it came with a strong south-wester, overhauled and passed us, signalling "*Archibald Russell*, fifty-four days out from Buenos Ayres, bound for Cape Borda." It was too magical to believe.

On February 26 we gazed on distant cliffs of rock and earth—Kangaroo Island—and the tiny cluster of dwellings round the lighthouse at Cape Borda. Then we entered St. Vincent's Gulf on a clear, hot day, marvelling at the tree-clad shores and the smoke of many steamers.

Our coming had been signalled from Cape Borda and when the pilot stepped on board he brought with him a telegram from Sir Samuel Way, Lieutenant-Governor of South Australia, welcoming us home. Sir John Lewis, President, and Mr. Piper, ex-president of the South Australian Geographical Society were there to meet us.

The welcome home—the voice of the innumerable strangers—the hand-grips of many friends—it chokes one— it cannot be uttered.

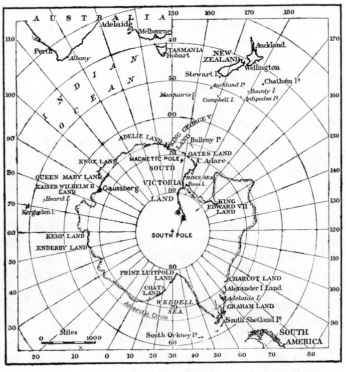

Map of the Antarctic Regions as known at the Present Day.

An official reception was reserved for three days later when the University Hall overflowed with friends and the Governor-General Lord Denman, arrived expressly from Melbourne and read a message of congratulation just received from His Majesty the King.

APPENDIX I

THE STAFF

G. F. AINSWORTH, 33 years of age;* single; born Sydney, N.S.W.; services loaned to the Expedition by the Commonwealth Meteorological Bureau.

R. BAGE, 23 years of age; single; born Melbourne; engineering graduate of Melbourne University; lieutenant in Royal Australian Engineers, on leave for the duration of the Expedition.†

F. H. BICKERTON, 22 years of age; single; born Oxford, England; expert motor engineer; Fellow of the Royal Geographical Society.

J. H. BLAIR, 24 years of age; single; born Scotland; first-mate's certificate in merchant service.

L. R. BLAKE, 21 years of age; single; born England; resident of Queensland; on leave from the Geological Survey Department, Brisbane. Killed in the War.

J. H. CLOSE, 40 years of age; married; born Sydney, N.S.W.; saw active service in the Matabele and South African wars; Fellow of Royal Geographical Society.

P. E. CORRELL, 19 years of age; single; born Adelaide; science student of Adelaide University; mechanic.

J. K. DAVIS, 28 years of age; single; born Ireland; extra-master's certificate, merchant service; joined Sir Ernest Shackleton's Expedition (1907–9) as chief officer of the *Nimrod*, acting subsequently as master.

G. DOVERS, 21 years of age; single; born Sydney, N.S.W.; surveyor in Commonwealth service.

F. J. GILLIES, 35 years of age; single; born Cardiff, Wales; chief engineer's certificate, merchant service.

P. GRAY, 22 years of age; single; born England; first officer's certificate, merchant service.

H. HAMILTON, 26 years of age; single; born Napier, New Zealand; science graduate of Otago University.

W. H. HANNAM, 26 years of age; single; born Sydney; science diploma of Technical College, Sydney; mechanic and wireless operator.

* The ages quoted in this Appendix refer to those at the date of joining the Expedition, and are approximate.

† Since killed whilst on active service, Gallipoli 1915.

C. T. HARRISSON, 43 years of age; married; born Hobart; biological collector and artist.*

C. A. HOADLEY, 24 years of age; single; born Melbourne; mining engineering graduate of Melbourne University.

A. J. HODGEMAN, 26 years of age; single; born Adelaide; articled architect; draughtsman in Government Works Department, Adelaide; on leave for the period of the expedition.

J. G. HUNTER, 23 years of age; single; born Sydney; science graduate of Sydney University; assistant demonstrator Biological Department, Sydney University.

J. F. HURLEY, 24 years of age; single; born Sydney; photographer.

S. N. JEFFRYES, 27 years of age; single; born Towoomba, Queensland; wireless operator.

S. E. JONES, 24 years of age; single; born Queensland; graduate in Medicine, Sydney University.

A. L. KENNEDY, 22 years of age; single; born Adelaide; engineering graduate of Adelaide University.

C. F. LASERON, 25 years of age; single; born Sydney; science diploma, Technical College, Sydney; collector to the Technological Museum, Sydney.

A. L. McLEAN, 26 years of age; single; born N.S.W.; graduate in arts and medicine of Sydney University.

C. T. MADIGAN, 23 years of age; single; born South Australia; engineering graduate Adelaide University; Rhodes Scholar, Oxford University.

D. MAWSON, 30 years of age; single; born Bradford, England; from early age resident in Sydney, N.S.W., graduate of science and mining engineering of Sydney University; doctor of science, Adelaide University; lecturer in certain geological subjects, Adelaide University; Geological investigations in New Hebrides Islands, 1903; a member of Shackleton's 1907–9 Expedition.

X. MERTZ, 28 years of age; born Basle, Switzerland; doctor of Law of the University of Berne; ski runner and mountaineer.

C. P. DE LA MOTTE, 20 years of age; single; born Bulli, N.S.W.; second officer's certificate, merchant service.

M. H. MOYES, 25 years of age; single; born South Australia; science graduate of Adelaide University.

H. D. MURPHY, 32 years of age; single; born Melbourne; one time scholar in History of Oxford University.

B. E. S. NINNIS, 23 years of age; single; born London; lieutenant Royal Fusiliers. (Son of Inspector-General Ninnis, R.N., one time of the *Alert* and *Discovery* Arctic Expedition.)

C. A. SANDELL, 25 years of age; single; born England; mechanic and operator Commonwealth Telegraph Service, Sydney.

* Afterwards appointed biologist to the Commonwealth Fisheries steamer *Endeavour* and lost his life when the vessel foundered with all hands, December 1914.

A. J. SAWYER, 26 years of age; single; born New Zealand; wireless telegraphist, Australian Wireless Company.

F. L. STILLWELL, 23 years of age; single; born Melbourne; engineering graduate of Melbourne University.

A. D. WATSON, 24 years of age; single; born N.S.W.; science graduate of Sydney University.

E. N. WEBB, 22 years of age; single; born Christchurch; associate of civil engineering of Canterbury University.

L. A. WHETTER, 29 years of age; single; born New Zealand; graduate in medicine of Otago University.

F. WILD, 38 years of age; single; born England; member of the National Antarctic Expedition (Capt. R. F. Scott) of 1901–4, and of Sir Ernest Shackleton's Expedition 1907–9 (one of the party to reach within 114 statute miles of the South Geographic Pole).

ACKNOWLEDGMENTS

REFERENCE has been made to the large part played by Professors T. W. E. David and Orme Masson in the organization and finances of the Expedition throughout its whole period. Professor G. C. Henderson gave his strong support to the promotion of the Expedition and in appealing for Government support. Sir Ernest Shackleton, besides assisting in the raising of funds for the enterprise, took a personal interest in its welfare, helping us by many acts of kindness in those early and critical days when preliminary arrangements were being made in London. In South Australia Sir Samuel Way was indefatigable in his support and in approaching the State Government for financial assistance.

To these gentlemen and all others mentioned in the Preface, the Expedition owes a special debt of gratitude, and it was by their united labours that the undertaking was made possible.

Finance.

The Expedition has many friends and helpers in all those who have themselves contributed to the expenses. Apart from the list of subscribers of the largest sums, outlined elsewhere in this volume, there are scores of others whose names will be recorded in the final audited statement in preparation to appear in connection with the series of Scientific Results now going to press. To all these benefactors we wish to express our gratitude.

I wish to mention that the whole of the proceeds from all the assets of the Expedition such as the profit from the sale of film-rights, from public lectures delivered by myself, and from the publication of this book are entirely paid into the Expedition funds and devoted to the settlement of outstanding accounts.

Scientific Equipment.

The scope of the scientific work necessitated extensive purchases, and these were amplified by loans from many scientific bodies and individuals, for which we are duly thankful.

Numerous instruments for surveying and navigation were loaned by the Royal Geographical Society and by the Admiralty. In this connection we are indebted to Admiral Purey Cust and to Dr. Scott Keltie and Mr. Reeves.

An assortment of oceanographical gear was generously supplied through H.S.H. The Prince of Monaco, from the Institut Oceanographique of Monaco. Dr. W. S. Bruce made similar donations and supervised the construction of our largest deep-sea dredge. The three-thousand-fathom tapered steel cables and mountings, designed to work the deep-water dredges, were supplied by Messrs. Bullivant. Appliances were also loaned by Mr. J. T. Buchanan of the *Challenger* Expedition and by the Commonwealth Fisheries Department. The self-recording tide-gauges we employed were the property of the New South Wales Government, obtained through Mr. G. Halligan.

The taxidermists' requirements, and other necessaries for the preservation of zoological specimens, were for the most part purchased, but great assistance was rendered through Professor Baldwin-Spencer by the National Museum of Melbourne and by the South Australian Museum, through the offices of Professor Stirling.

Articles of equipment for botanical work were loaned by Mr. J. H. Maiden, Director of the Botanical Gardens, Sydney.

A supply of heavy cameras for base-station work and light cameras for sledging was purchased from Messrs. Newman and Guardia; our stock being amplified by many private cameras, especially those belonging to F. H. Hurley, photographer to the Expedition. Special Lumière plates and material for colour photography were not omitted, and, during the final cruise of the *Aurora*, P. E. Correll at his own expense employed the Paget process for colour photography with good results.

The programme of magnetic work was intended to be as extensive as possible. In the matter of equipment we were very materially assisted by the Carnegie Institute through Dr. L. A. Bauer. An instrument was also loaned through Mr. H. F. Skey of the Christchurch Magnetic Observatory. A full set of Eschenhagen self-recording instruments was purchased, and in this and in other dispositions for the magnetic work we had to thank Dr. C. Chree, Director of the National Physical Laboratory, and Dr. C. C. Farr of University College, Christchurch. Captain Chetwynd kindly assisted in arrangements for the ship's compasses.

Two complete sets of Telefunken wireless apparatus were purchased from the Australasian Wireless Company. The motors and dynamos were got from Buzzacott, Sydney, and the masts were built by Saxton and Binns, Sydney. Manilla and tarred-hemp ropes were supplied on generous terms by Melbourne firms (chiefly Kinnear).

The meteorological instruments were largely purchased from Negretti and Zambra, but a great number were loaned by the Commonwealth Meteorological Department (Director, Mr. H. A. Hunt) and by the British Meteorological Office (Director, Dr. W. N. Shaw).

For astronomical work the following instruments were loaned, besides transit-theodolites and sextants: a four-inch telescope by the Greenwich Observatory through the Astronomer Royal; a portable transit-theodolite by the Melbourne Observatory through the Director, Mr. P. Baracchi; two stellar sidereal chronometers by the Adelaide Observatory through the Astronomer, Mr. P. Dodwell.

The apparatus for bacteriological and physiological work were got in Sydney, in arrangements and suggestions for which our thanks are due to Dr. Tidswell (Microbiological Laboratory) and Professor Welsh of Sydney University.

Apart from the acquisition of the instruments, there were long preparations to be made in the arrangement of the scientific programme and in the training of the observers. In this department the Expedition was assisted by many friends.

Thus Professor W. A. Haswell (Biology), Professor T. W. Edgeworth David (Geology), and Mr. H. A. Hunt (Meteorology), each drew up instructions relating to his respective sphere. Training in astronomical work at the Melbourne Observatory was supervised by Mr. P. Baracchi, Director, and in magnetic work by the Department of Terrestrial Magnetism, Carnegie Institute (Director, Dr. L. A. Bauer). Further, in the subject of magnetics, we have to thank especially Mr. E. Kidston of the Carnegie Institute for field tuition, and Mr. Baldwin of the Melbourne Observatory for demonstrations in the working of the Eschenhagen magnetographs. Professor J. A. Pollock gave us valuable advice on wireless and other physical subjects. At the Australian Museum, Sydney, Mr. Hedley rendered assistance in the zoological preparations. In the conduct of affairs we were assisted on many occasions by Messrs. W. S. Dun (Sydney), J. H. Maiden (Sydney), Robert Hall (Hobart), G. H. Knibbs (Melbourne) and by the presidents and members of the councils of the several Geographical Societies in Australia (more particularly Mr. Piper, Mr. Grummer, Mr. Sachell and Dr. J. C. Vercoe)—as well, of course, as to those of the Royal Geographical Society, London (especially Major Darwin, Lord Curzon, Mr. Douglas Freshfield and Dr. Scott Keltie).

Medical Equipment.
Messrs. Burroughs & Wellcome (drugs), Messrs. Allen & Hanbury (surgical instruments).

General Stores and Equipment.
A large quantity of coal was consumed by the *Aurora* in steaming her fifty thousand odd miles, and we were greatly helped by large gifts of this commodity gratuitously placed at our disposal by several friends including Mr. John Brown (N.S.W.), Mr. Dyce Murphy (Melbourne), the Lithgow Coal Association, and the Crown Preserved Fuel Co. (briquettes).

Through the offices of Mr. C. A. Bang we were indebted to "De Forenede Dampskilbsselskab" of Copenhagen for the transport of the dogs from Greenland. While the dogs remained in Hobart Mr. Thomas Tabart, Chief Quarantine Officer, took a personal interest in their welfare and gave up much of this time to see that they were properly cared for.

The largest of our huts, that erected in Adelie Land, was presented, jointly, by the timber merchants of Sydney. The hut which found its way to Queen Mary Land was the gift of Messrs. T. Anthony of Melbourne.

The following firms contributed valuable additions to the equipment:

British Imperial Oil Co. (Shell petrol); British American Tobacco Co. (cigarettes, cigars and tobacco); Bryant and May (matches); Jaeger (clothing); Eagley(clothing); Burberry (windproofs); Perdriau Rubber Co. (rubber boots); Athlone Woollen Mills (overcoating); Albion Woollen Mills (rugs); Collins Bros, (blankets); Messrs. Johnson (oil skin coats); Acetylene Corporation (acetylene equipment); Bingham & Co. (calcium carbide); Dee Oil Co. (engine oil); Wakefield & Co. (lubricating oil); Flexible Metallic Tubing Co. (gas tubing); Macfarlane & Robinson (fireproof ware); Queen's Stores Co. (fireproof ash bags); British Aluminium Co. (aluminium ware); Vacuum Oil Co. (lubricating oil); Messrs. Chubb (safe); Mappin & Webb (cutlery and electro ware); Messrs. Singer (sewing machines); Steel Trucks, Ltd. (portable trucks); Gamages (sporting gear); Sames & Co. (piano); Gramophone Co. (gramophones); Humber Co. (cycle wheels); Smith Premier Co. (type writer); Griffin (Photographic equipment); Paget Plate Co. (photo graphic plates); Kodak Co., of Australia (plates); Cowles & Dun (firearms); Carl Zeiss (binoculars); G. B. Kent (brushes); Winsor & Newton (artists' materials); John Sands (stationary); Ludowici & Son (leather goods); Millwall & Sons (fishing tackle); Spratts (dog biscuits); Allen Taylor (timber for sledges); Worsfold (skis); Lever Bros. (soap); Pears Ltd. (toilet soap); Price (candles); Smith & Wellstood (cooking range), Metters (range).

Food Stuffs.

We are grateful to the following firms for contributions of food stuffs:

Messrs. Cadbury (cocoa); Bovril (pemmican); Glaxo Ltd. (glaxo); Colonial Sugar Refining Co. (sugar, syrup and spirit); Colman (flour and mustard); Hartley (jam); Keiller & Son (marmalade); Plasmon Co. (plasmon and plasmon biscuits); "Te Sol" Co. (tea); Griffiths Bros. (tea and coffee); Armitage & Co. (coffee); Messrs. Rose (lime juice); Huttons ("Pineapple" brand bacon and ham); Flemington Meat Preserving Co. (canned soups and meat); Sydney Meat Preserving Co. (canned meat); Baynes Bros. (canned meat); Ramornie Meat Co. (canned meat); Border Preserving Co. (canned rabbit); Cook & Co. (salt beef and pork); Partridge & Twiss (canned meat); Brand & Co. (sauces); Mason & Co. (pickles); Eschoffier (soups); Hugon (suet); Conrad (suet); C. & E. Morton (canned fish); Laver Bros. (canned vegetables and fruit); Jones Bros. (canned fruit); Nestle (condensed milk); Parsons Bros., & Co. (prepared cereals); Bird & Co. (baking powder, custard powder, etc.); Arnott Bros. (biscuits); Swallow & Ariell (biscuits); Jacob & Co. (fancy biscuits); Patria Biscuit Fabriek (fancy biscuits); Colac Dairying Co. (butter); Cerebos (salt); Castle Salt Co. (salt); Trufood Co. (milk preparations); Fullers (sweet stuffs); Batger (preserved fruit); Farrah Ltd. (sweet stuffs); Horlick (malted milk); Seager (preserved meats); Neaves (health diet); Brown & Poison (cornflour); Schweppes (mineral waters); Köpke (Port wine); Burgoyne (wine); Marmite

Co. (vegetable extract); Messrs. Foster & Co. (dried peas); Eggo Ltd. (dried eggs), Barclay, Perkins & Co. (stout); Groves & Whitnall Ltd. (ale).

Anyone requiring full details of the food stuffs, their variety and quantity, is referred to Appendix VII of the first edition of this work.

Publication of Scientific Results.

The lasting reputation of the Expedition and the usefulness of the undertaking is, of course, founded upon the detailed knowledge acquired of the regions visited, which forms matter to be published as the Scientific Results. Owing to the fact that there is no wide sale for such publications the expense of production has to be faced. Unfortunately the outbreak of war dismissed all possible sources of revenue that might have contributed to this object, and we were most anxiously concerned with the problem of permanently recording the discoveries of the Expedition.

At this juncture Sir Samuel Way, Mr. T. Smeaton, M.P., and representatives of scientific institutions in South Australia kindly brought the case before the State Government through the Premier, the Hon. Crawford Vaughan. As a result, the Government agreed to print the manuscripts at the Government's Printing Office. The publication is in the hands of Mr. R. E. E. Rogers, the Government Printer. The Government of New South Wales, through the Hon. W. A. Holman, is assisting by the reproduction of certain special illustrations including colour plates; these are being prepared by Mr. W. A. Gullick, the Government Printer, Sydney, whose department is noted for such work.

The whole publication will comprise a large number of volumes, several parts of which have already appeared.

Professor W. A. Haswell has kindly undertaken to edit the biological section which forms a large portion of the whole. Contributions towards the cost of preparing the material have been made by the British Association, the Royal Society, and the New Zealand Government, the latter through the Premier, the Rt. Hon. W. F. Massey.

APPENDIX III

GLOSSARY

Ablation.—The surface waste of snow, névé or ice by natural causes, such as melting or evaporation.

Air-Tractor.—An engine dragging itself (and load) forward through the air. In the case of the air-tractor sledge, though it rested on the ice, the dragging force was exerted in the air by the propeller.

Arête.—A sharp ascending ridge of a mountain.

Barrier.—A term which has been rather loosely applied in the literature of Antarctic Exploration. Formerly it was used to describe a formation which is mainly shelf-ice, known as the Great Ross Barrier. Confusion arose when "Barrier" came to be applied to the seaward ice cliff (resting on rock) of an extensive sheet of land-ice (the ice-cap itself) and when it was also employed to designate a line of consolidated pack-ice. Spelt with a small "b" the term is a convenient one, so long as it carries its ordinary meaning; it seems unnecessary to give it a technical connotation.

Bergschrund.—See *Glacier.*

Blizzard.—The term as applied in this book means a high wind at a low temperature, accompanied by drifting, not necessarily falling snow.

Brash or *Brash-ice.*—Small floating fragments, the debris from the wreck of larger pieces, typically observed bordering a tract of pack-ice.

Calving (of icebergs).—This term is applied alike to the breaking off of an iceberg from a glacier and of smaller pieces from a parent iceberg.

Crevasse.—A crack or rift in a glacier.

Declination (magnetic).—At the magnetic poles, situated respectively near the northern and southern extremities of the earth, a magnetized needle (the compass) if freely suspended will stand vertically—on one extremity at the North Magnetic Pole, on the other at the South Magnetic Pole. Halfway between these poles it assumes a horizontal position (the magnetic equator) always, of course, pointing to the poles. Elsewhere on the surface of the earth it will be directed towards both magnetic poles but dip towards the nearest; the degree of dip or vertically being a measure of the distance from the latter. As the magnetic poles do not correspond with the Geographic poles (termini of the axis of the earth) the direction indicated on the compass is not the true north and south, but differs from it by an angle referred to as the *declination* which is specific for any particular spot on the earth's surface.

Dip (magnetic).—The angle of the vertical inclination of a freely suspended magnetized needle; see *Declination*.

Erratic (in glaciology).—A rock which has been transported by ice from its original position.

Field-ice.—See *Floe*.

Finnesko.—The fur boots worn by the Laplanders. They are made of reindeer skin, worn with the fur outside, are soft and roomy, and, as they are designed for walking through soft snow, have no hard sole as have ordinary boots.

Floe or *Floe-ice.*—The comparatively flat, frozen surface of the sea, intersected by cracks and channels of open water (leads). The term *field-ice* or *ice-field* has been applied frequently, in the past, to floe-ice formations of such great area as to extend beyond the horizon as viewed from the mast-head.

Flying-fox (in haulage).—A device for facilitating the haulage of materials, either on the flat or from one elevation to another, employing a stretched rope or cable on which to suspend the burden.

Glacier.—The term in its scientific usage includes any extensive land-ice formation. The familiar form is of course the valley type illustrated by the glaciers of Switzerland. Thus it is that, to the popular mind, a glacier is regarded as "a river of ice." At the head of such a glacier there is a snow catchment area which feeds it; in this snow-field the surface is smooth and unbroken, for, there, the ice is comparatively stagnant. The location at the head of the glacier, where, by more rapid motion, it tends to draw away from the ice of the snow-field, is indicated by a fissure (crevasse) of exceptional size, termed the *bergschrund*. The ice moves slowly downhill in these valleys, a few feet to a few hundred feet per year, carrying along with it, upon it or embedded in it, quantities of rock debris originating from the floor or the sides of its channel; accumulations of this debris (morainic matter) are referred to as *moraines*. In its onward motion, thus shod with morainic matter, the glacier polishes and grooves (striates) the rock of its bed.

Glacier-tongue.—See *Shelf-ice*.

Ground-ice.—Ice formed on the bed of a river, lake or sea, while the water as a whole remains unfrozen.

Iceberg.—A loose mass of ice floating in the sea, originally broken from a glacier (it is therefore fresh-water ice).

Ice-blink.—A peculiar brightness in the sky along the horizon, which shows itself over an ice-field; it is the effect of the reflection of the light by the glittering white surface.

Ice-cap.—A continuous covering of ice capping the land such as occurs in polar regions.

Ice-fall.—An interruption in a glacier caused by an abrupt change of slope in its bed. It corresponds to a waterfall in the case of a river.

Ice-foot.—A platform of ice rigidly attached along the shore of polar lands. The formation is composed of adhering floe-ice, with additions, in greater or lesser volume, of snow and frozen spray. The line of demarkation between it and the floe (frozen surface of the sea) is a crack (*tide crack*) which is the result of differential movement between the immovable ice-foot and the floe-ice which rises and falls with the tide.

Ice ship, to.—To replenish the ship's fresh-water supply by taking ice on board which, when melted, is run into the ship's tanks.

Lead.—A narrow track of open water traversing the pack-ice or the otherwise solid floe; see *Floe-ice.*

Mock-sun.—A spot on a solar halo (ring round the sun due to refraction of the rays traversing an atmosphere loaded with fog or ice particles) at which the light is intensified often, assuming a perfect image of the sun.

Névé.—The compacted snow of a snow-field; a stage in the transition between soft, loose snow and glacier-ice.

Nunatak.—An island-like outcrop of rock projecting through a sheet of enveloping land-ice.

Oceanography.—The study of the ocean, including the shape and character of its bed, the temperature and salinity of the water at various depths, the force and set of its currents, and the nature of the creatures and plants which haunt its successive zones.

Pack or *Pack-ice.*—An extensive field of loose ice on the surface of the sea, drifted together under the influence of winds and currents. It is composed in the main of fragments of floe-ice, to which may be added material from the disintegration of bergs, and bergs themselves. It is spoken of as "close pack" or "open pack" according as the components are pressed close together or not.

Pancake-ice.—Small circular pieces of floe-ice with edges upturned. Such a form is the result or the freezing of the surface of the sea (the development of floe-ice) under other than still conditions. A slight swell breaks up the floe-ice as it forms and the bumping one against the other on every side of the pieces, still somewhat pliable, rounds and turns up the edges.

Piecrust (surface).—Refers to a thin crust which often forms on soft snow; though frozen hard it is not sufficiently hard to support a heavy weight, and one's feet break through in a most annoying and often painful manner.

Saennagras.—A grass from Scandinavia which when dried is used in boots, especially finnesko, to keep the feet warm.

Sastrugi.—Irregularities due to wind on the surface of an expanse of snow. They may be ripples and waves of accumulation or ridges and furrows of erosion chiselled out of a hard surface by the abrasive action of wind-borne drift-snow. Sastruga (sing.); sastrugi (pl.).

Séracs.—Sharp irregular ridges or pinnacles of ice which appear on the surface of a glacier where it rides over an unusually rough or inclined bottom. A field of such pinnacles, jammed together in broken confusion, is called sérac-ice.

Shelf-ice.—The term as originally propounded by Dr. Otto Nordenskjöld refers to thick, floating, fresh-water ice formations pushing out from the land and continuous with an extensive land-ice formation. They are thus shelf-like extensions of the land-ice. Narrow strips of shelf-ice such as the floating, seaward extensions of certain glaciers may be referred to as *glacier-tongues.*

Snow-blind light.—A term applied by members of the Expedition to the diffused light on days when the sky was evenly over-cast, rendering almost invisible the detail of snow and ice surfaces owing to absence of contrast.

Snow-blindness.—An acute inflammation of the eye (conjunctivitis) due to the glare reflected from the snow. In severe cases the retina may become completely exhausted and permanent blindness result.

Sub-Antarctica.—A term used to denote the zone of the Southern Hemisphere between the South Temperate Regions and the ice-encased Antarctic area. It is characterized by its almost Antarctic forms of life rather than by specific latitude limits. Roughly, however, it is the belt of ocean and contained islands between the vicinity of the 50th and 60th parallels of south latitude.

Tide-crack.—See *Ice-foot.*

Water-sky.—The dark appearance of sky over open water, seen from a distance on the ice; see *Ice-blink.*

The following colloquial words or phrases occurring in the narrative were largely determined by general usage:

To depot = to cache or to place a stock of provisions in a depot; drift = drift-snow; fifty-mile wind = a wind of fifty miles an hour; burberry = "Burberry gabardine" or specially prepared wind-proof clothing; whirly (pl. whirlies) = whirlwind carrying drift-snow; glaxo = "Glaxo" (a powder of dried milk); primus = "primus" stove used during sledging; hoosh = a thick soup in which pemmican is the most important item; tanks = bags of water-proof material for holding sledging provisions; ramp (snow) = an evenly inclined bank of snow usually accumulated on the leeward side of an obstacle from which it tapers away to nothing; radiant (cloud) = an appearance noted in the case of parallel bands of cloud (especially cirro-stratus) which, owing to perspective, present the appearance of radiating from a point on the horizon.

In the following list of animals the specific names are placed against the popular titles as used throughout the text.

BIRDS

Emperor penguin	*Aptenodytes forsteri.*
King penguin	*Aptenodytes patagonica.*
Adelie penguin	*Pygoscelis adeliæ.*
Royal penguin	*Catarrhactes schlegeli.*
Victoria penguin	*Catarrhactes pachyrhynchus.*
Gentoo or Rockhopper penguin	*Pygoscelis papua.*

Birds *(continued)*

Sclater penguin	*Eudypes sclateri.*
Wandering albatross	*Diomedea exulans.*
Mollymawk	*Diomedea melanophrys.*
Sooty albatross	*Phoebetria fuliginosa.*
Giant petrel or nelly	*Ossifraga gigantea.*
MacCormick's skua gull	*Megalestris maccormicki.*
Southern skua (Macquarie Island)	*Megalestris antantica.*
Antarctic petrel	*Thallasoeca antarctica.*
Silver-grey petrel	*Priocella glacialoides.*
Cape pigeon	*Daption capensis.*
Snow petrel	*Pagodroma nivea.*
Lesson's petrel	*Oestrelata lessoni.*
Wilson petrel	*Oceanites oceanicus.*
Storm petrel (Mother Gary's chicken)	*Fregetta melanogaster.*
Cape hen	*Majaqueus æquinoctialis.*
Small prion or whale bird	*Prion banksii.*
Crested tern	*Sterna sp.*
Dominican gull	*Larus dominicanus.*
Macquarie Island shag	*Phalacrocorax traverse.*
Mutton bird	*Puffinus griseus.*
Maori hen or "weka"	*Ocydromus scotti.*

Seals

Sea-elephant	*Macrorhinus leoninus.*
Sea-leopard	*Stenorhynchus leptonyx.*
Sea-lion	*Otaria cyronii.*
Weddell seal	*Leptonychotes weddelli.*
Crab-eater seal	*Lobodon carcinophagus.*
Ross seal	*Ommatophoca rossi.*

Whales

Rorqual, finner, or blue whale	*Balaenoptera sibbaldi.*
Killer whale	*Orca gladiator.*

INDEX